MAR 2010

W9-CJQ-452

DISCARD
FCPL discards materials
that are outdated and in poor condition.
In order to make room for current,
in-demand materials, underused materials
are offered for public sale.

HISTORY OF
THE ANCIENT AND MEDIEVAL WORLD

SECOND EDITION

VOLUME 11

INDEX

Marshall Cavendish
Reference
New York

Marshall Cavendish
99 White Plains Road
Tarrytown, New York 10591

www.marshallcavendish.us

© 2009 Marshall Cavendish Corporation

All rights reserved. No part of this book may be reproduced or utilized in any form or by any means, electronic or mechanical, including photocopying, recording, or by any information storage and retrieval system, without prior written permission from the publisher and copyright holder.

Library of Congress Cataloging-in-Publication Data

History of the ancient and medieval world / [edited by Henk Dijkstra]. -- 2nd ed.
     v. cm.
 Includes bibliographical references and index.
 Contents: v. 1. The first civilizations -- v. 2. Western Asia and the Mediterranean -- v. 3. Ancient Greece -- v. 4. The Roman Empire -- v. 5. The changing shape of Europe -- v. 6. The early Middle Ages in western Asia and Europe -- v. 7. Southern and eastern Asia -- v. 8. Europe in the Middle Ages -- v. 9. Western Asia, northern Europe, and Africa in the Middle Ages -- v. 10. The passing of the medieval world -- v. 11. Index.
 ISBN 978-0-7614-7789-1 (set) -- ISBN 978-0-7614-7791-4 (v. 1) -- ISBN 978-0-7614-7792-1 (v. 2) -- ISBN 978-0-7614-7793-8 (v. 3) -- ISBN 978-0-7614-7794-5 (v. 4) -- ISBN 978-0-7614-7795-2 (v. 5) -- ISBN 978-0-7614-7796-9 (v. 6) -- ISBN 978-0-7614-7797-6 (v. 7) -- ISBN 978-0-7614-7798-3 (v. 8) -- ISBN 978-0-7614-7799-0 (v. 9) -- ISBN 978-0-7614-7800-3 (v. 10) -- ISBN 978-0-7614-7801-0 (v. 11)
 1. History, Ancient. 2. Middle Ages. 3. Civilization, Medieval. I. Dijkstra, Henk.
 D117.H57 2009
 940.1--dc22
                                        2008060052

Printed in Malaysia

12 11 10 09 08 7 6 5 4 3 2 1

General Editor: Henk Dijkstra

Marshall Cavendish
Project Editor: Brian Kinsey
Publisher: Paul Bernabeo
Production Manager: Michael Esposito

Brown Reference Group
Project Editor: Chris King
Text Editors: Shona Grimbly, Charles Phillips
Designer: Lynne Lennon
Cartographers: Joan Curtis, Darren Awuah
Picture Researcher: Laila Torsun
Indexer: Christine Michaud
Managing Editor: Tim Cooke

PICTURE CREDITS

Cover: A 14th-century-CE manuscript illustration depicting a scene from *The Song of Roland* (Topham: British Library).
Volume Contents: A 15th-century-CE manuscript illustration of two armies holding discussions in front of walled cities (Topham: British Library/HIP).

SET CONTENTS

VOLUME 1: THE FIRST CIVILIZATIONS

Early Humans
The Age of the Megaliths
The Bronze Age
The Iron Age
The Sumerians
Egypt's Old Kingdom
Egypt's Middle Kingdom
Egypt's New Kingdom
The Babylonians

VOLUME 2: WESTERN ASIA AND THE MEDITERRANEAN

The Hittites
Bronze Age Greece
The Minoans
Mycenae and Troy
The Phoenicians
The Assyrians
The Israelites
The Persians
The Dark Age and Greek Expansion
Sparta and Athens

VOLUME 3: ANCIENT GREECE

From Tyranny to Democracy
Greek Religion
The Birth of Drama
The Persian Wars
The Age of Pericles
The Great Philosophers
The Peloponnesian War
Macedon and Alexander the Great
After Alexander
The Greek Legacy

VOLUME 4: THE ROMAN EMPIRE

Early Rome
Rome's Early Wars and Conquests
The Punic Wars
Revolution and Reform
The End of the Republic
The Age of Augustus
The Julio-Claudian Emperors
Expanding the Empire
Daily Life in Rome

VOLUME 5: THE CHANGING SHAPE OF EUROPE

The Edges of the Empire
The Decline of Rome
The Disintegration of the Empire
Constantinople: A New Capital
The Rise of Christianity
The Barbarian Invaders
Life under the Barbarians
The Reign of Justinian
The Development of Christian Theology
The Appeal of Monasticism

VOLUME 6: THE EARLY MIDDLE AGES IN WESTERN ASIA AND EUROPE

The New Persian Empire
Mohammed and Islam
The Rise of Islam
The Caliphate
The Riches of Islam
The Age of Charlemagne
The Carolingian Empire
Feudal Europe
The Holy Roman Empire

VOLUME 7: SOUTHERN AND EASTERN ASIA

The Early History of China
Early Chinese Thinkers
China's Imperial Dynasties
The Emergence of Japan
India's First Civilizations
Hinduism: The Religion of India
The Buddha and Buddhism
India in the Middle Ages
Southeast Asia
Cultures of the Pacific

VOLUME 8: EUROPE IN THE MIDDLE AGES

The Reconquista and Christian Expansion
Growth of Urban Europe
France and England
Popes and Emperors
Rulers of the 13th Century
Crises in the Late Middle Ages
Leagues and Alliances
The Hundred Years' War
The Wars of the Roses
The Rise of Burgundy

VOLUME 9: WESTERN ASIA, NORTHERN EUROPE, AND AFRICA IN THE MIDDLE AGES

The Early Byzantine Empire
The Middle and Late Byzantine Empire
The Crusades
The Vikings
From Kiev to Moscow
The Mongols
Turkish Empires and the Islamic World
The Rise of the Ottomans
Africa's Early Cultures
The Rise and Fall of African Empires

VOLUME 10: THE PASSING OF THE MEDIEVAL WORLD

Pre-Columbian Cultures
The Maya
The Aztecs
The Incas
Peoples of North America
European Expansion
The Golden Age of Exploration
Scholasticism and Humanism
The Renaissance
The World in the Early 16th Century

VOLUME 11: INDEX

Time Line
Glossary
Major Historical Figures
Resources for Further Study
    Books
    Web Sites
Thematic Indexes
    Arts and Culture
    Everyday Life
    Geographical Locations
    Government and Politics
    People
    Religion
    Technology
    Trade and Economy
    Wars and Battles
Comprehensive Index

VOLUME CONTENTS

Time Line   1446

Glossary   1464

Major Historical Figures   1484

Resources for Further Study
  Books   1492
  Web Sites   1500

Thematic Indexes
  Arts and Culture   1506
  Everyday Life   1511
  Geographical Locations   1515
  Government and Politics   1521
  People   1525
  Religion   1533
  Technology   1538
  Trade and Economy   1541
  Wars and Battles   1544

Comprehensive Index   1548

TIME LINE

EUROPE AND WESTERN ASIA		AFRICA, EASTERN ASIA, AND THE AMERICAS	
		c. 2 million BCE	*Homo habilis* and *Homo erectus* evolve.
		c. 38,000 BCE	Humans first begin to inhabit Southeast Asia.
c. 30,000 BCE	Earliest cave paintings created.	c. 30,000 BCE	Lapita culture develops in New Guinea.
		c. 28,000 BCE	Hunters from Asia enter North America over land bridge between Siberia and Alaska.
c. 24,000 BCE	Figurine known as Venus of Willendorf carved in central Europe (modern Austria).		
		c. 17,000 BCE	First nomadic Asian hunters enter Central America.
c. 10,000 BCE	First permanent settlements established in western Asia by people of Natufian culture.	c. 10,000 BCE	End of Ice Age; land bridge between Alaska and Siberia submerged by Bering Strait.
c. 8500 BCE	First farmers cultivate oats and barley in Syria; Neolithic period begins.	c. 7500 BCE	Jomon period, marked by distinctive pottery, begins in Japan.
c. 6000 BCE *(left margin)* c. 6000 BCE	First settled European farmers in Crete and Greece.	c. 6000 BCE	First farmers in southern Asia.
c. 5000 BCE	Semitic-speaking people start to move into southern Mesopotamia.	c. 5000 BCE	Emergence of Yang-shao culture in China.
c. 4000 BCE	Funnel-beaker culture flourishes in central Europe.		

EUROPE AND WESTERN ASIA		AFRICA, EASTERN ASIA, AND THE AMERICAS	
c. 3500 BCE	Bronze Age begins in the Caucasus.	c. 3500 BCE	Llamas domesticated in Peru.
c. 3100 BCE	Work begins on ritual circle at Stonehenge, England.	c. 3100 BCE	Bronze Age reaches China.
c. 3000 BCE	First settlement appears at Troy. Dawn of Minoan culture on Crete.	c. 3000 BCE	Earliest known American pottery produced in Ecuador and Colombia.
c. 2900 BCE	Single-grave people replace funnel-beaker people in northern Europe.		
c. 2800 BCE	Invaders with knowledge of metalwork arrive in Greek mainland.	c. 2700 BCE	Silk production begins in China.
		c. 2600 BCE	Inhabitants of present-day Peru begin to mummify their dead. Earliest Indus Valley civilization develops.
		c. 2500 BCE	Pottery is made in Savannah River Valley in North America.
c. 2335 BCE	Sargon the Great founds Akkadian Empire, builds city of Akkad, and unites Mesopotamia.	c. 2200 BCE	Establishment of first Chinese dynasty, the Xia.
c. 2150 BCE	Akkadian Empire ends.	c. 2150 BCE	In Egypt, Old Kingdom comes to end as power of pharaoh diminishes; First Intermediate period begins.
c. 2100 BCE	Migrants from central Asia arrive on Greek mainland.	c. 2100 BCE	People of the Ban Chiang culture in Thailand begin to make bronze artifacts.
		c. 2047 BCE	Mentuhotep II reunites Egypt.
2004 BCE	Elamites sack Ur; end of Sumerian period.		

c. 2600 BCE

EUROPE AND WESTERN ASIA		AFRICA, EASTERN ASIA, AND THE AMERICAS	
		c. 2000 BCE	Bronze Age begins in northern Africa. Rice cultivated by Phung Nguyen culture in northern Vietnam. Long-shan culture evolves in Yellow River Valley in China.
c. 2000 BCE	Indo-European peoples arrive in Greece from central Asia. Distinct Assyrian culture emerges in northern Mesopotamia.		
		1962 BCE	Sesostris I becomes king of Egypt.
c. 1900 BCE	Metalworkers in British Isles begin using bronze.	c. 1850 BCE	Long-shan period comes to end in China.
c. 1800 BCE	Unetician culture reaches height of influence in central Europe.	c. 1800 BCE	India's great Indus Valley cultures start to decline. Previously fertile Sahara becomes desert.
c. 1792 BCE	Hammurabi ascends to throne of Babylon; carves out huge empire over course of next 42 years.	c. 1766 BCE	Shang dynasty begins rule of Yellow River Valley in China.
c. 1700 BCE	Hittites begin using iron for weapons and tools.	c. 1630 BCE	Asiatic Hyksos kings take control in northern Egypt; Second Intermediate period begins.
c. 1600 BCE	Mycenae becomes major power on Greek mainland.	c. 1600 BCE	Poverty Point culture established in present-day Louisiana.
c. 1500 BCE	Tumulus culture replaces Unetician culture in parts of Europe.	c. 1500 BCE	Aryans enter India from central Asia. First Vedas composed. Olmec civilization emerges on coast of Gulf of Mexico.
c. 1450 BCE	Minoan civilization comes to end. Palaces burned down.		

c. 1600 BCE

	EUROPE AND WESTERN ASIA		AFRICA, EASTERN ASIA, AND THE AMERICAS	
	c. 1250 BCE	Mycenaean era comes to end, possibly as result of invasion from the north. Troy VIIa, the Troy of Homer, destroyed.	c. 1250 BCE	Olmec center established at San Lorenzo.
	c. 1200 BCE	Hallstatt culture emerges in present-day Austria.	c. 1200 BCE	Orally transmitted Vedas first written down.
	c. 1100 BCE	Phoenicia becomes dominant maritime power in Mediterranean. Greece enters Dark Age.	c. 1100 BCE	Iron Age begins in India.
			c. 1075 BCE	New Kingdom comes to end in Egypt.
	c. 1050 BCE	Troy VIIb destroyed; city abandoned for centuries.	c. 1050 BCE	Shang dynasty in China ousted by Zhou.
c. 1000 BCE	c. 1000 BCE	King David makes Jerusalem capital of Kingdom of Israel.	c. 1000 BCE	Caste system emerges in India. Copper industry flourishes in southern Congo. Lapita culture reaches Fiji. Nubia gains independence from Egypt.
	c. 950 BCE	Dorian invaders settle on Eurotas Plain; over next two centuries, they form city-state of Sparta.		
	c. 900 BCE	Etruscan civilization develops in central Italy.	c. 900 BCE	First Brahmanas (Hindu sacred texts) composed. Small tribal kingdoms, known as *janapadas*, develop on Gangetic Plain.
	c. 850 BCE	Greeks begin migrations to Cyprus, Crete, Aegean islands, and Anatolia.		
	c. 800 BCE	Poet Homer believed to have written *Iliad* and *Odyssey* around this time.	c. 800 BCE	Early Upanishads appended to Vedas.
	753 BCE	Traditional date given for founding of Rome.		
	c. 700 BCE	City of Byzantium founded. Scythians migrate into southern Russia from homeland in central Asia.	c. 700 BCE	Iron Age begins in Egypt.

EUROPE AND WESTERN ASIA		AFRICA, EASTERN ASIA, AND THE AMERICAS	
c. 600 BCE	Iron Age arrives in northern Europe.	c. 600 BCE	City of Teotihuacán emerges in Mexico.
c. 586 BCE	Jerusalem captured by Babylonians.	c. 563 BCE	Siddharta Gautama (later known as the Buddha) born.
559 BCE	Cyrus the Great ascends Persian throne; later conquers Medes to absorb lands into Persian Empire.	551 BCE	Kongqiu (known in West as Confucius) born.
539 BCE	Babylon falls to Persians.	529 BCE	Egypt comes under Persian rule.
c. 510 BCE	Rome becomes republic after overthrow of last king, Tarquin the Proud.		
c. 500 BCE	La Tène culture emerges in Switzerland.	c. 500 BCE	Zapotec people become powerful in Mexico. Magadha becomes leading state in India. Dong Son culture emerges in Vietnam.
490 BCE	Persian forces defeated by Greeks at Battle of Marathon.	c. 490 BCE	Chinese philosopher Lao-tzu dies.
		c. 483 BCE	The Buddha dies.
		479 BCE	Confucius dies.
		c. 475 BCE	Period of the Warring States begins in China.
387 BCE	Plato establishes Academy in Athens.	c. 383 BCE	Buddhists split into two factions.
371 BCE	Thebes defeats Sparta at Battle of Leuctra.	c. 371 BCE	Birth of Confucian philosopher Mencius.
356 BCE	Alexander the Great born in Pella, Macedonia.		

c. 500 BCE

	EUROPE AND WESTERN ASIA		AFRICA, EASTERN ASIA, AND THE AMERICAS	
			c. 350 BCE	Cities and states develop among the Maya people of Central America. Crossbow invented in China.
	332 BCE	Alexander the Great seizes Tyre and founds city of Alexandria in Egypt.		
	323 BCE	Alexander dies from fever.	321 BCE	Mauryan period begins in Magadha, India.
			c. 300 BCE	Tiwanaku civilization emerges in Andes.
	280 BCE	Greek general Pyrrhus wins two costly victories over Rome; finally defeated eight years later.	268 BCE	Ashoka becomes emperor of India.
	260 BCE	Rome defeats Carthage at Battle of Mylae.	c. 260 BCE	Ashoka converts to Buddhism.
c. 250 BCE	c. 250 BCE	Aristotle studies at Museum in Alexandria, Egypt.	c. 250 BCE	Jomon period ends in Japan. Theravada Buddhism established in Ceylon.
	218 BCE	Hannibal crosses Alps and enters Italy with army of 40,000 men.	221 BCE	Period of the Warring States ends. Shi Huang Di becomes first emperor of China at start of Qin dynasty.
	216 BCE	Hannibal inflicts massive defeat on Roman army at Battle of Cannae.	213 BCE	Qin adopt legalism as state philosophy. Shi Huang Di orders burning of books.
			206 BCE	Rebellion by Liu Bang leads to downfall of Qin dynasty and marks beginning of Han period.
			204 BCE	Great Wall of China completed.
	c. 200 BCE	Germanic tribes move southward, threatening borders of Roman Empire.	c. 200 BCE	Composition of Laws of Manu, early Hindu script.

EUROPE AND WESTERN ASIA		AFRICA, EASTERN ASIA, AND THE AMERICAS	
		185 BCE	Mauryan Empire ends in India; Shunga dynasty begins.
146 BCE	Carthage destroyed by Roman army; Carthaginian territory becomes Roman province of Africa.	**c. 140 BCE**	Wu Ti becomes emperor of China; Han dynasty reaches height of its power.
		c. 136 BCE	Han dynasty officially adopts Confucianism as Chinese state philosophy.
		c. 110 BCE	China subjugates northern Vietnam, which becomes province of Annam.
		c. 100 BCE	First Chinese historical work, *Shih-chi*, written.
85 BCE	Troy taken by Romans; city later becomes important trading port within Roman Empire	**80 BCE**	Jains split into Digambara and Shvetambara sects.
49 BCE	Julius Caesar crosses Rubicon River and marches on Rome at head of army.	**c. 50 BCE**	El Mirador emerges as principal Maya lowland center in Guatemala. In India, Ayurveda becomes established as a holistic medical system.
44 BCE	Julius Caesar assassinated in senate on ides of March.	**c. 37 BCE**	Temple of Hathar completed in Egypt.
		23 BCE	Earliest description of sumo wrestling in Japan.

	EUROPE AND WESTERN ASIA		AFRICA, EASTERN ASIA, AND THE AMERICAS	
9 CE	**9 CE**	Germanic tribes under Arminius defeat Romans in Teutoburg Forest.	**9 CE**	Wang Mang, a usurper, establishes short-lived Xin dynasty in China.
	14 CE	Roman emperor Augustus dies; succeeded by Tiberius.	**14 CE**	Famine in China.
	43 CE	Roman emperor Claudius annexes Britain.	**43 CE**	Vietnam becomes a colony of China.

EUROPE AND WESTERN ASIA		AFRICA, EASTERN ASIA, AND THE AMERICAS	
		c. 50 CE	Aksum emerges in Ethiopia.
117 CE	Roman Empire reaches greatest extent under Trajan.	c. 100 CE	Inhabitants of Indonesia begin to migrate eastward and settle in Micronesia and Polynesia.
216 CE	Baths of Caracalla open in Rome.	c. 200 CE	Iron Age methods spread to eastern and central Africa.
		220 CE	Second Han period ends in China.
251 CE	Goths cross Danube and defeat Roman general Decius.	c. 240 CE	Prophet Mani has vision urging him to spread new religious faith.
		265 CE	Jin (Chin) dynasty established in China.

	EUROPE AND WESTERN ASIA		AFRICA, EASTERN ASIA, AND THE AMERICAS	
c. 300 CE	c. 300 CE	Slavs start to settle in Russia.		
	312 CE	Constantine becomes western emperor; converts to Christianity around this time.	c. 320 CE	Gupta dynasty begins in India.
	324 CE	Constantine makes Byzantium his capital city.		
	330 CE	Byzantium becomes official capital of Roman Empire and is renamed Constantinople.	335 CE	Samudra Gupta begins conquest of more than 20 other kingdoms in India to become chakravartin (king of the world).
	361 CE	Julian the Apostate becomes emperor; attempts to reestablish old Roman religion.	375 CE	Chandragupta II begins reign that brings Gupta Empire in India to height of its power.
	395 CE	Roman Empire splits on death of Theodosius I.		

EUROPE AND WESTERN ASIA		AFRICA, EASTERN ASIA, AND THE AMERICAS	
		c. 400 CE	Hinduism develops into approximately modern form. Ghana develops into empire. First settlers arrive on Easter Island.
402 CE	Visigoths invade Italy. Roman garrison withdraws from Britain.	c. 402 CE	Chinese Buddhist monks make pilgrimages through India and Ceylon.
410 CE	Visigothic king Alaric sacks Rome.		
445 CE	Attila murders brother Bleda and becomes sole king of Huns.		
450 CE	Marcian becomes eastern emperor on death of Theodosius II.	c. 450 CE	Avesta (Zoroastrian texts) compiled.
c. 480 CE	Roman scholar Boethius born. Benedict born in Nursia, Italy.	c. 480 CE	Hindu Tantrism develops in India.
537 CE	Hagia Sophia inaugurated in Constantinople.	c. 500 CE	Buddhism established in China and Thailand. Maya commence construction of Chichén Itzá in Mexico.
c. 550 CE	Kiev emerges as leading city in Russia.	c. 550 CE	Buddhism imported to Japan.
570 CE	Prophet Mohammed born in Mecca.		
622 CE	Mohammed flees Mecca on September 20.	618 CE	Chinese Tang period begins after end of Sui dynasty.
636 CE	Bedouin warriors defeat Byzantine forces at Battle of Yarmuk River.	c. 650 CE	Paper money first circulated in China around this time.

c. 450 CE

EUROPE AND WESTERN ASIA		AFRICA, EASTERN ASIA, AND THE AMERICAS	
661 CE	Umayyads establish first caliphate with Damascus as capital.	**c. 675 CE**	Srivijaya kingdom starts to dominate maritime trade around Malay Archipelago.
680 CE	Battle of Karbala causes lasting rift between Shi'ite and Sunni Muslims.	**702 CE**	Japan adopts state system similar to that of China as result of Taika Reforms.
710 CE	Arabs capture Samarkand.	**710 CE**	Heijo becomes Japan's first fixed capital.
711 CE	Arabs cross from northern Africa; begin conquest of Spain.		
c. 750 CE **750 CE**	Abu al-Abbas defeats Umayyads at Battle of Great Zab River; start of Abbasid dynasty.	**c. 750 CE**	Pala dynasty begins in Bengal. Teotihuacán destroyed by fire in Mexico.
762 CE	Al-Mansur transfers capital of caliphate to Baghdad from Damascus.		
800 CE	Charlemagne is crowned Holy Roman emperor.	**c. 800 CE**	Khmer state begins to flourish in present-day Cambodia. Maya from Guatemalan lowlands move to highlands and into Yucatán Peninsula. Chimú kingdom becomes powerful on coast of Peru. Polynesians settle in New Zealand.
804 CE	Charlemagne finally subdues Saxons.		
813 CE	Al-Mamun becomes caliph; encourages study of Greek philosophy. Charlemagne crowns only surviving son, Louis, co-emperor.		
814 CE	Charlemagne dies; son Louis the Pious inherits empire.		
832 CE	Al-Mamun founds Bayt al-Hikma (House of Wisdom) in Baghdad.		

EUROPE AND WESTERN ASIA		AFRICA, EASTERN ASIA, AND THE AMERICAS	
860 CE	Harald Finehair inherits small kingdom; eventually becomes first sole king of Norway.		
865 CE	Vikings capture Eboracum (modern York), England.		
c. 878 CE	Danelaw created in English midlands.	c. 900 CE	Toltecs become major power in central and southern Mexico.
910 CE	Monastery founded at Cluny, France.		
911 CE	Danish Viking Rollo becomes first duke of Normandy.		
982 CE	Erik the Red reaches Greenland.		
988 CE	Russia adopts Orthodox Christianity.		
c. 1000 CE	Mahmud begins campaigns in Persia, Afghanistan, and India that lead to creation of Ghaznavid Empire.	c. 1000 CE	Leif Eriksson lands in America. Chichén Itzá captured by Toltecs. Anasazi and Mississippian peoples emerge in North America around this time.
1016 CE	England united with Denmark and Norway under Cnut the Great.	c. 1010 CE	*The Tale of Genji* written in Japan.
1039 CE	Ferdinand I of Castile and León begins Reconquista of Iberian Peninsula.	1024 CE	Muslim troops destroy Hindu temple at Somnath.
1054 CE	Great Schism between eastern and western Christian churches.		

c. 1000 CE

EUROPE AND WESTERN ASIA		AFRICA, EASTERN ASIA, AND THE AMERICAS	
1066 CE	Norman conquest of England.		
1071 CE	Turks defeat Byzantine forces at Battle of Manzikert.		
1088 CE	First European university founded at Bologna, Italy.		
1095 CE	Pope Urban II launches First Crusade.	**c. 1100 CE**	Zen Buddhism established in Japan. In Cambodia, work begins on Khmer temple of Angkor Wat. First Incas settle in Cuzco Valley.
1167 CE	Lombard League formed in northern Italian Peninsula.		
1187 CE	Saladin captures Jerusalem. Pope Gregory VIII calls Third Crusade.	**1192 CE**	Minamoto Yoritomo becomes shogun (military ruler) of Japan. Muslims capture Delhi.
1198 CE	Pope Innocent III initiates Fourth Crusade. Order of Teutonic Knights founded.	**c. 1200 CE**	Nomadic Mexica people settle on Lake Texcoco, a region dominated by Tepanecs. Anasazi complete settlement of Pueblo Bonito.
1204 CE	Constantinople sacked during Fourth Crusade.		
		1206 CE	Mamluk dynasty begins rule from Delhi.
1215 CE **1215 CE**	English barons force King John to allow Magna Carta. Frederick II becomes Holy Roman emperor. Fourth Lateran Council outlaws trial by ordeal.	**1215 CE**	Genghis Khan captures Yenking (modern Beijing).
		1227 CE	Genghis Khan dies; succeeded by son Ogotai.
		1235 CE	Kingdom of Mali founded in western Africa.
1240 CE	Kiev sacked by Mongols.		
1250 CE	Population of Europe reaches between 70 million and 100 million.	**1250 CE**	Mamluks take power in Egypt.

EUROPE AND WESTERN ASIA	AFRICA, EASTERN ASIA, AND THE AMERICAS
1256 CE Il-Khanate established.	
1258 CE Mongols sack Baghdad.	
1260 CE Iceland becomes part of Norwegian Empire.	
1261 CE Fall of Latin Empire of Constantinople.	
1265 CE Rebel baron Simon de Montfort defeated by Prince Edward at Battle of Evesham in England.	**1279 CE** Mongol leader Kublai Khan completes conquest of China.
1281 CE Osman I takes control of small emirate in Anatolia, sowing seeds for Ottoman Empire.	**1281 CE** Typhoon destroys Mongol force during attempted invasion of Japan.
	1290 CE Mamluk dynasty ends in Egypt.
1302 CE Christian armies lose last stronghold in Holy Land.	**c. 1300 CE** Anasazi and Mississippian peoples decline and disappear.
1309 CE Papacy moves from Rome to Avignon.	**1313 CE** Khan of Golden Horde converts to Islam.
1337 CE Start of Hundred Years' War between England and France.	
1346 CE English forces defeat French at Battle of Crécy.	**c. 1345 CE** Tenochtitlán and other Aztec cities emerge.
1347 CE Black Death reaches Europe; around one-third of population dies over next five years.	
1356 CE English army defeats French at Battle of Poitiers.	

1281 CE

EUROPE AND WESTERN ASIA		AFRICA, EASTERN ASIA, AND THE AMERICAS	
1360 CE	Murad I takes power; Ottoman Empire expands into Balkans and Anatolia.	1368 CE	Ming dynasty begins.
1369 CE	Burgundy and Flanders join forces through marriage of respective rulers.	1371 CE	Chinese retake Yenking (modern Beijing).
1378 CE	Ciompi workers rebel in Florence.		
1381 CE	Peasants' Revolt in England.		
1382 CE	Moscow captured by Mongols of the Golden Horde.	1398 CE	Mongols under leadership of Tamerlane attack Delhi.

c. 1400 CE

1402 CE	Tamerlane defeats Ottomans at Battle of Ankara.	c. 1400 CE	Hausa and Yoruba peoples dominate along Niger River. Aztecs oust Tepanecs as major power in Central America.
1410 CE	Combined forces of Poland and Lithuania defeat Teutonic Knights at Battle of Tannenberg.		
1419 CE	Henry the Navigator founds academy at Sagres, Portugal.		
1429 CE	English siege of Orléans lifted by Joan of Arc.		
1435 CE	Burgundy and France make peace with Treaty of Arras.		
1446 CE	Italian architect Filippo Brunelleschi, pioneer of perspective, dies.		

EUROPE AND WESTERN ASIA		AFRICA, EASTERN ASIA, AND THE AMERICAS	
c. 1450 CE	First flowering of Italian High Renaissance.	c. 1450 CE	Malacca becomes first Southeast Asian state to adopt Islam. Songhai succeeds Mali in western Africa.
1453 CE	End of Hundred Years' War. Ottomans capture Constantinople.		
c. 1454 CE	Gutenberg Bible published in Germany.		
1455 CE	Wars of the Roses start in England.		
1461 CE	Loss of Trebizond marks end of Byzantine Empire.	c. 1458 CE	Aztecs conquer Mixtec cities.
1469 CE	Lorenzo the Magnificent becomes ruler of Florence.		
1477 CE	Burgundians defeated by French and Swiss forces at siege of Nancy.		
1479 CE	Aragon and Castile united by Ferdinand and Isabella. Final phase of Reconquista of Iberia.		
1481 CE	Formalization of confederacy that forms basis of modern Switzerland.		
1485 CE	English king Richard III dies at Bosworth Field. Russia ends tributes to Mongols.	1487 CE	Bartolomeu Dias rounds Cape of Good Hope.
1488 CE	Great Swabian League formed.		
1492 CE		1492 CE	Christopher Columbus reaches New World, landing on island of San Salvador.

EUROPE AND WESTERN ASIA		AFRICA, EASTERN ASIA, AND THE AMERICAS	
		1493 CE	Huayna Capac becomes Inca king; expands territory into southern Andes.
1494 CE	Treaty of Tordesillas creates north-south line in Atlantic Ocean to provide boundary between regions of Portuguese and Spanish exploration.	1498 CE	Vasco da Gama reaches India by sailing around southern Africa.
1505 CE	Leonardo da Vinci completes *Mona Lisa*.	c. 1500 CE	Pedro Álvares Cabral reaches South America. Five Indian nations form League of the Iroquois around this time.
1509 CE	Humanist author Erasmus writes *In Praise of Folly*.	1510 CE	Portuguese establish trading post in Goa, India.
1514 CE	Ottomans defeat Safavids at Battle of Chaldiran.	1511 CE	Portuguese capture Malacca.
1516 CE	Thomas More writes *Utopia*.		
1517 CE	Protestant Reformation begins.	1517 CE	Portuguese reach China via Atlantic and Indian oceans.
1519 CE 1519 CE	Leonardo da Vinci dies.	1519 CE	Spanish force under Hernán Cortés lands on east coast of Aztec Empire.
1520 CE	Süleyman I takes power in Ottoman Empire; arts and culture flourish during his 46-year reign. Martin Luther excommunicated.	1520 CE	Portuguese explorer Ferdinand Magellan becomes first European to enter Pacific Ocean.
1521 CE	Ottoman army under Süleyman I takes city of Belgrade.	1521 CE	Aztec forces overwhelmed by Spanish forces under Cortés; end of Aztec Empire and culture.

EUROPE AND WESTERN ASIA		AFRICA, EASTERN ASIA, AND THE AMERICAS	
1522 CE	Ottomans drive Knights Hospitaller from island of Rhodes.		
1523 CE	Niccolò Machiavelli publishes *The Prince*.	**1525 CE**	Spanish forces conquer Maya in Guatemala. Epidemic kills half of Inca population.
		1526 CE	Mughals overthrow Delhi Sultanate.
1528 CE	Albrecht Dürer, one of first artists of Northern Renaissance, dies.		
1530 CE	Coronation of Holy Roman Emperor Charles V unites Burgundy, Spain, and German Empire under single ruler.	**1531 CE**	Chichén Itzá falls to Spanish explorers.
1533 CE **1533 CE**	Accession of Ivan the Terrible, first "Czar of All the Russias."	**1533 CE**	Spanish topple Inca Empire.
1538 CE	Ottoman fleet commanded by Khayr ad-Din defeats Christian fleet at Battle of Preveza.		
1546 CE	Protestant reformer Martin Luther dies.		
1547 CE	Accession of Edward VI to English throne heralds increase in number of grammar schools.	**1549 CE**	Jesuit missionary Francis Xavier arrives in Japan; arrival leads to establishment of Christianity there.
1550 CE	Vasari's *Lives of the Artists* published.		
1555 CE	Süleyman signs peace treaty with Safavids.		

	EUROPE AND WESTERN ASIA		AFRICA, EASTERN ASIA, AND THE AMERICAS	
	1582 CE	Gregorian calendar adopted in Christian countries.	**1584 CE**	English make first attempt to colonize North America.
	1588 CE	Spanish Armada attempts unsuccessfully to conquer England.	**1591 CE**	Moroccans conquer Songhai.
c. 1600 CE	**c. 1600 CE**	Portuguese naval power declines; Dutch and Flemish maritime trade increases.	**c. 1600 CE**	Dahomey founded in central Africa.
	1616 CE	English playwright William Shakespeare dies.	**1607 CE**	English establish Jamestown Colony in Virginia.
	1643 CE	Italian composer Claudio Monteverdi dies.	**1620 CE**	*Mayflower* takes first Puritans to North America; they settle in Massachusetts.
	1649 CE	King Charles I executed; England ruled by Lord Protector Oliver Cromwell.	**1642 CE**	Abel Tasman sights New Zealand.
	1660 CE	Monarchy restored in England.	**1644 CE**	Manchu dynasty succeeds Ming dynasty in China.
	1776 CE	United States declares independence from Britain.	**1687 CE**	Mughals conquer Golconda.
	1789 CE	French Revolution begins.	**1720 CE**	Tuscarora join League of the Iroquois.
			1722 CE	Jacob Roggeveen discovers Easter Island.
			1769 CE	English mariner James Cook arrives in Tahiti.
			1879 CE	British defeat Zulus.

GLOSSARY

Abbasids dynasty of caliphs formed by descendants of Mohammed's uncle Abbas; ruled from Baghdad (750–1258 CE) until it was sacked by Mongols. Accorded a purely religious function in Egypt, Abbasids held power there from 1261 to 1517 CE.

Abrittus site of battle in which the Roman emperor Decius was defeated and killed by the Goths in 251 CE; modern Razgrad, Bulgaria.

Achaemenids Persian 27th dynasty of Egypt (525–404 BCE); founded by Cambyses II of Persia and named after his family, the Achaemenids. Darius I was a member of this dynasty.

acropolis fortified part of an ancient Greek city. The most famous such fortress is the Acropolis in Athens, where various large temples were built, including the Parthenon.

Actium place on the Greek north-west coast near where Octavian defeated the fleet of Antony and Cleopatra in 31 BCE. This victory gave Octavian definitive power as Roman emperor.

adobe type of brick made from sun-baked mud and straw.

Adonis in Greek mythology, a young mortal man of outstanding beauty; favorite of Aphrodite.

Adrianople site of battle in 378 CE in which 20,000 Visigoths defeated and killed the Roman emperor Valens and most of his troops; present-day Edirne, Turkey.

aedilis government officials in the Roman republic; equivalent to magistrate. *Aediles* oversaw public order, the market, water, grain supplies, and games. Initially, they

were officers at the temple of Diana in the Latin League.

Aegean Sea part of the Mediterranean Sea that separates mainland Greece from Asia Minor (part of modern Turkey).

Aeneas mythical hero who escaped the ruins of Troy and settled in Italy. His story is the subject of Virgil's epic poem the *Aeneid*.

Ahura Mazda Zoroastrian god of light and truth.

ajaw hereditary Mayan monarch who ruled a city-state.

Akhetaton city built by Akhenaton to replace the old Egyptian capital at Thebes; modern Amarna, Egypt.

Akkadians Semitic people who flourished in the third millennium BCE; named after Akkad, the capital of their empire.

Alans originally a Persian steppe people who settled in Scythia in the fourth century BCE. Conquered by the Huns, they later became allies.

Alba Longa city in southern Latium; considered the mother city of Rome; according to legend, freed by Romulus and Remus from a usurper; destroyed around 650 BCE.

Albigensians Christian heretics in southern France in the 12th and 13th centuries CE. They were attacked by the Albigensian Crusade in 1209 CE and were finally destroyed by the Inquisition.

Alemanni southern Germanic people; threatened Roman borders and invaded Gaul in the third century CE; conquered eastern Gaul in the

fourth century CE; defeated by the Frankish king Clovis I.

Alexandria greatest city of the ancient world. It lies on the Mediterranean Sea on the western edge of the delta of the Nile River and was founded in 332 BCE by Alexander the Great.

Allah Arabic word for God.

Almohads Islamic reformers from northern Africa who drove the Almoravids out of southern Spain in 1146 CE, establishing a strong caliphate.

Almoravids fundamental Muslim tribe from the southern Sahara who conquered northern Africa and aided the Muslims in Córdoba against the Christians between 1086 and 1146 CE.

Amarna Letters archive of clay tablets written in Babylonian cuneiform script; found at Akhetaton.

Ameratsu Japanese sun goddess from whom the imperial family claims direct descent.

Amorites Semitic people who invaded Mesopotamia from the north and northwest around 2000 BCE. They were slowly absorbed into the Mesopotamian population.

Amulius mythical usurper of his older brother, Numitor, as king of Alba Longa; separated his niece, Rea Silvia, from her twin children, Romulus and Remus.

Anatolia another name for Asia Minor (part of modern Turkey).

Angkor Wat temple complex in Khmer capital; built around 1100 CE;

famous monument in present-day Cambodia.

Antigonids descendants of Demetrius Poliorcetes; ruling dynasty of Macedonia from 306 to 168 BCE.

Anubis ancient Egyptian god of the dead; depicted as a jackal or as a man with the head of a jackal.

apanage region in the French Empire controlled by the younger brothers of the French king. Burgundy was an *apanage* until the Hundred Years' War.

Apennines range of hills and mountains that forms the spine of the Italian Peninsula.

Apollo Greek god of the sun, oracles, music, poetry, and justice; son of Zeus. The god of medicine, Apollo could also choose to inflict disease as punishment.

Aquae Sextiae Roman city in Gaul; modern Aix-en-Provence, France.

Aquileia city in northeastern Italy; founded as a Roman colony in 181 BCE to prevent barbarian incursions.

Aquitania area of Gaul between the Pyrenees and the Garonne River.

Arabia desert peninsula lying to the east of the Mediterranean Sea.

Aragon Christian kingdom in northeastern Spain, south of the Pyrenees.

Aramaeans Semitic people who invaded southern Mesopotamia (Babylonia) around 1100 BCE. They slowly assumed the Babylonian culture and constituted a large part of the population.

Aramaic Semitic language that was widely spoken in western Asia until displaced by Greek after the conquests of Alexander the Great.

Arcadia mountainous region of the central Peloponnese, Greece.

archons magistrates in Athens, beginning around the seventh century BCE. Elected annually, their duties comprised legislation, the dispensation of justice, the conduct of religion, and military affairs.

Arianism doctrine of fourth-century-CE theologian Arius; held that Jesus Christ was not of the same substance as God, but merely the best of created beings.

Ariminum town on Adriatic coast of Italy; site of modern city of Rimini.

Armenia region of the Transcaucasus between the Black Sea and the Caspian Sea.

Armorica Latin name for northwestern Gaul, now Brittany.

Arretium ancient town in western central Italy; now the city of Arezzo.

Artemisium, Battle of Persian naval victory over the Greeks in 480 BCE.

Aryans prehistoric inhabitants of Iran and northern India.

Ascanius mythical son of Aeneas; according to legend, the founder of Alba Longa, a city near Rome.

Assyrians people of northern Mesopotamia whose independent state, established in the 14th century BCE, became a major power in the region.

Astarte Canaanite and Phoenician goddess of procreation, fertility, and love. She was originally equated with the Semitic goddess Ishtar and later associated with the Greek goddess Aphrodite. Astarte was also connected with Baal and was worshipped as the mother-goddess until Roman times.

astrolabe device used by sailors to take sightings of the sun and stars for navigational purposes. The astrolabe was circular in shape and was marked in degrees around its circumference. Sailors used astrolabes to calculate their ships' latitude (their distance to the north or the south of the equator).

Athens preeminent city-state of ancient Greece.

Aton Egyptian sun god Re when worshipped in the form of the disk of the sun.

Attica region of central Greece. Its chief city was Athens.

Australopithecus "southern ape"; an upright-walking hominid from around 4 million years ago; found in Africa.

avatar from *avatara*, Sanskrit for "descent"; in Hinduism, the incarnation of a deity in human or animal form. The term usually refers to any of the 10 principal manifestations of the god Vishnu.

ayllu administrative area within the Inca Empire.

Aztecs Mesoamerican people who controlled a large empire in central and southern Mexico from the 14th to the 16th century CE. The Aztec Empire came to an end in 1521 CE, when it came under attack from the Spanish conquistador Hernán Cortés.

ba in ancient Egyptian religion, one of the three main aspects of the soul, along with ka (the sum of a person's physical and intellectual qualities) and akh (the spirit in the hereafter).

Babylon city in southern Mesopotamia that was the center of an Amorite empire under Hammurabi. Later, Babylon continued as the cultural and political capital of the region. From 612 to 539 BCE,

Babylon was the capital of the Neo-Babylonian Empire.

Babylonian Captivity 14th-century-CE period when the popes resided in Avignon because Italy was divided by feuds among noblemen. Avignon became a bureaucratic center of corrupt popes and prelates.

Bacchiads aristocratic family that ruled the city-state of Corinth in the seventh century BCE.

Bactrians people from the ancient country of Bactria, which lay between the mountains of the Hindu Kush and the Amu Darya (ancient Oxus River) in what is now part of Afghanistan, Uzbekistan, and Tajikistan.

Badr, Battle of battle near Medina in 624 CE that was Mohammed's first military victory. It damaged Meccan prestige, strengthened the political position of Muslims in Medina, and established Islam in Arabia.

Baghdad city built by Al-Mansur to appease the Persian Muslims; center of trade, industry, and Persian culture; destroyed by the Mongols.

Balearic Islands group of islands in the western Mediterranean Sea. The largest are today known as Mallorca, Minorca, Ibiza, and Formentera.

Bantu people of Africa, south of the equator, who speak related languages. After around 1000 BCE, they occupied large portions of Africa, leaving the area around Lake Chad and mixing with agricultural people.

basileus title of the Byzantine emperor, regarded as the head of Christendom and God's representative on Earth.

Bayt al-Hikma (House of Wisdom) library and translation institute in Abbasid Baghdad.

Bedouin nomadic people of the Arabian Desert; converted to Islam around 622 CE; dominated non-Islamic population under the Umayyads; forced to yield power to the Abbasid dynasty around 750 CE.

bell-beaker people Neolithic people who spread from Spain to northern Africa and western and central Europe between 2600 and 2000 BCE.

Berbers descendants of the pre-Arab inhabitants of northern Africa.

Black Death plague that originated in Asia and ravaged Europe between 1347 and 1351 CE, killing around one-third of the population.

Blues political party in Constantinople that organized important horse races against the Greens. Despite the lack of a clear political program, they had great influence on politics and religion.

Bosporus strait, 19 miles (30 km) long, that joins the Black Sea and the Sea of Marmara.

Brahma paramount Indian god; preacher of the Vedas; appears in Hinduism as part of the trinity of Brahma the creator, Vishnu the restorer, and Shiva the destroyer.

broadside simultaneous discharge of all the guns on one side of a ship.

bronze copper-tin alloy widely used by 1700 BCE.

Bronze Age period during which bronze became the most important basic material; began around 3500 BCE in western Asia and around 1900 BCE in Europe.

Buddhism religion founded by Siddharta Gautama, called the Buddha; rejected much of Hinduism, including priestly authority, the Vedic scriptures, sacrificial practices, and the caste system. Its goal is nirvana (release from all desire and from the cycle of life, death, and rebirth). The major schools of Buddhism are Theravada and Mahayana.

Bulgaria region and nation of the Balkans that constituted the strongest empire in eastern Europe in the 9th and 10th centuries CE. Incorporated into the Byzantine Empire in 1018 CE, Bulgaria rebelled in 1185 CE, forming another empire, which collapsed in the 14th century CE.

Burgundy region of eastern France that became a powerful independent state in the 15th century CE. Its main city is Dijon.

Busta Gallorum site of decisive battle in 552 CE where the Byzantine general Narses defeated the Goths, who were led by their Christian king, Totila; modern Gualdo Tadino, Italy.

Buyids native dynasty that ruled in western Iran and Iraq in the period between the Arab and Turkish conquests (945–1055 CE).

Byblos first city in pre-Phoenician Levant to trade with Egypt. Around 1200 BCE, it was superseded as a trading center by Sidon and Tyre. Byblos was the center of the Astarte-Tammuz cult in Roman times.

Byzantium ancient Greek city on the shore of the Bosporus; later known as Constantinople; modern Istanbul.

Calais port on the north coast of France; conquered by the English king Edward III after the Battle of Crécy in 1346 CE; remained an English bridgehead on the mainland of Europe until the 16th century CE.

Caledonia area of northern Britain; present-day Scotland.

caliph from *khalifah*, Arabic for "successor"; religious and political

leader of Islam; successor to Mohammed. Competing caliphs divided the Islamic states.

caliphate office and realm held by a caliph.

Campania region of southern Italy between the modern cities of Naples and Salerno.

Canaanites Semitic tribes who settled in Palestine and the western Levant in the third millennium BCE and mixed with the native population. They maintained separate city-states. Around 1200 BCE, their territory was infiltrated by Israelites and Philistines.

Cannae town in southeastern Italy; site of the worst defeat in Roman history. Hannibal surrounded a Roman army there and destroyed it in 216 BCE.

Capetians ruling house of France from 987 to 1328 CE. The Capetians all descended from Robert the Strong (died 866 CE).

Cappadocia district in east-central Anatolia; now part of Turkey.

Capua major Greek colony in southern Italy; first Greek colony to side with Hannibal in the Second Punic War.

caravel small, highly maneuverable, trading ship.

Carchemish Hittite trading city on the Euphrates River. After the fall of the Hittite Empire around 1200 BCE, it became the most important Neo-Hittite state. Carchemish was later conquered by the Assyrians.

Carpi ancient Dacian people who inhabited the Carpathian Mountains in modern Romania.

carrack type of trading ship that was characterized by a large stern, a large central rudder, and three or more masts.

Carthage city in northern Africa on the shores of the Mediterranean Sea; now a suburb of Tunis.

Carthusians monastic order that stressed penance, solitude, and asceticism; founded at the end of the 11th century CE.

cartouche oval frame enclosing the hieroglyphs of the name of an Egyptian sovereign.

cassava plant grown by the Maya, who used its sap to make an alcoholic drink.

Castile originally a Christian kingdom in northern Spain; in the 11th century CE, annexed León and spread Castilian culture throughout the Iberian Peninsula.

Cathars heretical Christian sect that flourished in western Europe in the 12th and 13th centuries CE. The Cathari believed that there are two principles, one good and one evil, and that the material world is evil.

Celts name given to a group of people occupying central and western Europe (from the British Isles to Hungary) by 1000 BCE. Bearers of the Celtic civilization are the Hallstatt and La Tène cultures; the Urnfield culture also has Celtic characteristics.

censor office in the Roman republic to which two ex-consuls were elected for five-year terms. They estimated the number of citizens for purposes of categorization, taxation, and military service, and they judged moral behavior.

Ceres Roman goddess of agriculture.

Chaeronea, Battle of conflict in which Philip II of Macedon defeated Thebes and Athens in 338 BCE.

Chalcedon ancient port on the Bosporus; overshadowed by its proximity to Byzantium.

Chalcolithic period time when copper first began to be used to make tools and weapons, prior to the Bronze Age.

Chaldeans Aramaean people from southern Mesopotamia who caused the fall of Assyria in the seventh century BCE.

Cham Austronesian-speaking carvers and temple builders who prospered until they were subdued by the Vietnamese in the 15th century CE.

chaski runners who were used to relay messages from one part of the Inca Empire to another. The runners were stationed at regular intervals along the empire's roads.

chinampa artificial island created by the Aztecs in Lake Texcoco. The Aztecs made *chinampas* out of mud and used them to grow crops such as corn.

choregi Greek sponsors of theatrical productions and competitions.

Christendom in the Middle Ages, the Christian world of western Europe. The main threat to Christendom came from the Islamic empires of western Asia and northern Africa.

Cimbrians people who invaded southern France and Spain around 111 BCE; defeated by Gaius Marius.

Ciompi Rebellion uprising of Florentine workers in the woolen industry in 1378 CE.

Cistercians monastic order founded in 1098 CE in France.

Classic period period of American history that lasted roughly from 300 to 900 CE.

Clermont, Council of public meeting called by Pope Urban II to announce the First Crusade.

Cloaca Maxima the first public sewer in Rome; completed in the third century BCE.

Cluny abbey near Mâcon, Burgundy, France, founded in 910 CE. The Cluniac movement that originated there strongly influenced the Roman Catholic Church, particularly monasticism, for the next 250 years.

codex (plural: codices) book made by the Aztecs and Maya; provided a largely pictorial record of their cultures; produced both before and after the Spanish conquest in the 16th century CE.

comedy originally, any play or literary composition with a nontragic ending.

comos procession of Greek citizens during which they wore masks and danced and sang; often part of festivals in honor of Dionysus.

Concordat of Worms compromise in 1122 CE between Pope Calixtus II and Holy Roman Emperor Henry V on investiture. The church was accorded the right to elect and invest bishops but only in the presence of the emperor, who retained the right to confer any land and wealth attached to the bishopric.

conquistador leader of the Spanish forces that conquered parts of Central America and South America in the 16th century CE.

Constance, Council of council (1414–1418 CE) that ended the schism and forced a number of popes to abdicate.

Constantinople name for Byzantium (present-day Istanbul), which became the (Christian) residence of the emperor Constantine in 330 CE. In

395 CE, it became the capital of the eastern Roman Empire.

consul one of two co-leaders of republican Rome. Each consul served only one year in office at a time.

copper reddish brown metallic element; chemical symbol Cu.

Corcyra ancient name for the Greek island of Corfu.

Corinth city of the Peloponnese, around 50 miles (80 km) west of Athens.

Corinthian War conflict that lasted from 395 to 387 BCE between Sparta and an alliance among Thebes, Athens, Corinth, and Argos, initially supported by Persia.

Corupedium, Battle of fought in 281 BCE, the decisive confrontation between the successors to Alexander the Great.

Council of 500 originally conceived by Cleisthenes and fully realized by Solon, a political decision-making body in Athens consisting of 10 groups, each of 50 men, chosen by lot.

Crannon, Battle of confrontation in 322 BCE in which Macedonian forces under Antipater defeated rebellious Greek forces led by the Athenians.

Crécy town near the northern coast of France; site where the French army, consisting of knights, was destroyed in 1346 CE by the English infantry, opening the way for Edward III to conquer Calais.

crop rotation farming system in which fields are divided into groups (typically of three) in which a different one is left fallow every year so that it may regenerate.

Croton Greek colony in the south of the Italian Peninsula in which

Pythagoras settled around 530 BCE; the modern city of Crotone, Italy.

crusades military expeditions undertaken by Christians from the end of the 11th century to the end of the 13th century CE, primarily to recover the Holy Land from Muslim control.

Ctesiphon capital of the ancient Persian Empire.

cuneiform script consisting of characters pressed into clay with the use of styluses. It was used by the Sumerians and the Semites, though created by the native Mesopotamians. It started as images but evolved into a syllabic script.

cuprite mineral composed of copper oxide (chemical formula CuO); minor ore of the metal copper.

Cuzco capital of the Inca Empire.

Cycladic civilization Bronze Age civilization from around 3300 to 1000 BCE on the Greek Cyclades islands.

Cynics from the Greek *kunikoi*. Followers of Diogenes and Antisthenes, they protested the material interests of established society. Holding virtue to be the only good, they stressed independence from worldly needs and pleasures and led austere lives.

Cyrenaica coastal district of southern Mediterranean Sea; former Greek colony; now part of Libya.

Dacia area of the Carpathian Mountains and Transylvania, in present-day Romania.

Damascus ancient capital of a city-state in Roman times; conquered variously by David of Israel, Assyrian Tiglath-pileser III in 732 BCE, and Alexander the Great in 333–332 BCE; part of the Seleucid kingdom until taken by Pompey the Great in

64 BCE. Made a Christian bishopric in the first century CE, it was taken over by Muslims in 635 CE and by Turks in 1056 CE. Damascus was besieged by the Christians in 1148 CE. In 1154 CE, it fell to the Egyptians. It was the headquarters of Saladin during the Third Crusade.

Danegeld direct tax introduced by Aethelred the Unready, an Anglo-Saxon king; paid as annual tribute to the Vikings (Danes).

Danelaw Viking kingdom in north-eastern England.

Danube river of eastern Europe that rises in the Black Forest in Germany and flows 1,770 miles (2,850 km) through the Balkans to the Black Sea.

dead reckoning system used by sailors to calculate the position of a ship in terms of longitude.

Delhi Sultanate principal Muslim sultanate in northern India from 1206 to 1526 CE.

Delian League (477–404 BCE) voluntary alliance of Athens and Ionian city-states in Asia Minor, the Aegean islands, and colonies in Thrace to rid themselves of Persians remaining after the Persian War; dominated by Athens; dissolved after the Peloponnesian War.

Delos one of the Cyclades, a group of islands in the Aegean Sea.

Delphi city in central Greece; site of an Apollo sanctuary and an oracle. The utterances of Pythia, the priestess of the oracle, had great influence on personal and political life.

Demeter Greek goddess of the earth and agriculture.

democracy from the Greek *demos* (people) and *kratein* (to rule); government by the people, either directly or through elected representatives. This form of government arose at the end of the sixth century BCE in Athens.

diadochs military commanders who succeeded Alexander the Great.

dictator magistrate appointed by the Roman senate; given unlimited authority in matters of state and war for six months.

Dionysia Greek annual festival in honor of Dionysus; characterized by processions, poetry competitions, and theatrical performances.

Dionysus Greek god of wine, ecstasy, reproduction, life force, chaos, and death.

dithyramb ancient Greek hymn of praise to the god Dionysus.

Dnieper fourth longest river in Europe; flows 1,367 miles (2,200 km) from the Valdai Hills to the west of Moscow to the Black Sea.

Dniester river of eastern Europe that rises on the north side of the Carpathian Mountains and flows for 840 miles (1,352 km) south and east (through modern Ukraine and Moldova) to the Black Sea.

Dodona site, near Epirus in north-western Greece, of an oracle devoted to the god Zeus.

dolmen Neolithic burial chamber constructed from two or more great stone slabs set edgewise in the earth and a flat stone roof.

Domesday Book land registry in which all property of the inhabitants of England was registered for tax purposes; introduced during the reign of William I.

Dominican member of a Christian order of friars founded by Saint Dominic of Spain in 1216 CE; also known as the Black Friars.

Donatists northern African Christians who believed that the holy sacraments could be administered only by priests who were without sin; named for their leader, Donatus (died c. 355 CE); outlawed as heretics.

Dong Son culture that emerged around 2000 BCE; by 500 BCE, proficient in metallurgy and at producing distinctive bronze drums; named for a village in northern Vietnam where artifacts were first discovered.

Dorians people from Macedonia and northern Greece who conquered parts of the Peloponnese and Crete between 1200 and 1000 BCE.

Early Dynastic period era of Egyptian history, also known as the Archaic period, when the pharaohs developed an effective system of ruling the whole of Egypt; lasted from around 2925 to 2650 BCE.

earthenware vessels and containers made of baked clay; in widespread use for cooking and storage by Neolithic cultures.

Eboracum Roman name for their fortification in northern England; later became the Viking town of Yorvick and finally the modern city of York.

ecclesia the tribal meeting of Athens open to all citizens that, after Cleisthenes' reforms, made the final political decisions on internal and foreign affairs.

Elam ancient country in western Asia, roughly equivalent to modern southwestern Iran.

Elea ancient town in Italy founded by Greek refugees; famous for its school of philosophy; modern Velia.

Eleusinian Mysteries secret religious rites in ancient Greece that involved the worship of the goddess Demeter.

Eleusis city on the Greek coast near Athens where mysteries were held between around 600 and 400 BCE.

ensi governor of a Sumerian city-state; temple king and ruler of the city on behalf of the deity and the temple.

Ephesus Ionian city in ancient Anatolia (part of modern Turkey).

Ephesus, Council of meeting of Christian leaders in 431 CE that confirmed Mary's status as the Mother of God.

Epic of Gilgamesh ancient poem written in the Akkadian language. The earliest surviving written version was inscribed in cuneiform script in the seventh century BCE.

Epicureanism philosophy founded by Epicurus (341–270 BCE). Its central tenets were the pursuit of happiness and the avoidance of pain.

Epidamnus colony on the Adriatic coast in part of what is now Albania; founded in the fifth century BCE by Greeks from Corcyra.

Epidaurus small but important city-state of ancient Greece; situated in the northeastern Peloponnese.

Epirus ancient kingdom occupying the coastal region of northwestern Greece and southern Albania.

Etruscans ancient people of central Italy whose civilization emerged around 900 BCE, before the founding of Rome.

Euphrates river of western Asia that flows from the mountains of western Asia to the Persian Gulf. Its lower reaches form the western edge of Mesopotamia.

Eurymedon river in Asia Minor; site of a major battle in 466 BCE between the Persians and the Delian League.

Ezo northern part of Japan roughly coextensive with modern Hokkaido.

fasces symbol of the Roman magistrates' legal authority; ax head projecting from a bundle of wooden sticks tied together with a red strap.

Fatimids Shi'ite dynasty of caliphs in northern Africa (909–1171 CE); descended from Mohammed's daughter Fatima; conquered Egypt and founded Cairo around 969 CE.

Fifth Crusade (1217–1221 CE) expedition that conquered Lisbon in 1217 CE and Damietta in Egypt in 1219 CE. Against the pope's wishes, the crusaders tried to conquer Egyptian territory in exchange for Jerusalem, but their attempt ended in failure.

First Crusade (1095–1099 CE) led by Godfrey of Bouillon and Raymond of Toulouse; conquered Edessa, Tripoli, Antioch, and Jerusalem, making them Christian kingdoms.

Flanders region on the North Sea coast; made part of Charlemagne's empire in the 9th century CE. Under independent counts, it developed into a regional power. In the 11th century CE, the counts of Flanders were vassals for both the French crown and the Holy Roman Empire. A duchy of the French king, beginning in the 12th century CE, it was economically dependent on England for its textile manufacture. When Edward III prohibited the export of wool in 1337 CE, Flanders rebelled against France; the uprising was crushed in 1340 CE.

flint hard type of stone found in calcium and chalk layers; easily chipped to make tools; widely used in the Paleolithic and Mesolithic ages.

flower war war waged by the Aztecs with the specific goal of capturing people for sacrifice.

foederati "the federated"; foreigners allied with the Romans; populated and patrolled land at imperial borders; provided troops for the Roman army.

Fourth Crusade (1202–1204 CE) expedition by French knights; captured Byzantium with the aid of Venice and founded a western-style empire.

Franciscan member of a Christian order of friars founded by Saint Francis of Assisi in 1209 CE. Originally, Franciscans made a vow to adhere to a life of strict poverty, but this requirement was later modified.

fresco type of painting in which the paint is applied to wet plaster; usually decorated walls or ceilings.

Frigidus River, Battle of battle in which Theodosius defeated Eugenius in 394 CE, thereby becoming emperor of both the eastern and western Roman empires.

Fujiwara period (858–1060 CE) era during which Japan was ruled by the Fujiwara family.

funnel-beaker culture culture that flourished around 2500 BCE in northern and central Europe; named for the characteristic shape of its earthenware.

Galatia ancient district in central Anatolia (part of modern Turkey).

Ganesh Hindu god.

Garonne river of southwestern France that rises in the Spanish central Pyrenees and flows 357 miles (575 km) to its confluence with the Dordogne River. From that point to the Atlantic Ocean, 45 miles (72 km) to the north, the estuary of the combined rivers is known as the Gironde.

Gaugamela, Battle of military confrontation in 331 BCE in which

Alexander the Great defeated Darius III of Persia.

Germanic tribes people from north-western Europe who migrated south-ward, beginning around 200 BCE.

Ghibellines (Waiblingen) supporters of the House of Hohenstaufen and proponents of the rule of a strong Holy Roman emperor over the church; ultimately defeated by their long-term enemies, the Guelphs.

Gnosticism philosophical and reli-gious movement that was prominent in the Greco-Roman world in the second century CE. It had a profound influence on developing Christianity.

Golden Horde western part of the Mongol Empire. At its peak, it included most of European Russia.

Golden Horn inlet of the Bosporus that forms a natural harbor at Constantinople (modern Istanbul).

Gordian knot according to Greek legend, a complex knot that could only be untied by the man destined to become king of Asia. The young Alexander the Great cut it with one blow of his sword.

Goths a German group in the third century CE. Living in Dacia, they were feared plunderers threatening the Roman borders. In the fourth century CE, the West Goths were driven back by the Huns. The Romans allowed them to settle below the Danube River. In 410 CE, they attacked Rome under the leadership of Alaric. The East Goths were conquered by the Huns and moved to Hungary.

grammar school educational estab-lishment that was open to secular pupils as well as trainee priests.

Granicus River, Battle of military confrontation between Alexander the Great and the Persian Empire near Troy in Asia Minor in 334 BCE.

Great Swabian League alliance between the cities of Swabia, the Rhineland, Bavaria, and Franconia; formed under the protection of the emperor Frederick III in 1488 CE.

Great Wall of China defensive barrier that extended for 4,160 miles (6,700 km) along the country's northern and eastern frontiers; completed in 204 BCE.

Greek fire secret Byzantine weapon, used especially against Arabs at sieges of Constantinople in the seventh and eighth centuries CE. Its main con-stituent, naphtha (a highly combustible hydrocarbon), burned spontaneously when sprayed onto enemy ships.

Greens party in Constantinople influential in politics and religion; organized horse races against the Blues party; comprised traders and working-class people.

Guelphs (Welfs) supporters of the House of Guelph and proponents of a monarchy with little influence, powerful vassals, and an autonomous church. From 1125 CE, they fought the Ghibellines and eventually defeated the last scion of the Hohenstaufen family.

guilds organizations of merchants and artisans; supervised working conditions and the quality and price of manufacture. Only guild members were allowed to practice in the cities.

Gupta Empire dynasty that ruled much of India (c. 320–550 CE) after a period of instability following the fall of the Mauryans.

Gur town founded by the Sassanian king Ardashir I to commemorate his victory over the Parthian king Artabanus; modern Firuzabad, Iran.

Gutians Iranian mountain people who invaded the Akkadian Empire repeatedly between around 2230 and 2100 BCE.

Hades god of the underworld and brother of Zeus; also the name of the underworld itself.

Hadith Arabic for "story"; companion book to the Koran; guide for Muslim daily life; details incidents in Mohammed's life and his maxims.

Hagia Sophia great domed Church of the Holy Wisdom in Constantinople; designed by Anthemius of Tralles and Isidorus of Miletus; built between 532 and 537 CE under Emperor Justinian.

Hallstatt culture central European culture of the late Bronze and early Iron ages; flourished around 800 to 500 BCE.

hand-ax Paleolithic tool originally made of flint. Increasingly made of other stones, it was refined throughout the Paleolithic period.

Han dynasty ruling dynasty of China (206 BCE–220 CE); restored the agrarian economy and introduced Confucianism as the state religion; defeated the Huns and undertook expeditions across the Chinese borders. Government tasks were fulfilled by state officials from the class of large landowners called mandarins.

Hanseatic League union of free cities in northern Germany that promoted their own interests in trade; formed in the 12th century CE. The leading Hanseatic centers included Bremen, Hamburg, and Lübeck. The league later grew to include non-German cities, such as Riga, Stockholm, and Szczecin.

Hanukkah Jewish midwinter festival that commemorates the restoration of

Jewish rites in the temple at Jerusalem by Judas Maccabaeus.

Hausa people of northwestern Nigeria and southern Niger.

hegira Arabic for "flight"; journey of Mohammed from Mecca to Medina, September 20, 622 CE; used as the first date of the Muslim calendar; the starting point of Islam.

Heiji Disturbance confrontation in Japan in 1159 CE in which the Taira clan overcame the Minamoto clan. The Taira became the major power in the land for a generation.

Heijo city in Nara that became Japan's first fixed capital in 710 CE. The capital had previously moved around with the emperor.

Hejaz region of Arabian Peninsula along the Red Sea coast.

Heliopolis city of ancient Egypt and site of a great temple to the sun god Re.

Helladic culture Bronze Age culture from around 3300 to 1000 BCE on the Greek mainland.

hemlock poisonous herb; commonly thought to have been the cause of Socrates's death.

Hephthalites nomadic people, originally from the Mongolian steppes, who created an empire in Persia and India in the sixth century CE.

Heracles greatest and strongest of Greek mythological heroes; also known as Hercules.

Hermes Greek god of travelers, shepherds, trade, and cunning. The son of Zeus and the messenger of the gods, he guided souls to the underworld.

hieroglyphs oldest Egyptian script. It was originally based on images, but later, as a result of the need to represent abstract concepts, it developed into a combination of ideograms, syllable signs, and letters.

Hinduism predominant religion in India, originating from Brahmanism; characterized by belief in many gods headed by Brahma, Shiva, and Vishnu.

Hittites people from Asia Minor who spoke an Indo-European language and settled in Asia Minor around 2000 BCE. They expanded their territory politically southward into Syria, Mesopotamia, and Canaan between 1650 and 1350 BCE. The Hittite Empire disappeared around 1200 BCE after the rise of Assyria and invasions by the Sea Peoples.

Hohenstaufens German dynasty that ruled the Holy Roman Empire in the 12th and 13th centuries CE.

Holy Roman Empire title adopted in the 13th century CE in an effort to reinstate the Roman Empire. Mainly comprised of German states, its first emperor, Otto the Great, was crowned in 962 CE. By 1100 CE, the empire included the kingdoms of Italy, Bohemia, Burgundy, and Germany. It lasted until 1806 CE.

Homo erectus hominid who walked upright and lived between 500,000 and 150,000 years ago in Africa, Asia, and Europe; first hominid species to be found outside Africa; includes Java man (*Pithecanthropus*) and Peking man; used tools, made shelters, and utilized fires.

Homo habilis hominid who walked upright and lived around 2 million years ago, at the same time as *Australopithecus*; first hominid species to be found in association with manufactured tools.

Homo sapiens sapiens modern man; developed around 100,000 years ago; displaced Neanderthals around 30,000 years ago.

hoplites soldiers in the Greek heavy infantry, armed with swords, lances, and the large round shields known as hoplons.

Horatius legendary Roman hero who singlehandedly defended a bridge in Rome against the forces of Lars Porsenna and the entire Etruscan army.

Hormuz island in the Strait of Hormuz, between the Persian Gulf and the Gulf of Oman; site of battle in which Ardashir defeated the Parthians and killed Artabanus in 224 CE.

Horus Egyptian sun god and son of Osiris; represented as a falcon.

huaca sacred object worshipped by the Incas. *Huacas* could take the form of natural phenomena such as rocks, human-made objects, or the mummified remains of sacred people.

humanism school of thought that stressed the artistic, intellectual, and scientific achievements of humankind. With its secular outlook, humanism contrasted with earlier ways of looking at the world that centered around humanity's relationship with God.

Hundred Years' War (1337–1453 CE) war between France and England, which still possessed areas in France. The immediate cause was a dispute about the succession to the French throne. By 1453 CE, England had lost all territory in France except for Calais.

Huns central Asiatic people noted for horsemanship and ferocity in battle; drove the Visigoths from Ukraine (c. 370 CE); conquered eastern and central Europe in the fifth century CE; seized western Europe under Attila (c. 450 CE).

Hurrians tribe from east-central Asia that settled in northern Mesopotamia

around 1800 BCE. The Hurrians founded the Mitanni Empire ruled by a militarily superior Indo-European elite. After around 1200 BCE, they settled in Urartu and from there conquered parts of Syria and Phoenicia.

Hwang He (Hwang Ho; Yellow River) China's second longest river; flows for 3,395 miles (5,464 km) from the Plateau of Tibet to the Yellow Sea.

Hyksos Asiatic people who settled in Egypt during the 17th century BCE. They later ruled the kingdom.

Iberians non-Celtic Iron Age people of Spain and southern France. The high point of their culture was from the fifth to the third century BCE.

ice ages climatic episodes characterized by a great drop in temperature, the expansion of ice caps at regions of higher latitude, and changes in flora and fauna.

I Ching (Yi Jing; **Book of Changes)** Chinese divination manual; traditionally attributed to Confucius.

iconoclasm policy of destroying religious images (icons); introduced in the eighth century CE by the Byzantine emperor Leo III.

Il-Khanate Mongol dynasty that ruled in Persia in the 13th and 14th centuries CE.

Illyria ancient region of the Balkans; part of modern Albania.

imam Arabic for "leader"; the head of the Muslim community.

Inanna Sumerian fertility goddess; daughter of Anu (the god of heaven and ruler of the gods). She merged with the Semitic god Ishtar during the Akkadian Empire and became the goddess of love and fertility.

Incas people who lived on the west coast of South America and ruled a vast empire that reached the height of its power in the 15th century CE. The empire stretched from present-day Ecuador in the north to central Chile in the south.

Indies vague term used by people in the Middle Ages to describe a number of different places in Asia, including China, Japan, and the Spice Islands. Many of the great explorers of the 15th and 16th centuries CE undertook their voyages to try to find a westbound route to the Indies.

Indo-European languages common family of European and Asiatic (Indian) languages.

Indus river of south Asia that flows 1,800 miles (2,900 km) from southwestern Tibet to the Arabian Sea near modern Karachi (Pakistan).

interdict papal sanction whereby citizens of the territory of a sinner are excluded from religious ceremonies; allowed the pope to pit the religious populace against the perpetrator.

Intiwatana Inca temple associated with the worship of the sun.

investiture controversy dispute over the appointment of clergy by lay people. It was resolved in favor of the church at the Concordat of Worms in 1122 CE.

Ionia coastal region of southwestern Anatolia (part of modern Turkey) that contained several Greek city-states.

Ionians Greek tribe driven from the mainland (except Attica) by the Dorians; settled on the Greek islands and on the west coast of Asia Minor in the ninth century BCE.

iron metallic element (chemical symbol Fe) that can be made into tools, weapons, and ornaments. It is

extracted from iron ore by heating and hammering it for long periods. Iron was being processed in Anatolia, western Asia, by 3000 BCE. Iron is easier to work with than bronze.

Iron Age period during which major tools and weapons were made of iron; followed the Bronze Age. The Hittites formed the first Iron Age culture around 1700 BCE. Between 1200 and 600 BCE, ironworking spread over Asia and Europe.

Ishtar Semitic war goddess who merged with Inanna and became the goddess of love and fertility.

Islam monotheistic religion worshipping Allah; founded by Mohammed in the seventh century CE. Its tenets are recorded in the Koran.

Israelites Semitic tribes who infiltrated Canaan in the second millennium BCE. They probably stayed in Egypt or in the border area between around 1650 and 1214 BCE. After 1200 BCE, they conquered Canaan, according to the Bible. They lived in a loose alliance of tribes but joined under a king around 1000 BCE.

isthmus narrow strip of land, bordered on two sides by water, that joins two larger land masses.

Jacquerie farmers' rebellion in 1358 CE led by "Les Jacques," peasants in the region surrounding Paris, against their lords after years of oppression and their defeat by the English at Poitiers; finally crushed by Charles II.

Jagiellon dynasty rulers of Poland-Lithuania, Bohemia, and Hungary who wielded great power and influence in east-central Europe in the 15th and 16th centuries CE.

Jainism religion of India that teaches a path to spiritual purity and enlightenment through a disciplined mode of

life founded on nonviolence to all living creatures; founded by Vardhamana (Mahavira) around the sixth century BCE.

Janissaries army of slaves and Christian prisoners of war who were indoctrinated with Turkish culture and military discipline. They stood as the basis for the military successes the Turks enjoyed between 1360 and 1826 CE. Janissary revolts took place from the 17th century CE onward.

Jason Greek mythological hero who sailed in the *Argo* in search of the Golden Fleece.

jihad Arabic for "holy war"; Muslim duty to expand Allah's realm, to propagate Islam; led to the conquering of Mesopotamia, Syria, Egypt, northern Africa, central Asia, and Spain in the seventh and eighth centuries CE.

Jomon period (c. 7500–250 BCE) early era of arts and crafts in Japan.

Kaaba Arabic for "cube"; stone cube in Mecca originally considered holy by most Arabs for its more than 300 statues. Mohammed considered it a religious relic of Allah built by Ishmael and condemned the polytheism. Although driven away in 622 CE, he returned to purge it in 629 CE, making it the central temple of Islam.

Karbala, Battle of battle in which the Umayyad military defeated the forces of the grandson of the prophet Mohammed. The battle secured the power of the Umayyad dynasty.

karma Sanskrit for "fate, work"; a person's acts and their consequences in a subsequent existence. In Buddhism, karma is considered the result of actions that define the kind of rebirth that occurs, not as punishment, but for evolution. In Hinduism, karma means cause and effect, bearing in this life the consequences of actions taken in previous lives.

Khmer ethnolinguistic group that emerged around 800 CE; now constitutes most of the population of Cambodia.

Kiev capital of the Russian Empire of Vladimir and Yaroslav; flourishing trade center and seat of the Byzantine Church; destroyed by the Mongols in 1240 CE.

Knights Hospitaller society of Christian knights who fought the Muslims. The order grew out of the 11th-century-CE pilgrims' hospital in the Holy Land. When noblemen of the brotherhood became the leaders, the order took on a military character.

Knights Templar religious military order established at the time of the crusades to protect Christian pilgrims to the Holy Land. The order was destroyed in 1307 CE.

Knossos Minoan settlement housing a large palace from the Second Palace period until around 1300 BCE.

Koran scripture of Islam; regarded by the faithful as being revealed to Mohammed over 22 years and recorded by scribes; written in verses organized into 114 chapters, called *suras*; contains the history of Mohammed, references to the Bible, and principles of Islamic law.

Kush kingdom of southern Egypt; part of modern Sudan. In the Late period, the Kushites ruled Egypt.

Lagash Sumerian city-state that constituted an empire in Mesopotamia in the 22nd century BCE.

Lapita culture named after a site in New Guinea at which was found a type of fired pottery dating from around 30,000 BCE.

lar (plural: lares) Roman family deity; originally gods of the fields.

Lars Porsenna legendary sixth-century-BCE Etruscan king who besieged Rome in an unsuccessful attempt to restore a monarchy.

La Tène culture Celtic Iron Age culture (c. 500–40 BCE); named for the site in Switzerland at which its artifacts were first discovered.

Late period era, from around 671 BCE, when Egypt was ruled by a succession of foreign powers: the Kushites, the Assyrians, the Persians, and finally, in 332 BCE, the Greeks under Alexander the Great.

Latin League ethnic religious federation of Latin cities on the Italian Peninsula; fought the Etruscans in the sixth century BCE; abolished in 338 BCE, following rebellion against Roman domination.

latitude distance of a place or object to the north or south of the equator; measured in degrees.

Latium region of the Italian Peninsula between the Tiber River and the Apennine Hills; the home of the original Latin people.

League of the Iroquois Confederation of tribes who lived in the northeast of the present-day United States. The league originally consisted of five tribes—the Mohawk, Oneida, Onondaga, Cayuga, and Seneca.

León 10th-century-CE Christian kingdom in northwestern Spain; absorbed by Castile in the 11th century CE.

Leptis Magna ancient city in northern Africa on the Mediterranean coast 62 miles (100 km) southeast of modern Tripoli (Libya).

lictor attendant who waited on Roman magistrates and carried the ceremonial fasces.

Linear A script found on Minoan clay tablets in the palace complexes. Never deciphered, the script is probably a syllabic script and a simplified form of hieroglyphs.

Linear B script found on Mycenaean clay tablets on the Greek mainland and in Knossos. It is a syllabic script based on the characters of Linear A. It was not deciphered until 1953 CE.

Linearbandceramik culture Neolithic culture of northern and central Europe dating from around 5000 BCE; recognized by its pottery decorations of distinct wavy or zigzag patterns.

logogram picture used to represent a word; used by Mesoamerican people such as the Olmecs.

Logos divine force—also known as reason—that the Stoics in ancient Greece believed directed the universe and humankind.

Loire longest river in France; flows for 634 miles (1,020 km) from the Massif Central north and west to the Atlantic Ocean.

Lombard League alliance of Italian cities that rebelled against Frederick I Barbarossa in 1167 CE after he revoked their royal privileges of coinage, tolls, and administration of justice.

Lombards central European Germanic people; conquered most of Italy in 568 CE, leaving Byzantine rule only on the coast and in the south. The Lombard Empire was subjected by Charlemagne in the eighth century CE.

longitude distance of a place or object to the east or west of any given meridian; measured in degrees.

Long-Shan (Lung-shan) Neolithic culture of central China (c. 2000–

1850 BCE); named after the site in Shandong Province where its remains were first discovered.

lost-wax casting process used for making metal ornaments. In the lost-wax method, a wax model was made, then covered in clay and placed in an oven. The wax melted, leaving a hollow clay mold that could be filled with molten metal to create an ornament.

Lotharingia kingdom belonging to Lothair (ruled 855–869 CE); dissolved after the king's death in 869 CE; modern Lorraine, France.

Lucius Junius Brutus legendary figure who expelled Tarquin the Proud from Rome and founded a republic.

lugal political leader in the Sumerian city-states.

Lugdunum Roman name for a major city in east-central Gaul; modern Lyon, France.

Lupercalia (wolves' feasts) Roman festival named for the wolves' skins worn by the participating priests.

lute stringed instrument played by plucking the strings; popular during the Renaissance.

Lydia ancient province of Anatolia (part of modern Turkey). Its capital was Sardis.

Macedon alternatively, Macedonia; region of northeastern Greece that was for a short time during the fourth century BCE the most powerful state in the eastern Mediterranean region.

Macedonian Wars four conflicts (214–205 BCE, 200–197 BCE, 171–168 BCE, 149–148 BCE) between the Roman republic and the kingdom of Macedonia.

Machu Picchu Inca city located in the mountains 50 miles (80 km)

northwest of Cuzco. Machu Picchu was discovered by archaeologist Hiram Bingham in 1911 CE and has since become a major tourist attraction.

madrigal type of song featuring a number of different voices; popular during the Renaissance.

Maghreb region of northern Africa bordering the Mediterranean Sea and at one time also comprising Spain.

Magna Carta document—issued by John, king of England, under pressure from his barons in 1215 CE—that set down the rights and obligations of king and barons and formed the basis of political evolution in the country.

Magyars Finno-Ugric people who occupied the middle basin of the Danube River in the ninth century CE; ancestors of modern Hungarians.

Maia in Greek mythology, the eldest of the Pleiades and the mother of Zeus's son, Hermes.

Mamertines mercenaries from Campania who fought on behalf of Syracuse but then deserted the city-state and seized Messana (modern Messina, Sicily) around 288 BCE; later joined forces with the Carthaginians, thereby precipitating the First Punic War.

Mamluks originally slaves hired as mercenaries by caliphs in Cairo to maintain order in the 12th century CE; gained power in 1250 CE; dominated Egypt until the start of the 16th century CE.

Manichaeism religion founded by Mani in Mesopotamia; combines elements of Christianity, Zoroastrianism, Buddhism, and others; postulates two competing principles of good (referred to as light, God, the human soul) and evil (as seen in darkness, the devil, the human body). Mani considered knowledge of light through his

teachings and an ascetic way of life as the way to salvation. The Manichaeans were persecuted by Persian kings and Roman emperors.

Mantinea ancient city in Arcadia; site of two battles. The first Battle of Mantinea, in 418 BCE, was the largest land battle of the Peloponnesian War. In the second Battle of Mantinea (362 BCE), Thebes defeated the allied forces of Athens and Sparta.

Marathon city on the east coast of Attica where the Persians suffered a devastating defeat in 490 BCE by a small Athenian army under Miltiades.

Marduk Babylonian sun god. He became god of the state under Hammurabi and was considered the creator of Earth and god of wisdom.

mare nostrum literally, "our sea"; Roman name for the Mediterranean Sea.

Mari Semitic commercial center on the middle course of the Euphrates River. Its first flowering ended with the conquest by Sargon I, after which Mari was ruled by Akkad, Ur, and Ashur. Between around 1780 and 1760 BCE, Mari was again independent but was destroyed around 1760 BCE.

Mars Roman god of war.

Maurya major kingdom in India (c. 321–185 BCE). The Mauryan Empire reached the height of its power and influence during the reign of Ashoka (ruled 268–233 BCE).

Maya people who lived in present-day southern Mexico, Belize, and Guatemala. Their culture flourished between around 300 BCE and 1525 CE.

Medes nomadic horsemen who settled in Persia during the second millennium BCE. From around 700 BCE, they dominated a loose federation of tribes, including the Persians. Together with Babylon, they were responsible for the fall of the Assyrian Empire in 610 BCE.

Medina Arabian oasis town to which Mohammed fled in 622 CE; originally named Yathrib; renamed Madinat al-Nabi (the city of the prophet), or Medina. Mohammed converted its already largely monotheistic Jewish population, becoming its theocratic leader. Medina waged war against Mecca until 628 CE.

megaliths large stone monuments.

Memphis city in Lower (northern) Egypt; residence of the pharaohs during the Old Kingdom and during the time of the Ramesside kings.

menhirs pillarlike stone monuments or megaliths that may have marked sacrificial sites.

meridian circle or half-circle of the earth, passing through or ending at the poles.

Meroë capital of the ancient Nubian Empire; on the eastern bank of the Nile River, around 125 miles (200 km) northeast of present-day Khartoum (Sudan).

Merovingians Frankish dynasty (481–751 CE) that ruled an area of Europe roughly corresponding to modern France.

Mesoamerica region of Central America, stretching roughly from present-day central Mexico in the north to Honduras in the south, that was home to a number of pre-Columbian cultures. Among the most famous Mesoamerican civilizations were those of the Aztecs and the Maya.

Mesopotamia area in western Asia surrounding the Euphrates and Tigris rivers. (The word comes from the Greek meaning "between two rivers.") The first agricultural settlements were founded there around 4500 BCE.

Messana modern Messina, Sicily; site of an ancient Greek colony.

Messenia basin of the Pamisos River in the southwestern Peloponnese conquered by Sparta in the seventh century BCE.

Middle Kingdom period of Egyptian history, from around 2150 to 1550 BCE, during which unity was restored by the Theban kings.

Milvian Bridge, Battle of decisive battle in which Constantine defeated Maxentius in 312 CE.

Ming dynasty Chinese dynasty (1368–1644 CE) under which the empire was extended substantially.

Minoan civilization Bronze Age civilization on Crete from around 3300 to 1000 BCE, divided into the period before the palaces (3300–1900 BCE), the palace periods (1900–1200 BCE), and the period after the palaces (1200–1000 BCE).

Mitanni Hurrian kingdom that flourished in northern Mesopotamia from around 1500 to 1350 BCE.

Mixtecs Mesoamerican people who lived in the Oaxaca Valley from the 10th century CE.

Moesia Roman province comprised of lands that are now Serbia, part of Macedonia, and part of Bulgaria.

Moguntiacum military camp on the banks of the Rhine River established by the Romans around 14 BCE.

monastery ascetic community of monks led by an abbot under strict regulations. In the east, Basil was the founder of monasticism; in the west,

the movement was founded by Benedict of Nursia.

Mongols Asian tribes of horsemen who originally came from lands to the north of China; united by Genghis Khan in 1190 CE; conquered central Asian Islamic states, China, Russia, and the Delhi Sultanate in the 12th and 13th centuries CE.

Monophysitism fifth-century-CE doctrine—from the Greek *monos* (single) and *physis* (nature)—that contended that Jesus Christ had only a single nature, which was divine, not human. That idea conflicted with the orthodox doctrine that Christ was at once human and divine.

monopoly exclusive control of the supply of a product or service.

Moscow city that became the seat of Byzantine Russian Christianity after the fall of Kiev. Moscow separated from the Mongols in the 14th century CE and assumed the leadership of all the Russian principalities. After the conquest of Byzantium, Moscow became the new Christian center.

Mucius Scaevola legendary Roman hero who is said to have saved the city from an attack by the forces of Lars Porsenna.

Mughals Muslim dynasty that ruled India (1526–1857 CE); founded by Babur, a descendant of Genghis Khan.

mummification method of preserving human remains by embalming.

Muses in Greek—and later in Roman—mythology, nine sister goddesses (daughters of Zeus) who inspired human artistic creativity: Calliope (epic poetry), Clio (history), Erato (lyric poetry), Euterpe (music), Melpomene (tragedy), Polyhymnia (sacred poetry), Terpsichore (dancing), Thalia (comedy), Urania (astronomy).

Muslims worshippers of Allah; members of Islam.

Mycenae Bronze Age settlement on the Peloponnese where a palace fortress was built after 1450 BCE.

Nahuatl language of the Aztecs.

Navarre Christian kingdom in northern Spain. Pushed into the Pyrenees over the 11th century CE, it became increasingly involved in French politics. Its last king, Henry IV, was the founder of the French royal dynasty of the Bourbons.

Neanderthal archaic branch of *Homo sapiens* classified today as *Homo sapiens Neanderthalensis*; lived between 75,000 and 30,000 years ago in Europe and Asia.

Nedao, Battle of battle on the banks of the Nedava River in Pannonia in which a Germanic alliance defeated the Huns in 455 CE.

Neolithic period era that lasted from around 8000 to 2000 BCE; characterized by a shift from hunting and gathering to domestication of plants and animals.

Neoplatonism third-century-CE school of Greek philosophy.

Nestorianism doctrine of Nestorius (c. 382–451 CE), patriarch of Constantinople (428–431 CE). He postulated that Jesus Christ acted as a single person but did not have conjoined divine and human natures, being purely human on earth and purely god in heaven. In consequence, he contended that Mary could not be called Mother of God; she begot the man Jesus, while God begot his divine aspect. This doctrine gained followers, notably in the New Persian Empire, against the orthodox Christian belief that Christ has two distinct natures, divine and human, joined in both person and substance. In the fifth

century CE, Nestorianism spread throughout the Byzantine Empire but was declared heretical by the Council of Ephesus (431 CE). The Nestorians became powerful in Persia, India, China, and Mongolia in early medieval times.

New Kingdom period of Egyptian history that lasted from around 1550 to 1075 BCE.

New Persian Empire ruled by the Sassanid dynasty; founded by Ardashir in 224 CE; conquered by Arabs in 651 CE; notable for coexistence of many religions, including Christianity, Nestorianism, and Manichaeism.

New World European term for the Americas.

Nicaea, Council of convoked by Constantine I in 325 CE; defined Christian doctrine.

Nicene Creed statement of faith that is accepted by all Christian churches—eastern Orthodox, western Roman Catholic, and Protestant.

Nika Revolt uprising (January 13–18, 532 CE) in Constantinople of the Greens and the Blues, who turned the population against Justinian. The population appointed a new emperor and destroyed the city center. Belisarius suppressed the revolt with mercenaries.

Nile world's longest river at 4,132 miles (6,650 km). The river flows north from central Africa into Egypt, where in the final part of its course it forms a delta before reaching the Mediterranean Sea. During the annual rainy season in central Africa, the Nile River floods its banks, rendering the surrounding valley fertile and suitable for agriculture and horticulture.

Nineveh city of the ancient Assyrian Empire; situated on the Tigris River opposite modern Mosul (Iraq).

Nisibis city in ancient Armenia ceded to the Persian king Shapur II by the Roman emperor Jovian in 364 CE; modern Nusaybin, Turkey.

Normandy area in western Gaul given in fief to the Normans in 911 CE and where they established an empire. Norman nobles established a kingdom in southern Italy and Sicily in the early 11th century CE. The Norman duke William the Conqueror conquered England in 1066 CE. In 1204 CE, Normandy was incorporated into the French Empire.

Normans "North men" or Vikings; Nordic people (Danes, Norwegians, and Swedes) who variously raided, traded, and settled on the coasts and rivers of Europe, Greenland, and North America in the eighth and ninth centuries CE.

Novgorod Russian trading post and manufacturing center for the German *hansas*, which monopolized trade in the North Sea and the Baltic Sea. Novgorod came under Mongol threat in the 13th century CE. Ivan III conquered the city in 1478 CE.

Nubia region in Africa, extending from the Nile River Valley to the shores of the Red Sea, southward to Khartoum, and westward to the Libyan Desert. The southern part of Nubia included Kush.

Numantia Celtiberian stronghold until 133 BCE, when it fell to the forces of the Roman general Scipio Aemilianus; near modern Soria, Spain.

Numidia region of northern Africa; roughly equivalent to modern Algeria.

Numitor legendary king of Alba Longa; grandfather of Romulus and Remus; deposed by his younger brother, Amulius.

obsidian type of glass formed by the cooling of molten lava. Mesoamerican people used obsidian to produce decorative objects, tools, and weapons.

Old Kingdom period of Egyptian history that lasted from around 2650 to 2150 BCE.

Olmecs Mesoamerican people who lived on the coast of the Gulf of Mexico from around 1500 BCE. Today, the Olmecs are best known for the giant stone heads that they carved out of basalt.

optimates conservative senatorial aristocracy during the later Roman republic (c. 133–27 BCE).

Orléans city in the French duchy of Berry on the side of Charles VII and beleaguered by the English in 1428 and 1429 CE. In 1429 CE, the city was freed by a French army led by Joan of Arc.

Osiris ancient Egyptian god of death and the underworld.

Ostia ancient town at the mouth of the Tiber River; port of Rome.

Ostrogoths Germanic tribe from Ukraine; subjected by the Huns; migrated to Hungary in the fifth century CE; established a kingdom in Italy under Theodoric (493 CE); defeated under Totila (552 CE).

Paleolithic period era that lasted from around 1.6 million years ago to 10,000 BCE.

Palmyra ancient city in south-central Syria, 130 miles (210 km) northeast of Damascus.

Pannonia Roman province roughly corresponding to present-day eastern Austria, western Hungary, and parts of Croatia, Serbia, and Slovenia.

Parnassus mountain of central Greece; in Greek mythology, the home of Apollo and the Muses.

Parni nomadic tribe living to the east of the Caspian Sea. Its members founded the Parthian Empire.

Parthenon temple on the Athenian Acropolis dedicated to Pallas Athena; built between 447 and 438 BCE.

Parthia kingdom founded around 240 BCE; part of present-day Afghanistan and Iran.

Parthians inhabitants of Parthia; acclaimed for their equestrian skills; regularly waged war with the Roman Empire; conquered by rebelling Persians, who founded the New Persian Kingdom (224 CE).

patrician in Rome, an aristocrat; often a member of the ruling class.

patron someone who commissions a work of art and pays for its production. Many of the great paintings and statues of the Renaissance were created under the patronage of the Italian nobility.

Peasants' Revolt uprising of English laborers in 1381 CE (during the reign of Richard II) against taxation and the maximum wage.

Pechenegs seminomadic Turkic people who occupied the steppes to the north of the Black Sea; threatened Byzantium in the 10th century CE.

Peloponnese large, mountainous peninsula joined to the mainland of Greece by the Isthmus of Corinth.

Peloponnesian War (431–404 BCE) conflict of hegemony between Athens (generally allied with the Ionians) and Sparta (allied with the Dorians). The direct cause was a conflict about the island of Corcyra (modern Corfu). The army of Sparta annually destroyed Attica, while the Athenian fleet plundered the Peloponnesian coasts. Sparta finally triumphed over Athens with help from the Persians.

Pergamum ancient Greek city in Asia Minor; near modern Izmir, Turkey.

Period of the Warring States last period (c. 475–221 BCE) of the Zhou (Chou) dynasty during which war was a constant fact of life, although trade, agriculture, and urbanization evolved simultaneously. Legislation and philosophy, such as Confucianism, legalism, and Taoism also developed at this time. At the end of the Period of Warring States, China was reunited.

Persephone daughter of Demeter, the goddess of agriculture. Her recurring abduction by Hades and return from the underworld symbolize the growth and decay of life.

Persepolis important center of the Persian kingdom of the Achaemenids. From the reign of Darius, it was also a major royal citadel with multicolumned halls. Persepolis was destroyed by Alexander the Great.

Persis ancient country in western Asia (present-day southwestern Iran). Its name derives from that of the Parsua, a nomadic people who settled there in the seventh century BCE.

perspective technique, developed in the Renaissance, that allows artists to create the illusion of three-dimensional space within their paintings.

Petra ancient city of western Asia in present-day Jordan; center of an Arab kingdom in Hellenistic and Roman times.

phalanx battle array used by the ancient Greeks and Macedonians, consisting of a number of rows of heavily armed infantry soldiers. Thebans later introduced the diagonal phalanx, which had more rows on one side.

pharaoh Egyptian king, who also acted as legislator, military general, and religious leader.

Philistines Indo-European maritime people who settled in coastal Canaan at the end of the 13th century BCE. They drove the Israelites and the Canaanites out from the coastal area, forcing the Israelite tribes to organize centrally. King David of Israel and Judah ended their expansion.

Phoenicia country north of modern Israel and Lebanon consisting of mountains and a narrow coastal strip. It was inhabited by local groups, mainly Canaanites. After Egyptian rule (c. 1500–1350 BCE) and Hittite rule (c. 1350–1200 BCE), Phoenicia became independent around 1100 BCE. Phoenician forests were used for shipbuilding and timber export.

Picts ancient people of Great Britain; driven into Scotland by Romans and Britons.

plebeian any citizen of Rome who was not a patrician (aristocrat); member of the lower classes.

Pleistocene epoch period between 1.8 million and 10,000 years ago during which the ice ages occurred.

Po longest river in Italy; rises in the western Alps and flows 405 miles (652 km) to the Adriatic Sea, which it enters south of Venice.

podestas hired strong men used by Frederick I Barbarossa against Lombard cities.

Poitiers city in central France; site where Edward the Black Prince of England destroyed the French army in 1356 CE with an army of archers and lancers and John the Good, the French king, was taken prisoner.

polis (plural: *poleis*) independent Greek city-state.

polyphonic music music consisting of a number of different melodic lines played simultaneously.

Popol Vuh Mayan manuscript that is also known as the Book of the Community. The *Popol Vuh* contained the Maya's account of the creation of the world.

populares patrician political group in the late Roman republic that drew support from the masses against the ruling oligarchy.

Portugal western region of the Iberian Peninsula given to Henry of Burgundy and his wife, Theresa, by Alfonso I, king of Castile, in 1093 CE. Their son Alfonso Henriques rebelled against Theresa in 1128 CE. He proclaimed himself to be the king in 1139 CE and was officially granted the throne as Alfonso I by the dominant Portuguese nobility in 1143 CE.

Poseidon Greek god of the sea, earthquakes, and volcanic phenomena; creator of the horse; brother of Zeus.

Postclassic period period of American history that lasted roughly from 900 to 1540 CE.

potsherd fragment of pottery, usually one that has been unearthed by archaeological excavation.

Praetorian Guard imperial bodyguard in ancient Rome.

praetors political leaders of the Roman republic; later became known as consuls.

Preclassic period period of American history that lasted roughly from 1500 BCE to 300 CE.

pre-Columbian people or a culture that existed in the Americas prior to the continents' discovery by Christopher Columbus in 1492 CE.

prehistory period of human history before the development of writing; knowledge of this time is based on

archaeological sources and scientific dating methods.

Prester John mythical Christian ruler of an unspecified land in the East. Western nations hoped that he would join forces with them against the Mongols and the Muslims.

prytanes 10 groups of 50 men from the Council of 500; formed the daily administration of Athens for one-month periods.

pueblo housing complex made by the peoples of the southwestern United States. Pueblos were made out of stone and adobe bricks.

pulque sacred Aztec drink; made out of fermented cactus juice.

Punic War, First (264–241 BCE) war between Rome and Carthage for supremacy in the western Mediterranean. Rome adopted seafaring armies to defeat the Carthaginian power at sea. By introducing grappling, they defeated the Carthaginians. Carthage then ceded Sicily to Rome.

Punic War, Second (218–201 BCE) war between Rome and Carthage (under Hannibal) for supremacy in the western Mediterranean.

Punic War, Third (149–146 BCE) war between Rome and Carthage for supremacy in the Mediterranean. The Romans destroyed Carthage in 146 BCE.

Punjab region of northwestern India. Its name derives from Persian words meaning "five rivers."

pyramid building with a square base and four triangular sides. The Aztecs and the Maya both built pyramids. In Mesoamerican cultures, pyramids were used as venues for human sacrifice. In Egypt, pyramid construction reached its height between around 2600 and 2400 BCE.

Qin (Ch'in) dynasty rulers of north-western China who took control of the whole country in 221 BCE. They established a central government and replaced the old feudal system with direct administration by bureaucratic officials.

quadrant device used by sailors to help them navigate. The quadrant was shaped like a triangle, with two straight edges and one curved edge. By using a quadrant, a sailor could calculate his ship's latitude (its distance to the north or south of the equator).

quaestor Roman official who originally assisted consuls in criminal justice; eventually, financial manager.

Quetzalcoatl major Aztec deity; represented as a feathered serpent. The Aztecs believed that Quetzalcoatl had appeared on Earth as a god-king and that he would one day return.

quipu piece of knotted string used for administrative purposes in the Inca Empire.

Re Egyptian sun god. The pharaoh was considered his son and ascended to his heavenly empire after death.

Rea Silvia legendary daughter of Numitor, king of Alba Longa; became a Vestal Virgin; mother of Romulus and Remus.

Reconquista Spanish for "reconquest"; Christian reconquering of occupied Spain from the Muslims (11th–13th centuries CE).

relief figurative sculpture that projects from a supporting background, which is usually a plane surface.

Renaissance period of European history marked by an increased interest in the works of classical writers, scientific advances, and a flourishing of the arts. Historians disagree about when the Renaissance started and

ended, but it is generally agreed that the period was at its height between around 1450 and 1525 CE.

res publica **(public things)** republic; Roman state (c. 510–27 BCE) governed by two annually elected consuls. Citizens exercised influence through popular assemblies and the senate.

rhetors orator-politicians in Athens. With their rhetorical gifts, they had great influence on Athenian politics.

Rhine river of western Europe that flows 865 miles (1,390 km) from the eastern Swiss Alps to the North Sea.

Rhodes largest of the Dodecanese, a group of islands in the Aegean Sea off the eastern coast of mainland Greece.

Rhone river that flows 505 miles (813 km) from its source in Switzerland, through France, to the Mediterranean Sea.

Romulus and Remus legendary twin sons of the war god Mars. Separated at birth from their mother, Rea Silvia, they were suckled in infancy by a she-wolf. They later co-founded the city of Rome. Romulus then killed Remus and became the first king of Rome.

Roncesvalles village in Navarre (northern Spain) near which the Basques massacred the rearguard of Charlemagne's army in 778 CE.

Rubicon small stream separating Gaul from the central Roman republic. When Julius Caesar crossed it in 49 BCE—in defiance of a law that forbade provincial generals from leaving the territories to which they were assigned—he precipitated a three-year civil war. At the end of the conflict, Caesar himself was in control of the Roman world.

Sabines ancient people who lived in mountains to the east of the Tiber

River. According to legend, their women were carried off by the men of Rome.

Salamis island on the western coast of Attica where the Persian fleet was defeated by the Greeks in 480 BCE.

Samarra town on the Tigris River that became the capital of the Abbasid caliphate in 836 CE.

samurai member of the Japanese warrior caste that rose to power in the 12th century CE and dominated the Japanese government until the Meiji Restoration in 1868 CE.

Sanskrit old Indo-Aryan language widely used in northern India as early as 1800 BCE.

Sassanids dynasty of kings (224–651 CE); captured Mesopotamia and eastern Syria from the Byzantines in the fourth century CE; conquered Jerusalem in 614 CE; defeated by Alexius in 628 CE.

satrap provincial governor in the Achaemenian Persian Empire.

satyr play Greek dramatic work with a heroic mythological theme, like a tragedy, but with a humorous tone and a chorus of satyrs (goatlike male companions of Pan and Dionysus who roamed the woods and mountains). Satyr plays formed the last part of a tetralogy and were thus always performed after three tragedies.

Saxons ancient people of northern Germany; conquered parts of England in the fifth and sixth centuries CE.

schism 14th-century-CE division in the church that occurred when the cardinals elected Clement VII as pope because they were dissatisfied with Urban VI. During this time, there were two popes, one in Avignon and one in Rome. Both were supported by competing secular rulers who

expanded their influence in this manner.

Scholasticism philosophical movement that began to flourish in western Europe around 1100 CE; attempted to reconcile church doctrine with the teachings of certain Greek philosophers, particularly Aristotle.

scurvy disease caused by a lack of vitamin C. Scurvy afflicted sailors on many voyages of exploration, because of the lack of fresh fruits and vegetables in their diets.

Scythians herdsmen of Iranian stock who migrated from central Asia to southern Russia (principally the Crimea) in the eighth century BCE.

Sea Peoples groups who threatened the eastern Mediterranean coast, including the Nile Delta, during the time of the Ramesside kings of Egypt. The Philistines were one of the Sea Peoples.

Second Crusade (1145–1148 CE) authorized by the pope after the Turks had conquered Edessa and threatened Jerusalem. The Christians unsuccessfully besieged Damascus and returned home empty-handed.

secular referring to the physical, rather than the spiritual world; non-religious.

Seleucid Empire empire that, between 312 and 64 BCE, extended from Thrace on the edge of the Black Sea to the western border of India. It was formed by Seleucus I Nicator from the remnants of Alexander the Great's realm.

Seljuks Turks who named themselves after their leader; captured Baghdad from the Shi'ites; established power in Persia around 1055 CE; conquered Anatolia in 1071 CE. Their kingdom disintegrated by the end of the 12th century CE.

Semites people residing in northern and southern Mesopotamia. They spoke a language different from the Sumerians and were largely rural dwellers. They founded the Akkadian Empire around 2335 BCE. The Akkadian and Sumerian civilizations rapidly became one.

senate college of magistrates; the highest authority in the Roman republic.

Separatists group of English Puritans who rejected the teachings of the Church of England and set up a colony in North America.

Septimania ancient territory between the Garonne and Rhone rivers in southwestern France.

Severan dynasty Roman dynasty established by Septimius Severus (ruled 197–211 CE); lasted until 235 CE.

Shang dynasty the earliest Chinese dynasty (c. 1766–1050 BCE) of which there are documentary records. The main part of the realm was centrally governed while autonomous vassals were allowed to control outlying areas. Most of the inhabitants were peasants who leased lands in exchange for labor.

Shi'ites supporters of Mohammed's son-in-law Ali; seceded from orthodox Islam after the murder of Hussein in 680 CE. Shi'ites (from *shi'ah*, Arabic for "partisan") believe that their leaders (imams) are divinely guided and have the right to Muslim leadership.

Shintoism indigenous Japanese religion based on the worship of forefathers. The sun goddess, Ameratsu, the first mother, was the most prominent of the goddesses. The emperor was revered as her leading priest and her son.

Shiva Hindu god of destruction and reproduction; member of the Hindu

trinity with Vishnu and Brahma; frequently manifests in female aspects, Parvati and Kali.

shogun originally the title given to the chief military commander of Japan; from 1192 CE, the hereditary title of honor for the emperor; continued to exist until 1868 CE.

Shu dynasty Chinese dynasty (221–263 CE) that rivaled the Han dynasty in southwestern China.

Sicilian Vespers rebellion in 1282 CE by the Sicilians against French rule. During the uprising, all Frenchmen in Palermo were killed. Sicily offered the crown to Peter of Aragon.

Sidon city on the Phoenician coast that was a powerful trading center (c. 1400–700 BCE). Phoenicians were often called Sidonians.

Silk Road ancient overland trade route that extended for 4,000 miles (6,400 km) and linked China and the West. First used as a caravan route, the road ran from Xi'an, China, along the Great Wall, through the Pamir Mountains, into Afghanistan, and on to the eastern Mediterranean Sea, where goods were taken onward by boat. On westbound journeys, the principal cargo was silk; wool, gold, and silver were the main commodities carried in the opposite direction.

simony sale of church offices to the highest bidder.

Sixth Crusade (1228–1229 CE) expedition led by Frederick II, during which he obtained Jerusalem by negotiating with the Muslims.

Skeptics Greek school of philosophy founded around 300 BCE; from *skeptikos* (inquiring); denied the possibility of real knowledge; considered inquiry to be always a process of doubting and judgments to be only of relative value.

Song (Sung) dynasty Chinese dynasty (960–1279 CE) that established its capital at Kaifeng in northern Henan (Honan) Province.

Songhai state in western Africa (present-day Mali, Niger, and Nigeria) that flourished as a trading nation in the 15th and 16th centuries CE.

Sophists fifth-century-BCE itinerant teachers of philosophy, politics, and rhetoric in Greece; noted for skill in clever but fallacious argument and persuasive rhetoric; provided instruction for a fee; most considered truth and morality relative; first to systematize education. Notable sophists were Hippias of Elis, Protagoras, Gorgias, and Prodicus of Ceos.

Sparta city-state in the southern Peloponnese; isolated agricultural land power, resistant to external influences; oligarchy; fought Athens in the Peloponnesian War.

Spice Islands islands in Indonesia; so called because they were the source of nutmeg, cloves, and mace; present-day Moluccas.

SPQR initials, written on the standards of Roman legions, representing a Latin phrase meaning "for the senate and people of Rome."

Stoicism school of philosophy founded by Zeno of Citium in Athens in the third century BCE. At its core was the belief that people should do what is required of them by nature and accept their lot.

Stone Age earliest period of human civilization, from around 2 million BCE to around 3500 BCE.

Sumerians people who settled in southern Mesopotamia (Sumer). They lived in independent city-states dominated by a temple economy. Lugalzaggisi tried to create a unified Sumerian state, but the rise of the Akkadian Empire around 2335 BCE prevented this.

Sunnis orthodox Muslims who follow the Sunna (the body of Islamic custom).

Syracuse Corinthian colony on Sicily; flourished culturally and commercially in the fifth century BCE and dominated the other Sicilian colonies. Syracuse resisted Athenian siege and defeated Athens with the help of Sparta (414–413 BCE).

Taika Reforms period in Japan (645–702 CE) during which landownership was abolished and the power of the emperor's family was extended throughout society.

talent unit of weight and money used by Hebrews, Egyptians, Greeks, and Romans. Its exact value varied from place to place; in Attica, one talent weighed around 57 pounds (25.8 kg).

Taoism (Daoism) Chinese philosophy originated by Lao-tzu (Laozi) around 500 BCE; emphasizes inner harmony with nature and submission to the Tao (Dao; the Way).

Teotihuacán city in central Mexico that was the center of a large state by around 600 CE. The population of the city at this time was approximately 200,000 people.

tepee conical dwelling used by Native Americans. Tepees were made from animal skins.

Teshup Hurrian storm god who was adopted by the Hittites. He was the husband of the Hittite sun goddess Arinna and was considered the king of the heavens.

Teutoburg Forest, Battle of battle in which Roman legions commanded by Publius Quinctilius Varus were annihilated by German tribes led by

Arminius in 9 CE. The defeat effectively ended the Romanization of Germany to the east of the Rhine River. The site is located near present-day Osnabrück, Germany.

Teutonic Knights order of knights in northern Germany and the Baltic states. Founded in 1198 CE, they were defeated at the Battle of Tannenberg in 1410 CE. By the end of the 15th century CE, they had lost their political influence.

theology study of religion.

Thera volcanic island north of Crete where a Minoanlike civilization existed during the Bronze Age. A volcanic eruption destroyed Thera around 1500 BCE.

Thermopylae mountain pass between Thessaly and central Greece where Leonidas and hundreds of Spartans died covering the retreat of the Greek army from the Persians in 480 BCE.

Third Crusade (1187–1192 CE) followed the capture of Jerusalem in 1187 CE. Frederick I Barbarossa, Philip II Augustus, and Richard the Lionheart traveled to Palestine. Christians conquered the fortress of Acre, but Jerusalem remained in Turkish hands. Mutual strife forced the Christians to return home.

Thrace region of the southeastern Balkans. Its exact extent has varied throughout history, but it is generally regarded as being bounded by the Danube River to the north, the Black Sea to the east, the Aegean Sea to the south, and the mountains of the central Balkans to the west.

Tiber river that flows through Rome; second longest river in Italy after the Po.

Tigris river of western Asia that flows 1,180 miles (1,900 km) from eastern Turkey to the Persian Gulf.

Titus Tatius legendary king of the Sabines who combined his realm with Rome and ruled with Romulus.

Tiwinaku civilization that arose in the mountains of central Bolivia around 300 BCE.

tlatoani head of the Aztec state.

Toltecs Mesoamerican people who built up an empire in central Mexico in the 10th and 11th centuries CE. The empire was based around the city of Tula.

tomahawk club- or axlike weapon used by Native Americans.

tribune in the ancient Roman republic, a political representative of the plebeians.

tribus **(district)** division where Roman citizens were registered on the basis of landholdings and assessed taxes called *tributum*.

trireme ancient galley ship with three banks of oars.

Troy ancient city of northwestern Anatolia (part of modern Turkey); reputed destruction by Greek forces formed the basis of Homer's epic poem the *Iliad*.

Tyre Phoenician city situated on an island off the coast of Lebanon. Tyre was a booming trade city from the 10th century BCE and founded many colonies, including Carthage.

uji Japanese clans forming a tribal society worshipping their own god. The emperor stood at the head of all clans, and political battles between clan leaders caused unrest.

Umayyads dynasty of caliphs in Damascus from the Umayyad clan that dominated the Arab world, including non-Islamic population (c. 661–750 CE); ousted by the Abbasids.

Vandals eastern Germanic people who migrated to Gaul and Spain in the fifth century CE; founded a kingdom in northern Africa in 429 CE; plundered Rome in 455 CE; defeated by Emperor Justinian I in 534 CE.

Vikings Scandinavian seafaring warriors who raided and colonized wide areas of Europe from the 9th century to the 11th century CE. Some of them settled in northern France, where they became Normans.

Visigoths Germanic people from Ukraine; driven out by the Huns; settled south of the Danube River as *foederati* (allies) of Rome; rebelled in 378 CE; plundered Rome under Alaric in 410 CE; established a kingdom in Spain conquered by the Arabs in 711 CE.

Volga longest river in Europe; flows 2,193 miles (3,530 km) from northwest of Moscow to the Caspian Sea.

Wars of the Roses (1455–1485 CE) series of dynastic civil wars between the houses of Lancaster and York, who were contending for the English throne.

Xia (Hsia) dynasty China's first ruling dynasty; traditionally established by Yu the Great around 2200 BCE.

Yangtze world's third longest river; flows 3,400 miles (5,470 km) from the Plateau of Tibet to the East China Sea. Its fertile lower valley was the cradle of Chinese civilization.

Zhou (Chou) dynasty Chinese dynasty that ousted the Shang dynasty around 1050 BCE; ruled for almost a millennium until it was succeeded by the Qin (Ch'in) dynasty in 221 BCE.

MAJOR HISTORICAL FIGURES

Abu Bakr (c. 573–634 CE) first leader of Islam after the death of the prophet Mohammed in 632 CE; began jihad, seizing Syrian territory from the Persians.

Aeschylus (525–456 BCE) Greek playwright; author of the *Oresteia* trilogy and *The Persians*.

Aethelred the Unready king of the English between 978 and 1016 CE; failed to prevent the Danish conquest of the country.

Aethelstan first king of a united England; ruled between 924 and 939 CE.

Agrippa (c. 63–12 BCE) deputy of the Roman emperor Augustus; defeated Mark Antony at the Battle of Actium in 31 BCE.

Ahmose pharaoh from 1550 to 1525 BCE; drove the Hyksos from Egypt and conquered their territory in western Asia; subjugated the Kushites.

Akhenaton pharaoh from 1353 to 1335 BCE; introduced the monotheistic cult of Aton to Egypt; built a new royal residence at Akhetaton.

Alaric I king of the Visigoths from around 370 to 410 CE; sacked Rome in 410 CE.

Alcibiades (c. 450–404 BCE) Athenian politician and military commander whose policies contributed to his city's defeat by Sparta in the Peloponnesian War (431–404 BCE).

Alexander the Great king of Macedonia; ruled between 336 and 323 BCE; son of Philip II; conquered the Persian Empire (334–330 BCE); conquered Syria and Egypt (333 BCE); invaded the Indus Valley (327 BCE).

Alexius I Comnenus Byzantine emperor between 1081 and 1118 CE; partially restored the strength of the empire after its defeats by the Normans and the Turks in the 11th century CE.

Alfonso I first king of Portugal; ruled between 1139 and 1185 CE; conquered Lisbon from the Muslims (1147 CE); secured Portuguese independence from León (1139 CE).

Alfonso III king of Portugal from 1248 to 1279 CE; recaptured the Algarve from the Muslims.

Alfred the Great king of Wessex, a Saxon kingdom in southwestern England, between 871 and 899 CE; prevented England from falling to the Danes.

Alp Arslan Seljuk sultan who ruled between 1063 and 1072 CE; conquered Georgia, Armenia, and much of Asia Minor.

Ambrose, Saint (c. 340–397 CE) bishop of Milan; opponent of the Arian heresy.

Amenemhet I pharaoh from 1991 to 1962 BCE; restored unity to Egypt after the civil war that followed the death of his predecessor.

Amenemhet III pharaoh from 1843 to 1797 BCE; brought Egypt's Middle Kingdom to a peak of prosperity.

Anastasius I Byzantine emperor from 491 to 518 CE; supporter of Monophysitism.

Anthony, Saint (c. 251–356 CE) first Christian monk.

Antigonus (382–301 BCE) Macedonian general who co-founded the Antigonid dynasty.

Archilochus (c. 700 BCE) Greek poet from the island of Paros.

Archimedes (c. 287–212 BCE) Greek mathematician and inventor killed during the sacking of Syracuse by the Romans.

Ardashir I king of Persia from 224 to 241 CE.

Aristophanes (c. 450–388 BCE) early Greek comic playwright.

Aristotle (384–322 BCE) Greek philosopher and scientist.

Arnold of Brescia (c. 1100–1155 CE) popular preacher who criticized the church's political power. His sermons caused a rebellion in Rome in 1146 CE, after which the senate regained its power. Pope Hadrian IV and Frederick I Barbarossa conspired to have Arnold executed.

Artabanus V king of Parthia from 213 to 224 CE.

Ashoka Mauryan emperor who ruled between 268 and 233 BCE; contributed to the spread of Buddhism across India.

Attila king of the Huns between 434 and 453 CE; conquered western Europe; defeated in Gaul by Romans and Visigoths in 451 CE; plundered Italy in 452 CE.

Augustine of Hippo, Saint (354–430 CE) Christian convert, bishop, theologian, and author of *The City of God*.

Augustus (63 BCE–14 CE) originally named Octavian; first emperor of Rome; ruled from 27 BCE until his death.

Averroës (1126–1198 CE) also known as Ibn Ruhd; Córdoba-born Muslim writer on religious law, philosophy, and medicine.

Avicenna (980–1037 CE) also known as Ibn Sina; born in Bukhara; author of *Kitab ash-shifa* (Book of Healing) and *Al-Qanan fi at-tibb* (The Canon of Medicine).

Barents, Willem (c. 1550–1597 CE) Dutch navigator who died while attempting to discover a northeastern route to the Indies.

Becket, Thomas archbishop of Canterbury (1162–1170 CE); opponent of Henry II, who took away the authority of the ecclesiastical courts; murdered in 1170 CE.

Belisarius sixth-century-CE Roman general; conquered the Vandals in Africa in 533–534 CE; defeated the Ostrogoths in Italy in 540 CE.

Benedict of Nursia, Saint (c. 480–547 CE) monk from Umbria (Italy); founded Benedictine monastic order.

Bindusara Mauryan emperor between around 293 and 268 BCE; extended his power far into southern India; father of Ashoka.

Bleda (died 445 CE) nephew of Roas, king of the Huns; along with his brother Attila, succeeded Roas; murdered by Attila.

Brunelleschi, Filippo (1377–1446 CE) Florentine architect who designed the dome of the city's cathedral.

Cabral, Pedro Álvares (c. 1467–1520 CE) Portuguese navigator who, by chance, discovered the eastern coast of South America.

Cai Lun (Ts'ai Lun) Chinese court eunuch; traditionally credited as the first maker of paper, in 105 CE.

Caligula Roman emperor from 37 to 41 CE; succeeded by Claudius I.

Cambyses II king of the Medes and Persians; ruled between 529 and 522 BCE; son of Cyrus the Great; conquered Egypt in 525 BCE.

Carter, Howard (1874–1939 CE) British archaeologist who, in 1922 CE, discovered the tomb of the Egyptian king Tutankhamen.

Cassiodorus (c. 490–583 CE) Roman statesman and author; stimulated the copying of manuscripts by monks.

Cassius, Gaius one of the assassins of Julius Caesar in 44 BCE.

Catiline (c. 108–62 BCE) Roman aristocrat who tried unsuccessfully to overthrow the republic in 63 BCE.

Cato the Elder (234–149 BCE) leading Roman politician who led the republic into war against Carthage.

Chandragupta Maurya founder of the Mauryan Empire and conqueror of the Indus Valley; ruled between around 321 and 293 BCE.

Charlemagne Frankish king from 768 to 814 CE; founded the Holy Roman Empire, of which he was emperor from 800 CE.

Charles Martel ruler of Austrasia (modern northeastern France and southwestern Germany) between 714 and 741 CE; fought against Alemanni, Bavarians, and Saxons; defeated an Islamic army near Poitiers in 732 CE.

Cicero, Marcus Tullius (106–43 BCE) Roman statesman and author. On the death of Julius Caesar, he took the side of Brutus.

Cleopatra queen of Egypt from 51 to 30 BCE; ruled successively with her two brothers, Ptolemy XIII (51–47 BCE) and Ptolemy XIV (47–44 BCE), and then with her son Ptolemy XV (44–30 BCE). A mistress of both Julius Caesar and Mark Antony, she and the latter committed suicide together after their defeat by Octavian (the future Roman emperor Augustus).

Clotilda (474–545 CE) Burgundian wife of Clovis I.

Clovis I king of the Franks between 481 and 511 CE; conquered most of Gaul; defeated Alemanni and Visigoths; converted in 496 CE.

Cnut (died 1035 CE) Danish king who united Denmark, England, and Norway into a single kingdom.

Columbus, Christopher (1451–1506 CE) Genoese mariner credited with being the first European to set foot in the Americas (although many people believe that Viking explorers did so several hundred years earlier).

Confucius (Kongqiu; K'ung) (551–479 BCE) Chinese philosopher and founder of Confucianism.

Constantine the Great Roman emperor between 306 and 337 CE; ruled initially in the west only but became absolute sovereign in 324 CE; built Constantinople; legalized Christianity.

Cortés, Hernán (1485–1547 CE) Spanish adventurer who led the force that brought down the Aztec Empire in 1521 CE.

Crassus, Marcus Licinius (c. 115–53 BCE) Roman politician who formed the first triumvirate with Julius Caesar and Pompey. After Crassus's death, the other two members became enemies and precipitated a civil war (49–45 BCE).

Croesus king of Lydia between 560 and 546 BCE; conquered Ionia and was in turn subjugated by the Persians; famous for his vast wealth.

Cyrus the Great king of the Persian Empire from 559 to 529 BCE and member of the Achaemenid dynasty. In 558 BCE, he obtained hegemony following an uprising against the Medes. He conquered Lydia in 547 BCE and the Neo-Babylonian kingdom around 539 BCE.

Darius I king of the Persian Empire between 521 and 486 BCE. He created political unity by dividing the empire into 20 satrapies, which were subject to central rule. He consolidated the borders, promoted trade, and developed an infrastructure. He was a follower of Zoroaster. He started the First Persian War, annexed Thrace and Macedonia, and undertook an expedition against Athens that ended in the Battle of Marathon.

David king of Israel and Judah between around 1000 and 965 BCE; successor to Saul. He defeated the Philistines, expanded the kingdom to its greatest size, seized Jerusalem from the Jebusites, and made it his capital.

Decius Roman emperor who ruled between 249 and 251 CE. The first systematic persecution of Christians took place during his reign.

Democritus fifth-century-BCE Greek philosopher.

Dias, Bartolomeu (1450–1500 CE) Portuguese mariner who was the first European to sail around the southern tip of Africa, which he named the Cape of Good Hope.

Diocletian Roman emperor between 284 and 305 CE.

Diogenes (c. 400–325 BCE) Greek philosopher; founded Cynicism.

Djoser pharaoh from around 2630 to 2611 BCE; presided over Egypt's first cultural flowering. The Step Pyramid was built for him at Saqqara.

Domitian Roman emperor who ruled between 81 and 96 CE; presided over a reign of terror.

Edward III king of England from 1327 to 1377 CE; proclaimed himself king of France in 1337 CE, thus sparking the Hundred Years' War; reshaped the English army.

El Cid (c. 1043–1099 CE) *El Cid Campeador* (The Lord Champion); born Rodrigo Díaz de Vivar; great Spanish warrior.

Eleanor of Aquitaine (c. 1122–1204 CE) heiress to the region of Aquitaine. When Louis VII of France had their marriage annulled, Eleanor married Henry II of England, giving him the western part of the French Empire.

Eratosthenes Greek mathematician and astronomer of the third and second centuries BCE who calculated the circumference of Earth.

Eriksson, Leif (c. 970–1020 CE) Norse explorer; first European to reach the shores of North America.

Euclid (c. 300 BCE) ancient Greek mathematician; known as the father of geometry.

Euripides (c. 485–406 BCE) Greek dramatist; author of more than 90 plays, including *Medea*.

Fabius, Quintus Maximus Verrucosus (died 203 BCE) Roman commander whose delaying tactics during the Second Punic War bought time for Rome to prepare to confront the Carthaginian army of Hannibal.

Firdawsi Persian poet who wrote *Shah-nama* (Book of Kings) around 1010 CE.

Frederick I Barbarossa Holy Roman emperor between 1152 and 1190 CE; as a scion of the Hohenstaufen family, made peace with the Guelph leader, Henry of Saxony; strengthened his power and removed many privileges from the princes and dukes of his realm; fought against the rebellious Lombard League, the Guelphs, and the pope; died during the Third Crusade.

Frederick II Holy Roman emperor between 1215 and 1250 CE; supported by Pope Innocent III; left the German noblemen to their own devices and harshly ruled the kingdom of Sicily; became king of Jerusalem in 1229 CE.

Gaiseric king of the Vandals between 428 and 477 CE.

Galerius Roman emperor between 305 and 311 CE; persecuted Christians and then issued an edict of tolerance.

Gama, Vasco da (c. 1460–1524 CE) Portuguese navigator who established an eastbound naval route from Europe to eastern Asia. He sailed around the southern tip of Africa and up the east coast as far as Kenya before crossing the Indian Ocean to reach Calicut.

Genghis Khan (c. 1162–1227 CE) first leader to unite the Mongols, whom he led on a campaign of conquest that took in China and some Islamic empires.

Go-Sanjo first Japanese emperor in more than a century not to be related to the Fujiwaras; ruled between 1060 and 1073 CE.

Gratian western Roman emperor between 367 and 383 CE.

Gudea ruler (*ensi*) of Lagash from around 2141 to 2122 BCE; famous for overseeing the construction of a temple to the god Ningirsu and

the building hymn celebrating his accomplishment.

Gutenberg, Johannes (c. 1390–1468 CE) German inventor of the movable type printing press. He used his invention to produce the Gutenberg Bible.

Hadrian Roman emperor who ruled from 117 to 138 CE, succeeding his uncle, Trajan. His rule was a period of consolidation of the vast empire.

Hamilcar Barca (c. 270–228 BCE) Carthaginian general who made peace with the Romans at the end of the First Punic War; father of Hannibal.

Hammurabi king of Babylon from around 1792 to 1750 BCE; defeated the kings of Larsa and Assur and conquered Mari; drew up a legal code and abolished the deification of kings.

Han Fei (Han-fei-tzu) (died 233 BCE) Chinese legalist philosopher whose works exerted a major influence on the development of autocratic government.

Hannibal (247–183 BCE) Carthaginian general who famously led an army with elephants over the Alps from Spain to Rome.

Harald Finehair first king of a united Norway; ruled between 860 and 930 CE.

Harun al-Rashid caliph who brought the Abbasid dynasty to the peak of its power; ruled between 786 and 809 CE.

Hatshepsut only female pharaoh; ruled Egypt from around 1473 to 1458 BCE.

Hattusilis I king of the Old Hittite kingdom between around 1650 and 1620 BCE; founded Hattusas; tried to protect Hittite power against the Hurrians in Syria and the mountain peoples in Anatolia.

Henry II first Plantagenet king of England; ruled between 1154 and 1189 CE; acquired the western part of the French Empire through his marriage to Eleanor of Aquitaine.

Henry the Navigator (1394–1460 CE) Portuguese monarch who sponsored many voyages of exploration.

Heraclius Byzantine emperor between 610 and 641 CE; began counteroffensive against Khosrow II in 622 CE; weakened the Persian Empire by his victories in the center of the realm in 627 CE.

Herod Roman-appointed king of Judaea from 37 to 4 BCE. Jesus was born during Herod's reign.

Herodotus (born c. 480 BCE) known as the father of Greek historiography. His work *History* viewed the battle between the Greeks and the Persians as a confrontation between eastern and western cultures.

Herophilus personal physician to Ptolemy I in the fourth century BCE; widely regarded as the father of the study of human anatomy.

Hesiod (c. 700 BCE) Greek epic poet; author of *Theogony* (or *Birth of the Gods*), on religion and mythology, and *Works and Days*, a sort of manual for farmers.

Hippocrates (c. 460–377 BCE) ancient Greek physician; known as the father of medicine.

Homer (c. 800 BCE) legendary Greek poet to whom the epics the *Iliad* and the *Odyssey* are attributed.

Honorius western Roman emperor between 395 and 423 CE; ruled from the age of 12 under the guardianship of Stilicho.

Huayna Capac Inca monarch who ruled between around 1493 and 1525

CE. During his reign, the empire reached its greatest extent.

Hugh Capet king of France between 987 and 996 CE; gradually unified the previously fragmented country. The Capetian dynasty that he founded endured until 1328 CE.

Hulagu Khan grandson of Genghis Khan; founded the Il-Khanate dynasty in 1256 CE; sacked Baghdad.

Hus, Jan (1372–1415 CE) Czech religious reformer; convicted of heresy at the Council of Constance and burned at the stake.

Imhotep Egyptian architect who lived in the 27th century BCE; built the Step Pyramid at Saqqara on the orders of the pharaoh Djoser. Imhotep was deified after his death.

Iname Japanese emperor of the Soga clan; ruled between 536 and 570 CE; early sponsor of Buddhism.

Ivan IV (the Terrible) first "Czar of All the Russias"; ruled between 1533 and 1584 CE; introduced an effective central administration and created an empire that incorporated non-Slav states.

Jerome, Saint (c. 345–420 CE) Dalmatian-born monastic leader who translated the Bible into Latin.

Joan of Arc (1412–1431 CE) French peasant girl who broke the English siege of Orléans and had Charles VII crowned king of France; captured by the English and burned at the stake as a heretic.

John I Tzimisces Byzantine emperor; ruled between 969 and 976 CE; consolidated power in the Balkans and Syria.

Judas Maccabaeus leader of the Maccabaean revolt against the Seleucid Empire (166–165 BCE).

Jugurtha king of Numidia from 118 to 105 BCE; fought against Rome for control of his realm in northern Africa.

Julian the Apostate Roman emperor between 361 and 363 CE; converted to paganism and limited the rights of Christians.

Julius Caesar (100–44 BCE) Roman general who conquered Gaul (58–50 BCE) and triumphed in the civil war of 49–45 BCE; dictator of Rome (46–44 BCE); assassinated by political opponents.

Justinian Byzantine emperor between 527 and 565 CE; built the Hagia Sophia. His generals Belisarius and Narses defeated the Ostrogoths.

Kalidasa Indian poet and dramatist; wrote in Sanskrit. His dates are uncertain, but he probably lived during the reign of the Gupta king Chandragupta II, who ruled between 375 and 414 CE.

Kammu Japanese emperor who ruled between 781 and 806 CE; moved the capital to Heian-kyo (modern Kyoto).

Kamose pharaoh from 1554 to 1550 BCE; tried to expel the Hyksos from the north and thwarted their attempts to form an alliance with the Kushites.

Kanishka king of the Kushan dynasty; ruled between around 100 and 130 CE; outstanding patron of Buddhism.

Khosrow I king of Persia between 531 and 579 CE.

Khosrow II king of Persia between 590 and 628 CE; seized Syria and Jerusalem from the Byzantines; defeated by Heraclius in 627 CE.

Kublai Khan Mongolian general and statesman; grandson of Genghis Khan; ruled between 1260 and 1294 CE. He conquered China and became the first emperor of its Yüan, or Mongol, dynasty. In that role, he promoted the integration of Chinese and Mongol civilizations.

Lao-tzu (Laozi) (c. 570–490 BCE) Chinese philosopher whose ideas are recorded in the *Tao Te Ching* (*Dao De Jing*; Classic of the Way and Its Virtue).

Leo III Byzantine emperor between 717 and 741 CE; sometimes known as Leo the Isaurian; gained the throne after several succession conflicts; withstood an Arab siege; made the Byzantine Empire a buffer against Islamic expansion.

Leonardo da Vinci (1452–1519 CE) painter, sculptor, architect, and scientist who embodied the spirit of the Renaissance. His best known paintings are the *Mona Lisa* and *The Last Supper*.

Leonidas (died 480 BCE) king of Sparta; killed at the Battle of Thermopylae with hundreds of Spartans covering the retreat of the main Greek army from the Persians.

Li Si (Li Ssu) (c. 280–208 BCE) Chinese statesman and philosopher; used his political theories to unite the warring states into the centralized Qin (Ch'in) dynasty (221–206 BCE).

Liu Bang (Liu Pang) army officer of nonaristocratic birth who proclaimed the Han dynasty in 206 BCE.

Louis VII king of France between 1137 and 1180 CE. By annulling his marriage to Eleanor of Aquitaine, he lost a large portion of his empire to Henry II of England.

Lugalzaggisi king of the Sumerian city-state of Umma in the 24th century BCE.

Lycurgus ninth-century-BCE Spartan lawgiver and probable author of the Spartan constitution.

Machiavelli, Niccolò (1469–1527 CE) Florentine diplomat and writer. His most famous work is *The Prince*, a guide on how to succeed in politics.

Magellan, Ferdinand (1480–1521 CE) Portuguese navigator who began the first circumnavigation of the world.

Manetho priest who drew up a history of Egypt in the third century BCE and divided the pharaohs into dynasties.

Mani (c. 216–276 CE) Persian prophet who founded Manichaeism.

Marcus Aurelius emperor of Rome between 161 and 180 CE.

Mark Antony (83–30 BCE) Roman general under Julius Caesar and later triumvir (43–30 BCE); became lover of Cleopatra, queen of Egypt, and was defeated with her by Octavian (the future emperor Augustus) in the last of the civil wars that destroyed the Roman republic.

Martin of Tours, Saint (c. 316–397 CE) bishop of Tours; one of the founders of monasticism.

Medici, Cosimo de' (1389–1464 CE) Florentine banker who was an important patron of the arts.

Medici, Lorenzo de' (1449–1492 CE) poet and patron of the arts; known as Lorenzo the Magnificent.

Menander (c. 341–291 BCE) Athenian comic dramatist; author of more than 100 plays.

Mencius (Mengzi) (c. 371–289 BCE) early Chinese philosopher who developed orthodox Confucianism.

Mentuhotep II pharaoh from 2061 to 2010 BCE; reunified Egypt around 2047 BCE by defeating his rivals and ushered in the period known as the Middle Kingdom.

Mercator (1512–1594 CE) Flemish cartographer (born Gerhard Kremer) who developed a way of representing the world accurately on a two-dimensional map.

Merneptah king of Egypt from 1213 to 1203 BCE; successfully defended his country against a serious invasion from Libya.

Michelangelo (1475–1564 CE) Italian painter, sculptor, and architect; responsible for the ceiling decorations of the Sistine Chapel.

Miltiades general who led Athenian forces to victory over the Persians at the Battle of Marathon in 490 BCE.

Mithridates king of Pontus (in northern Anatolia) from 120 to 63 BCE; led an uprising against Rome in Anatolia and Greece in 88 BCE; defeated by Sulla in 84 BCE.

Monteverdi, Claudio (1567–1643 CE) Venetian composer who played an important role in the development of the opera.

Montezuma II Aztec emperor between 1502 and 1520 CE; ruled at the time of the arrival of the Spanish conquistador Hernán Cortés; subsequently held captive by Cortés.

Montfort, Simon de (c. 1208–1265 CE) leader of the baronial revolt against King Henry III of England.

Mu'awiyah first Umayyad caliph; ruled between 661 and 680 CE; moved the capital of Islam from Medina to Damascus; opposed Ali and his followers; dominated Syria and Egypt. After Ali's death, he bought off Ali's son Hassan to become absolute sovereign of the Arabian Empire.

Muhammad ibn Tughluq sultan who briefly extended the rule of the Delhi Sultanate of northern India over most of the subcontinent; ruled between 1325 and 1351 CE.

Mursilis I Hittite king from around 1620 to 1590 BCE; conquered parts of Syria and razed Aleppo and Babylon.

Mursilis II Hittite king from around 1350 to 1320 BCE; resided in Hattusas; defended the Hittite Empire against surrounding states; conquered Asia Minor and fought the Egyptians.

Naram-Sin king of the Akkadian Empire from around 2254 to 2218 BCE; suppressed a rebellion by the Sumerian cities and conquered the areas surrounding Mesopotamia.

Narses sixth-century-CE Roman general of Justinian I; defeated the Ostrogoths in Italy in 552 CE.

Nebuchadnezzar II king of Neo-Babylonian Empire from 605 to 562 BCE; conquered Syria, Phoenicia, and Judaea; built Babylon into an impressive capital.

Nero Roman emperor from 54 to 68 CE; committed suicide. His rule is best known for its immorality and violence.

Oppert, Jules (1825–1905 CE) French pioneer of research into the Sumerian language.

Othman ibn Affan third caliph; ruled between 644 and 656 CE; son-in-law of the prophet Mohammed; founder of the Umayyad dynasty.

Ovid (43 BCE–17 CE) Roman poet; author of *Metamorphoses*; banished from Rome by the emperor Augustus.

Pachomius (c. 290–346 CE) founder of monastic commune in Egypt.

Paul of Thebes (c. 230–341 CE) first Christian hermit; Egyptian who fled persecution by Decius.

Pericles (c. 495–429 BCE) democratic leader of Athens during its Golden Age.

Philip II Augustus king of France; ruled between 1180 and 1223 CE; annexed French territories that had previously been apportioned to the English king; expanded his powers by instituting a nonfeudal government system; forged the French kingdom into a powerful unity.

Pizarro, Francisco (c. 1471–1541 CE) Spanish conquistador who led the forces that conquered the Incas.

Plato (c. 428–348 BCE) ancient Greek philosopher who, with Aristotle and Socrates, laid the foundations of subsequent Western thought.

Pliny the Younger (c. 61–113 CE) author of nine books of letters on a wide range of contemporary issues.

Plutarch (c. 46–120 CE) Greek biographer who wrote *Parallel Lives*, in which leading Greeks and Romans are discussed in pairs.

Pocahontas daughter of the Native American chieftain Powhatan; saved the life of the English settler John Smith.

Polo, Marco (c. 1254–1324 CE) Venetian merchant and traveler who reached China and met the Mongol emperor Kublai Khan.

Pompey (106–48 BCE) Roman statesman and general; a triumvir (61–54 BCE); first an associate and later an enemy of Julius Caesar.

Powhatan Native American chieftain who conquered and subsequently ruled over a number of tribes in present-day Virginia between around 1575 and 1600 CE.

Pythagoras (c. 580–500 BCE) Greek philosopher and mathematician whose

religious, political, and philosophical doctrines influenced Plato.

Raleigh, Walter (c. 1554–1618 CE) English adventurer who organized several expeditions to settle the eastern coast of North America.

Ramses II pharaoh of Egypt from 1279 to 1213 BCE. Among his numerous building projects were his own temple, the Ramesseum, and the expansion of the residence in Avaris.

Raymond of Toulouse (1042–1105 CE) southern French nobleman; one of the leaders of the First Crusade.

Richard I (the Lionheart) king of England; ruled between 1189 and 1199 CE; took part in the Third Crusade; warred against Philip II Augustus of France.

Robert Guiscard (c. 1015–1085 CE) Norman adventurer who became duke of Apulia and extended Norman rule over Naples, Calabria, and Sicily; laid the foundations of the kingdom of Sicily.

Roger II first king of Sicily; ruled between 1130 and 1154 CE.

Romulus Augustulus last western Roman emperor; deposed in 476 CE.

Sargon II king of the Assyrians between 722 and 705 BCE; subjugated the Syrian and Phoenician coastal cities; became the king of Babylon.

Sargon the Great founded the Akkadian Empire around 2335 BCE; based his power on the state monopoly of raw materials.

Sennacherib king of the Assyrians between 704 and 681 BCE.

Sesostris I pharaoh from 1962 to 1926 BCE during the Middle Kingdom period; brought Egypt to the height of its prosperity.

Sesostris III pharaoh from 1878 to 1843 BCE; ended the power and independence of the local administrators; established a centralized system of royal supervisors; expanded Egyptian territory into Palestine.

Shapur I king of Persia between 241 and 272 CE; expanded the New Persian Empire to the Himalayas; conquered Armenia; defeated the Byzantines in Antioch, taking many Syrian prisoners of war. Christianity spread throughout his realm.

Shapur II king of Persia between 309 and 379 CE; captured parts of eastern Syria and Mesopotamia from the eastern Roman Empire; defeated Julian in 363 CE; brought the New Persian Empire to its apex.

Shi Huang Di (Shi Huang Ti) regional ruler who declared himself emperor of China and founded the Qin (Ch'in) dynasty; emperor between 221 and 210 BCE.

Siddharta Gautama (c. 563–483 BCE) Nepalese holy man and teacher; founder of Buddhism.

Sima Yan (Ssu-ma Yen) emperor of China; seized the throne in 265 CE, establishing the Jin (Ching) dynasty; reunited the north and south of the country by 280 CE. The dynasty remained stable until 290 CE.

Socrates (469–399 BCE) Athenian philosopher. His ideas were passed down through the writings of Plato.

Solon sixth-century-BCE Athenian law reformer who abolished debt slavery in 594 BCE; expanded participation of all free citizens in government.

Sophocles (c. 496–406 BCE) Greek playwright; author of tragedies.

Spartacus (died 71 BCE) gladiator who deserted from the Roman army and led a slave rebellion (73–71 BCE).

Süleyman I sultan of the Ottoman Empire; ruled between 1520 and 1566 CE; conquered Rhodes and Belgrade; reorganized the state and tolerated different religions.

Sulla, Lucius Cornelius (138–78 BCE) Roman dictator who tried to strengthen the republic after its first civil war (88–82 BCE).

Suppiluliumas I Hittite king who ruled from around 1358 to 1323 BCE; expanded the Hittite Empire to its greatest size; conquered Syria; fought the Mitanni.

Tamerlane (Timur the Lame) Mongolian ruler between around 1369 and 1405 CE; subjected the Mongols in the west; conquered territory in Persia, India, Syria; spread Islam.

Tarquin the Proud traditionally the seventh and last king of Rome; ruled from 534 to 510 BCE.

Theodora Byzantine empress (ruled 527–548 CE); wife of Justinian I; a Monophysite.

Theodoric the Great king of the Ostrogoths between 471 and 526 CE.

Theodosius I eastern and then eastern and western Roman emperor; ruled between 379 and 395 CE.

Thomas Aquinas (1225–1274 CE) Scholastic philosopher and theologian. His best-known work is *Summa Theologiae* (Summary of Theology), which is a catalog of contemporary Christian thought.

Thomsen, Christian (1788–1865 CE) Danish archaeologist who devised the division of early human history into three ages: the Stone Age, the Bronze Age, and the Iron Age.

Thucydides (c. 460–400 BCE) Greek historian of the Peloponnesian War.

Tiglath-pileser III king of the Assyrians between around 746 and 727 BCE; conquered Babylon and was crowned its king.

Tutankhamen pharaoh from around 1332 to 1323 BCE; left the royal residence at Akhetaton and resumed the cult of deities to reduce the chaos and dissatisfaction that had been created by Akhenaton. Tutankhamen's grave was left untouched and contained precious funerary treasures.

Urban II pope who proclaimed the First Crusade in 1095 CE; served between 1088 and 1099 CE.

Vacarius, Roger (c. 1120–1200 CE) teacher of law at Oxford; produced a nine-volume study of Justinian's legal code.

Valens eastern Roman emperor; ruled between 364 and 378 CE.

Vima Kadphises Kushan emperor who conquered the Indus Valley and much of the Gangetic Plain; ruled between around 75 and 100 CE.

Virgil (70–19 BCE) Roman poet; author of the *Aeneid*, an epic of the foundation of Rome by fugitives from the sacking of Troy.

Wang Mang government official who overthrew the Han dynasty and founded the short-lived Xin dynasty; ruled between 9 and 23 CE.

William I (the Conqueror) first Norman king of England; ruled between 1066 and 1087 CE; defeated King Harold at the Battle of Hastings; established a centralized monarchy, granting estates to loyal followers but retaining power; ordered the compilation of the Domesday Book.

Woolley, Leonard (1880–1960 CE) British archaeologist who excavated the ancient city of Ur in Mesopotamia; also worked on the excavation of the Hittite city of Carchemish.

Xanthippus third-century-BCE Spartan general who fought for Carthage in the First Punic War.

Xavier, Francis (1506–1552 CE) first Jesuit missionary to establish Christianity in Japan.

Xenophon (431–350 BCE) Greek historian; author of the *Anabasis*, an account of how Greek mercenaries attempted to seize the Persian throne.

Xerxes I king of Persia between 486 and 465 BCE; destroyed Athens in 480 BCE during the Second Persian War.

Yazdegerd III last Sassanid king of Persia; ruled between 632 and 651 CE.

Yazid I caliph between 680 and 683 CE; son and successor of Mu'awiyah.

Zeno (c. 335–263 BCE) Greek Cypriot who founded the Stoic school of philosophy.

Zhao Kuangyin (Chao K'uang-yin) Chinese general who seized the throne in 960 CE and declared himself the first Song (Sung) emperor.

RESOURCES FOR FURTHER STUDY

BOOKS

Abbasid Caliphate

El-Hibri, Tayeb. *Reinterpreting Islamic Historiography: Harun al-Rashid and the Narrative of the Abbasid Caliphate*. New York, 1999.

Le Strange, G. *Baghdad during the Abbasid Caliphate: From Contemporary Arabic and Persian Sources*. New York, 1972.

Africa

Le Tourneau, Roger. *The Almohad Movement in North Africa in the Twelfth and Thirteenth Centuries*. Princeton, NJ, 1969.

Merrills, A.H. (ed.). *Vandals, Romans and Berbers: New Perspectives on Late Antique North Africa*. Burlington, VT, 2004.

Quigley, Mary. *Ancient West African Kingdoms: Ghana, Mali, and Songhai*. Chicago, IL, 2002.

Alexander the Great

Cartledge, Paul. *Alexander the Great: The Hunt for a New Past*. Woodstock, NY, 2004.

Fildes, Alan. *Alexander the Great: Son of the Gods*. Los Angeles, CA, 2002.

Fuller, J.F.C. *The Generalship of Alexander the Great*. New York, 1960.

Gergel, Tania (ed.). *Alexander the Great: Selected Texts from Arrian, Curtius, and Plutarch*. New York, 2004.

Green, Robert. *Alexander the Great*. New York, 1996.

Heckel, Waldemar. *The Wars of Alexander the Great, 336–323 BC*. New York, 2003.

Prevas, John. *Envy of the Gods: Alexander the Great's Ill-Fated Journey across Asia*. Cambridge, MA, 2004.

Archaeology

Bahn, Paul (ed.). *The Atlas of World Archaeology*. New York, 2000.

Hodder, Ian. *Theory and Practice in Archaeology*. New York, 1992.

Maisels, Charles. *The Near East: Archaeology in the Cradle of Civilization*. London, England, 1993.

Arianism

Newman, John Henry. *The Arians of the Fourth Century*. Notre Dame, IN, 2001.

Wiles, Maurice F. *Archetypal Heresy: Arianism Through the Centuries*. New York, 1996.

Williams, Rowan. *Arius: Heresy and Tradition*. Grand Rapids, MI, 2002.

Art

Boardman, John. *The Diffusion of Classical Art in Antiquity*. London, England, 1994.

Boardman, John (ed.). *The Oxford History of Classical Art*. New York, 1993.

Doumas, Christos. *The Wall-Paintings of Thera*. London, England, 1992.

Robertson, Martin. *The Art of Vase-Painting in Classical Athens*. New York, 1992.

Aztecs

Gruzinski, Serge. *The Aztecs: Rise and Fall of an Empire*. New York, 1992.

Townsend, Richard F. *The Aztecs*. London, England, 2000.

Babylon

Oates, Joan. *Babylon*. London, England, 1986.

Saggs, H.W.F. *Babylonians*. London, England, 2000.

Schomp, Virginia. *Ancient Mesopotamia: The Sumerians, Babylonians, and Assyrians*. New York, 2005.

Yoffee, Norman. *The Economic Role of the Crown in the Old Babylonian Period*. Malibu, CA, 1977.

Bedouin

Losleben, Elizabeth. *The Bedouin of the Middle East*. Minneapolis, MN, 2003.

Berbers

Brett, Michael, and Elizabeth Fentress. *The Berbers*. Cambridge, MA, 1996.

Merrills, A.H. (ed.). *Vandals, Romans and Berbers: New Perspectives on Late Antique North Africa*. Burlington, VT, 2004.

Bronze Age

Anthony, David W. *The Horse, the Wheel, and Language: How Bronze-Age Riders from the Eurasian Steppes Shaped the Modern World.* Princeton, NJ, 2007.

Barber, Robin. *The Cyclades in the Bronze Age.* London, England, 1987.

Dickinson, Oliver. *The Aegean Bronze Age.* New York, 1994.

Drews, Robert. *The End of the Bronze Age: Changes in Warfare and the Catastrophe ca. 1200 B.C.* Princeton, NJ, 1993.

Forsyth, Phyllis Young. *Thera in the Bronze Age.* New York, 1997.

Manning, Sturt. *Absolute Chronology of the Aegean Early Bronze Age.* Sheffield, England, 1995.

Shanower, Eric. *Age of Bronze* (three volumes). Orange, CA, 2001.

Warren, Peter, and Vronwy Hankey (eds.). *Aegean Bronze Age Chronology.* Bristol, England, 1989.

Burgundy

Boulton, D'Arcy Jonathan Dacre, and Jan R. Veenstra (eds.). *The Ideology of Burgundy: The Promotion of National Consciousness, 1364–1565.* Boston, MA, 2006.

Carthage

Brown, Shelby. *Late Carthaginian Child Sacrifice and Sacrificial Monuments in Their Mediterranean Context.* Sheffield, England, 1991.

Lancel, Serge. *Carthage: A History.* Oxford, England, 1995.

Soren, David, Aicha Ben Abed Khader, and Hedi Slim. *Carthage: Uncovering the Mysteries and Splendors of Ancient Tunisia.* New York, 1990.

Cathars

Lansing, Carol. *Power and Purity: Cathar Heresy in Medieval Italy.* New York, 1998.

Martin, Sean. *The Cathars: The Most Successful Heresy of the Middle Ages.* New York, 2005.

Rahn, Otto (translated by Christopher Jones). *Crusade against the Grail: The Struggle between the Cathars, the Templars, and the Church of Rome.* Rochester, VT, 2006.

Charlemagne

Barbero, Alessandro (translated by Allan Cameron). *Charlemagne: Father of a Continent.* Berkeley, CA, 2004.

Sypeck, Jeff. *Becoming Charlemagne: Europe, Baghdad, and the Empires of AD 800.* New York, 2006.

———. *The Holy Roman Empire and Charlemagne in World History.* Berkeley Heights, NJ, 2002.

Wilson, Derek A. *Charlemagne: A Biography.* New York, 2006.

China

Cotterell, Arthur. *Ancient China.* New York, 2005.

Fisher, Leonard Everett. *The Great Wall of China.* New York, 1986.

Gascoigne, Bamber. *The Dynasties of China: A History.* New York, 2003.

Hardy, Grant. *The Establishment of the Han Empire and Imperial China.* Westport, CT, 2005.

Hirth, Friedrich. *The Ancient History of China, to the End of the Chou Dynasty.* Freeport, NY, 1969.

Lewis, Mark Edward. *The Early Chinese Empires: Qin and Han.* Cambridge, MA, 2007.

Pavan, Aldo. *Yellow River: The Spirit and Strength of China.* New York, 2007.

Sawyer, Ralph D. *The Art of the Warrior: Leadership and Strategy from the Chinese Military Classics: With Selections from the Seven Military Classics of Ancient China and Sun Pin's Military Methods.* Boston, MA, 1996.

———. *Fire and Water: The Art of Incendiary and Aquatic Warfare in China.* Boulder, CO, 2003.

Thorp, Robert L. *China in the Early Bronze Age: Shang Civilization.* Philadelphia, PA, 2006.

Crusades

Madden, Thomas F. *The New Concise History of the Crusades.* Lanham, MD, 2006.

Miller, David. *Richard the Lionheart: The Mighty Crusader.* New York, 2003.

O'Callaghan, Joseph F. *Reconquest and Crusade in Medieval Spain.* Philadelphia, PA, 2003.

Pegg, Mark Gregory. *A Most Holy War: The Albigensian Crusade and the Battle for Christendom*. New York, 2008.

Rahn, Otto (translated by Christopher Jones). *Crusade against the Grail: The Struggle between the Cathars, the Templars, and the Church of Rome*. Rochester, VT, 2006.

Strayer, Joseph Reese. *The Albigensian Crusades*. Ann Arbor, MI, 1992.

Early Civilizations
Burke, John, and Kaj Halberg. *Seed of Knowledge, Stone of Plenty: Understanding the Lost Technology of the Megalith Builders*. San Francisco, CA, 2005.

Cotterell, Arthur (ed.). *The Penguin Encyclopedia of Ancient Civilizations*. New York, 1988.

Curtis, Gregory. *The Cave Painters: Probing the Mysteries of the World's First Artists*. New York, 2007.

Dorling Kindersley Publishing. *Early Humans*. New York, 2005.

Haywood, John. *Ancient Civilizations of the Near East and Mediterranean*. Armonk, NY, 1997.

Hynes, Margaret. *The Best Book of Early People*. New York, 2003.

Leakey, Richard E. *The Origin of Humankind*. New York, 1994.

Maisels, Charles. *The Emergence of Civilization*. London, England, 1990.

Mithen, Steven J. *After the Ice: A Global Human History, 20,000–5000 BC*. Cambridge, MA, 2004.

Oates, David, and Joan Oates. *The Rise of Civilization*. Oxford, England, 1976.

Redman, Charles. *The Rise of Civilization*. San Francisco, CA, 1978.

Renfrew, Colin. *The Emergence of Civilization: The Cyclades and the Aegean in the Third Millennium B.C.* London, England, 1972.

Rudgley, Richard. *The Lost Civilizations of the Stone Age*. New York, 1999.

Scarre, Christopher, and Brian M. Fagan. *Ancient Civilizations*. Upper Saddle River, NJ, 2008.

Steward, Julian (ed.). *Irrigation Civilizations: A Comparative Study*. Washington, DC, 1955.

Time-Life Books. *Ancient Civilizations, 3000 BC–AD 500*. Alexandria, VA, 1998.

Cuneiform
Hooker, J.T. *Reading the Past: Ancient Writing from Cuneiform to the Alphabet*. London, England, 1990.

Walker, C.B.F. *Cuneiform*. Berkeley, CA, 1987.

Egypt
Baines, John, and Jaromir Malek. *Atlas of Ancient Egypt*. New York, 2002.

Brier, Bob. *Egyptian Mummies: Unraveling the Secrets of an Ancient Art*. New York, 1994.

Chadwick, Robert. *First Civilizations: Ancient Mesopotamia and Ancient Egypt*. Oakville, CT, 2005.

Clayton, Peter A. *Chronicle of the Pharaohs: The Reign-by-Reign Record of the Rulers and Dynasties of Ancient Egypt*. New York, 1994.

Hawass, Zahi A. *The Golden Age of Tutankhamun: Divine Might and Splendor in the New Kingdom*. New York, 2004.

Hoffman, Michael A. *Egypt before the Pharaohs*. New York, 1979.

Honan, Linda. *Spend the Day in Ancient Egypt: Projects and Activities that Bring the Past to Life*. New York, 1999.

James, T.G.H. *A Short History of Ancient Egypt: From Predynastic to Roman Times*. Baltimore, MD, 1998.

Langley, Andrew. *Ancient Egypt*. Chicago, IL, 2005.

Oakes, Lorna, and Philip Steele. *Everyday Life in Ancient Egypt and Mesopotamia*. London, England, 2006.

Reeves, C.N., and Richard H. Wilkinson. *The Complete Valley of the Kings: Tombs and Treasures of Egypt's Greatest Pharaohs*. New York, 1996.

Robins, Gay. *Women in Ancient Egypt*. Cambridge, MA, 1993.

Romer, John. *The Great Pyramid: Ancient Egypt Revisited*. New York, 2007.

Ross, Stewart. *Ancient Egypt*. Milwaukee, WI, 2005.

Shaw, Ina (ed.). *The Oxford History of Ancient Egypt*. New York, 2003.

Silverman, David P. (ed.). *Ancient Egypt*. New York, 2003.

Time-Life Books. *Egypt: Land of the Pharaohs*. Alexandria, VA, 1992.

Wilkinson, Toby (ed.). *The Egyptian World*. New York, 2007.

Eleanor of Aquitaine
Weir, Alison. *Eleanor of Aquitaine: A Life*. New York, 2000.

Eriksson, Leif
Kimmel, Elizabeth Cody. *Before Columbus: The Leif Eriksson Expedition*. New York, 2003.

Klingel, Cynthia Fitterer, and Robert B. Noyed. *Leif Eriksson: Norwegian Explorer*. Chanhassen, MI, 2003.

Etruscans
Barker, Graeme, and Tom Rasmussen. *The Etruscans*. Malden, MA, 1998.

Bonfante, Larissa (ed.). *Etruscan Life and Afterlife*. Detroit, MI, 1986.

Pallottino, Massimo. *The Etruscans*. Harmondsworth, England, 1978.

Spivey, Nigel, and Simon Stoddart. *Etruscan Italy: An Archaeological History*. London, England, 1990.

Fatimids
Walker, Paul E. *Exploring an Islamic Empire: Fatimid History and Its Sources*. London, England, 2002.

France
Bradbury, Jim. *Philip Augustus: King of France, 1180–1223*. New York, 1998.

Duby, Georges. *France in the Middle Ages, 987–1460: From Hugh Capet to Joan of Arc*. Cambridge, MA, 1991.

Dunbabin, Jean. *France in the Making, 843–1180*. New York, 2000.

Geary, Patrick J. *Before France and Germany: The Creation and Transformation of the Merovingian World*. New York, 1988.

Hallam, Elizabeth M., and Judith Everard. *Capetian France, 987–1328*. New York, 2001.

Parker, Geoffrey. *The Grand Strategy of Philip II*. New Haven, CT, 1998.

Wood, Charles T. *The French Apanages and the Capetian Monarchy, 1224–1328*. Cambridge, MA, 1966.

Gama, Vasco da
Bailey, Katharine. *Vasco da Gama: Quest for the Spice Trade*. New York, 2007.

Subrahmanyam, Sanjay. *The Career and Legend of Vasco da Gama*. New York, 1997.

Genghis Khan
Hartog, Leo de. *Genghis Khan: Conqueror of the World*. New York, 2004.

Iggulden, Conn. *Genghis: Birth of an Empire*. New York, 2007.

Nicolle, David. *The Mongol Warlords*. New York, 1990.

Weatherford, J. McIver. *Genghis Khan and the Making of the Modern World*. New York, 2004.

Goths
Wolfram, Herwig (translated by Thomas J. Dunlap). *History of the Goths*. Berkeley, CA, 1998.

Greece
Alcock, Susan E., John F. Cherry, and Jaś Elsner (eds.). *Pausanias: Travel and Memory in Roman Greece*. New York, 2001.

Allen, Reginald E. (ed.). *Greek Philosophy: Thales to Aristotle*. New York, 1991.

Biers, William R. *The Archaeology of Greece: An Introduction*. Ithaca, NY, 1996.

Boardman, John. *The Greeks Overseas: Their Early Colonies and Trade*. London, England, 1980.

Boardman, John, and David Finn. *The Parthenon and Its Sculptures*. London, England, 1985.

Bury, J.B., and Russell Meiggs. *A History of Greece*. London, England, 1975.

Cartledge, Paul. *The Spartans: The World of the Warrior-Heroes of Ancient Greece, from Utopia to Crisis and Collapse*. Woodstock, NY, 2003.

Chadwick, John. *The Decipherment of Linear B*. London, England, 1967.

Cook, R.M. *Greek Painted Pottery*. London, England, 1972.

Coulton, J.J. *Greek Architects at Work*. Ithaca, NY, 1977.

Davis, Victor (ed.). *Hoplites: The Classical Greek Battle Experience*. New York, 1991.

Dinsmoor, W.B. *The Architecture of Ancient Greece: An Account of Its Historic Development*. New York, 1975.

Economakis, Richard (ed.). *Acropolis Restorations*. London, England, 1994.

Evans, Arthur. *The Palace of Minos at Knossos* (four volumes). Oxford, England, 1921–1935.

Forrest, W.G. *The Emergence of Greek Democracy*. London, England, 1966.

Green, Peter. *Alexander to Actium: The Hellenistic Age*. London, England, 1990.

Habicht, Christian. *Pausanias' Guide to Ancient Greece*. Berkeley, CA, 1998.

Hadas, Moses. *Greek Drama*. New York, 1965.

Heath, Thomas Little. *Aristarchus of Samos, the Ancient Copernicus: A History of Greek Astronomy to Aristarchus, together with Aristarchus's Treatise on the Sizes and Distances of the Sun and Moon*. Oxford, England, 1913.

Isager, Signe, and Jens Erik Skydsgaard. *Ancient Greek Agriculture: An Introduction*. London, England, 1992.

Jameson, Michael, Curtis Runnels, and Tjeerd van Andel. *A Greek Countryside: The Southern Argolid from Prehistory to the Present Day*. Stanford, CA, 1994.

Kahn, Charles H. *Anaximander and the Origins of Greek Cosmology*. Indianapolis, IN, 1994.

Morris, Ian. *Burial and Ancient Society: The Rise of the Greek City-State*. New York, 1987.

Morris, Ian (ed.). *Classical Greece: Ancient Histories and Modern Archaeologies*. New York, 1994.

Plutarch (translated by Robin Waterfield). *Greek Lives: A Selection of Nine Greek Lives*. New York, 1998.

Pollitt, J.J. *Art and Experience in Classical Greece*. Cambridge, England, 1972.

Rasmussen, Tom, and Nigel Spivey (eds.). *Looking at Greek Vases*. New York, 1991.

Ridgway, David. *The First Western Greeks*. New York, 1992.

Sekunda, Nick. *Marathon 490 BC: The First Persian Invasion of Greece*. Westport, CT, 2005.

Shanks, Michael. *Art and the Early Greek State: An Interpretive Archaeology*. New York, 1999.

Smith, Helaine L. *Masterpieces of Classic Greek Drama*. Westport, CT, 2006.

Strauss, Barry S. *The Battle of Salamis: The Naval Encounter that Saved Greece—and Western Civilization*. New York, 2004.

Wiles, David. *The Masks of Menander: Sign and Meaning in Greek and Roman Performance*. New York, 1991.

Hagia Sophia
Mainstone, R.J. *Hagia Sophia: Architecture, Structure, and Liturgy of Justinian's Great Church*. New York, 1988.

Hellenism
Bentwich, Norman De Mattos. *Hellenism*. Philadelphia, PA, 1919.

Bowersock, Glen W. *Hellenism in Late Antiquity*. Ann Arbor, MI, 1996.

Hittites
Bryce, Trevor. *The Kingdom of the Hittites*. New York, 2005.

Gurney, O.R. *The Hittites*. Baltimore, MD, 1952.

Macqueen, J.G. *The Hittites and Their Contemporaries in Asia Minor*. London, England, 1996.

Hundred Years' War
Ayton, Andrew, and Philip Preston. *The Battle of Crécy, 1346*. Woodbridge, England, 2005.

Green, David. *The Battle of Poitiers, 1356*. Charleston, SC, 2002.

Huns
Kennedy, Hugh. *Mongols, Huns, and Vikings: Nomads at War*. London, England, 2002.

Man, John. *Attila: The Barbarian King who Challenged Rome*. New York, 2006.

Thompson, E. A. *The Huns*. Cambridge, MA, 1996.

Ice Age
Bahn, Paul. *Journey Through the Ice Age*. Berkeley, CA, 1997.

Incas
D'Altroy, Terence N. *The Incas*. Malden, MA, 2002.

Inuits
Houston, James A. *Treasury of Inuit Legends*. Orlando, FL, 2006.

Islam
Dakake, Maria Massi. *The Charismatic Community: Shi'ite Identity in Early Islam*. Albany, NY, 2007.

El-Hibri, Tayeb. *Reinterpreting Islamic Historiography: Harun al-Rashid and the Narrative of the Abbasid Caliphate*. New York, 1999.

Hawting, G.R. *The First Dynasty of Islam: The Umayyad Caliphate, AD 661–750*. New York, 2000.

Nicolle, David. *Yarmuk, AD 636: The Muslim Conquest of Syria*. Westport, CT, 2005.

Nomachi, Kazuyoshi. *Mecca the Blessed, Medina the Radiant: The Holiest Cities of Islam*. New York, 1997.

Swarup, Ram. *Understanding the Hadith: The Sacred Traditions of Islam*. Amherst, NY, 2002.

Japan
Habu, Junko. *Ancient Jomon of Japan*. New York, 2004.

Mason, R.H.P. *A History of Japan*. New York, 1974.

Sansom, George Bailey. *A History of Japan* (three volumes). Stanford, CA, 1958–1963.

Seagrave, Sterling. *The Yamato Dynasty*. New York, 1999.

Underwood, Alfred Clair. *Shintoism: The Indigenous Religion of Japan*. London, England, 1934.

Knights Templar
Rahn, Otto (translated by Christopher Jones). *Crusade against the Grail: The Struggle between the Cathars, the Templars, and the Church of Rome*. Rochester, VT, 2006.

Ralls, Karen. *Knights Templar Encyclopedia*. Franklin Lakes, NJ, 2007.

Kublai Khan
Man, John. *Kublai Khan: From Xanadu to Superpower*. London, England, 2006.

Rossabi, Morris. *Khubilai Khan: His Life and Times*. Berkeley, CA, 1988.

Magellan, Ferdinand
Bergreen, Laurence. *Over the Edge of the World: Magellan's Terrifying Circumnavigation of the Globe*. New York, 2003.

Kramer, Sydelle. *Who Was Ferdinand Magellan?* New York, 2004.

Maya
Schele, Linda, and David Freidel. *A Forest of Kings: The Untold Story of the Ancient Maya*. New York, 1992.

Sharer, Robert J., with Loa P. Traxler. *The Ancient Maya*. Stanford, CA, 2006.

Mesopotamia
Adams, Robert McC. *The Evolution of Urban Society: Early Mesopotamia and Prehispanic Mexico*. Chicago, IL, 1966.

Bancroft Hunt, Norman. *Historical Atlas of Ancient Mesopotamia*. New York, 2004.

Chadwick, Robert. *First Civilizations: Ancient Mesopotamia and Ancient Egypt*. Oakville, CT, 2005.

Lloyd, Seton. *The Archaeology of Mesopotamia*. London, England, 1978.

McIntosh, Jane. *Ancient Mesopotamia: New Perspectives*. Santa Barbara, CA, 2005.

Moorey, P.R.S. *Ancient Mesopotamian Materials and Industries: The Archaeological Evidence*. Oxford, England, 1994.

Oakes, Lorna, and Philip Steele. *Everyday Life in Ancient Egypt and Mesopotamia*. London, England, 2006.

Postgate, Nicholas. *Early Mesopotamia: Society and Economy at the Dawn of History*. London, England, 1992.

Roaf, Michael. *Cultural Atlas of Mesopotamia and the Ancient Near East*. New York, 1990.

Schomp, Virginia. *Ancient Mesopotamia*. New York, 2005.

Minoan Crete
Cadogan, Gerald. *Palaces of Minoan Crete*. London, England, 1976.

MacGillivray, J.A. *Sir Arthur Evans and the Archaeology of the Minoan Myth*. New York, 2000.

Mongols

Halperin, Charles J. *Russia and the Golden Horde: The Mongol Impact on Medieval Russian History*. Bloomington, IN, 1985.

Kennedy, Hugh. *Mongols, Huns, and Vikings: Nomads at War*. London, England, 2002.

Morgan, David. *The Mongols*. New York, 1986.

Montfort, Simon de

Hutton, W.H. (ed.). *Simon de Montfort and His Cause, 1251–1266: Extracts from the Writings of Robert of Gloucester, Matthew Paris, William Rishanger, Thomas of Wykes, and Others*. New York, 1888.

Maddicott, J.R. *Simon de Montfort*. New York, 1994.

Mughals

Berinstain, Valerie. *India and the Mughal Dynasty*. New York, 1998.

Eraly, Abraham. *The Mughal Throne: The Saga of India's Great Emperors*. London, England, 2003.

Mycenae

Chadwick, John. *The Mycenaean World*. New York, 1976.

Mylonas, George E. *Mycenae and the Mycenaean Age*. Princeton, NJ, 1966.

Taylour, William. *The Mycenaeans*. New York, 1983.

Normans

Crouch, David. *The Normans: The History of a Dynasty*. London, England, 2002.

Houben, Hubert (translated by Graham A. Loud and Diane Milburn). *Roger II of Sicily: A Ruler Between East and West*. New York, 2002.

Loud, Graham. *Conquerors and Churchmen in Norman Italy*. Brookfield, VT, 1999.

Olmecs

Coe, Michael D., and Richard A. Diehl. *In the Land of the Olmec*. Austin, TX, 1980.

Diehl, Richard A. *The Olmecs: America's First Civilization*. London, England, 2004.

Peloponnesian War

Kagan, Donald. *The Peloponnesian War: Athens and Sparta in Savage Conflict, 431–404 BC*. London, England, 2003.

Thucydides (translated by Steven Lattimore). *History of the Peloponnesian War*. Indianapolis, IN, 1998.

Persia

Olmstead, A.T. *History of the Persian Empire: Achaemenid Period*. Chicago, IL, 1948.

Phoenicians

Aubet, Maria Eugenia. *The Phoenicians and the West: Politics, Colonies, and Trade*. New York, 1993.

Moscati, Sabatino (ed.). *The Phoenicians*. Milan, Italy, 1988.

Polo, Marco

Bergreen, Laurence. *Marco Polo: From Venice to Xanadu*. New York, 2007.

Holub, Joan. *Who Was Marco Polo?* New York, 2007.

Humble, Richard. *The Travels of Marco Polo*. New York, 1990.

Rome

Baker, G.P. *Sulla the Fortunate: Roman General and Dictator*. New York, 2001.

Balsdon, J.P.V.D. *Life and Leisure in Ancient Rome*. New York, 1969.

Bennett, Julian. *Trajan: Optimus Princeps*. Bloomington, IN, 2001.

Boatwright, Mary Taliaferro, Daniel J. Gargola, and Richard J.A. Talbert. *A Brief History of Ancient Rome: Politics, Society, and Culture*. New York, 2005.

Bonner, Stanley Frederick. *Education in Ancient Rome: From the Elder Cato to the Younger Pliny*. Berkeley, CA, 1977.

Champlin, Edward. *Nero*. Cambridge, MA, 2003.

Charlesworth, M.P. *Trade Routes and Commerce of the Roman Empire*. New York, 1970.

Dio, Cassius (translated by Ian Scott-Kilvert). *The Roman History: The Reign of Augustus*. New York, 1987.

Gibbon, Edward. *The Decline and Fall of the Roman Empire*. New York, 1983.

Harl, Kenneth W. *Coinage in the Roman Economy, 300 B.C. to A.D. 700*. Baltimore, MD, 1996.

Hodge, A. Trevor. *Roman Aqueducts and Water Supply.* London, England, 1992.

Holland, Tom. *Rubicon: The Last Years of the Roman Republic.* New York, 2005.

Kulikowski, Michael. *Rome's Gothic Wars: From the Third Century to Alaric.* New York, 2007.

Livy (translated by T.J. Luce). *The Rise of Rome: Books One to Five.* New York, 1998.

Livy (translated by Betty Radice). *Rome and Italy: Books Six to Ten.* New York, 1982.

Luecke, Janemarie. *Rape of the Sabine Women.* Sanbornville, NH, 1978.

MacMullen, Ramsay. *Paganism in the Roman Empire.* New Haven, CT, 1981.

Mahoney, Anne. *Roman Sports and Spectacles: A Sourcebook.* Newburyport, MA, 2001.

Meijer, Fik (translated by Liz Waters). *The Gladiators: History's Most Deadly Sport.* New York, 2004.

Scarre, Christopher. *The Penguin Historical Atlas of Ancient Rome.* New York, 1995.

Wiseman, T.P. *Remus: A Roman Myth.* New York, 1995.

Russia
Halperin, Charles J. *Russia and the Golden Horde: The Mongol Impact on Medieval Russian History.* Bloomington, IN, 1985.

Madariaga, Isabel de. *Ivan the Terrible: First Tsar of Russia.* New Haven, CT, 2005.

Martin, Janet. *Medieval Russia: 980–1584.* New York, 2007.

Payne, Robert, and Nikita Romanoff. *Ivan the Terrible.* New York, 1975.

Skrine, Francis Henry, and Edward Denison Ross. *The Heart of Asia: A History of Russian Turkestan and the Central Asian Khanates from the Earliest Times.* London, England, 1899.

Sumerians
Kramer, Samuel Noah. *The Sumerians: Their History, Culture, and Character.* Chicago, IL, 1963.

Time-Life Books. *Sumer: Cities of Eden.* Alexandria, VA, 1993.

Vanstiphout, H.L.J. *Epics of Sumerian Kings: The Matter of Aratta.* Boston, MA, 2004.

Tamerlane
Marozzi, Justin. *Tamerlane: Sword of Islam, Conqueror of the World.* London, England, 2004.

Nicolle, David. *The Mongol Warlords: Genghis Khan, Kublai Khan, Hulegu, Tamerlane.* New York, 1990.

Teutonic Knights
Nicolle, David. *Teutonic Knight, 1190–1561.* New York, 2007.

Urban, William L. *The Teutonic Knights: A Military History.* St. Paul, MN, 2005.

Troy
Schlitz, Laura Amy. *The Hero Schliemann.* Cambridge, MA, 2006.

Woods, Michael. *In Search of the Trojan War.* Berkeley, CA, 1985.

Ur
Zettler, Richard L., and Lee Horne (eds.). *Treasures from the Royal Tombs of Ur.* Philadelphia, PA, 1998.

Uruk
Liverani, Mario (edited and translated by Zainab Bahrani and Marc Van De Mieroop). *Uruk: The First City.* Oakville, Ontario, Canada, 2006.

Vikings
Hall, R.A. *The World of the Vikings.* New York, 2007.

Haywood, John. *The Penguin Historical Atlas of the Vikings.* New York, 1995.

Kennedy, Hugh. *Mongols, Huns, and Vikings: Nomads at War.* London, England, 2002.

Roesdahl, Else (translated by Susan M. Margeson and Kirsten Williams). *The Vikings.* New York, 1998.

Visigoths
Collins, Roger. *Visigothic Spain, 409–711.* Malden, MA, 2004.

Heather, Peter (ed.). *The Visigoths from the Migration Period to the Seventh Century: An Ethnographic Perspective.* Rochester, NY, 1999.

WEB SITES

AMERICAS

American Museum of Natural History
A wealth of information on anthropology and paleontology
http://www.amnh.org

Anasazi
Web site that includes a wealth of information about the Anasazi and provides links to material about other North American desert peoples
http://www.desertusa.com/ind1/du_peo_ana.html

Conquistadors
Web site that provides biographies of the Spanish adventurers who brought down some of the great civilizations of Mesoamerica
http://www.pbs.org/conquistadors/index.html

Inuit
Part of an extensive Web site that is concerned with all aspects of Canadian history and culture
http://www.civilization.ca/educat/oracle/modules/dmorrison/page01_e.html

Sioux
Web site that is dedicated to the history of the Native American people and their present-day affairs
http://www.nativeamericans.com/Sioux.htm

EGYPT

Ancient Egypt
Web site that is dedicated to ancient Egypt and Egyptology
http://www.ancientegypt.co.uk

Ancient Egyptian Gods
Web site that provides facts about 12 of the most important Egyptian gods
http://www.bbc.co.uk/history/ancient/egyptians/gods_gallery_01.shtml

Cleopatra
Biography of the Egyptian queen; includes links to discussions of many aspects of Egyptian life and culture
http://www.egyptologyonline.com/cleopatra.htm

Pharaohs
Web site that provides a full list of the ancient rulers
http://www.touregypt.net/kings.htm

Secrets of the Pharaohs
Web site that accompanies a PBS series investigating some of the mysteries of ancient Egypt
http://www.pbs.org/wnet/pharaohs/about.html

Tutankhamen's Tomb
Guide to the treasures of the pharaoh's tomb
http://www.nationalgeographic.com/egypt

EUROPE IN THE MIDDLE AGES

Alfred the Great
Outline of the king's reign; includes links to his writings and accounts of the lives of other English monarchs
http://www.royalinsight.gov.uk/output/Page25.asp

Avignon Papacy
Web site that gives an overview of the papacy during the period of its absence from its traditional seat in Rome
http://www.the-orb.net/textbooks/nelson/avignon.html

Becket
Web site that gives a short biographical account of the life of the archbishop of Canterbury
http://www.bbc.co.uk/history/historic_figures/becket_thomas.shtml

Black Death
Web site that contains information about the epidemic that ravaged Asia and Europe in the 14th century CE
http://www.insecta-inspecta.com/fleas/bdeath

Cathars
Introduction to the beliefs of the heretical group; includes links to further articles on the Albigensian Crusade
http://www.languedoc-france.info/12_cathars.htm

Chanson de Roland
Original French text of the 11th-century-CE poem; includes an English translation and commentary
http://www.orbilat.com/Languages/French/Texts/Period_02/1090-La_Chanson_de_Roland.htm

Charlemagne
Extensive biography of the Frankish leader who united much of western Europe under his rule
http://www.historyworld.net/wrldhis/PlainTextHistories.asp?historyid=aa20

Cistercians
Introduction to the monastic movement that was founded in France in the 11th century CE and is still thriving today
http://www.osb.org/cist/intro.html

Crécy
Illustrated description of the English victory over France in one of the key battles in the Hundred Years' War
http://www.battlefield-site.co.uk/crecy.htm

Crusades
Web site that outlines the origins of the crusading ideal
http://www.medievalcrusades.com

Einhard: The Life of Charlemagne
Online English-language edition of the classic biography of Charlemagne, translated by Samuel Epes Turner
http://www.fordham.edu/halsall/basis/einhard.html

Francis of Assisi
Web site that contains links to a number of biographies of the Christian saint
http://www.franciscan-archive.org/patriarcha

Frederick Barbarossa
Essay on the life of the Holy Roman emperor
http://www.authorama.com/famous-men-of-the-middle-ages-22.html

Gnosticism
Comprehensive introduction to the structure and significance of the religious movement and its worldview
http://www.webcom.com/gnosis/gnintro.htm

Great Schism
Account of the rift between the eastern and western Christian churches in 1054 CE
http://mb-soft.com/believe/txc/gschism.htm

Hagia Sophia
Photographs and description of the "mother church" of all eastern Christians
http://www.byzantines.net/epiphany/hagiasophia.htm

Iconoclasm
Essay on icons and iconoclasm in Byzantium
http://www.metmuseum.org/toah/hd/icon/hd_icon.htm

Ivan the Terrible
Web site that provides an introduction to the reign of the great Russian czar
http://www.mnsu.edu/emuseum/history/russia/ivantheterrible.html

Joan of Arc
Web site that provides a biographical summary, trial testimony, letters, and other documents related to the life of the French martyr
http://www.joanofarc.info

Knights Hospitaller
Information about the religious military order that played a key role in the crusades
http://www.middle-ages.org.uk/knights-hospitaller.htm

Luther, Martin
Web site that provides a time line covering the life of the religious reformer
http://www.pbs.org/empires/martinluther

Magellan, Ferdinand
Web site that outlines the career of the navigator whose last voyage culminated in the first circumnavigation of the world
http://www.bbc.co.uk/history/historic_figures/magellan_ferdinand.shtml

Magna Carta
Web site that includes a facsimile of the document that altered the course of English history
http://www.bl.uk/treasures/magnacarta/index.html

Medici
Illustrated chronology of the influential Florentine family
http://www.channel4.com/history/microsites/H/history/i-m/medici.html

Merovingians
Introduction to the Frankish royal line
http://www.ordotempli.org/the_merovingians.htm

Normans
Web site that explains who the Normans were and where they came from; provides further resources
http://www.historyonthenet.com/Normans/normansmain.htm

Polo, Marco
Web site that is devoted to the traveler's life
http://www.silk-road.com/artl/marcopolo.shtml

Reconquista
Time line that charts the Christian reclamation of the Iberian Peninsula from the forces of Islam
http://www.ucalgary.ca/applied_history/tutor/eurvoya/timeline.html

Scholasticism
Web site that outlines the ideals of the movement
http://www.philosophypages.com/hy/3f.htm

Teutonic Knights
Web site that traces the history of the military religious order
http://www.the-orb.net/encyclop/religion/monastic/opsahl2.html

RESOURCES FOR FURTHER STUDY

Thomas Aquinas
Web site that provides a biography of the 13th-century-CE scholar and saint
http://plato.stanford.edu/entries/aquinas

Wars of the Roses
Time line with links to articles about the rulers and other leading participants in the English civil conflict
http://www.warsoftheroses.com

GREECE

Aeschylus
Biography of the Greek playwright; includes links to all of his works currently in print
http://www.imagi-nation.com/moonstruck/clsc3.htm

Alexander the Great
Web site that is dedicated to the Macedonian general; includes more than 400 photographs, as well as links to hundreds of additional sites
http://www.isidore-of-seville.com/Alexanderama.html

Athenian Democracy
Analysis of the Athenian political system
http://www.bbc.co.uk/history/ancient/greeks/greekcritics_01.shtml

Delian League
Web site that details the history of the Athenian confederation that was formed as protection against the Persian Empire
http://www.bbc.co.uk/dna/h2g2/A14481777

Diadochs
Web site that is dedicated to the lives of the successors to Alexander the Great
http://www.livius.org/di-dn/diadochi/war02.html

Eleusinian Mysteries
Account of the rituals conducted by ancient Greeks in honor of the goddess Demeter
http://www.pantheon.org/articles/e/eleusinian_mysteries.html

Euripides
Short biography of the playwright and numerous links to discussions of his work
http://www.theatredatabase.com/ancient/euripides_001.html

Greek Dialects
Guide to the major linguistic variants of the Greek language; includes a family tree
http://www.columbia.edu/~rcc20/greece3.html

Greek Philosophy
Contains discussions of Greek philosophical thought
http://www.iep.utm.edu/g/greekphi.htm

Greek Religion
Resources for the study of all aspects of Greek religion
http://www.greekreligion.org

Hellenistic Greece
Guide to the Hellenistic age
http://www.wsu.edu/~dee/GREECE/HELLGREE.HTM

Hesiod
Facts about the life of the ancient Greek poet
http://ancienthistory.about.com/cs/people/p/hesiod.htm

Homer
Introduction to the poet's work
http://www.wsu.edu/~dee/MINOA/HOMER.HTM

Hoplites
Description of the hoplites' equipment and function in battle
http://digilander.libero.it/tepec/the_athenian_hoplite.htm

Macedonian Wars
Account of the conflicts between Rome and Macedonia
http://www.livius.org/ap-ark/appian/appian_macedonia1.html

Menander
Introduction to the work of the father of comedy
http://www.theatrehistory.com/ancient/menander001.html

Muses
Introduction to the functions of the nine Greek goddesses
http://ancienthistory.about.com/library/bl/bl_myth_europe_grecoroman_muses.htm

Mycenaeans
History of the Mycenaean culture
http://www.historywiz.com/mycenaean-mm.htm

Persian Wars
General overview of the conflict
http://www.socialstudiesforkids.com/subjects/persianwars.htm

Sophocles
Biography of the ancient Greek playwright
http://www.imagi-nation.com/moonstruck/clsc1.htm

Spartacus
Web site that separates the biographical facts from the legend of the rebel slave leader
http://www.channel4.com/history/microsites/R/real_lives/spartacus.html

Thermopylae
Detailed account of one of the key battles in ancient Greek history
http://www.historynet.com/magazines/military_history/3038411.html

Trireme
History of the development of the Greek warship
http://home-3.tiscali.nl/~meester7/engtrireme.html

ISLAMIC WORLD

Abbasids
Article about the family that formed the last Arab caliphates; includes dates for the various caliphs
http://i-cias.com/e.o/abbasids.htm

Bedouin
Web site that covers all aspects of the culture and history of the desert-dwelling people
http://www.geographia.com/egypt/sinai/bedouin.htm

Berbers
Web site that gives a short and accessible introduction to the history and significance of the people who lived in northern Africa before the arrival of the Muslims
http://i-cias.com/e.o/berbers.htm

Islam
Web site that provides an outline of Muslim beliefs
http://www.bbc.co.uk/religion/religions/islam

Mecca
Description of the city; includes a list of key dates
http://i-cias.com/e.o/mecca.htm

Ottomans
Web site that details the history of the Ottomans from their rise in the 13th century CE to their downfall 700 years later
http://www.wsu.edu/~dee/OTTOMAN/OTTOMAN1.HTM

Sunni and Shi'ite Muslims
Essay explaining the origin of the central split in the Muslim world
http://hnn.us/articles/934.html

MESOPOTAMIA

Ancient Sumeria
Aspects of life in ancient Sumeria
http://history-world.org/sumeria.htm

Code of Hammurabi
Online English version of the full text
http://www.wsu.edu/~dee/MESO/CODE.HTM

Cuneiform
Interactive Web site about cuneiform writing
http://www.upennmuseum.com/cuneiform.cgi

Mesopotamia
Web site that features separate sections on Assyria, Babylonia, and Sumer
http://www.mesopotamia.co.uk

Umayyads
Short account of the first Muslim dynasty
http://www.princeton.edu/~batke/itl/denise/umayyads.htm

Ur
Illustrated history
http://www.mnsu.edu/emuseum/archaeology/sites/middle_east/ur.html

ROME

Etruscans
Web site that is dedicated to the people whose culture once dominated central Italy
http://www.mysteriousetruscans.com

Hamilcar Barca
Life and achievements of the founder of Carthage's empire in Spain
http://www.livius.org/ha-hd/hamilcar/hamilcar2.html

Julian Calendar
Explanation of the dating system
http://www.nottingham.ac.uk/mss/learning/skills/dating/julian-gregorian.phtml

Julian the Apostate
Account of the life and historical significance of the Roman emperor who rejected Christianity
http://www.roman-empire.net/collapse/julian.html

Julius Caesar
Biography of the Roman general and political leader
http://www.vroma.org/~bmcmanus/caesar.html

Pompeii
Description and photographs of the city that was destroyed by Mount Vesuvius
http://www.mnsu.edu/emuseum/archaeology/sites/europe/pompeii.html

Punic Wars
Web site that is dedicated to the wars between Rome and Carthage
http://www.wsu.edu/~dee/ROME/PUNICWAR.HTM

Roman Army
Detailed description of the history and evolution of the Roman armed forces
http://www.roman-empire.net/army/army.html

Roman Emperors
Online encyclopedia of Roman rulers
http://www.roman-emperors.org

Roman Gladiatorial Games
Web site that gives an account of the evolution of the games and describes the different types of gladiators
http://depthome.brooklyn.cuny.edu/classics/gladiatr

Roman Religion
Guide to Roman religious practices; includes links to articles on other aspects of life in ancient Rome
http://www.classicsunveiled.com/rome1/html/religion.html

Sulla
Biography of the Roman dictator
http://www.roman-empire.net/republic/sulla.html

SOUTHERN AND EASTERN ASIA

Ancient China
Web site that contains photographs of a number of ancient Chinese artifacts as well as interactive features
http://www.ancientchina.co.uk/menu.html

Angkor Wat
Web site that includes a wealth of photographs of the Cambodian temple complex
http://whc.unesco.org/en/list/668

Aryans
Web site that discusses the true origins of these mysterious and influential Asian people
http://www.iranchamber.com/history/articles/aryan_people_origins.php

Babur
Web site that is devoted to the life and times of the first Mughal emperor, who imposed his rule on most of northern India in the early 16th century CE
http://www.bbc.co.uk/religion/religions/islam/history/mughalempire_2.shtml

Genghis Khan
Web site that describes the journey of the Mongol leader from his native land to the gates of Vienna.
http://www.fsmitha.com/h3/h11mon.htm

Golden Horde
Web site that provides an introduction to the Mongol Empire
http://www.ucalgary.ca/applied_history/tutor/islam/mongols/goldenHorde.html

Great Wall of China
Web site that provides information about the wall's construction and history
http://www.travelchinaguide.com/china_great_wall

Gupta Empire
Web site that gives the historical background of the empire and supplies links to information about other civilizations
http://www.wsu.edu/~dee/ANCINDIA/GUPTA.HTM

Hinduism
Web site that provides an outline of the basic Hindu beliefs
http://www.bbc.co.uk/religion/religions/hinduism

Jainism
Web site that provides an outline of the basic Jainist beliefs
http://www.bbc.co.uk/religion/religions/jainism

Khmer Culture
Web site that is devoted to the culture of ancient Cambodia
http://www.khmerculture.net

Ming dynasty
Web site that provides an overview of the period and links to related sites on the later imperial dynasties
http://www.mnsu.edu/emuseum/prehistory/china/later_imperial_china/ming.html

Mongols
Web site that gives a highly illustrated account of the individuals and policies that turned the steppe nomads into the lords of the largest Eurasian empire in history
http://afe.easia.columbia.edu/mongols

Silk Road
Story of one of the world's most historically important trade routes and its influences on the cultures of China, central Asia, and Europe
http://www.ess.uci.edu/~oliver/silk.html

Taj Mahal

Web site that captures the majesty of the great building in Agra, India, and explains its significance

http://www.pbs.org/treasuresoftheworld/a_nav/taj_nav/main_tajfrm.html

WESTERN AND CENTRAL EUROPE BEFORE THE MIDDLE AGES

Alaric

Biography of the Goth leader

http://www.bbc.co.uk/history/ancient/romans/enemiesrome_gallery_01.shtml

Attila

Web site that provides an outline of the Hun leader's life

http://www.bbc.co.uk/dna/h2g2/A292402

Boudicca

Description of the life and times of the woman who led the Iceni against the Roman occupiers of Britain

http://mysite.wanadoo-members.co.uk/parsonal/boudicca.htm

Celtic Art

Descriptions and illustrations of a wide range of ancient Celtic art forms, from body decoration to megaliths

http://www.freeceltic.com

Funnel-Beaker Culture

Overview with suggestions for further study

http://www.comp-archaeology.org/TRB.htm

Goths

English translation of Jordanes's sixth-century-CE history of the Goths

http://www.ucalgary.ca/~vandersp/Courses/texts/jordgeti.html

Huns

Web site that describes the origins of the Asian people and their influence on Europe

http://www.imninalu.net/Huns.htm

Iberia

History of early Spain

http://www.fordham.edu/halsall/sbook1p.html

Iron Age in Western Europe

Web site that includes photographs of La Tène artifacts

http://www.hp.uab.edu/image_archive/uj/ujk.html

Lombards

Web site that provides a brief description of the people's origins and achievements

http://www.hyw.com/books/history/Langobar.htm

Magyars

Essay on the forebears of the modern Hungarian people; includes suggestions for further reading

http://www.geocities.com/egfrothos/magyars/magyars.html

Stone Age Institute

Web site that highlights the latest anthropological and archaeological research into the period

http://www.stoneageinstitute.org

Vandals

History of the Germanic people and their effect on the history of Rome

http://www.roman-empire.net/articles/article-016.html

Venus of Willendorf

Web site about the famous prehistoric figurine

http://witcombe.sbc.edu/willendorf/willendorfdiscovery.html

Vikings

Web site that contains information about every aspect of Viking life

http://www.bbc.co.uk/history/ancient/vikings

Visigoths

Web site that provides an account of the Visigoths' contribution to history and their relationships with other peoples of Europe

http://www.friesian.com/germania.htm

ARTS AND CULTURE

Page numbers in *italics* refer to illustrations. Page numbers in **bold** refer to entire chapters.

A

Abelard, Peter **8**:1040, **10**:1384
About Nature (Anaximander) **3**:354
Academy, Plato's **3**:365, 367, 413, **5**:633, *634*, 639
Acharnians (Aristophanes) **3**:378
Achilles and the Turtle (paradox) **3**:360
actors **3**:318, 321, 322, 323, **5**:674
Aeneid (Virgil) **2**:200, **4**:438, 512
Aeschylus **3**:318, 322–323, 349
Agamemnon (Aeschylus) **3**:*322*, 322
Ajax (Sophocles) **3**:323
Alcuin **6**:804, *806*, 806, 807
Almagest (Ptolemy) **10**:1390–1391
alphabets
    Africa and **9**:1264
    Cyrillic **9**:1177, 1212
    Greek **2**:207, 248–249, 252
    Linear B script **2**:*252*
    Phoenicians and **2**:203–204, 207
    see also writing
Amarna Letters **1**:101, 103–104, **2**:230–231
amphora, Egyptian **1**:*99*
amulet, Viking **9**:*1203*
Anaxagoras **3**:348, 356, *358*, 362
Anaximander **3**:354
Anaximenes **3**:354–355, *355*
ancient knowledge, rediscovery of **10**:*1390*, 1398
Antigone (Sophocles) **3**:323, 324
Antisthenes **3**:366
Apology (Plato) **3**:364
Apotheosis of Claudius, The (cameo) **4**:*523*
Arcadia, poetry and **3**:406–407
Archimedes **3**:408, *410*, **4**:*473*, 473, **10**:1390
architecture
    Africa and **9**:*1270*
    Assyrian **2**:213, 215, 220
    Byzantine Empire and **5**:672, **9**:1180
    Greece and **3**:298, 311–312, 349, 351
    India and **7**:960, 961, **10**:*1364*, 1419
    Islamic world and **6**:763, 767, 769
    mathematics and **3**:407
    Minoan **2**:173, 174
    Mycenaean **2**:187
    Norman **8**:*1022*
    Ottoman Turks and **9**:1255
    Palatine Chapel and **6**:807

pre-Columbian cultures and **10**:1302, 1304, 1309, 1315, 1333, 1342, 1345–1347
    Renaissance and **10**:1401, 1402, 1406, *1409*, 1409
    Spain and **6**:*763*
archives, Hittites and **2**:159, 161
Aristophanes **3**:325, 349, 364, *378*, 378
Aristotle **3**:*353*, 367, 367, **10**:*1388*, 1389, 1391, 1404
    Alexander the Great and **3**:384
    Islamic world and **6**:782, 783
    preserving knowledge of **5**:661
    Sophists and **3**:361, 412
    Thales of Miletus and **3**:354
artists, Renaissance and **10**:1402, 1403
arts
    Africa and **9**:1259, 1262, 1263, *1267*
    Assyrians and **2**:215, 216, 220
    Babylonians and **1**:*111*
    Benedict and **5**:700
    Byzantine Empire and **9**:1166–1167, 1174–1175
    Celtic **1**:46, *52*
    China and **7**:903
    Cycladic people and **2**:165–166, 169
    early humans and **1**:7, 11, *12*
    Egypt and **1**:71, 77, 92, 103
    Hittites and **2**:156, 158–159
    India and **7**:940, 942, 960, 961, 965, 966
    Islamic culture and **6**:766, 767, 772
    Japan and **7**:906
    Macedonian Renaissance and **9**:1180
    Mari and **1**:*114*
    medieval Europe and **8**:1093, 1096, 1099
    Minoans and **2**:170, 178–180
    Neolithic period and **1**:14–15, *15*
    Ottoman Turks and **9**:1255
    Pacific islands and **7**:987, 988
    Persians and **2**:240
    pre-Columbian cultures and **10**:1305, 1319, 1333
    Renaissance and **10**:1398, 1400–1401, 1402, 1403–1404, 1406–1407
    Roman Empire and **4**:525, 527
    Southeast Asia and **7**:978
    see also crafts and craftspeople

B

Bayeux Tapestry **8**:*1049*
bell-beaker pottery **1**:*19*
Bessarion, Basilius **10**:*1390*, 1390–1391

black-figure pottery **3**:301, *308*
blood games **4**:551–552
Blues **5**:623–624, 627, 671
Book of Kings **6**:*732*, 732
Book of Roads and Kingdoms (El Bekri) **9**:1270
books **10**:1387, 1391–1392, *1392*–1393, 1394
Botticelli, Sandro **10**:1403
Bramante, Donato **10**:1406
Brancacci, Felice **10**:1403
"bread and circuses" **4**:531, 548–553
bronze artifacts
    Akkadian **1**:*62*
    Bronze Age and **1**:*35*, *37*, *40*
    Celtic **1**:*51*
    China and **1**:*33*, **7**:*871*
    Greek **3**:*301*
    Hallstatt culture and **1**:*39*
    Persian **2**:*242*
    Phoenician **2**:*216*
    Southeast Asia and **7**:974, *975*
    statuettes **7**:*896*, *898*, *903*, *966*
Brunelleschi, Filippo **10**:*1399*, 1401, 1404
burial practices
    Assyrians and **2**:219
    Babylonians and **1**:117
    Bronze Age and **1**:38, 39
    Celtic people and **1**:46, 52, **2**:257
    Cycladic people and **2**:165, 166–167
    Dark Age Greece and **2**:246
    Egypt and **1**:73–74, *75*, 75, 77, 82, 84–85, 95–96, *97*
    funnel-beaker culture and **1**:22, 24, 24–25
    Hallstatt culture and **1**:48
    India and **7**:927
    Japan and **7**:909
    Latium and **4**:443
    Maya and **10**:1322
    Mycenaeans and **2**:185–187, 188, 190
    Natufian culture and **1**:11
    Persians and **2**:244
    Roman Empire and **4**:550
    Rössen culture and **1**:18, *21*
    Scythian people and **1**:51
    Sumerian people and **1**:57–58
    Urnfield culture and **1**:39–40
Buridan, Jean **10**:1391

C

cameos **4**:*523*, **6**:*730*
Canterbury Tales, The (Chaucer) **10**:1394
Carolingian Renaissance **6**:806–807
carpets **6**:781, **9**:*1231*
Castagno, Andrea de **10**:1401

cave paintings **1**:7, 11, *12*, **10**:1307
Caxton, William **10**:1394
ceramic artifacts **1**:*99*, **10**:*1315*, *1320*, *1322*, *1340*
chalice, Byzantine **9**:*1169*
Chalice of Tassilo **6**:*803*
chansons de geste (songs of heroic deeds) **6**:801, **10**:1394
chariot races **4**:552–553, *553*
Chaucer, Geoffrey **10**:1394
chivalry **6**:734, 799, 823, **8**:1018
Choerilus **3**:321
chorus, Greek drama and **3**:318, 320–321
Chronicle of the Famous and Invincible Knight, Cid Ruy Diaz **8**:*1021*
Chu Hsi **7**:887
classical antiquity **10**:1404
clay bowl, Nubian **9**:*1262*
Cleanthes **3**:413
cloisoinné brooch, Viking **9**:*1206*
Clouds, The (Aristophanes) **3**:364, 378
clubs, Hippodrome and **5**:623–624, 627
codices **10**:1319, 1328
coffin texts **1**:84
comedy **3**:318, 320, 325, 378, 407
Confucianism **7**:884–886, 887, 890, 910, 975
    Buddhism and **7**:892, 902
    China and **7**:877, 881, 882, 893, 901
    legalism and **7**:891, 893
    Taoism and **7**:888, 889
Confucius **7**:877, 882, *883*, *884*, 884–886, *886*, 889, 894
Coptic language **9**:1258
Coronation of Poppea (Monteverdi) **10**:*1407*, 1407
courses of study, medieval universities and **10**:1386–1388
crafts and craftspeople
    Anasazi people and **10**:1350
    Aztecs and **10**:1327, 1333
    Celtic people and **1**:46, 50
    copper and **1**:32
    Egypt and **1**:86
    Etruscans and **4**:445
    Franks and **6**:*793*
    Goths and **5**:*645*
    Greece and **3**:302–303
    Hallstatt culture and **1**:45, 47
    Hittites and **2**:156
    Huns and **5**:*649*
    Iberian people and **1**:50
    India and **7**:920, 925
    Islamic world and **6**:779, 780–781
    Maya and **10**:1314, 1316, 1319
    medieval Europe and **8**:1041, 1043, 1086

Mixtec people and 10:1310
Mycenaeans and 2:189
Neolithic period and 1:15
Phoenicians and 2:198, 200
pre-Columbian cultures and
10:1302, 1304, 1305,
1305–1306
Renaissance and 10:1403
Rome and 4:466, 548
Tarascan people and 10:1310
see also arts
cultural influences
African kingdoms and 9:1275
Alexander the Great and 3:395
Bulgarian Empire and 9:1177
Byzantine Empire and 9:1167
England and 8:1048–1049
Germanic peoples and 5:658, 665
Greece and 3:352, 402–403,
404–413
Kushan India and 7:931
Latium and 4:444
Mongols and 9:1238, 1240
Pacific islands and 7:985
Roman Empire and 4:504, 546–
547
Russia and 9:1212
Seleucid dynasty and 3:401
Sicily and 8:1023, 1025
Southeast Asia and 7:975, 978
cuneiform writing
Akkadian 1:60–61
Assyrians and 2:208
Babylonians and 1:119
Greeks and 2:252
Hittites and 2:150, 161
Mesopotamians and 2:204
Sumerian 1:67, 68, 68, 69
cup, Mycenaean 2:*192*
Cynics 3:366, 413

D
Dafne (Peri) 10:1407
Damon 3:348
dance *see* music and dance
Dance of Apollo with the Muses
(Peruzzi) 3:*411*
Dante Alighieri 10:1394
David (Michelangelo) 10:1404
death mask, Mycenaean 2:*183*
Death of Socrates, The (David)
3:*363*
Democritus 3:361
Diagoras of Melos 3:352
Diogenes 3:*353*, 365, *366*, 366
disputations, education and 10:1387
dithyramb (poem) 3:318, 320
divination 7:*887*, 887, 889
Divine Comedy, The (Dante) 4:*459*,
10:1394
Donatello 10:1401
drama 3:**318–325**, 378, 384, 407,
7:*907*, 963, 8:1021
dramatists 3:321–322, *322*, 325, 407
Duomo (cathedral), Florence
10:*1399*

Dürer, Albrecht 10:*1408*,
1408–1409

E
education
Abbasid caliphate and 6:772
Alexander the Great and 3:384
Alfred the Great and 6:820
Aristotle and 3:367
Babylonians and 1:119
Bulgarian Empire and 9:1177
Carolingian Empire and 6:804,
806
China and 7:882, 887, 894–
895, 903
Confucianism and 7:884–885
Egyptians and 1:108
Frederick II and 8:1070
gladiators and 4:551
Greek philosophy and 3:356, 361,
364, 367, 411
humanism and 10:1400
Jerome and 5:696
Laws of the Twelve Tables and
4:453
Mali and 9:1271
medieval Europe and 8:1043,
10:1366, 1384, 1400
military training and 10:1328
Museum of Alexandria and
3:404, 406–407
Persians and 2:244
Plato's Academy and 3:365, 367
pre-Columbian cultures and
10:1327, 1328, 1331, 1353
Rome and 4:556–557
Scholasticism and 10:1384, 1386–
1390
Sparta and 2:263
Sumerians and 1:65, 69
Taoism and 7:888
Egyptian language 9:1264
Einhard 6:798, 802, 803, 806–807,
808
El cantar de mío Cid (The
Song of the Cid) 8:1021
El Cid 8:*1021*, 1021
Electra (Sophocles) 3:323
enamel plaque, French 9:*1163*
entertainment 4:531, 548, 548–553,
8:1031, 1043
see also drama; music and dance
Epicureanism 3:412–413
Epicurus 3:412–413, *413*
Epiphany, The (Giotto) 10:1402
Erasmus, Desiderius 10:1397
ethics 3:362–363, 411, 412, 7:886
Eumenides (Aeschylus) 3:323
Euridice (Peri) 10:1407
Euripides 3:324–325, *325*, 349,
356, 378

F
festivals 4:511, 527, 549–550
Ficino, Marsilio 10:1401
Five Chariots sculpture 7:965

Five Classics 7:887
Four Books 7:887
Four Noble Truths 7:948, 950–
951
Fra Angelico 10:1401
freedom of thought 10:1388, 1390
frescos
chariot races and 4:*553*
Cycladic people and 2:*169*, 169
Italian 3:*311*, 5:*687*
Mani and 6:*731*
Minoans and 2:*177*, 178, *179*,
179, *181*
music and dance and 4:557
Pompeii and 4:*537*
Renaissance and 10:*1401*,
1403–1404
Roman 4:*509*, 9:*1161*
frieze, Persian 2:*237*
Frogs (Aristophanes) 3:325

G
games
Maya and 10:*1317*, 1317, 1318
Rome and 4:*500*, 511, *549*,
549–550, 551–552, *552*–
553
Georgics (Virgil) 4:512
Ghiberti, Lorenzo 10:1401
Giorgione 10:1406
Giotto 10:1402
glass lamps, Mamluk 9:*1240*
glassware, Phoenicians and 2:200
goblet, Greek 2:*164*
gold artifacts
African 9:*1267*
Akkadian 1:*61*
Byzantine 9:*1173*
Celtic 1:*46*
Greek 2:*164*, *166*
Hallstatt 1:*45*
Mycenaean 2:*183*
Phoenician 2:*207*
pre-Columbian cultures and
10:*1305*, *1310*
Scythian 1:*48*, *49*
Sumerian 1:*69*
Gozzoli, Benozzo 10:1401
Graces 3:412
grammar schools 10:1387
grave goods
Bronze Age and 1:38
Celtic people and 2:257
China and 7:873, 874, 876, *881*,
881
Cycladic people and 2:166–
167
Egyptian 1:*74*, 75, 84–85, 87
Hallstatt culture and 1:48
Japan and 7:909
Mycenaeans and 2:186, 190
pre-Columbian cultures and
10:*1305*, 1309
Scythian 1:49
Sumerian 1:57–58, 69
see also burial practices

Greek drama 3:**318–325**, 349,
407
Greek language 2:186
Greek legacy 3:**404–413**
Greek philosophy 3:**352–367**,
6:781–782, 9:1273, 10:1389,
1404
Greek warrior, statue of 3:*348*
Greens 5:623–624, 627, 671
Gregorian chant 5:700
griffin, Persian statue of 2:*245*
griots (singer-poets) 9:*1271*
Gundestrup Cauldron 1:*52*

H
Hagia Sophia 5:*621*, *668*, *672*,
672
Constantine I and 5:621
Macedonian Renaissance and
9:1180
mosaics and 9:*1159*, *1178*, *1180*
Nika Revolt and 5:671
Ottoman Turks and 9:1247
Hanging Gardens of Babylon
1:124–125, *125*
haniwa (terra-cotta sculptures)
7:909, *912*
Han-li Academy 7:901
Harmonica (Ptolemy) 3:410
harp, Sumerian 1:*55*
headband, Greek 2:*166*
Helios 3:357
Hellenism 3:402–403
Heraclitus 3:355, 362
Hero of Alexandria 3:408, *409*,
10:1390
hieratic writing 1:88
hieroglyphic writing
Africa and 9:1264
Egyptians and 1:*72–73*, 88, 2:204,
252
Hittites and 2:160–161, 203–
204
Minoans and 2:179, 180
Phoenicians and 2:203
pre-Columbian cultures and
10:1305, 1319
Hippodamas 3:349
Hippodrome 5:621, 622–624, 627,
671
Hippolytus (Euripides) 3:325
historians 3:*335*, 335, 352, 377,
4:456, 516, 524, 531, 7:886,
899
Historia Roderici (History of
Rodrigo) 8:1021
historical eras, labels for 10:1398,
1400
Holbein, Hans 10:1409
Homer 2:182, 193, 194, 256, 3:313,
4:557, 6:732
Homeric Hymns (Homer) 3:313
Horace 4:510, *511*, 511, 557
horse racing 5:622, 623, 624
humanism 10:**1384–1397**, 1398,
1400

I

I Ching (Book of Changes) 7:*887*, 887, 892

iconoclasm 6:761, 800, 811, 9:*1166*, 1166–1167, 1168, 1172, 1173, 1180

idealism, Plato and 3:367, 412

"ideal world," philosophy of 3:358

Iliad (Homer) 2:182, 192, 194, 248–249, 256, 3:313, 404, 6:732

"indivisibility of being" theory 3:358, 360

In Praise of Folly (Erasmus) 10:1397

Ionian philosophy 3:352, 354–355

Irnerius 10:1384

ivory carving, Byzantine 9:*1167*

ivory figurine, Minoan 2:*172*

J

jade artifacts 7:872, *875*, *989*, 10:*1304*, *1316*

Japanese language 7:912, 915

jar, Mycenaean 2:*191*

jewelry 1:*60*, 2:156, 179, 180, *207*, *251*, 10:*1358*

jug, Athenian 3:*349*

K

Kamares ware 2:173, 180

Knights (Aristophanes) 3:325, 378

L

Lady with an Ermine (da Vinci) 10:*1405*

languages

Africa and 9:1258, 1259, 1263, 1264, 1265

Amarna Letters and 1:101

Assyrians and 2:216

Behistun Inscription and 2:243

Bulgar people and 9:1177

Byzantine Empire and 9:1167

Carolingian Empire and 6:804, 806

Chinese 7:873

Egypt and 1:88, 103

England and 8:1049

Etruscans and 4:445

Europe and 10:1387–1388, 1393, 1394

Germanic peoples and 5:665

Ghazan Khan and 9:1238

Greece and 2:163, 246, 248, 250, 3:402

Hittites and 2:160

India and 7:940, 971

Islamic world and 6:759, 771, 773

Japanese 7:912, 915

Latium and 4:443

Mycenaeans and 2:186

Pacific islands and 7:988

pre-Columbian cultures and 10:1335, 1336, 1348, 1353–1354

Roman Empire and 4:540, 546–547

Semitic people and 2:222

Southeast Asia and 7:972

Sumerian people and 1:54

Lao-tzu 7:886, *888*, 888, *889*, 889, 890

Lascaux, France, cave paintings at 1:11, *12*

Lasso, Orlando di 10:1407, 1408

Last Supper, The (da Vinci) 10:1404, 1405

Late Egyptian language 1:103

Latin 10:1394

Laws (Plato) 3:367

learning and knowledge

Il-Khanate and 9:1238

medieval Europe and 10:1360, 1362, 1367, 1384–1397, 1418

Ottoman Turks and 9:1249, 1255

Plato and 3:367

preservation of 5:661, 665, 701

Skeptics and 3:412

Socrates and 3:362, 363–364

Songhai and 9:1272–1273

legalism, philosophy of 7:877, 879, 881, 891, 893

Leonardo da Vinci 10:1403, 1404, *1405*, 1405, 1406

Libation Bearers (Aeschylus) 3:323

liberal arts, study of 6:804, 806

libraries 2:221, 4:553, 5:693, 701, 6:782, 10:1392, 1401

Library of Alexandria 3:392, 398, 406, 407

Linear A script 2:179, 181, 186

Linear B script 2:186, *252*

lion, Hittite sculpture of 2:*159*

Li Si 7:891, *893*

literacy, medieval Europe and 10:1387, 1393, 1394

literature and writing

Africa and 9:1264, 1273

Alexander the Great and 3:384

Alfred the Great and 6:820

Assyrians and 2:211

Athens and 2:267, 3:301, 305, 349

Augustine and 5:686, 687

Babylonian 1:123

Buddhism and 7:*953*

chansons de geste (songs of heroic deeds) 6:801, 10:1394

China and 7:879, 882, 893, 901

Confucianism and 7:884, 887

Constantine VII and 9:1174–1175

Egypt's Middle Kingdom and 1:81, 82–83, 83–84, 88

Egypt's New Kingdom and 1:97, 101, 103–104

El Cid and 8:1021

Greece and 2:194, 248–249, 256, 257

Greek drama 3:318–325

Greek literature 6:782, 783

Greek religion and 3:313

hagiography 5:688, 690, 691

Hinduism and 7:943, 944

India and 7:927, 961, 963

Japan and 7:908–909, 912–913, 915

Kublai Khan and 9:1226

Mari Letters 1:115

medieval Europe and 10:1394, 1397

Museum of Alexandria and 3:404

Mycenaeans and 2:182

navigation and 2:202

One Thousand and One Nights 6:781

Ottoman Turks and 9:1255

Persians and 2:242–244, 6:730, 731, 732, 735

Polynesia and 7:988

preservation of 5:661, 701

Roman Empire and 4:510–511, 512, 524, 555–556, 557

Russia and 9:1212

Sparta and 2:258, 264

Sumerian 1:57

Theocritus and 3:406–407

Vedas and 7:935

Vikings and 9:1205

Lives of the Artists, The (Vasari) 10:1402, 1403

Livy 4:438, 510, 524

Logos 3:355, 413

lost-wax process 10:1310

Lun Yu (Sayings of Confucius) 7:884

Lyceum 3:367, 413

Lysistrata (Aristophanes) 3:378

M

Macedonian Renaissance 9:1180

madrigals 10:1407

Mahabharata 7:943, *944*, 944

Malayo-Polynesian languages 7:972

manners, Aztecs and 10:1331

manuscripts 5:661, *677*, 693

Manutius, Aldus 10:1393

Mari Letters 1:115, 2:224

Masaccio, Tommaso 10:*1401*, 1403–1404

masks, theatrical 3:318, *320*, 320, 321, 4:*555*

Masolino 10:1403

Medea (Euripides) 3:325

Medici, Cosimo de' 10:1401

Medici, Lorenzo de' 8:1096, 10:1396, 1401, 1403

Menander 3:325, *407*, 407, 4:557

Mencius 7:887, 890, *891*

Metaphysics (Aristotle) 3:354

metempsychosis 3:357

Michelangelo 8:1096, 10:1402, *1403*, 1404, 1406

Michelozzo 10:1401

mime, Roman theater and 4:555

Mirandola, Pico della 10:1401, 1403

models, Egyptian 1:*74*, *81*, 84–85, *86*, *91*

Mona Lisa (da Vinci) 10:1405

Monteverdi, Claudio 10:*1407*, 1407

More, Thomas 10:1397

mosaics

Byzantine Empire and 5:*667*, *673*, 674, 9:*1164*

Christianity and 5:*679*

Fourth Crusade and 9:*1193*

gladiators and 4:*551*

Hagia Sophia and 5:672, 9:*1159*, *1178*, *1180*

Macedonian Renaissance and 9:1180

Minoan 2:*171*

pre-Columbian cultures and 10:1310, 1315

Roman 2:*194*, 250, 3:*389*, 5:*591*

Rome and 4:*477*

in Saint Sophia's Cathedral 9:*1209*

Sumerian 1:56

in Umayyad Mosque 6:*767*

Venetian 2:*223*

Murasaki Shikibu 7:913

Muses 3:412

Museum of Alexandria 3:392, 398, 404, 406–407, *411*

music and dance

Africa and 9:1259, *1261*

Babylonians and 1:*117*

Egypt and 1:*90*

Greek drama and 3:320

Gregorian chant 5:700

Hittites and 2:158–159

Mali and 9:1272

medieval Europe and 10:1394

Ptolemy of Alexandria and 3:410

Pythagoras and 3:357, 358

religious festivals and 3:318

Renaissance and 10:1407–1408

Rome and 4:555, *557*

sankyo (musical instrument) 9:*1274*

Sioux people and 10:*1356*

Sparta and 2:264

Sufis and 9:1230, 1233

N

Nahuatl language 10:1335

Neoplatonism 5:683, 684, 6:783

"New Comedy," Greek 3:325

Nilo-Saharan languages 9:1259, 1264

Nilotic languages 9:1264

nobility of character, Confucianism and 7:885–886

No drama 7:*907*

"non-doing," Taoism and 7:888

North Semitic alphabet 2:204

O

Oceanic languages 7:988

Odyssey (Homer) 2:182, 192, 194, 248–249, 256, 3:313, 404, *406*, 6:732

Oedipus at Colonus (Sophocles) 3:323–324
Oedipus Rex (Sophocles) 3:323, *324*, 324
"Old Comedy," Greek 3:325
One Thousand and One Nights 6:*780*, 780, 781, 787
On Nature (Anaxagoras) 3:356
opera 10:*1407*, 1407
oral traditions 9:1264, 1271, 10:1336
orators 3:380
see also rhetoric
Oresteia trilogy (Aeschylus) 3:322–323
Orfeo (Monteverdi) 10:1407
origins of the world, Greek philosophers and 3:354, 355, 356
Ovid 4:510–511, *512*, 526

P

painting
Macedonian Renaissance and 9:1180
Minoans and 2:178
perspective and 10:1403–1404
portraits 10:1404, 1405, 1406
pre-Columbian cultures and 10:1305, 1308, 1315
Renaissance and 10:1402
Venice and 10:1406
Palestrina 10:1407
paradoxes, Greek philosophy and 3:360
Parmenides 3:355, 358, 360, 362–363
patrons, Renaissance and 10:1400–1401, 1403, 1404, 1405, 1406
Peace (Aristophanes) 3:378
Peri, Jacopo 10:1407
Persians (Aeschylus) 3:323
perspective, painting and 10:1403–1404
Petrarch 8:1088
petroglyphs 10:1351
Phaedo (Plato) 3:365
Phidias 3:349, 351
Philoctetes (Sophocles) 3:323
philosophy
China and 7:877, 879, **882–893**, 903
Christianity and 5:633, *634*, 639, 682–685
Greek 3:348, **352–367**, 411–413, 5:661
Hinduism and 7:964
humanism 10:1392–1393, 1395, 1396, 1397
Islamic world and 6:781–783
phonetic writing 1:68
pictographic writing 1:68, 10:*1328*, 1328
see also hieroglyphic writing
Pietàs (Michelangelo) 10:*1403*, 1404

Pillow Book, The (Sei) 7:913
Plato 3:*353*, 10:*1388*
Academy and 3:365, 367
democracy and 3:347–348
Heracles and 3:355
humanism and 10:1393, 1395
Islamic world and 6:782, 783
Neoplatonism 5:684
preserving knowledge of 5:661
Renaissance and 10:1404
Socrates and 3:362, 364, 365
Sophists and 3:361, 412
Sparta and 2:264
Platonic Academy, Florence 10:1393
playwrights *see* dramatists
Plutarch 3:384, 4:438
poetry
Bedouin people and 6:738
China and 7:887, 901
Greece and 3:318, 355, 358, 406–407, 412
Hinduism and 7:940, 944
India and 7:935, 961, 963
Islamic world and 6:766, 767, 9:1233
Japan and 7:912
medieval Europe and 6:798, 801, 10:1394
Persians and 6:732
Roman Empire and 4:556
see also literature and writings
Politian 10:1403
portrait painting 10:1404, 1405, 1406, 1409
pottery
African 9:1259, *1262*
bell-beaker culture and 1:*19*, 31
Bükk culture and 1:*16*
China and 7:870, 871–872
corded-ware culture and 1:31
Crete and 2:172
funnel-beaker culture and 1:18–19, 21
Greece and 3:296, *298*, 301, *308*
Hallstatt culture and 1:47
India and 7:924, 927
Japan and 7:906, *909*
Minoans and 2:170, 173, 180
Minyan people and 2:163
Neolithic period and 1:16–17
Pacific islands and 7:984, 987
pre-Columbian cultures and 10:1305, 1310, 1311, 1314, *1315*, *1323*, *1350*, 1350, *1352*
Rössen and Michelsburg cultures and 1:18
Sumerian people and 1:65
Thera and 2:168
printing presses 10:1391–1392, 1408
Prometheus Bound (Aeschylus) 3:323
Protagoras 3:349, 352

Ptolemy of Alexandria 3:*405*, 10:1390–1391, *1391*, 1397
Pyrrhon of Elis 3:412
Pythagoras 3:356–357, *358*, *359*
pyx, Córdoban 6:*773*
pyxis (jewelry box) 3:*350*

R

Raphael 10:*1404*, 1406
relief sculptures
Assyrian 2:*201*, *212*, *215*, 215, *221*, *231*
Greek 2:*262*, *265*, 3:*307*, *317*
Hittites and 2:158
India and 7:*928*, *940*, *961*
Palmyra and 5:*602*
Parthians and 6:*728*
Persians and 2:*233*, *239*, 240, 3:*338*, 5:*600*, 6:*729*, 729
Phoenician 2:205
Pictish 5:*664*
pre-Columbian cultures and 10:*1318*
Roman 4:*480*, *515*, *541*, *547*, *550*, 5:*605*, *681*
Sicily and 8:*1023*
Southeast Asia and 7:*973*
Syrian 5:597
Rembrandt van Rijn 10:1409
Renaissance 8:1093, 1094, 1096, 1099, 10:**1398–1409**
Republic, The (Plato) 3:347–348, 367
Resurrection of the Son of Theophilus (Masaccio) 10:*1401*, 1403–1404
Revellers (Aristophanes) 3:325
rhetoric 3:345, 361, 362, 411–412, 4:557
rhino horn cup, Chinese 10:*1414*
rock paintings, San people and 9:1262

S

sacerdotal writing 2:204
Sacrifice of Isaac (Caravaggio) 2:*226*
Sangallo, Giuliano da 10:1403
sankyo (musical instrument) 9:*1274*
Sanskrit 7:940, 971, 975
Sappho 2:*250*
satire 3:325, 378
satyr plays 3:320, 324
Scholasticism and humanism 10:**1384–1397**
School of Athens, The (Raphael) 3:*353*, 10:1404
School of Miletus 3:352, 354
sculpture
Assyrian 2:213, 215
Aztecs and 10:*1329*, 1333
Babylonian 2:*219*
Easter Island and 7:*986*, 986
Greek 2:*163*, *166*, 257, *259*, 267
Hittite 2:*151*, *152*, *154*, *155*, *158*, *159*

Mayan architecture and 10:1315
Minoan 2:179
Olmec people and 10:*1306*, *1307*, 1307
Persian 2:245
pre-Columbian cultures and 10:1305, 1307, 1310
Renaissance and 10:1404, 1406
Toltec people and 10:*1309*, 1309
see also relief sculptures
Sei Shonagon 7:913
Semitic languages 9:1258
Seven Against Thebes (Aeschylus) 3:323
Sforza, Ludovico 10:1404, *1405*, 1405
Shah-nameh (Book of Kings) 6:732
Shakespeare, William 3:407
shawabti figures 1:*87*
Shi-ji (Records of the Grand Historian) (Sima Qian) 7:886, 899
Shi Shu (Four Books) 7:887
silver artifacts 2:156, 7:*901*, *902*, 9:*1232*, 10:1421
Sima Qian 7:886, 899
Sindbad and the Old Man of the Sea 6:*780*, 780
Sistine Chapel 10:1406
skenes, Greek drama and 3:320
Skeptics 3:412, 5:683
slit-drums 10:1310
Socrates 3:348, 356, 361–365, *362*, *363*, 366, 373
Socratic irony 3:363
Song of Roland 6:798, *801*, 801
Sophism 3:348, 361, 362, 364, 411–412
Sophocles 3:323–324, 349
speechmaking, North American peoples and 10:1355
spelling and grammar, medieval Europe and 10:1394
sports 2:169, 177, 5:622, 624
see also games
stag, carving of 1:*15*
stained-glass windows 5:*697*, 6:*815*, 8:*1036*, *1067*
statues *see* relief sculptures; sculpture
statuettes 1:7, 2:165–166, *167*, 179, *190*, 248
Stoicism 3:413, 4:544, 555, 557
stone sculptures, pre-Columbian cultures and 10:*1306*, *1307*, *1309*, *1329*
Story of Sinuhe (Egyptian text) 1:83–84
student life, medieval Europe and 10:1384, 1386
Suppliants (Aeschylus) 3:323
Swahili 9:1264, 1275

T

Tale of Genji, The (Murasaki) 7:913
Tao 7:884, 885, 886, 888
Taoism 7:886, 888, 889, 890, 892
Tao Te Ching (Lao-tzu) 7:886, 888, 889, 892
tapestries 5:*646, 659*, 10:*1371*
teaching methods, medieval universities and 10:1387, 1388–1389
terra-cotta artifacts
  Africa and 9:*1257*
  Byzantine Empire and 9:*1181*
  China and 7:*881*, 881
  Greece and 2:*248*
  India and 7:920, *924, 926*
  Japan and 7:909, *912*
  Mycenaeans and 2:*190*, 190
  Nok people and 9:*1257*, 1261, 1263
  Phoenicians and 2:*197*
textual criticism 3:404, 406
Thales of Miletus 3:352, *354*
theater *see* drama
Theater of Dionysus 3:*321*
theaters 2:*254*, 3:318, 320, *321*, 4:553, 555
Theocritus 3:406–407
Thespis 3:318, 321

Thomas Aquinas 10:*1388, 1389*, 1389–1390
Three Doctrines 7:892
Thucydides 3:352
Tintoretto 10:1406
Titian 10:*1406*, 1406
Toscanelli, Paolo 10:1395, 1397
Trachiniai (Sophocles) 3:323
tragedy
  Aeschylus and 3:322–323
  Euripides and 3:324–325
  Greek drama and 3:318, 320, 321–322
  Roman theater and 4:555
  Sophocles and 3:323–324
tragoidos (goat bard) 3:318
translations
  of ancient texts 10:1390–1391, 1393
  of Bible 5:697
  of Greek literature 5:661

U

universities 10:1384, *1386, 1388*
Utopia (More) 10:1397

V

vacuum, Greek philosophy and 3:358, 360, 361
Vasari, Giorgio 10:1402, 1403

vase illustrations, Greek 3:*302, 303, 306, 313, 319, 336, 342, 369, 371, 406*
vases 2:*193, 251, 266*, 7:*904*
Venus of Brassempouy 1:7, *10*
Venus of Willendorf 1:7, *9*
Veronese 10:1406
Verrocchio, Andrea del 10:1403
Vespo della Beata Virgine (Monteverdi) 10:1407
Virgil 2:200, 3:406–407, 4:438, 510, 512, 526, 557
virtue 3:362, 413

W

wall paintings 9:1259, *1261*
Wasps (Aristophanes) 3:378
wooden sculptures 7:*987*, 9:*1175, 1271, 1276*
writing
  Africa and 9:1264
  Carolingian miniscule script and 6:806
  China and 7:873, 876, 877, 879, 899
  cuneiform 1:60–61, 67, *68*, 68, 69, 119
  demotic 1:88
  Germanic peoples and 5:658, 665
  Greeks and 2:248–249, 253, 3:315

hieratic 1:88
hieroglyphic 1:72–73, 88
Hittites and 2:150, 160–161
Indus Valley civilization and 7:920, 923
Japan and 7:910, *915*, 915
Minoans and 2:176, 179, 180–181
Mongols and 9:1222
Mycenaeans and 2:182, 186, 189
Persians and 2:236
Phoenicians and 2:203–204
phonetic 1:68
pictographic 1:68
pre-Columbian cultures and 10:1305, 1319, *1328*, 1328, 1336
printing press and 10:1391–1392
systems of 2:252
see also alphabets; literature and writing
Wu Jing (Five Classics) 7:887

X

Xenophanes 3:355, *357*
Xenophon 3:362
Xunzi 7:891

Z

Zeno of Citium 3:413
Zeno of Elea 3:360, 362–363

EVERYDAY LIFE

Page numbers in *italics* refer to illustrations. Page numbers in **bold** refer to entire chapters.

A

adultery, punishments for 5:635
agriculture
  Africa and 9:1256, 1258–1259, 1265, 1271
  Arabia and 6:738
  Assyrians and 2:211
  Aztecs and 10:1324, 1333
  Byzantine Empire and 9:1175
  China and 7:870–871, 873, 875, 877, 878, 897
  Cistercian Order and 8:1035
  climate change and 8:1084
  Crete and 2:172
  Cycladic people and 2:164–165
  development of states and 10:1414
  early humans and 1:6, 11, 14–15
  Egypt and 1:70, 78, 86, 87, 101
  Etruscans and 4:444
  Europe and 8:*1030*, 10:1416
  European settlers and 10:1381, 1383
  feudal Europe and 6:*821*, 821, *822*, 823, 8:1026, *1027*, 1028–1029, *1029*, *1030*
  funnel-beaker culture and 1:19
  Germanic people and 5:665
  Greece and 2:162, 258, 260, 261, 266, 3:*302*, 302–303, *306*, 370
  Greek colonies and 2:256
  Hittites and 2:156, 158
  Incas and 10:1340, 1342
  India and 7:918
  Islamic world and 9:1238, 1240
  Japan and 7:906, 911
  Linearbandkeramik culture and 1:17
  Maya and 10:1312, 1314, 1323
  Mesopotamia and 1:54
  Minoans and 2:175–176
  Mycenaeans and 2:189
  Neolithic period and 1:12, 13, 14–15, 16, 18
  North American peoples and 10:1350, 1352, 1357
  pre-Columbian cultures and 10:1304, 1311
  religious rituals and 10:1354–1355
  Roman Empire and 4:466, 476, *477*, 5:606
  Southeast Asia and 7:972, 974–975, 976–977
  Sumerian people and 1:65
  tools and 1:21–22, 42
  Vikings and 9:1205
animals, domesticated 8:1026, 1028, 10:1304, 1312, 1352
  Africa and 9:1258
  Crete and 2:172
  early humans and 1:9, 13, 14
  funnel-beaker culture and 1:19, 21
  Greece and 2:162
  medieval Europe and 8:1026, 1028
  Pacific islands and 7:987
  Persians and 2:243–244
  Polynesia and 7:988
  Scythian people and 1:49
  single-grave culture and 1:31
apprentices 8:1043
ayllu (family work unit) 10:1340

B

barbarian rulers **5:658–665**
baths 4:*524*, 553, *554*, 7:920
be (communities of workers) 7:909
Black Death 8:*1084*, 1084–1086, *1085*, *1086*, 1105,1108, 1109
blood games 4:551–552
blood money 5:662, 664
Blues 5:623–624, 627, 671
bread and circuses 4:531, 548–553
burial practices
  Assyrians and 2:219
  Babylonians and 1:117
  Bronze Age and 1:38, 39
  Celtic people and 1:46, 52, 2:257
  Cycladic people and 2:165, 166–167
  Dark Age Greece and 2:246
  Egypt and 1:73–74, *75*, 75, 77, 82, 84–85, 95–96, *97*
  funnel-beaker culture and 1:22, 24–25
  Hallstatt culture and 1:48
  India and 7:927
  Japan and 7:909
  Latium and 4:443
  Maya and 10:1322
  Mycenaeans and 2:185–187, 188, 190
  Natufian culture and 1:11
  Persians and 2:244
  Roman Empire and 4:550
  Rössen culture and 1:18, *21*
  Scythian people and 1:51
  Sumerian people and 1:57–58
  Urnfield culture and 1:39–40

C

camayo (social group) 10:1344
camels 6:*778*, 778, 779
carpets 6:781, 9:*1231*
caste system, India 7:923, 924–925, 927, 946
character, Roman 4:457–458
chariot races 4:552–553, *553*
chaski runners 10:1346, 1347
children
  Christianity and 5:635, 680
  Germanic peoples and 5:664–665
  Greece and 2:263, 268, 3:350
  military forces and 9:1230, 1236, 1255
  Minoans and 2:180
  Phoenicians and 2:206
  pre-Columbian cultures and 10:1331, 1343, 1353
  Rome and 4:551
  see also family life
cities and towns
  Africa and 9:1270
  Arabia and 6:736
  Babylon 1:124
  in early 16th century CE 10:1416
  East Francia and 6:830
  feudalism and 6:822
  government and 8:1131
  India and 7:918, 927, 971
  Latium and 4:443–444
  leagues and alliances and 8:1094
  medieval Europe and 8:1033–1034, 1036–1039, 1086
  pre-Columbian cultures and 10:1306–1307, 1315–1316, 1318, 1332, 1342, 1350
  Roman provinces and 4:547
  Rome and 4:508
  social classes and 8:1086
  Southeast Asia and 7:978, 980
  spread of Islam and 6:755
  Sumerian people and 1:54, 55
  Swabian League of Cities 8:1094
  see also towns and villages
client system 4:447
clothing 2:156, 179, 212
  Celtic people and 1:46
  Copper Age and 1:34
  Mari and 1:115
  pre-Columbian cultures and 10:1323, 1329, 1331, 1344–1345, 1353
clubs, Hippodrome and 5:623–624, 627
common people 10:1324, 1331, 1332, 1340, 1344, 1358, 1397
competition, Greece and 3:308, 318, 320, 323
court life
  Burgundy and 8:1129
  Carolingian Empire and 6:805, 806, 807
  Islamic world and 6:785
Mali and 9:1272
Mongols and 9:1224, 1225, 1226
crafts and craftspeople
  Anasazi people and 10:1350
  Aztecs and 10:1327, 1333
  Celtic people and 1:46, 50
  copper and 1:32
  Egypt and 1:86
  Etruscans and 4:445
  Franks and 6:*793*
  Goths and 5:*645*
  Greece and 3:302–303
  Hallstatt culture and 1:45, 47
  Hittites and 2:156
  Huns and 5:*649*
  Iberian people and 1:50
  India and 7:920, 925
  Islamic world and 6:*779*, 780–781
  Maya and 10:1314, 1316, 1319
  medieval Europe and 8:1041, 1043, 1086
  Mixtec people and 10:1310
  Mycenaeans and 2:189
  Neolithic period and 1:15
  Phoenicians and 2:198, 200
  pre-Columbian cultures and 10:1302, 1304, 1305, 1305–1306
  Renaissance and 10:1403
  Rome and 4:466, 548
  Tarascan people and 10:1310
crop rotations 3:302, 6:823, 8:1028
Cycladic people 2:169

D

debts 2:266–267, 3:294, 298, 403, 4:450, 455, 493, 5:664
dice set, Roman 4:*549*
diseases
  Black Death 8:*1084*, *1085*, *1086*, 1084–1086
  European conquests and 10:1421
  European settlers and 10:1381
  pre-Columbian cultures and 10:1311, 1335, 1347
  Roman Empire and 4:544, 5:604, 606
divorce 1:118, 2:161, 3:350, 4:510, 5:674
dogs 1:9, 2:243–244
dowries 1:118, 3:350, 10:1323
drainage projects 4:442

E

earthquakes, Constantinople and 5:619, 672
education
  Abbasid caliphate and 6:772
  Alexander the Great and 3:384

education (*continued*)
  Alfred the Great and 6:820
  Aristotle and 3:367
  Babylonians and 1:119
  Bulgarian Empire and 9:1177
  Carolingian Empire and 6:804,
    806
  China and 7:882, 887, 894–895,
    903
  Confucianism and 7:884–885
  Egyptians and 1:108
  Frederick II and 8:1070
  gladiators and 4:551
  Greek philosophy and 3:356, 361,
    364, 367, 411
  humanism and 10:1400
  Jerome and 5:696
  Laws of the Twelve Tables and
    4:453
  Mali and 9:1271
  medieval Europe and 8:1043,
    10:1366, 1384, 1400
  military training and 10:1328
  Museum of Alexandria and
    3:404, 406–407
  Persians and 2:244
  Plato's Academy and 3:365, 367
  pre-Columbian cultures and
    10:1327, 1328, 1331, 1353
  Rome and 4:556–557
  Scholasticism 10:1384, 1386–
    1390
  Sparta and 2:263
  Sumerians and 1:65, 69
  Taoism and 7:888
Egypt 1:86, 97, 108
employment
  actors 3:321
  cities and towns and 10:1416
  crafts and craftspeople and
    3:302–303
  Egypt and 1:108
  guilds and 8:1043
  Hittites and 2:158
  Hundred Years' War and 8:1102
  mercenaries 3:388–389
  Peasants' Revolt and 8:1109
  pre-Columbian cultures and
    10:1319, 1327, 1344
  Rome and 4:548, 549
  shoemakers 4:*550*
  Socrates and 3:362
  Sophists and 3:361
  specialization 1:36–37, 38, 70
  temples and 7:966
  see also agriculture; labor
entertainment 4:531, 548–553,
  8:1031, 1043

F

fairs, annual 8:1030–1032, *1032,
  1033*
family law 1:113
family life
  Augustus, Age of, and 4:509–510
  Christianity and 5:635

early Rome and 4:446
  Germanic peoples and 5:664–
    665
  legal system and 4:453
  military forces and 4:513
  pre-Columbian cultures and
    10:1312, 1322–1323, 1340,
    1346–1347, 1353
  Roman character and 4:458
  Roman emperors and 4:516, 518,
    523–524, 525, 527
famine 5:622, 8:1084, 10:1381
  see also food
farming *see* agriculture
fertility 2:244
festivals 4:511, 527, 549–550
feudalism 6:823
feudal manors 6:823
fines, Germanic peoples and 5:662,
  664
firearms, Japan and 7:917
fires, cities and 4:527–528, 535,
  548, 5:619
fishing 1:7, 7:975, 988, 10:1358
food
  Africa and 9:1256, 1262
  agricultural improvements and
    8:1028–1029
  China and 7:895, 911
  crusades and 9:1187
  distribution of 5:603, 612, 616,
    621–622
  Mongols and 9:1220
  Pacific islands and 7:987
  pre-Columbian cultures and
    10:1312, 1314, 1316, 1331,
    1333
  religious offerings 3:312
  Rome and 4:482, 490, 498
freemen 6:821, 7:911
funerals *see* burial practices

G

games
  Maya and 10:*1317*, 1317, 1318
  Rome and 4:*500*, 511, *549*, 549–
    550, 551–552, 552–553
  see also sports
gender roles, pre-Columbian
  cultures and 10:1323, 1331,
  1352, 1353, 1355
genealogy 9:1259, 1261, 10:1319
gift giving, caste system and
  7:925, 927
grain 1:11, 12, 4:481–482,
  508, 548–549, 5:586,
  621–622
grammar schools 10:1387
grave goods
  Bronze Age and 1:38
  Celtic people and 2:257
  China and 7:873, 874, 876,
    881, 881
  Cycladic people and 2:166–167
  Egyptian 1:*74*, 75, 84–85, 87
  Hallstatt culture and 1:48

Japan and 7:909
  Mycenaeans and 2:186, 190
  pre-Columbian cultures and
    10:*1305*, 1309
  Scythian 1:49
  Sumerian 1:57–58, *69*
  see also burial practices
grave robbery 1:96, 104
Greens 5:623–624, 627, 671
guilds 4:548, 550, 8:*1041*, 1087
  Black Death and 8:1086
  cities and towns and 8:1037,
    1041, 1043
  education and 10:1387
  Hundred Years' War and 8:1102,
    1104

H

helots (serfs) 2:258, 260
herding 1:31
Hittites 2:154, 159
horse racing 5:622, 623, 624
horses 1:49, 2:211, 251, 9:1220,
  1221, 10:1358
hospitium (visitors' rights) 5:658
household gods and goddesses
  3:312
household shrines 4:448, *449*
housing
  Anasazi people and 10:1348,
    1350, 1351
  Aztecs and 10:1331, 1332
  Babylonian Empire and 1:115
  barbarians and 5:658
  China and 7:870, 872
  Crete and 2:172
  Cycladic people and 2:169
  Egyptian 1:86, 97
  funnel-beaker culture and 1:19
  Greece and 2:162
  Hittites and 2:154
  Incas and 10:1342, 1346
  India and 7:918, 920
  Japan and 7:906
  Latium and 4:443–444, 445
  Linearbandkeramik culture and
    1:17
  Maya and 10:1312, 1316,
    1323
  Minoans and 2:173, 177
  Minyan people and 2:163,
    164
  Mongols and 9:*1223*
  Mycenae and 2:184
  Neolithic period and 1:13, 14–15
  North American peoples and
    10:1352, 1353, 1357, 1358
  Rome and 4:548, *556*
  Rössen and Michelsburg cultures
    and 1:18
  serfs and 6:823
  Skara Brae and 1:30
  students and 10:1386
  Sumerian people and 1:65
  Teotihuacán and 10:1308–1309
  Vikings and 9:1205, 1207

hunter-gatherers 7:871, 906,
  9:1256, 1259, 10:1312, 1350,
  1359
hunting
  early humans and 1:6, 8–10
  Egypt's New Kingdom and 1:*98*
  funnel-beaker culture and 1:19
  North American peoples and
    10:1352–1353, *1354*, 1354,
    1355, *1356*, 1358
  Persians and 6:734, *735*

I

immigration
  Athens and 3:308
  Constantinople and 5:616,
    618, 621, 666
  Egypt and 1:89
infanticide 2:263, 268
inheritance rights 5:664–665,
  6:809, 828, 830, 9:1212,
  1255
insults 5:662, 664
irrigation
  Arabia and 5:587
  Assyrians and 2:211
  China and 7:877
  Egypt and 1:80–81
  Latium and 4:444
  Mesopotamia and 1:54
  Persians and 2:245
  pre-Columbian cultures and
    10:1310, 1311, 1312, 1333,
    1350

J

jewelry 1:*60*, 2:156, 179, 180, *207*,
  251, 10:*1358*
journeymen, guilds and 8:1043

L

labor
  Black Death and 8:1086
  Buddhism and 7:954–955
  Egypt and 1:86, 97, 99, 100
  Incas and 10:1341
  India and 7:924–925
  monasteries and 5:692, 693, 694,
    700, 6:824, 826
  pyramids and 1:73–74
  see also employment
landownership
  Akkadian Empire and 1:61
  barbarians and 5:660
  Buddhist monasteries and 7:955
  Capetian dynasty and 6:828
  Carolingian Empire and 6:811,
    813
  Charles Martel and 6:792–793
  China and 7:875, 879, 897, 899,
    900, 901–902
  Christians and 5:628
  Egypt and 1:86, 94, 107
  feudalism and 6:808, 819, 821,
    823
  Franks and 6:788, 790

Greece and 2:255–256, 266,
  3:301, 403
Hittites and 2:155–156
Japan and 7:910, 911, 913, 917
Merovingian dynasty and 6:790
monasteries and 8:1035
Ottoman Turks and 9:1255
pre-Columbian cultures and
  10:1328, 1340
Roman Catholic Church and
  6:790
Roman Empire and 4:513,
  5:606
Rome and 4:476, 479–481,
  484
Vikings and 6:809
law enforcement, Incas and
  10:1347
looms 8:1030, *1031*
ludi magni (big games) 4:549–550
ludi saeculares (secular games) 4:511
luxury goods, trade and 8:1033

M
manners, Aztecs and 10:1331
marriage
  Athens and 2:268, 3:*350*
  Augustus Caesar and 4:510
  Buddha and 7:948
  Byzantine Empire and
    9:1165–1166, 1170
  Charlemagne and 6:796
  Code of Hammurabi and 1:113,
    118
  Constantine I and 5:635
  early Africa and 9:1261
  Edward IV of England and
    8:1120
  Egypt's New Kingdom and
    1:108
  Germanic peoples and 5:664, 665
  Hittites and 2:158, 161
  Khosrow I and 6:735
  Mohammed and 6:740–741
  Mongols and 9:1220
  Philip II Augustus and
    8:1066–1067
  pre-Columbian cultures and
    10:1323, 1340, 1344
  Rome and 4:441, 453
  social classes and 4:447, 451
  Sparta and 2:263
matrilineal societies 7:988
medicine
  Alexander the Great and
    3:384
  Alexandria and 3:410–411
  Athens and 3:372
  Babylonians and 1:119
  Black Death and 8:1085
  Hippocrates 3:352
  India and 7:926
  Islamic world and 6:783
  medieval Europe and 10:1390,
    1391
mental illness 4:518, 519, 520–521

migrations
  Africa and 9:1263, 1264, 1265
  early Byzantine Empire and
    9:1158, 1160–1161
  pre-Columbian cultures and
    10:1302, 1304, 1323, 1350,
    1352, 1357, 1359
Minoans and 2:174
models, Egyptian 1:*74, 81,* 84–
  85, *86, 91*
monastic rules 5:692, 693–694,
  699–701, 6:825, 826, 7:954
mowing tools 1:11

N
natural disasters 2:167, 168, 169,
  181, 192, 210, 4:535
nobility of character, Confucianism
  and 7:885–886
notaries 8:*1043*

O
"oath helpers" 5:662
obedience, monasteries and 5:694
offerings, religious 1:19, 24, 25, 85,
  3:312
olive oil 3:302

P
patrilineal societies 7:987
payments, government service and
  3:344
payments, trade and 2:202–203
perfume makers 6:*779*
Persians 2:244–245
personal appearance
  Egyptians and 1:108
  Hittites and 2:150, 156
  Minoans and 2:178–179
  pre-Columbian cultures and
    10:1323, 1331, 1345, *1358*
personal property, North American
  peoples and 10:1352
plague
  Black Death 8:*1084,* 1084–
    1086, *1085, 1086,* 1105,
    1108, 1109
  Peloponnesian War and 3:344,
    370–371, 372
  Rome and 4:544
plumbing and water supplies
  aqueducts 5:*620, 670,* 675, 676
  Constantinople and 5:619, 620
  Cycladic culture and 2:169
  Hittites and 2:154
  India and 7:918
  Khmer people and 7:976–977
  Minoans and 2:174, 175
  Mycenae and 2:184
  Persians and 6:735
  pre-Columbian cultures and
    10:1316, 1332
  Rome and 5:675, 676
  Saint Anthony's Monastery and
    5:*691*
police forces *see* public safety

population
  Black Death and 8:1084–1086
  China and 10:1419
  city-states and 8:1036, 1039
  Constantinople and 5:616, 618,
    9:1161
  crusades and 9:1182
  Dark Age Greece and 2:246
  Great Zimbabwe and 9:1276
  growth of 8:1026, 1082
  Iceland and 9:1204
  Neolithic period and 1:15
  North American peoples and
    10:1348, 1350, 1351
  pre-Columbian cultures and
    10:1307, 1332, 1336
  Rome and 4:548
postal service, Persians and 2:245
potlatch festivals 10:1358
pre-Columbian cultures 10:1322–
  1323, 1328, 1331, 1333,
  1354
professions, Sumerians and 1:69
  see also labor
property rights
  Athens and 2:267, 269
  Babylonians and 1:113
  early Byzantine Empire and
    9:1165
  early Rome and 4:449, 453, 550
  monasteries and 5:694, 700
  serfs and 6:823
  women and 5:664
  see also landownership
prostitution 5:674
public safety 4:509, 532, 550
punishments
  Assyrians and 2:212
  Aztecs and 10:1326–1327
  Code of Hammurabi and 1:113,
    115–116, 119
  Constantine I and 5:635
  early Rome and 4:441, 451,
    453
  Germanic peoples and 5:662,
    664
  Greece and 2:260
  Hittites and 2:161
  Persians and 2:244
  Roman republic and 4:490

R
relay runners, Incas and 10:1346,
  1347
Renaissance 10:1394, 1398
Roman Empire 4:520, 536,
  546–547, **548–557**
rules, university students and
  10:1386

S
scurvy, European explorers and
  10:1377
seasonal camps 1:6
serfs 5:606, 6:819, 821, 822, 823,
  8:1041

sewers *see* plumbing and water
  supplies
shoemakers 2:*266,* 3:*303,* 4:*550*
shudras (laborers and servants)
  7:925, 927, 946
slash-and-burn agriculture 1:16, 19,
  10:1312
slavery
  Africa and 9:1272, 1274–1275
  agriculture and 4:476
  Assyrians and 2:214
  Babylonians and 1:115
  Carthage and 4:469
  Celtic people and 1:50
  China and 7:877
  Christianity and 5:635
  debts and 4:453, 455
  early Rome and 4:446
  Egyptians and 1:86
  Germanic peoples and 5:664
  Greece and 2:253, 255, 266–
    267, 3:308, 347, 403
  Islam and 6:743
  Japan and 7:911
  Macedonia and 3:388
  Mycenaeans and 2:189
  Peloponnesian War and 3:376
  Portuguese traders and
    10:1367
  pre-Columbian cultures and
    10:1326–1327, 1358
  Punic Wars and 4:481
  Roman Empire and 5:606
  Spartacus and 4:489–490
  Sumerians and 1:57
  Vikings and 9:1196, 1205
social classes
  arts and 10:1400–1401, 1403
  Babylonian 1:113, 115–116
  Carolingian Empire and 6:808
  China and 7:873
  clothing and 10:1344–1345
  Constantinople and 5:623
  Egyptian 1:77, 86, 97, 99–100
  feudalism and 6:821–822
  Greece and 3:298, 299, 300–301,
    304, 367
  India and 7:918, 924–925, 927
  Islamic world and 6:743–744,
    768
  Japan and 7:911, 917
  landownership and 4:476
  medieval Europe and 8:1078,
    1086
  military forces and 4:484
  pre-Columbian cultures and
    10:1316, 1326
  Roman Catholic Church and
    6:825
  Rome and 4:446–455, 479–
    481, 481–482, 488, 492, 542,
    543
  Sumerian 1:56–57
  Vikings and 9:1205
social clubs 4:550
social mobility 6:822, 823

social structure
  barbarians and 5:658, 660
  Confucianism and 7:884,
    885–886, 890, 894
  early Africa and 9:1259, 1261
  Greece and 2:246, 251, 253, 258,
    260–261, 266–267
  Greek colonies and 2:256
  Hittites and 2:155–156
  Minoans and 2:175–177
  Mycenaeans and 2:189,
    191
  pre-Columbian cultures and
    10:1306, 1307, 1310,
    1318–1319, 1324, 1326–
    1327, 1340, 1343–1344,
    1353, 1357–1358
  Rome and 5:593–594,
    595
  Sparta 2:263–264
speechmaking, North American
  peoples and 10:1355
spinning 3:*349*
sports 2:*169*, 177, 5:622, 624
  see also games
student life, medieval Europe and
  10:1384, 1386

T
tailors 8:*1036*
tattoos 7:987
tenant farmers 5:606, 608
thetes (laborers) 2:266, 267, 3:304,
  344
towns and villages
  Athenian government and 3:307,
    308
  Bronze Age and 1:40
  Celtic people and 1:52
  Cycladic people and 2:167
  Egyptian 1:86
  funnel-beaker culture and
    1:19
  Greece and 2:162, 246, 249,
    251
  Hittites and 2:158
  Iberian people and 1:50
  Mesopotamia and 1:54
  Minoans and 2:177–178, *178*
  Minyan people and 2:164
  North American peoples and
    10:1350, 1352, *1355*, 1355
  Skara Brae 1:30
  Sparta and 2:263–264
  see also cities and towns

transportation 1:37, 10:1316,
  1327
traps and snares 1:9

U
Ulama ball game 10:*1317*, 1317,
  1318
untouchables 7:923, *925*, 959
urban Europe 8:**1026–1043**

V
Vikings 9:1205
villages *see* towns and villages
villas, Minoan 2:177–178
volcanoes 2:167, 168, 169, 181

W
wages 1:116, 8:1086, 1109
water supplies *see* plumbing and
  water supplies
wealth
  Assyrians and 2:208
  Athens and 3:348
  Greeks and 2:251, 269
  Minoans and 2:180
  Rome and 4:446, 449, 450,
    507, 548

weights and measures 1:119,
  2:212, 238, 7:879
wills 4:501, 515
wine 2:244
women
  Africa and 4:453, 9:1259
  Assyrians and 2:212
  Babylonian 1:113, 118
  Byzantine Empire and 5:674
  China and 7:903
  Egyptian 1:108
  Germanic peoples and
    5:664–665
  Greece and 2:263, *268*, 268,
    3:308, 321, 350
  Greek colonies and 2:256
  medieval Europe and 10:1387
  Minoans and 2:179
  pre-Columbian cultures and
    10:1344, 1345
  religious communities and 5:692
work *see* employment
wrestlers 2:*262*

Z
zeugitai (farmers) 2:266, 267,
  3:304, 344

GEOGRAPHICAL
LOCATIONS

Page numbers in *italics* refer to picture captions. Page numbers in **bold** refer to main articles.

A

Aachen 6:807
Abu Hureyra 1:12
Acre 8:1080, 9:1192, 1195, 1237
Adrianopole 9:1245
Aegean Sea 2:246, 254, 3:341, 6:780
Afghanistan 6:733
Africa 9:**1256–1265**, *1258*, **1266–1277**, 10:1364, 1410, 1416, 1420
　Berber peoples and 9:1234–1235
　Bronze Age and 1:45
　Byzantine Empire and 9:1163
　early humans and 1:6, 9
　Greeks and 2:254–255
　Islam and 6:759, 773, 774, 9:1230
　Ottoman Turks and 9:1242, 1255
　Phoenicians and 2:201, 202–203, 205
　Portuguese exploration of 10:1366–1367, 1369–1370
　Roman Empire and 4:474–475, 483, 498, 502, 503, 5:588–589, 671, 673
　temples 5:*613*
　trade and 10:1366, 1367, 1371, 1418
　Vandals and 5:652–653
Agrigentum 4:465, *467*
Akhetaton 1:101, 103
Akkad 1:59
Akkadian Empire 1:59–62, 114, 117
Akrotiri 2:167, 169
Aksum 9:1266, 1268–1269
Alba Longa 4:438, 440
Aleppo 2:150, 9:1190, 1228, 1238, *1239*
Alexandria 3:*392*, 392, 4:*507*
　Alexander the Great and 3:391
　Christianity and 5:632, 636–637
　cultural influence of 3:404, 406–407
　philosophy and 3:411–413
　Pompey's Pillar 3:*400*
　Ptolemy I and 3:398
　sciences and 3:407–411
al-Ghaba 9:1270
Allia, Battle of 4:462
American Samoa 7:*985*
Amphipolis 3:371, 373, 377
Amsterdam 10:1371
Anagni 8:1081, 1089

Anatolia
　Alexander the Great and 3:384–385, 389–390
　Byzantine Empire and 9:1165, 1171–1172, 1178–1179, 1181
　Constantinople and 5:618
　Etruscans and 4:445
　First Crusade and 9:1184, 1185, 1187–1188
　Greek settlers and 2:246, 254
　Hittites and 2:150
　Ionian rebellion 3:326–327
　Mongols and 9:1229, 1235
　Ottoman Turks and 9:1241, 1245, 1245–1246, 1252
　Palmyra and 5:602
　Persians and 3:309, 326, 381–382
　Rome and 4:482, 488–489, 513, 529, 538, 5:586
　Seleucid dynasty and 3:401
　Seljuk Turks and 9:1232, 1234, 1240–1241
　Troy and 2:192–195
Angra Mainyu 2:242, 243
Anjou 6:826
Ankara 9:1229
Antioch 3:399, 5:632, 6:729, 735, 9:1187, 1187–1188, *1188*, 1189
Anyang 7:876
Aquitaine 6:760, 768, 792, 812, 8:1107, 1113
Aquitania 5:643, 645
Arabia 10:1410, 1414, 1420
　before Islam 6:736, 738–739
　Ottoman Turks and 9:1242, 1252
　Roman Empire and 4:540, 5:587, 588, 677
Aragon 8:1016, 1017, 1018–1019
Archilochus 2:257
Argos 2:251, 3:373, 382
Armenia 4:513, 529, 540, 9:1176, 1228, 1229
Ashur 2:208, 210, 221
Asia 10:1302, 1304, 1348, 1416
　Alexander the Great and 3:388–389, 393–394
　Iron Age and 1:42
　Persians and 6:729
　Rome and 4:486, 5:589
　spread of Islam and 6:763
　see also specific countries
Assyria 1:101, 109, 120–121, 122, 2:*211*, 5:586
Aswan 9:1266
Athens 2:264–269, 3:**340–351**
　Acropolis 3:*300, 309*, 342, *347*, 349
　Alaric I in 5:*644*
　architecture and 3:349, 351

Athena and 3:301, 312, 351
　citizenship and 2:253
　coins and 3:303, *304*
　colonization and 2:251
　Corinth and 3:298, 382
　First Persian War and 3:329–330
　government and 3:298, 300–302, 304, 306–309
　Lamian War and 3:401–402
　Macedon and 3:383
　marriage and 3:350
　Mycenaeans and 2:182
　Peloponnesian War and 3:342, 344, **368–383**
　Persians and 2:239, 3:326, 327
　philosophy and 3:356, 361
　Second Persian War and 3:331, 333–334, 336, 337, *339*
　Sparta and 2:**258–268**
Attica 2:264, 3:300, 333–334, 336, 344
Austrasia 6:791
Austria 8:1094
　see also Holy Roman Empire
Avebury 1:*20*, 26–27, 28
Avignon 8:*1083*, 1087–1088, *1088*, 1089, 1091
Azores 10:1366, 1367

B

Babylon 1:101, **110–125**, 3:310, 399, 5:586
　Alexander the Great and 3:393, 395
　Assyrians and 2:210, 211–212, 216–217, 218–219, 220–221
　Greek philosophy and 3:352, 354
　Hittites and 1:42, 2:150, 153
　Israelites and 2:227, 231
　Judaism and 6:730
　Medes and 2:232
　Persians and 2:234, 239, 3:326
　Phoenicians and 2:199, 207
Bactria 3:401, 5:585, 586, 7:895, 929, 931
Badami 7:966
Baghdad
　Islamic world and 6:771, 782, 786
　Mongols and 9:1228, 1229, 1236, *1237*, 1240
　Seljuk Turks and 9:1232
　siege of 6:772, *775*
　Tigris River and 6:*787*, 787
　trade and 6:776
Bahamas 10:1374
Bahmani Sultanate 7:971
Balearic Islands 8:1025
Bali 7:967

Balkans 4:513–514, 5:649, 651, 9:1165, 1181, 1245, 1248, 1252, 10:1360
Baltic countries 8:1025, 1029, 1082, 1101, 9:1200–1201, 1203
Baluchistan 7:918
Bamberg 6:835
Barcelona 8:1016
Basiliscus 5:626
Bath 4:*524*
Bavaria 6:812, 819, 829, 832, 8:1094
Beaufort Sea 10:*1378*
Belgium 9:1276, 1277
Belgrade 9:1252, *1254*
Benin 9:1274, 1275
Bishapur 6:729
Bismark Archipelago 7:982
Bithynia 4:475, 488–489
Bohemia 6:835, 837, 8:1094, 1100
Bokhara 7:895
Borneo 7:967
Bornu 9:1273–1274
Britain 4:*524*
　Africa and 9:1275, 1277
　barbarian invaders and 5:663
　Pacific islands and 7:989
　Phoenicians and 2:200
　Roman Empire and 4:522–523, 528–529, 537–538, 542, *543*, 544, 5:582, 595, 663
　Southeast Asia and 7:981
　Vikings and 6:816, 819
　see also England
Brittany 5:663
Bruges 8:1039
Bulgaria 6:763, 9:1175, 1177, 1181, 1193, 1245, 1248
Burgundy 8:**1126–1133**, *1128*
　cultural achievements of 8:1093, 1094
　Franks and 6:826, 836
　Hundred Years' War and 8:1108, 1110, 1112, 1113
　Vikings and 9:1200
　Wars of the Roses and 8:1120, 1121
Burma *see* Myanmar
Bursa 9:1242, 1244
Byblos 1:77, 101, 2:196
Byzantine Empire 9:**1158–1167**, **1168–1181**
　Africa and 9:1269
　Charlemagne and 6:802, 803
　Christianity and 5:628–634, 636–637, 639, 6:761, 799–800, 811, 839, 840
　crusades and 8:1068, 9:1182, 1184, 1185, 1187, 1190

Byzantine Empire (*continued*)
European scholarship and 10:1390
Germanic peoples and 5:665
Holy Roman Empire and 6:832
Islam and 6:754, 755, 757, 763, 768, 776, 8:1014, 10:1360
Italy and 6:794, 795, 817, 8:1020, 1022, 1024
Justinian I and 5:**666–677**
naval power of 6:779–780
Ottoman Turks and 9:1242, 1244, 1246, 1246–1247, 1248
Persians and 6:734, 735, 752
Russia and 9:1203, 1210, 1215
Seljuk Turks and 9:1232, *1234*, 1234, 1240, 1241
Byzantium *see* Constantinople

C

Cahokia 10:1350
Cairo 6:774, 776, 786
Calais 8:1105, 1113
Caledonia 5:584
Cambodia 7:967, 976–977, *978*, 979
Canaan 2:196, 222, 225–226, 229
Cape Bojador 10:1366
Cape of Good Hope 10:*1369*, 1369–1370
Capri 4:518, *519*
Capua 4:460, 466, 473
Carchemish 2:155, 217
Caroline Islands 7:984
Carolingian Empire 6:**804–813**, 817–818, 818–819, 828, 832, 8:1026
Carthage 2:*203*, 5:*653*
Cato the Elder and 4:479
Etruscans and 4:456
Latium and 4:444
Phoenicians and 2:196, 199–200, 222
Punic Wars and 4:464–475, 481
Pyrrhus and 4:462
Roman Empire and 5:588–589
trade and 2:257
Vandals and 5:653, 671, 673
weapons and armor 4:*465*
Castile 8:1016, 1017, 1018, 1107
Castile-León 8:1018
Çatalhüyük 1:14–15, 30
Çayönü 1:14–15
central African kingdoms 9:1276–1277
Central America 1:14, 10:1302
Central Andean region 10:1304, 1305
Central and Southern Plateau region 9:1260
Ceuta 10:1366
Ceylon 7:929, 958, 965, 10:1371
Champagne region 8:1031, *1032*
Chan Chan 10:1311
Chang'an 7:901

Chang Jiang River *see* Yangtze River
Chichén Itzá 10:1309, 1315, 1316, 1317, 1318, *1319*, *1321*
China 7:**870–881**, *872*, **882–893**, **894–905**, 10:*1414*
agriculture in 1:14
Black Death and 8:1084
Bronze Age and 1:33, 35
Buddhism and 7:958, 959
European knowledge of 10:1360
exploration and 10:1420
Indian missionaries and 7:967
Iron Age and 1:41
Japan and 7:915
Ming dynasty and 10:1419, 1421
Mongols and 9:1222, 1223, 1224, 1226
Roman Empire and 5:589
Southeast Asia and 7:975, 978, 980
technology and 10:1365, 1391
trade and 6:776, 10:1371
warfare and 10:1416
Chittor 10:*1418*
Chopán 10:1315
Congo River Basin 9:1256, *1260*, 1260
Constantinople 5:**616–627**, *617*, *619*, *622*, *623*, *625*, 9:*1162*, *1164*, *1179*
Arcadius and 5:666
attacks on 9:1165, 1172
Christianity and 5:632, 6:839, 840
Constantine I and 5:611
crusades and 8:*1068*, 1068, 1082, 9:1168, 1179, 1181, 1187, 1192, *1193*, 1213
early 16th century CE and 10:1418
economy of 9:1160–1161
Germanic peoples and 5:649, 651, 653, 665
Islamic world and 6:762, 763, 10:1360
Moscow and 9:1215
Ottoman Turks and 9:1245, 1246–1247, *1250*
Persians and 6:734
Vikings and 9:1201, 1203, 1210
see also Byzantine Empire
Cook Islands 7:982
Córdoba 6:*770*, 770, *773*, 8:1016, 1017
Corfu 3:368, *370*, 370
Corinth 2:253, 254, 3:*297*, *345*
Corinthian War and 3:382
Peloponnesian War and 3:342, 368, 370
Temple of Apollo and 3:*299*
tyranny and 3:294, 295–296, 298
Corsica 4:469, 470, 5:653, 8:1025
Crete 2:167, 168, 170, 182, 204, 246, 3:310

Crimea 8:1084, 9:1214, 1217, 1228
Croton 3:356–357
Ctesiphon 5:585, *586*, 6:726
Cuba 10:1374
Cusco 10:*1346*
Cuzco 10:1302, 1336, 1340, 1343, *1346*, 1346
Cyprus 2:246, 250, 3:327, 339, 396, 6:763

D

Dacia 5:599, 601, 603
Dahomey 9:1275
Damascus
Assyrians and 2:216
crusades and 9:*1190*, 1190–1191
Islamic world and 6:754, 764, 767
Mongols and 9:1228
Persians and 6:735
trade and 6:776
weaving and 6:781
Damietta 9:1193, 1195
Danelaw 6:820, 9:1198
Danishmend emirate 9:1234, 1241
Daulatabd 7:969
Delhi 9:1229, 1232
Delhi Sultanate 7:963, 968–970, 10:*1418*
Delos 2:164, 167
Delphi 2:234, 3:313, 315, 331
Denmark 8:1097, 1098, 1098–1099, 1100, 9:1199, 1205
Dijon 8:1129
Djenné 9:*1270*, 1272
Dnieper River 9:1202, 1208, *1212*, 1223
Dougga 5:*588*
Dur Sharrukin 2:208, 218

E

east African kingdoms 9:1275–1276
East Anglia 9:1196, 1198
Easter Island 7:982, 985, *986*, 986
Eastern Highland region 9:1260
East Francia 6:813, 828–830
Eboracum 9:1196, 1198
Edessa 9:1188, 1189, 1190, 1191
Egypt 1:**70–77**, **78–91**, **92–109**
Africa and 9:1261, 1266, *1268*, 1268, 1274
Alexander the Great and 3:391, 392, 393
Alexandria and 3:404, 406–407
Assyrians and 2:220
astronomy and 3:354
Ayyubid Empire and 9:1234
Babylon and 1:124
Byzantine Empire and 9:1163, 1165
Christianity and 5:625, 688, 690, 691–692
crusades and 9:1191, 1193, 1195
Cycladic people and 2:167

Fatimid dynasty and 9:1188–1189
Hittites and 2:150, 152, 153
Indus Valley civilization and 7:920
Islam and 6:*745*, 755, 757, 774, 775
Israelites and 2:225, 226–227, 228, 229
Mamluk dynasty and 8:1082, 9:1195, 1236, 1236–1238
Minoans and 2:170, 179
Neolithic period and 1:16
Nile River 5:*587*
Ottoman Turks and 9:1242, 1251–1252, 10:1418
Palmyra and 5:602
Persians and 2:235–236, 238–239, 3:326
Phoenicians and 2:196, 198, 199, 201
Ptolemies and 3:396, 398, 402
Roman Empire and 4:543, 5:582, 586
Rome and 4:496, 497, 498, 503, 508
Sea Peoples and 2:192
Seljuk Turks and 9:1232, 1234
trade and 5:587, 589
writing and 2:204
Elam 1:60, 65–66, 110, 112, 121
Elis 3:373
El Mirador 10:1316
England
Christianity and 8:1025
France and 8:**1044–1057**, 1079
government and 8:1057, 1067, 1094, 1131
Hundred Years' War and 8:1085, 1102–1113, 1126
North America and 10:1378, 1380–1381, 1382, 1383
population growth in 8:1026
pre-Conquest 8:1046–1047
rulers of 6:820, 8:1067, 1076–1078
Vikings and 9:1196, 1198–1199, 1200
Wars of the Roses 8:**1114–1125**
see also Britain
Ephesus 3:303
Eritria 3:327, 329
Eshnunna 1:110, 111
Estonia 8:1101
Europe 6:**814–831**, 8:*1016*, **1026–1043**, *1028*
agriculture in 1:15
Arabic learning and 6:783, 784
Bronze Age and 1:33
Greek literature and 6:783
Iron Age and 1:41, 44–45
Islam and 6:759–762, 793, 9:1230
Japan and 7:917
Mesolithic period and 1:9, 10, 14
Mongols and 9:1227–1228
Neolithic period and 1:18
Ottoman Turks and 9:1242, 1245

raids on 6:814, 816, 819,
822–823, 832
Roman Empire and 5:582, 584
Southeast Asia and 7:980–981
trade and 2:257
see also specific countries
Ezo 7:912

F

Faiyum oasis 1:87
Federated States of Micronesia
7:982
Ferghana 7:895
Fertile Crescent 1:12, 14, 18
see also Mesopotamia
Fiji 7:982
Flanders 8:*1027,* 1102, 1104, 1130,
10:1408
Florence 8:1036, 1085, 1086, 1096,
10:1398, *1399,* 1400, 1402
France
Africa and 9:1275
Avignon popes and 8:1087–1088,
1091
Burgundy and 8:1126–1133
crusades and 9:1182, 1185, 1187
England and 8:**1044–1057,** 1076
exploration and 10:1379–1380
feudal territories of 6:813
Franks and 5:657
government and 8:1057, 1114,
1131
Greek colonies and 2:254
Holy Roman Empire and
6:832
Hundred Years' War and 8:1085,
1102–1113
leagues and alliances and 8:1094
Renaissance and 10:1409
rulers of 8:1066–1067, 1078–
1079, 1081
Southeast Asia and 7:981
Vikings and 9:1199–1200
Wars of the Roses and 8:1117,
1120, 1125
see also Carolingian Empire; West
Francia
Franconia 6:819
Frankfurt 8:1039, *1040*
Funan, kingdom of 7:975

G

Gades 2:196, 200
Gao 9:1271, *1272,* 1272
Gascony 8:1102, 1108
Gaul
Franks and 6:776
Gallic Wars and 4:494–495
Germanic peoples and 5:643,
652, 654, 657
Huns and 5:649–650
monasteries and 5:696
rebellion in 4:529, 531
Roman Empire and 4:496,
520–521, 5:601, 603, 606, 607,
612–613

Rome and 4:459–460, 462
trade and 2:257
Genoa 8:1025, 1036, *1038*
Georgia 9:1228, 1229
Germany
Burgundy and 8:1128, 1129
Carolingian Empire and 6:813
government and 8:1131
leagues and alliances and 8:1094,
1097
Poland and 8:1100
Roman Empire and 4:504, 514,
532, 538, 542, 544
see also East Francia; Holy Roman
Empire
Ghana 9:1269, 1270, 1271
Ghaznavid Empire 9:1232
Ghent 8:1039, 1102, *1105*
Gibraltar 6:759, *760*
Gla 2:182, 191
Gordium 3:390
Gournia 2:177, *178*
Granada 6:770
Great Britain *see* Britain
Great Rift Valley 9:1260, *1264*
Great Zimbabwe 9:*1275,* 1276
Greece
Africa and 9:1266, 1269
Alexander the Great and
3:**384–395**
Bronze Age and 1:33, 40–41,
2:**162–169**
Celtic people and 1:50
Christianity and 5:609
Constantinople and 5:616
cultural influence of 3:404–
413
Cycladic people and 2:167
Dark Age and expansion of
2:**246–257**
drama and 3:**318–325**
Egypt and 1:109, 3:396, 398
great philosophers and
3:**352–367**
Hellenism 3:402–403
Iron Age and 1:44
Julius Caesar and 4:496
Lamian War and 3:401–402
maps of 2:*248–249,* 3:*296, 329,
388, 399*
Mycenaeans and 2:182–192
Peloponnesian War and
3:**368–383**
Pericles, Age of, and 3:**340–351**
Persians and 2:238, 239
Persian Wars and 3:**326–339**
Phoenicians and 2:202
Scythian people and 1:48–49
trade and 1:49
Troy and 2:195
tyranny and democracy in
3:**294–309**
Vandals and 5:653
Visigoths and 5:642, *644*
Greenland 8:1026, 9:1204, 1206
Guangzhou 7:901

H

Haiman 7:896
Hajex region 6:768, 769
Hakata Bay 7:916
Hamburg 8:*1095*
Harappa 7:918, 920–921, *921*
Harran 2:221, 225, 226
Hattushash 2:150, 153, *154,* 154,
155, 159, 161
Hawaiian Islands 7:982, 985
Heijo 7:911–912
Herakleopolis 1:80–81
Herculaneum 4:535, 536
Hispaniola 10:1374, 1375
Holy Roman Empire 6:772,
832–845, *834*
Italy and 8:1022, 1023, 1039
Middle Ages and 8:1094
Philip II Augustus and 8:1055
popes and 8:1058, 1060–1065
rulers of 8:1058, 1060–1065,
1070, 1072–1073
Honshu 7:912
Hungary
Byzantine Empire and 9:1181
Conrad II and 6:837
crusades and 9:1185, 1187, 1192
Mongols and 8:1084, 9:1214,
1227
Ottoman Turks and 9:1245, 1252
Poland and 8:1100
Russia and 9:1213, 1216

I

Iceland 8:1098, 9:1203–1204, *1205*
Il-Khanate 9:1228–1229, 1235–
1236, 1238
Illium 2:195
Illyricum 5:642
India
Aksum and 9:1269
Alexander the Great and 3:394
Bronze Age and 1:33, 40
Buddhism and 7:892, **946–959**
Chinese exploration and 10:1420
colonial period 10:*1364*
European knowledge of 10:1360
first civilizations of 7:**918–931**
Hinduism 7:**932–945**
Islamic world and 6:763, 780,
783–784, 9:1232
Lao-tzu and 7:889
Manichaeism and 6:731
Middle Ages and 7:**960–971**
Mongols and 9:1223
Mughal Empire and 10:1418
Persians and 2:232, 6:726
Portugal and 10:1370, *1371,*
1371
Roman Empire and 5:589
Southeast Asia and 7:975
Tamerlane and 9:1229
trade and 5:587, 6:776
Zoroastrianism and 6:731
Indies 10:1372, 1375
Indochina Peninsula 7:972, 974

Indonesia 7:979, 980, 984, 9:1230
Indus River 3:394, 7:*922,* 928
Intermediate region 10:1304
Iran *see* Persia
Iraq *see* Mesopotamia
Ireland, Vikings and 6:816
Israel
kingdom of 2:*224,* 227, 231
Ottoman Turks and 9:1242
tribes of 2:227
see also Palestine
Istanbul *see* Constantinople
Italian cities 4:485–486, 490
Italy
Byzantine Empire and 6:800,
802, 9:1163, 1165, 1167, 1174,
1178, 1181
Carolingian Empire and 6:813
city-states and 8:1039, 1041
Constantinople and 5:618
culture and 8:1093
Greek colonies and 2:254, *255,*
256
Holy Roman Empire and 6:831,
832, 834–835, 836, 837,
8:1060–1063, 1073
Huns and 5:651
Islamic world and 6:817
Justinian I and 5:673, 675–676
leagues and alliances and 8:1096
Lombards and 6:794–795
Middle Ages and 8:1020, 1022,
1094
monasteries and 5:696
Renaissance and 8:1099, 10:1398,
1400–1404, 1405, 1406–1408
Theodoric the Great and 5:646,
648
trade and 3:296
see also Roman Empire; Rome

J

Jamestown Colony 10:1380–1381,
1382, *1383*
Japan 7:879, 901, **906–917,** *908,*
958–959, 10:*1416,* 1416,
1417
Java 7:*956,* 967, 975, 977, 979
Jericho 1:11, *13,* 13, 30
Jerusalem
Alexander the Great and 3:391
Assyrians and 2:219
Christianity and 5:632, 678
crusades and 6:*823,* 8:1014, 1068,
1069, 9:1182, 1188–1189, 1195
destruction of 4:535
Dome of the Rock 6:768, 769
Frederick II and 8:1073
geography and 10:1360, *1361,*
1368
Israelites and 2:230–231
Judas Maccabaeus and 3:400,
402
medieval maps and 10:1368
military forces of 9:1189–1190
Persians and 6:735

Jerusalem (*continued*)
  Phoenicians and 2:198
  Roman Empire and 4:491, 520,
    529, 541
  Saladin and 9:1191, *1192*
  Seljuk Turks and 9:1234
Judaea 4:508, 520, 529, 533, 538,
  541, 542
Judah, kingdom of 2:231

K

Kalahari Desert 9:1260, 1262
Kalinga 7:929, 930, 958
Kalyani 7:966
Kanem 9:1273–1274
Kanesh 2:150, 208
Kano 9:1272, 1273, 1274
Kausambi 7:927
Kazakhstan 7:874, 895
Kazembe 9:1276
Kephala *see* Knossos
Khan-balik 7:904
Khartoum 9:1266
Khmer state 7:976–977
Khoresm Empire 9:1223, 1234,
  1235
Kiev 9:**1208–1217**
  Hungary and 9:1216
  Mongols and 8:1101, 9:1227
  trade and 9:1208
  Vikings and 9:1201, 1202, 1203
Kievan Rus 9:1201, 1210, 1211
Kiribati 7:982
Kish 1:57
Knossos 2:170, 172, 173, *174*, 174,
  175, 175, 182
Kongo 9:1276
Korean Peninsula 7:896, 901, 906,
  909
Kosovo 8:1082, 9:1245, 1246
Kush *see* Nubia
Kushan India 7:929, 931, 960
Kyrgyzstan 7:874

L

Lagash 1:58, 62
Lake Texcoco 10:1324
Lascaux 1:11, *12*
Lasta 9:1269
Latium 4:443–444, 458, 460, 463
Latvia 8:1101
La Venta 10:1306, 1307
Lebanon 2:196, 5:602
León 8:1016, 1017, 1018
Leptis Magna 5:*593*, 593
Libya 1:106, 107, 109
Lindisfarne 6:*816*, 816, 9:1196,
  1198
Lisbon 10:*1370*, 1371
Lithuania 8:1082, 1084, 1100–1101,
  9:1215, 1216, 1217
Lombardy 8:1061, 1096
London 8:1039, 1117, 1118–1119
Lorraine 6:819, 832, 837
Lothal 7:920
Lotharingia 6:829–830

Low Countries 8:1128–1129
Lower Egypt 1:72
Lu 7:884
Lunda Empire 9:1276–1277
Luxor *see* Thebes
Lycia 4:522
Lydia 3:303, 326, 328, 336, 339

M

Macedonia 3:**384–395**, *388*, 4:476
  after Alexander the Great
    3:396–403
  Macedonian Empire 5:586
  Ottoman Turks and 9:1244
  Persians and 3:326
  Philip II and 3:383
  Phoenicians and 2:207
  Spartan Confederacy and 3:342
Machu Pichu 10:1302, *1342*, 1342
Madeira 10:1366, 1367
Magadha 7:927, 928, 929, 960
Malacca 7:980, *981*, 981
Malay Peninsula 7:975, 977
Mali 9:*1271*, 1271–1272
Manchuria 7:896, 901, 902
Mantinea 3:373
Mantua 8:1096
Maqurrah 9:1238
Mari 1:110, 111, 114, 2:210
Mariana Islands 10:1377
Marquesas Islands 7:982
Marshall Islands 7:982, 984–985
Massachusetts Bay Colony 10:1383
Mauretania 4:483, 522
Mauryan India 7:927–929, 930,
  960, 963, 965
Mayapán 10:1315, 1323
Mecca
  Adb al-Malik and 6:767, 768
  Africa and 9:1271
  Islam and 6:*740*, 749
  Mohammed and 6:736, 746, 747
  pre-Islamic Arabia and 6:738–739
Medina 6:736, 745–746, *747*, 764
Mediterranean Sea 6:779–780, 814,
  817, 8:1019, 9:1163, 1252,
  1253, 1255, 10:1360
Mehrgarh 7:918
Melanesia 7:982, 987
Memphis 1:73, 2:199
Mercia 9:1196, 1198
Meroë 5:*585*, 586, 9:1266, *1269*
Mesoamerican region 10:1304
Mesopotamia
  Aramaeans and 2:212
  Babylonians and 1:110–125,
    110–125
  Byzantine Empire and
    9:1175–1176
  Egypt and 1:72, 99
  Indus Valley civilization and
    7:918, 920
  Islamic world and 6:754, *755*, 768
  metalwork and 1:32
  Mongols and 9:1228, 1235
  Neolithic period and 1:16, 22

Ottoman Turks and 9:1242, 1252
Parthians and 5:584–585
Persians and 6:729
Roman Empire and 4:540,
  5:594–595, 596
Sumerians and 1:54
Tamerlane and 9:1229
Messana 4:464
Messenia 2:258
Micronesia 7:982, 984, 987–988
Milan 8:1061, 1096
Miletus 3:303, 327, 352, 354
Milos 2:167, 169
Minos 2:170, 176
Mitanni, kingdom of 1:99, 101, 120
Mitanni Empire 2:210
Mitla 10:1310
Mohenjo-Daro 7:918, *919*, 920,
  920–921, 923
Mongolia 9:*1221*
Monte Albán 10:1309
Morocco 10:1366
Moscow 9:1215, 1217
Mosul 1:*57*
Mount Vesuvius 4:535, 536
Mughal Empire 7:930, 970, 971,
  10:*1411*, 1414, *1418*, 1418
Muscovy 8:1084, 1101
Mwene Mutapa Empire 9:1276,
  1277
Myanmar 7:*953*, *958*, 958, 967,
  977, 978
Mycenae and Troy 2:**182–195**,
  187

N

Nabatean kingdom 6:736
Nabonidus 1:125, 2:234
Nabu-nasir 1:122, 2:216
Namib Desert 9:1260
Nancy 8:1132
Napata 9:1266
Naples 4:473, 5:675, 8:1019, 1096
Nara 7:917
Nauru 7:982
Navarre 8:1016
Nepal 7:950
Netherlands 10:1371, 1378,
  1409
Neustria 6:791
New Caledonia 7:982, 984
New Carthage 4:474
New England 10:1383
New Guinea 7:982, 984, 985
New Zealand 7:982, 985, 988,
  989, 10:1410
Nicaea 9:1187, 1242
Nicomedia 9:1242, 1244
Nile River 1:70, 78, 86, 5:*587*,
  9:1195, 1260, 1266
Nimrud 2:208, *209*, 213, 215, 216,
  217, *218*
Ninevah 1:122, 2:208, 218,
  219–220, *220*, 221, 232
Normandy 6:826, 8:1044, 1046,
  1113, 9:1200

North America 9:1206–1207,
  10:**1348–1359**, 1379–1381,
  1382, 1383, 1410
northern Europe 8:1025,
  1033–1034, 10:1408–1409
Northern Marianas Islands
  7:982
Northern Plateau region 9:1260
Northumbria 9:1196, 1198
Norway 8:1098, 1098–1099, 1100,
  9:1199, 1204, 1205
Novgorod
  Estonia and 9:1217
  fortifications and 8:*1101*,
    9:*1214*
  government and 9:1211
  Kiev and 9:1213
  Mongols and 8:1101, 9:1214
  Moscow and 9:1215, 1217
  trade and 9:1208
Nubia
  Africa and 9:1266, 1268
  Egypt and 1:77, 83, 87, 89, 92,
    94, 95, 109, 9:*1268*
  pottery and 9:*1262*
  pyramids and 5:*585*, 9:*1269*
  Roman Empire and 5:586, 588

O

Ottoman Empire, map of
  9:*1244*
Oyo 9:1275

P

Pacific islands 7:*984*, 10:1410
Pacific Ocean 10:1377–1378
Pagan kingdom 7:978, *980*
Pakistan 7:874, 966
Palau 7:982
Palenque 10:1315
Palestine
  Byzantine Empire and 9:1181
  crusades and 8:1082, 9:1182,
    1187, 1195
  Egypt and 1:92, 94
  Ottoman Turks and 9:1252
  Palmyra and 5:602
  Philistines and 2:222
  Seleucid dynasty and 3:400
  Seljuk Turks and 9:1234
  Umayyad caliphate and 6:768
Palmero 8:1022
Palmyra 5:*597*, 601, *602*, 603
Pamir 7:901
Pamplona 6:798
Pannonia 5:666, 669
Paris 6:832, 8:1039, 1112, 1113,
  9:1199–1200, *1201*
Parthia 4:496, 513, 529, 540, 544,
  6:728
Pasargadae 2:234, *236*, 3:393
Pataliputra 7:960
Pavia 6:796
Pergamum 3:401, 4:476, 482
Persepolis 2:*240*, 240, *241*, *245*,
  3:*338*, 390, 393

Persia
  Babylon and 1:125
  Byzantine Empire and 9:1165
  Egypt's New Kingdom and
    1:109
  Islam and 6:753, 768, 769, 771
  Islamic world and 9:1232,
    1234, 1238, 1240, 10:1415,
    1418
  Khoresm Empire and 9:1223
  Mongols and 9:1228, 1229,
    1235–1236, 1240
  Ottoman Turks and 9:1252
  Tamerlane and 9:1229
Persian Empire 6:726–735
  Achaemenid dynasty and 6:726
  Byzantine Empire and 6:752
  Islam and 6:751, 754, 755, 757,
    776
  map of 2:235
  taxation and 6:779
Persian Gulf 3:394–395
Persis 6:726, 728
Peru 1:14
Petén region 10:1312
Philae 9:1266
Philippines 7:982, 10:1377
Piraeus 3:349, 370, 371, 372
Pisa 8:1025, 1034, 1036–1037
Pithekoussai 2:256
Plymouth Colony 10:1381, 1383
Pola Island 7:985
Poland 6:835, 836, 8:1084, 1100–
    1101, 9:1213, 1216, 1217, 1227
Polynesia 7:974, 982, 983, 985, 985,
    988
Pompeii 4:449, 531, 535, 536, 537,
    553, 556
Pontus 4:485, 486
Portugal
  Africa and 9:1275, 1276, 1277
  exploration and 8:1093, 10:1362,
    1364, 1366–1367, 1369–1371
  medieval Europe and 8:1020
  Pacific islands and 7:988–989
  pre-Columbian cultures and
    10:1311
  Southeast Asia and 7:981
  Tordesillas, Treaty of, and
    10:1375–1376
  trade and 10:1417, 1418
Pskov 9:1215, 1217
Punt 1:77, 98
Punta Arenas 10:1380
Pylos 2:182, 187, 191

R

Rheims 8:1112
Rhodes 3:396, 4:476, 9:1195, 1195,
    1251, 1252, 1255
Roanoke Island 10:1380
Roman Empire
  Africa and 9:1266, 1269
  barbarians and 5:640–657
  Charlemagne and 6:799, 808
  China and 7:899

Christianity and 5:609, 634, 636,
    687, 695–696
daily life under barbarian rulers
    in 5:658–665
decline of 5:590–603
disintegration of 5:604–615
edges of 5:582–589
Germanic peoples and 1:53
India and 7:931
Islamic world and 6:751
Persians and 6:728, 729, 733,
    734
  see also Byzantine Empire; Holy
    Roman Empire; Rome
Rome
  Augustus, Age of, and 4:504–515
  Aurelian Wall 5:603
  Byzantine Empire and 5:675,
    676
  Celtic people and 1:50, 52
  Christianity and 5:609, 678
  city of 4:508–509
  daily life and 4:548–557
  early history of 4:438–455
  early wars and conquests by
    4:456–463
  end of the republic 4:488–
    503
  expanding the empire 4:532–
    547
  fires in 4:527–528, 535, 548
  Germanic people and 1:53
  Holy Roman Empire and
    6:834–835, 840, 843, 844
  Islamic world and 6:780
  Julio-Claudian emperors and
    4:516–531
  legal system and 5:664
  maps of 4:491, 534
  medieval Europe and 8:1037–
    1039, 1040, 1060–1061
  origins of 4:438
  popes and 8:1088–1089
  Punic Wars and 4:464–475
  Renaissance and 10:1398, 1406
  republic and 4:447–455, 488–
    503
  revolution and reform and
    4:476–487
  Vandals and 5:653
  Visigoths and 5:643, 645
  warfare and 4:456–463
  see also Italy; Roman Empire
Roussillon 6:762
Rum 9:1234, 1241
Russia 8:1101, 9:1175, 1177,
    1208–1217, 1223, 1227–1228
Rwanda 9:1275–1276

S

Sabaea 9:1268–1269
Safavid Empire 10:1414, 1415,
    1418, 1419
Sahara Desert 5:589, 9:1260
Salonika 9:1246
Samaria 2:217, 231

Samarkand 6:763, 7:895, 9:1223,
    1228, 1229
Samarra 6:776, 786, 787
Samoa 7:982, 984
Samos 3:331, 356
San Lorenzo 10:1306–1307
San Salvador 10:1374
Santorini see Thera
Sarai 9:1215, 1228
Sarasvati-Ghaggar river system
    7:923
Sardinia 4:469, 470, 5:653, 8:1019,
    1025
Sardis 2:234, 3:327
Satavahanihara 7:929
Saudi Arabia 6:775
Saxony 6:819, 829, 836, 8:1094
Scandinavia 8:1082, 1098–1100,
    9:1196, 1201, 1205
Scotland 8:1077, 1098
Seleucid Empire 4:476
Serbia 9:1177, 1245
Seville 6:760, 8:1017
Shandong Peninsula 9:1222
Siberia 10:1302, 1304, 1348
Sicily
  Aragon and 8:1019
  Byzantine Empire and 5:673,
    9:1163
  Greece and 2:254, 3:296,
    373–374, 376
  Holy Roman Empire and
    8:1060, 1063, 1064, 1070,
    1072, 1073–1075, 1096
  Innocent III and 8:1065
  medieval Europe and 6:817
  Mongols and 9:1200
  Normans and 8:1023, 1025
  Ottoman Turks and 9:1255
  Punic Wars and 4:467, 468–469,
    470, 473
  Rome and 4:462, 464–465
  Saracens and 8:1020, 1022
  Vandals and 5:653
Silbury Hill 1:28, 31
Sinai Peninsula 1:83
Skara Brae 1:30, 30
Society Islands 7:982
Solomon Islands 7:982
Songhai 9:1272–1273, 10:1418
Sont Strait 8:1097
south African kingdoms 9:1277
South America 5:677, 10:1302,
    1336–1347, 1375–1376, 1377,
    1410, 1419, 1421
Southeast Asia 7:972–981, 974,
    9:1226
Spain
  absolute monarchies and 8:1094
  barbarian invaders and 5:643,
    645, 652, 660
  Byzantine Empire and 5:618,
    676, 9:1163
  Carthage and 4:469, 470–471,
    474
  Charlemagne and 6:798, 801

Charles Martel and 6:792
crusades and 9:1182
Greece and 2:254
Incas and 10:1342, 1347
Islamic Spain 8:1016–1020, 1021,
    1082, 1099
Islamic world and 6:759–760,
    768, 770, 771, 785, 9:1235,
    1238
Phoenicians and 2:196, 200
pre-Columbian cultures and
    10:1311, 1323, 1333, 1334,
    1335
Reconquista and 6:762,
    8:1016–1020, 1082
Rome and 4:482, 488, 493, 496,
    499, 504, 513, 529, 531
smiths in 6:780–781
Southeast Asia and 7:981
Tordesillas, Treaty of, and
    10:1375–1376
weapons and 10:1419, 1421
Sparta
  Athens and 2:258–268, 261,
    3:302, 340, 342, 348
  citizenship and 2:253
  Cleomenes III and 3:403
  colonization and 2:251
  First Persian War and 3:329, 330
  military forces of 2:265
  Peloponnesian War and 3:342,
    344, 368–383
  Persians and 2:239, 3:326
  Plataea, Battle of, and 3:337
  Second Persian War and 3:331,
    334, 336
  Thermopylae, Battle of, and
    3:333
  Troy and 2:182
  tyranny and 3:294
Spice Islands 7:980, 981, 10:1362,
    1363, 1371, 1376, 1377
Spitsbergen Islands 10:1378
Stabiae 4:535, 536
Stonehenge 1:26, 29, 29
Strait of Magellan 10:1377, 1380
Straits of Malacca 7:976
Sumatra 7:967, 975
Sumer 1:62, 123, 2:208, 225
Susa 2:221, 3:390, 393, 395
Swabia 6:819, 829, 8:1094
Sweden 8:1098, 1098–1099, 1100,
    9:1199, 1200–1201, 1203, 1205,
    1217
Switzerland 8:1132
Syracuse 2:254, 254, 3:373–374,
    375, 376, 408, 4:464, 473
Syria
  Aramaeans and 2:212
  Assyrians and 2:215–216, 217,
    219
  Ayyubids and 9:1234
  Babylonians and 1:124
  Byzantine Empire and 9:1165,
    1175–1176
  Christianity and 5:625

Syria (continued)
 Hittites and 2:150, 152, 153
 Islamic world and 6:768
 Jewish people and 3:400
 Mongols and 9:1229, 1236
 Neo-Hittites and 2:155
 Ottoman Turks and 9:1242,
  1252
 Palmyra and 5:602
 Persians and 6:729
 Phoenicians and 2:196
 religious beliefs and 2:159,
  5:596
 Rome and 4:475, 490, 495,
  513, 540
 Seleucid dynasty and 3:399,
  5:586
 Seljuk Turks and 9:1232
 Semitic people and 2:222
 spread of Islam and 6:754, 757

T
Tahiti 7:982, 987, 989
Tamralipti 7:967
Tarentum 3:374, 4:461–462, 463,
 464, 473
Tarunza 2:152
Tell es-Sultan 1:13
Tenochtitlán 10:1324, 1325, 1332,
 1332, 1333, 1416, 1419
Teotihuacán 10:1302, 1303,
 1307–1309, 1308, 1316
Texcoco 10:1324

Thailand
 Ayutthaya dynasty and 7:977
 Bronze Age and 1:33, 35
 Buddhism and 7:954, 958
 Chiang Mai dynasty and 7:977
 early humans and 7:972
 statues 7:947, 976
 Thai people 7:978
Thasos 2:257
Thebes (Egypt) 1:81, 91, 92, 95,
 100, 103, 106, 107, 109
Thebes (Greece) 3:342, 382, 382–
 383
 Macedonia and 3:386, 388
 Mycenaeans and 2:182
Thera 2:167, 168, 168, 169
Thessaloniki 9:1177, 1181,
 1245
Thingvellir 9:1205
Thrace 4:522, 5:649
Thurii 3:349, 4:461
Tiber River 4:448, 508
Tibet 7:901, 959, 963
Tigris River 6:787
Tikal 10:1313, 1315, 1316
Timbuktu 9:1271, 1273
Tirnova 9:1245
Tiryns 2:182, 184, 187, 189
Tlacopán 10:1324
Toledo 8:1016, 1017
Tonga 7:982
Toulouse 8:1025
Tres Zapotes 10:1306, 1307

Tripoli 9:1189, 1255, 1273
Troy 2:182–183, 192–195, 195,
 4:438
Tuamotu Archipelago 7:982
Tula 10:1309
Tunisia 5:588
Turkestan 6:763, 776, 7:901
Turkey 6:775
Tuvalu 7:982
Tyre 2:196, 197–198, 200, 204, 206,
 3:391
Tzintzuntzan 10:1310

U
Ugarit 2:196, 206, 252
Ujjain 7:927
Ukraine 9:1210
Upper Egypt 1:72
Ur 1:57–58, 114, 2:225
Urartu 2:216, 217
Uruk 1:54, 57, 62, 65, 123
Uru-Salem see Jerusalem
Uxmal 10:1315, 1317

V
Valencia 8:1021
Valley of the Kings 1:95–96, 96,
 97
Venice
 Byzantine Empire and 8:1082,
  9:1181
 Fourth Crusade and 8:1068,
  9:1192

Middle Ages and 8:1096
Ottoman Turks and 9:1245,
 1246
Polo, Marco, and 8:1098, 9:1225,
 10:1363
Renaissance and 10:1406–1407
spice trade and 10:1362–1363
Venus 4:537
Vermandois 8:1054
Vienna 9:1216, 1252
Vietnam 7:896, 901, 972, 974, 975,
 977, 977–978, 980
Vijayanagar, kingdom of 7:971
Vinland 9:1207
Volga River 9:1203, 1208

W
Wadai 9:1273, 1274
Wagadou see Ghana
Wales 8:1077
Wessex 6:820, 9:1196, 1198
west African kingdoms
 9:1274–1275
West Francia 6:813, 828

Y
Yagul 10:1310
Yangtze River 7:878, 878
Yathrib see Medina
Yellow River 7:878, 898
Yemen 9:1269
Yenking 9:1222
Yin 7:873, 876

GOVERNMENT AND POLITICS

Page numbers in *italics* refer to illustrations. Page numbers in **bold** refer to entire chapters.

A

Abbasid caliphate 6:772–773
absolute monarchies 8:1057, 1072, 1094, 1114, 10:1416
Africa 9:1259, 1270, 1272
Akkadian Empire 1:61
alliances
 Achaean League 3:403
 Athens and 3:340
 Corinthian League 3:385
 Delian League 3:341, 342, 368, 370
 Peloponnesian League 3:368, 370, 373
 Peloponnesian War and 3:368
 Rome and 4:458, 463
 Spartan Confederacy 3:342
 see also foederati (allies); leagues and alliances
anarchy, democracy and 3:347–348
archons 2:266, 269, 3:320, 344, 344–345
aristocracy
 Burgundy and 8:1128
 Carolingian dynasty and 6:795, 804, 811, 826–827
 Charlemagne and 6:808, 810
 Charles Martel and 6:793
 China and 7:875, 877, 879
 Confucianism and 7:885
 democracy and 3:304
 England and 8:1048–1049
 France and 8:1079
 Greece and 3:296, 298, 299, 300–301
 India and 7:924, 925
 Japan and 7:911
 luxury goods and 8:1033
 Merovingian dynasty and 6:788, 790–791
 Middle Ages and 8:1094, 1131
 Salian dynasty and 6:837, 843, 844, 844–845
 social classes and 6:822
 tyranny and 3:294, 295
 see also nobility
Aristotle 3:367
assemblies of the three orders 8:1131

Assyrians 2:213, 217
Athens 2:266, 267, 269, 3:298, 300–302, 304, 306–309, 344–348, 378–380
Aztecs 10:1326, 1334

B

bailiffs, Philip II Augustus and 8:1057
barbarian invaders 5:658, 660
Bedouin nomads 6:738
Burgundy 8:1128, 1129
Byzantine Empire 9:1163–1164, 1167, 1174, 1175

C

caliphs
 Abu al-Abbas 6:769, 771
 Abu Bakr 6:751, 752
 Adb al-Malik 6:767–768
 Ali 6:756–757
 Córdoba and 6:770
 Harun al-Rashid 6:787
 Mahdi, Al- 6:787
 Mamun, Al- 6:787
 Mansur, Al- 6:771–772
 Mu'awiyah 6:757
 Mu'tasim, Al- 6:786
 Mutawakkil, Al- 6:*786*
 Omar bin Khattab 6:752, 754
 Shi'ite Muslims and 6:773, 758, 774
 Sunni Muslims and 6:758
 Walid, Al- 6:768
calpullis (administrative units) 10:1327
Canuleian Law 4:451
capitularies, Charlemagne and 6:810
charters, cities and 8:1034, 1039, 1041
Chibcha people 10:1310
China 7:875, 877, 879, 893, **894–905**
cities and towns 6:822, 8:1034, 1036–1037, 1039, 1041, 1094, 1096, 1131
citizenship
 Athens and 2:266, 269, 3:307–308, 308–309, 346, 350
 Christians and 4:530
 Constantinople and 9:1161
 Greek poleis and 2:253
 Italian cities and 4:485, 486, 490

medieval Europe and 8:1041, 10:1397
 military forces and 4:512
 Rome and 4:460, 463, 499, 508, 522, 5:595
 Sparta and 2:258, 260, 260–261, 262, 3:403
civil servants 1:100, 4:476, 479, 8:1063
civil service exams 7:887, 893, 894–895, 901, 911
client system 4:447
communes 8:1034, 1036–1039, 1060
 see also cities and towns
concilium plebis (council of the plebians) 4:451, 455, 480
Confucianism 7:882, 884, 885–886, 887, 890, 891, 893
Constantine 5:612
Constantinople 5:619, 624
constitutions 2:262–263, 3:304, 344, 7:910
consuls 4:448, 453, 458, 474, 492, 493, 504, 8:1036
Corinthian League 3:385
corruption
 caliphate and 6:764
 England and 8:1116
 government 4:476, 479, 491–492, 9:1163, 1164, 1166
Council of 500 3:304, 306, 307–308, 344
counts, Carolingian Empire and 6:808, 810, 811, 812–813

D

deification, Roman emperors and 4:511, 520, *523*, 525, 535, 537, 538, 540, 544, 5:608
delatores (informers) 4:518–519, 537
Delian League 3:341, 342, 368, 370
democracy, Greece and 3:304, 306–309, 344, 346–348, 378–379, 380
development of states 10:1414
diadochs 3:396, 398, 399, 401
dictators, Rome and 4:453–454, 461–462, 472, 487, 498–500
Diet of Besançon 8:1061
Diet of Würzburg 6:844
divisions, Roman Empire and 5:607–608, 613–614, 615, 616, 632, 666

Domesday Book 8:1026, 1050
dominium mundi (sovereignty over the world) 8:1064, 1067, 1075, 1081
dukedoms 6:819, 828–830, 837
duma (council) 9:1211
dynastic succession *see* succession
dynasties, Egyptian 1:76, 82, 89, 92

E

ecclesia (public assembly) *see* public assembly
Edict of Milan 5:611, 628, 635
Egypt 1:73, 77, 83, 86, 87, 89, 3:398
 Middle Kingdom 1:86, 87, 89
 New Kingdom 1:94, 97, 99
 Old Kingdom 1:77
elections 3:306, 4:448, 449, 450, 9:1218, 1224
emperors
 Charlemagne 6:799–800, 802–803
 China and 7:870, 877, 895–897, 897–898, 902
 Henry II of Germany 6:835
 Japan and 7:908, 909, 910–911, 912, 916–917
 Otto II and 6:832
 Otto III and 6:834
 Otto the Great and 6:831
 popes and 6:839, 841–842, 843–844, 843–845, 8:1058–1069
 see also kings
emperors, Byzantine
 Anastasius I 5:625, *627*, 627, 669
 Arcadius 5:641, 642, 666, 668
 Constantius II 5:612–613, 625, 630, 631, 633
 Hippodrome and 5:622, 624
 Jovian 5:613, 634
 Justin 5:669, 674
 Justinian I 5:639, 654, **666–677**, *667*, *673*
 Leo I 5:626, 653, 669
 Theodosius II 5:618, 649, 666, 668, *680*
 Valens 5:614, 620, 630, 631, 640, 643
 Zeno 5:*626*, 626, 645–646, 647, 653, 669
emperors, Roman
 Alexander, Severus 5:597–598
 Antoninus Pius 4:543–544

emperors, Roman (*continued*)
  Augustus Caesar **4:504–515,** *505, 506, 508*
  Byzantine Empire and 9:1158
  Caligula 4:516, 519–521
  Caracalla 5:595–596
  Claudius I 4:516, 521–524
  Commodus 5:590, 592
  Constantine 5:610–612, *611*
  Domitian 4:535–538
  Galba, Sulpicius 4:529, 532, *535*
  Gaul and 5:601
  Gratian 5:614–615, 634, 636, 643
  Hadrian 4:*533*, 540, 542–543
  Julian the Apostate 5:612–613, 632, 633, *636*, 654
  Julius Caesar 4:488, *489*, 492, 493–496, *494*, 497, 498–501
  Macrinus, Marcus Opellius 5:596
  Marcus Aurelius 4:544–546
  Maximinus 5:598
  Nero 4:516, *517*, 524–525, 527–529, 531
  Nerva, Marcus Cocceius 4:538
  purchase of the emperorship 5:592
  Severus, Septimius 5:592–595
  soldier emperors 5:599, 601
  tetrarchy and 5:607–608, 610–611
  Tiberius 4:516–519
  Titus 4:535
  Trajan 4:538–540
  Vespasian 4:533–535
  Vitellus, Aulus 4:532–533
empires and unions 10:1356, 1418–1419, 1421
England 8:1049, 1052, 1057, 1067, 1076, 1077–1078, 1094, 1119, 1131
  parliament 8:1076, 1077, 1108, 1118, 1131
  rulers of 6:820, 8:1067, 1076–1078
equestrians 4:481, 488, 507, 542, 543, 5:594, 596, 601
Estates General 8:1079, 1105, 1107, 1131, 1132
Etruscans 4:445
Europe 10:1384, 1393, 1396, 1397

F

family law 1:113
feudal Europe 6:814–831

feudalism
  Carolingian Empire and 6:808
  China and 7:882, 900
  cities and towns and 8:1034, 1041
  crusades and 9:1182
  daily life and 6:823
  England and 8:1048–1049
  Franks and 6:793
  Hittites and 2:155–156
  Holy Roman Empire and 6:831, 8:1058, 1060, 1063
  leagues and alliances and 8:1094
  Peasants' Revolt and 8:1109
  Philip II Augustus and 8:1054, 1057
  primogeniture and 6:828
  religion and 6:823–824, 825
  rise of 6:819, 821
  Roman Catholic Church and 8:1014, 1061
  social classes and 6:821–822
  warfare and 6:822–823
finances, Roman Empire and 5:592, 595–596, 603, 604
fines, Germanic peoples and 5:662, 664
fiscal problems, Philip IV (Philip the Fair) and 8:1079
foederati (allies) 5:588, 643, 645, 652, 654, 660
foreign relations
  Amarna Letters and 1:101, 103–104
  Babylonians and 1:110
  Egypt and 1:72, 77, 98, 99
  Mycenaeans and 2:191
  Phoenicians and 2:199
  France 8:1044, 1057, 1078, 1079, 1114, 1131
  leagues and alliances and 8:1094
  rulers of 8:1066–1067, 1078–1079, 1081

G

general assembly, Charlemagne and 6:807–808
Germany 8:1094, 1097, 1131
governors, provincial 4:507–508, 546
Great Swabian League 8:1094
Great Yasa 9:1220
Greece 2:249, 251, 253, 262–263, **3:294–309, 340–351**

H

hereditary rule, tyranny and 3:294–295
Hittites 2:155, 158
Holy Roman Empire 8:1061, 1063, 1072
Hundred Years' War 8:1105, 1107

I

Iceland 9:1204
Illyrian emperors 5:601, 603, 606–607
imperial dynasties, China **7:894–905**
imperial orb and sword, German 6:*833*, 835
imperial provinces, Roman 4:507–508
Incas 10:1339–1340, 1343, 1346
India 7:928, 931
investiture controversy 6:839, 841–842, 843–844, 845, 8:1058, 1064

J

Japan 7:910, 910–911, 914, 917

K

kingdoms
  Africa and 9:1263, 1266–1277
  India and 7:927, 963, 965–966
  Southeast Asia and 7:975–976
  Spain and 8:1016, 1017, 1018–1019
kings
  Assyrians and 2:215
  China and 7:875, 890
  early Rome and 4:440–442
  feudal Europe and 6:821, 826–827
  Francia and 8:1044
  Germanic tribes and 5:582, 660
  Greece and 2:253, 258, 262, 263
  Hekau-chasut (desert kings) 1:89–90
  Hittites and 2:155, 157, 159, 160
  Israelites and 2:230
  Julius Caesar and 4:500
  Minoans and 2:173, 174, 175
  Mycenaeans and 2:188, 189
  Phoenicians and 2:197
  pre-Columbian cultures and 10:1326, 1340, 1340–1341, 1343, 1344
  Rome and 4:444, 446, 458
  Sumerian people and 1:56–57
  see also emperors, Byzantine; emperors, Roman

L

land reforms 4:479–481
law enforcement, Incas and 10:1347
laws *see* legal systems
Laws of Manu 7:939–940
Laws of the Twelve Tables 4:453
leaders, North American peoples and 10:1355, 1356
League of the Iroquois 10:1356
leagues and alliances 8:1094–1101

legalism, philosophy of 7:877, 879, 881, 891, 893
legal systems
  Africa and 9:1272, 1273
  Assyrians and 2:212
  Athens and 2:267, 269
  Byzantine Empire and 5:674, 9:1163–1164, 1165–1166, 1174
  China and 7:877, 898, 901
  Christianity and 5:635
  Christians and 4:530
  cities and towns and 8:1034, 1041
  Code of Hammurabi 1:111–117
  comitia centuriata and 4:450
  education and 10:1384
  Egyptian 1:105
  England and 8:1049, 1052
  feudal Europe and 6:820, 8:1031
  France and 8:1078
  Germanic peoples and 5:660, 662, 664–665
  Greece and 2:253, 261–262, 3:294, 298, 301, 364–365, 380
  Hittites and 2:161
  India and 7:928
  Islamic world and 6:761, 766
  Justinian I and 5:676–677, *677*
  Mongols and 9:1220
  morality laws 4:510
  Ottoman Turks and 9:1249, 1250, 1255
  Persians and 2:238, 239
  plebians and 4:451, 452, 452–454, 455
  Pompey and 4:496
  quaestors and 4:451
  reform movements and 4:481
  Roman Empire and 4:518–519
  Russia and 9:1211, 1212
  Severus, Septimius, and 5:594
  Stoicism and 4:557
  Sumerian 1:63, 111
  Verres, trial of, and 4:491–492
Licinian-Sextian Laws 4:452–455
Lombard League 8:1062, 1070
Lycurgan Constitution 2:262–263

M

Machiavelli, Niccolò 10:1396
magistrates 4:450, 451, 452, 546
Magna Carta 8:1067, 1076
major domus (chief official) 5:660
major palatii (mayor of the palace) *see* mayors, Merovingian dynasty and

Maya 10:1312, 1314, 1315
Mayflower Compact 10:1381, 1383
mayors, Merovingian dynasty and 6:790–791
Middle Ages
leagues and alliances during 8:1094–1101
popes and emperors during 8:1058–1069
rulers of the 13th century CE 8:1070–1081
Mohammed 6:747–748
Mongols 9:1218, 1220, 1222, 1224, 1238, 1240
Mycenaeans 2:189

N
nation-states, development of 10:1414
nobility
Athens and 2:266, 269
Aztecs and 10:1324, 1326, 1327, 1331, 1332
civil strife and 4:486–487
clothing and 10:1344–1345
Greek poleis and 2:249, 251, 253
Incas and 10:1340, 1344
Kiev and 9:1213
landownership and 4:476
Minoans and 2:175
North American peoples and 10:1358
political power of 4:488
reform movements and 4:479, 481, 482
senate, Roman, and 4:455
Vikings and 9:1205
see also aristocracy; kings; patricians
nomarchs (provincial governors) 1:77, 78, 80, 83
North American peoples 10:1353, 1355

O
oaths of allegiance 6:808, 810, 819, 821, 842
oligarchy 3:298, 348, 378–380, 8:1036–1037
ostracism, Athens and 3:306, 342
Ottoman Turks 9:1245, 1249, 1250, 1255

P
Pacific islands 7:987
Paderborn, diet at 6:797, 798
Papal States 8:1064, 1065, 1072, 1096
parliament, English 8:1076, 1077, 1108, 1118, 1131
patricians 4:446, 446–447, 448, 449, 452
Peace of Anatolius 5:649
Peace of Antalcidas 3:382

Peace of Nicias 3:373, 378
peace treaties 4:469, 474–475, 478, 513
Peloponnesian League 3:368, 370, 373
Pericles, Age of 3:340–351
Persians 2:236, 238, 245
pharaohs
afterlife and 1:85
Egypt's Middle Kingdom 1:78, 80, 83, 89, 91
Egypt's New Kingdom 1:99, 100
Egypt's Old Kingdom 1:73, 74
literature and 1:88
Philip II Augustus, development of France and 8:1044, 1052, 1054–1055, 1057
Phoenicians 2:197
phylae (governmental divisions) 3:306, 307
Plato 3:367
plebians
Clodius, Publius Pulcher, and 4:494
concilium plebis (council of the plebians) 4:451, 455, 480
Domitian and 4:536–537
early republic and 4:450–451
early Rome and 4:446, 446–447
legal system and 4:452–455
political power of 4:488
senate and 4:449
political intrigue, Louis XI and 8:1130
political power
barbarian invaders and 5:660
Buddhist monasteries and 7:955
Byzantine Empire and 9:1158
Carolingian Empire and 6:826–827
conquered people and 4:463
democracy and 3:304
development of states and 10:1415–1416
English parliament and 8:1108
Inquisition and 8:1019–1020
Japan and 7:909, 913–914
Machiavelli, Niccolò, and 10:1396
mandalas and 7:975–976
Merovingian dynasty and 6:788, 790–791
Mongol China and 9:1224
pre-Columbian cultures and 10:1323, 1326
religious beliefs and 10:1415
Roman Catholic Church and 6:824–825, 835, 8:1058, 1061, 1064, 1075, 1081, 1086, 9:1170, 1191
Roman emperors and 4:493, 496, 504, 506, 515, 517, 522

Rome and 4:450–451, 458, 488
social classes and 4:446–455, 488
trade guilds and 4:550
western schism and 8:1089
popes and emperors 8:1058–1069
postal service, Persians and 2:245
praetors 4:453, 470
see also consuls
Prince, The (Machiavelli) 10:1396, 1397
princeps (first citizen) 4:506
see also emperors, Roman
provinces 4:470, 507–508, 546
Provisions of Oxford 8:1076
prytane system (government administration) 3:307–308
public assembly
Athens and 2:267, 269, 3:304, 306–307, 308–309, 344, 345, 380
early Rome and 4:449–550, 451–452
Sparta and 2:262–263
see also senate, Roman

Q
quipucamayoc (imperial administrators) 10:1341, 1343

R
reform movements, Roman republic and 4:479–481, 481–482, 490
regencies
Han dynasty and 7:896–897, 898–899
Macedonian Empire and 3:396
Nero and 4:524–525
Renaissance 8:1099
republic, Roman 4:447–455, 488–503
revolution and reform, Rome and 4:476–487
rhetoric 3:345, 361, 362, 411–412, 4:557
Rome 4:458, 8:1037–1039, 1060
early government of 4:440–442, 444, 446
republic and 4:447–455, 488–503
revolution and reform and 4:476–487
see also emperors, Roman; senate, Roman
rulers of the 13th century CE 8:1070–1081
ruling classes
Bronze Age and 1:38
Celtic people and 1:50, 52
Egypt and 1:73, 78, 80, 81

Hallstatt culture and 1:48
Scythians and 1:51
Sumerians and 1:56–57
Russia 9:1211, 1215, 1217

S
second triumvirate 4:502–503
Seljuk Turks 9:1241
senate, Roman
Christianity and 5:634, 636
civil strife and 4:486
Curia 4:455
decline of Rome and 5:590, 598
early republic and 4:448, 449
early Rome and 4:440
emperors and 4:496, 498, 500–501, 504, 506–507, 517, 522, 531, 533–534, 535–536, 538–539, 544
first triumvirate and 4:495
kings and 4:444, 446
military forces and 4:493
plebians and 4:454–455
reform movements and 4:480–481, 482
Samnites and 4:460
succession of Roman leadership and 4:532
Southeast Asia 7:975–976
Sparta 2:253, 261–263
Spartan Confederacy 3:342
speechmaking, North American peoples and 10:1355
spending, government 4:516–517, 520, 531, 532–533, 534, 539, 5:595
succession
Antonine emperors and 4:538
Byzantine Empire and 5:624, 669, 6:763, 9:1158
caliphs and 6:755–756, 756–757, 758, 764, 771, 772
Capetian dynasty and 6:827, 827–828
Carolingian Empire and 6:803, 811, 812–813, 817–818
Chinese dynasties and 7:875, 896–899
Holy Roman Empire and 8:1058
Hundred Years' War and 8:1102–1113
Julio-Claudian emperors and 4:516, 517–518, 519, 521
Mamluk dynasty and 9:1237–1238
Merovingian dynasty and 6:788
Mongols and 9:1218, 1227
political leadership and 10:1340, 1415–1416
Roman leadership and 4:515, 532, 543, 5:590, 595, 598, 599, 603, 610–611, 612

succession (*continued*)
  Russia and **9:**1212–1213
  Wars of the Roses and **8:1114–1125**

T
Taoism **7:**888
taxation
  Assyrians and **2:**216, 217
  barbarian invaders and **5:**658
  Byzantine Empire and **5:**608, 612, 676, **9:**1161, 1164, 1170, 1175
  China and **7:**877, 879, 894, 895, 896, 897, 901–902, 904
  cities and towns and **8:**1034, 1039
  Egypt and **1:**77, 86, 105
  England and **8:**1050, 1056, 1067, 1109, 1116
  France and **8:**1079, 1081
  Greece and **3:**301
  Hittites and **2:**158
  Holy Roman Empire and **8:**1072
  Incas and **10:**1341
  India and **7:**928
  Islamic world and **6:**746, 759, 768
  Japan and **7:**911, 913
  Kievan Rus and **9:**1211
  Mongols and **9:**1220, 1222, 1226
  Ottoman Turks and **9:**1249, 1250
  Persians and **2:**238, 245, **6:**735
  Roman Empire and **4:**508, 525, 534, 546, **5:**595, 596, 604
  Rome and **4:**476, 479, 534
tax collectors **5:**604
Teotihuacán **10:**1308
tetrarchy **5:**607–608, 610
theocracy, Tibet and **7:**959
Theodoric the Great **5:**646, 648
Tibet **7:**959
tribal councils, Germanic peoples and **5:**660
tribunes **4:**451, 480, 506
tyranny and democracy **3:294–309**
tyrants **2:**253, **3:**326, 327, 345, 367, 378–380, 403, **4:**442

V
viziers (chief ministers) **1:**77, 78, 94, 99
voting **3:**306, **10:**1355

PEOPLE

Page numbers in *italics* refer to picture captions. Page numbers in **bold** refer to main articles.

A

Abbas **6**:769
Abd ar-Rahman **6**:770, 771, 798
Abd ar-Rahman III **6**:770
Abderrahman **6**:743–744
Abdul Aziz ibn Saud **6**:775
Abelard, Peter **8**:1040, **10**:1384
Abraham **2**:225–226, *226*, **5**:*679*, **6**:742, 748, 749
Abu al-Abbas **6**:769, 770, 771, 785
Abu Bakr **6**:743, *750*, 751, 752, 758
Abu-Lu'lu'ah **6**:755
Abu Muslim **6**:769, 771
Abu Talib **6**:740, 744
Adad-nirari I **2**:210
Adad-nirari II **2**:212
Adalbero **6**:827
Adam **5**:*685*, 685, **6**:742
Adb-Allah **6**:739–740
Adb al-Malik **6**:767–768, 769
Adelaide **6**:834
Adeodatus **5**:682
Adhemar of Le Puy **9**:1184, 1187
Adrian I **6**:796
Adrian II **9**:1177
Aelfgifu **8**:*1047*
Aeschines **3**:383
Aeschylus **3**:318, 322, 322–323, 349
Aethelred I **6**:820
Aethelred the Unready **6**:816, **8**:*1046*, **9**:1198–1199
Aethelstan **8**:*1046*, 1046
Aethelwulf **6**:820
Aetius, Flavius **5**:650, 651
Agaja **9**:1275
Agamemnon **2**:182, 183, 194
Agesilaus II **3**:*381*, 381–382
Agnes of Meran **8**:1067
Agrippa **4**:503, 515
Agrippina **4**:523–524, *525*, 525
Agum II **1**:120
Ahenobarbus, Domitius **4**:524
Ahiram **2**:207
Ahmad Baba **9**:1273
Ahmose I **1**:91, 92, 94–95
Ahuitzotl **10**:1334
Aidan **6**:816
Aisha **6**:756
Ajax **2**:*251*
Akhenaton **1**:92, *100*, 101, *102*, 102–103, 103–104
Akhtal, Al- **6**:766
Akhthoes **1**:80
Alaric I **5**:*641*, 641–643, *644*, 660, 666
Alaric II **5**:645, 657

Ala-ud-Din Bahman Shah **7**:971
Ala-ud-Din Khalji **7**:970
Albert of Mecklenburg **8**:1099
Albinus, Clodius **5**:592–593, 594
Albrecht of Bavaria **10**:1408
Alcibiades **3**:*373*, 373–374, *374*, 376
Alcuin **6**:804, *806*, 806, 807
Alexander III **8**:1061–1062, 1062–1063
Alexander IV **3**:396
Alexander VI **10**:1375
Alexander Nevsky **8**:*1101*, 1101, **9**:1214, 1217
Alexander the Great **3**:**384–395**, 396
   in artworks **3**:*385, 389, 390, 391, 394*
   Chaeronea, Battle of, and **3**:383
   Egypt and **1**:109, **4**:497
   Hellenism and **3**:402
   India and **7**:928
   Persepolis and **2**:240
   Persians and **2**:232, 239, 240, 241, **6**:731
   Phoenicians and **2**:207
Alexius III **8**:1068
Alexius IV **8**:1068
Alexius V **8**:1068
Alexius Comnenus **9**:1179, 1181, 1182, *1185*, 1185, 1187
Alfonso I **8**:*1015*, 1020
Alfonso III **8**:1020
Alfonso VI **8**:1017, 1021
Alfred the Great **6**:816, *820*, 820, **9**:1198
Ali **6**:*741*, 743, 756, 758, 769
Ali Dunamami **9**:1274
Ali Gaji **9**:1274
Alp Arslan **9**:1179, 1232
Alypius **5**:695
Ambedkar, Bhimrao Ramji **7**:959
Ambrose **5**:636, *638*, 683, *684*
Amenemhet I **1**:82–83
Amenemhet II **1**:87
Amenemhet III **1**:87, 89, *90*
Amenhotep I **1**:95
Amenhotep II **1**:99
Amenhotep III **1**:99, 101
Amenhotep IV *see* Akhenaton
Amin, Al- **6**:772
Amulius **4**:438
Amyitis **1**:125
Amyntas **3**:386
Anastasius (patriarch) **9**:1166
Anastasius I **5**:625, *627*, 627, 669, **9**:1162
Anaxagoras **3**:348, 356, *358*, 362
Anaximander **3**:354
Anaximenes **3**:354–355, *355*
Anchises **4**:*442, 513*
Ancus Marcius **4**:440–441, 442

Andrew Bogolyubsky **9**:1211
Andriscus **4**:478
Anittas **2**:150
Ankhesenaten **1**:104
Anna **9**:1203, 1212
Anthemius of Tralles **5**:672
Anthony of Egypt **5**:688, *690*, 690, 691, 692
Antigonus Gonatas **3**:*397*, 399, 401–402
Antigonus Monophthalmos **3**:398
Antinous **4**:543
Antioch III **4**:475, 476
Antiochus I **3**:401
Antiochus III **5**:586
Antipater **3**:388, 401
Antisthenes **3**:366
Antoninus Pius **4**:543–544, *544*
Aper **5**:606
Apophis **1**:92
Appius Claudius **4**:462
Aratus of Sicyon **3**:403
Arcadius **5**:641, 642, 666, 668, **9**:1158
Archidamus II **3**:370
Archilochus **2**:257
Archimedes **3**:408, *410*, **4**:473, **6**:782, **10**:1390
Ardashir I **6**:726, 727, 730
Arduin of Ivrea **6**:835
Ariadne **5**:626, 669, **9**:1162
Aristarchus of Samos **3**:409
Aristides **3**:341
Aristogeiton **3**:*305*, 305
Aristophanes **3**:325, 364, 349, *378*, 378
Aristotle **3**:*353*, 367, 367, **10**:*1388*, 1389, 1391, 1404
   Alexander the Great and **3**:384
   Ibn Sina and **6**:783
   Mamun, Al-, and **6**:782
   preserving knowledge of **5**:661
   Sophists and **3**:361, 412
   Thales of Miletus and **3**:354
Arius **5**:624, 629, 629–630, 631, **6**:788
Arminius **4**:514
Arnold of Brescia **8**:1038, 1039, 1040
Arnulf **6**:818
Árpád **6**:*818*
Arsaces **5**:585
Artabanus V **6**:726
Artaphernes **3**:327
Artaxerxes **3**:390
Artevelde, Jacob van **8**:1102, 1104
Arthur **5**:*663,* 663
Arthur of Brittany **8**:1054
Artorius **5**:663
Ascanius **4**:438

Ashoka **7**:928–929, 930, 958, 960, 963
Ashurbanipal **2**:220–221, *221*
Ashurnasirpal II **2**:212–213
Ashur-uballit I **2**:210
Ashur-uballit II **2**:221
Askia Muhammad I **9**:*1272*, 1272, 1273
Askold **9**:1201, 1210
Asser **6**:820
Astyages **2**:233–234
Atahuallpa **10**:1347
Ataulf **5**:643
Athanasius of Alexandria **5**:629, 630, 688, 690, 691, 695–696
Atreus **2**:188
Attila **5**:649–651, *650, 652*
Augustine **5**:633, 680, 682–685, *684, 686*, 686, 687, 696, **9**:*1166*
Augustus Caesar **4**:**504–515**, *505, 506, 508*, **5**:582, 586, 588
Aulus Hirtius **4**:502
Aurelian **5**:601, 602, 603, *606*
Aurelius Carus **5**:606
Aureolus **5**:601
Averroës **6**:783
Avicenna *see* Ibn Sina
Avidius Cassius **4**:544, 545–546
Axayacatl **10**:1334
Aya **1**:104, 105

B

Babak **6**:726
Babur **7**:970, *971*, **9**:1229, 1232, **10**:*1411*, 1418
Bahram I **6**:733
Bahram V **6**:734
Baldwin I (Constantinople) **9**:1192
Baldwin I (Jerusalem) **9**:1188, 1189
Baldwin II (Constantinople) **9**:1192–1193
Baldwin of Flanders **8**:1068
Baldwin Iron-Arm **6**:809
Bardiya **2**:236
Barents, Willem **10**:1378
Bar Kochba **4**:541, 542
Barocci, Federico **4**:*513*
Basil (father of Basil of Caesare) **5**:695
Basil I **6**:817, **9**:1173–1174
Basil II **9**:*1176*, 1176, 1178, 1203, 1210, 1212
Basiliscus **5**:626
Basil of Caesarea **5**:692, 692–695, *694*
Bassianus *see* Elagabalus

Batu Khan **9**:1214, *1215*, 1227, 1228

Baybars I **6**:775, **8**:1082

Bayezid I **9**:1245–1246, *1247*, 1248

Bayezid II **9**:1249

Beaufort, Margaret **8**:1125

Becket, Thomas **8**:*1053*, 1053

Béhanzin **9**:1275

Bela IV **9**:1227

Belisarius **5**:654, 670, 671, 673, 675, *676*, **9**:1163, 1164

Belshazzar **1**:125

Benedict VII **6**:835

Benedict VIII **8**:1023

Benedict IX **6**:837

Benedict XI **8**:1087

Benedict XIII **8**:*1091*, 1091, 1092

Benedict of Nursia **5**:688, 697, *699*, 699–701, *701*, **6**:*824*, 825, 826, **8**:1035

Berengar II **6**:*830*

Berno **6**:826

Bessarion, Basilius **10**:*1390*, 1390–1391

Bilal **6**:743

Bimbisara **7**:927

Bindusara **7**:928

Bingham, Hiram **10**:1342

Bismarck, Otto von **6**:845

Blanche of Castile **8**:1078

Bleda **5**:649

Bocchoris **1**:109

Bocchus I **4**:483

Boethius **5**:661, **6**:820

Bohemond of Taranto **9**:1187, 1188

Boleslav I **6**:835

Boniface **6**:794, 797

Boniface VIII **8**:*1081*, 1081, 1087

Bonifacius **5**:652

Boris I **9**:1177

Boris II **9**:1177

Botticelli, Sandro **10**:1403

Boudicca **4**:528–529, *530*

Bougainville, Louis-Antoine de **7**:989

Bourdin, Maurice **6**:844

Brackenbury, Robert **8**:1124

Bramante, Donato **10**:1406

Brancacci, Felice **10**:1403

Britannicus **4**:524, 525

Brunelleschi, Filippo **10**:*1399*, 1401, 1404

Bruno of Cologne **8**:1035

Brutus, Lucius Junius **4**:442

Brutus, Marcus Junius **4**:*498*, 500–501, 502

Bubnov, Alexander **9**:*1216*

Buckingham, duke of **8**:1124, 1125

Buddha **7**:*911*, 942, **946–959**, *947*, *952*, *956*, *958*

 Great Renunciation **7**:*949*, 949
 life of **7**:948, 949, 950

Mahayana Buddhism and **7**:956–957

 teachings of **7**:950–954

Bukka Raya I **7**:971

Buridan, Jean **10**:1391

Burrus, Afranius **4**:524, 525, 527

Byron, John **7**:989

C

Cabot, John **10**:1378

Cabral, Pedro Álvares **10**:1375, *1377*

Cadamosto, Alvise **10**:1367

Caesarion **4**:497, 498, 503

Cagnacci, Guido **4**:*501*

Caligula **4**:516, 519–521, *520*, *521*

Calixtus **6**:844

Callias **3**:342

Callixus **5**:682

Cambyses I **1**:109, **2**:233

Cambyses II **2**:235–236, 244, **3**:309, 326

Camphausen, Wilhelm **6**:*844*

Cano, Juan Sebastian del **10**:1377, 1379

Canute *see* Cnut

Cão, Diogo **10**:1369

Capac Yupanqui **10**:1339

Capelianus **5**:598

Caracalla **5**:593, 595–596

Caractacus **4**:522

Caretena **5**:656

Carinus **5**:606, 607

Carl of Durazzo **8**:1091

Carloman (son of Charles Martel) **6**:794

Carloman (son of Louis the Stammerer) **6**:818

Carloman (son of Pépin I) **6**:795, 796

Carnarvon, Lord **1**:104

Carter, Howard **1**:104, *105*

Carteret, Philip **7**:989

Cartier, Jacques **10**:1379–1380

Cassander **3**:401

Cassian, John **5**:696

Cassiodorus **5**:*661*, 661

Cassius **4**:500–501, 502

Castagno, Andrea de **10**:1401

Catilina, Lucius Sergius **4**:492, *493*

Cato the Elder **4**:458, 479, 492, 498, 499

Cato the Younger **4**:557

Caxton, William **10**:1394

Celestine III **8**:1065

Cetshwayo **9**:1277

Chandragupta I **7**:960

Chandragupta II **7**:960

Chandragupta Maurya **7**:928

Charlemagne **6**:*772*, 795–799, *796*, *800*, *802*, 802–803, *806*, *808*, *810*

 Abbasid caliphate and **6**:772
 Byzantine Empire and **9**:1170, 1171

Carolingian dynasty and **6**:791

Carolingian Empire and **6**:804

chanson de geste (song of heroic deeds) and **6**:801

 government of **6**:807–808, 810–811

 iconoclasm and **6**:811

 intellectual pursuits and **6**:806

 Italy and **8**:1020

 reliquary of **6**:*789*

 Roman Empire and **6**:836

 throne of **6**:*807*

 Vikings and **6**:809, **9**:1199

Charles II (Alençon) **8**:1106

Charles II (Navarre) **8**:1107

Charles IV (France) **6**:827, **8**:1102

Charles IV (Holy Roman emperor) **8**:*1110*

Charles V (France) **8**:1107, 1108, *1110*, 1126

Charles V (Holy Roman emperor) **8**:1133, **9**:1253

Charles V (Spain) **10**:1376, 1377

Charles VI (France) **8**:1108, 1110, 1126

Charles VII (France) **8**:1110, 1112, 1113, 1114, 1126, 1128

Charles Martel **6**:760, 761, 768, 791, 792–793, *794*, *795*, 804

Charles of Anjou **8**:*1074*, 1074–1075

Charles of Lorraine **6**:827

Charles the Bald **6**:812, *813*, 813, 814, *815*, 821, **8**:1044

Charles the Bold of Burgundy **8**:1120, 1129–1132, *1130*

Charles the Fat **6**:818, *819*, **9**:1200

Charles the Simple **6**:818, 818–819, 827, **8**:1046, **9**:1200

Chaucer, Geoffrey **10**:1394

Cheng Ho **10**:*1420*, 1420

Cheops **1**:74

Childeric I **5**:654

Childeric III **6**:794

Choerilus **3**:321

Chrysippus **3**:413

Chu Hsi **7**:887

Cicero, Marcus Tullius **3**:335, **4**:491–492, *492*, 494–495, 501, 502, **5**:683

Cimon **3**:341, 341–342

Cinna **4**:486

Claudius, Appius Pulcher **4**:480

Claudius I **4**:516, 521–524, *522*, *523*

Claudius II **5**:601

Cleanthes **3**:413

Cleisthenes **3**:304, 309

Clement II **6**:837, *841*

Clement III **6**:843, **8**:1063

Clement V **8**:1080, 1081, 1087–1088

Clement VII **8**:1089

Cleomenes III **3**:403

Cleon **3**:371, 373, 378

Cleopatra **4**:*497*, 497, 498, *499*, *501*, 503, **5**:586

Clodia Pulchra **4**:510

Clodius, Publius Pulcher **4**:494–495, 496, 549

Clotilda **5**:654, *656*, 656

Clovis I **5**:645, *646*, 654, *655*, 656, 657, *659*, **6**:788, *791*

Cnut **6**:816, **8**:1046, *1047*, **9**:1199, *1200*

Cnut IV of Denmark **8**:1066

Colonna, Sciarra **8**: *1081*, 1081

Columbus, Christopher **10**:1372, *1373*, 1374–1375, 1395, 1397

Commodus **4**:546, **5**:590, 592

Commodus, Lucius Ceonius **4**:543

Confucius **7**:877, 882, *883*, *884*, 884–886, *886*, 889, 894

Conrad II **6**:836, *839*

Conrad III **9**:1190

Conrad IV **8**:1073

Conradin **8**:1073, 1074

Conrad of Franconia **6**:828–829

Conrad of Hohenstaufen **8**:1058

Constance of Sicily **8**:1063

Constans I **5**:632–633

Constantine I **5**:610–612, *611*, 629, *630*, *632*, **9**:*1161*

 Arianism and **5**:625
 baptism and **5**:680
 Christianity and **5**:628
 Constantinople and **5**:616
 Nicaea, Council of, and **5**:628–630, *631*
 popes and **6**:800, 802
 Roman Empire and **9**:1158

Constantine IV **6**:762

Constantine V **6**:811, **9**:1168

Constantine VI **9**:1168, 1170

Constantine VII **9**:1174–1175, *1175*

Constantine VIII **9**:1176, 1178

Constantine IX **9**:1178

Constantine XI **9**:1181, 1247

Constantius **5**:607, 610

Constantius II **5**:612–613, 625, 630, 631, 633

Cook, James **7**:986, 987, 989

Copernicus, Nicolaus **3**:*410*

Corbulo **4**:529

Corneille, Pierre **8**:1021

Cortés, Hernán **10**:1333, 1334, *1335*, 1335, 1419

Crassus, Marcus Licinius **4**:490, 493–494, 496, **6**:728

Croesus **2**:234, 244, **3**:*328*, 328

Cubells, Salvador Martínez **6**:*761*

Cyaxares **2**:232

Cypselus **3**:294, 296, 297

Cyrus **1**:125

Cyrus the Great **2**:207, 233–234, *236*, *238*, **3**:326, 328

D

Daia, Maximinus **5**:610, 611
Dalai Lama **7**:*959, 959*
Damasus I **5**:697
Damon **3**:348
Dampier, William **7**:989
Daniel **5**:695
Daniel Nevsky **9**:1215
Däniken, Erich von **7**:986
Dante Alighieri **10**:1394
Darius I **2**:236, 238–239, **3**:305, *332, 393,* **6**:726
  Behistun Inscription and **2**:243
  death of **3**:330
  Ionian rebellion and **3**:329
  military forces of **2**:237
  Persepolis and **2**:240
  warfare and **3**:326
Darius III **2**:239, 241, **3**:*389,* 390–391, 393–394, 395
David **2**:230, 231
Davis, John **10**:1378
Decebalus **4**:538, 539
Decius **5**:*599,* 599, 601
Deioces **2**:232
Demaratus **3**:329, **4**:441
Demetrius Poliorcetes **3**:398
Democritus **3**:317, 361
Demosthenes **3**:371, *382,* 383, 386, 401
Dengizich **5**:651
Desiderius **6**:796
Devi **7**:930
Diagoras of Melos **3**:317, 352
Dias, Bartolomeu **10**:1369–1370
Dingane **9**:1277
Diocletian **5**:606–608, *607,* 610, *611,* 628, **9**:1158
Diodorus **1**:46
Diodorus Siculus **2**:206
Diogenes **3**:*353, 365, 366,* 366
Dionysius of Halicarnassus **4**:456
Dir **9**:1201, 1210
Djefai-Hapi **1**:85
Djoser **1**:73, 75
Dmitry Donskoy **9**:1215
Domitian **4**:535–538, *538,* **5**:678
Domna, Julia **5**:593, 595, 596, 597
Donatello **10**:1401
Drusus **4**:518
Drusus, Marcus Livius **4**:485
Drusus, Nero Claudius **4**:514
Duilius **4**:467
Dürer, Albrecht **10**:*1408,* 1408–1409

E

Edmund Langley **8**:1114, 1116
Edmund of Rutland **8**:1118
Edward (Black Prince) **8**:1105, 1107

Edward I **8**:*1076,* 1076, 1077–1078, 1081
Edward III **8**:1033, *1034*
  Bretigny, Treaty of, and **8**:1107, 1108
  Crécy, Battle of, and **8**:1106
  Hundred Years' War and **8**:1102, 1104, 1105
  Richard III and **8**:1125
  Wars of the Roses and **8**:1114, 1116
Edward IV **8**:1117, 1118, 1119–1222
Edward V **8**:1123, 1124
Edward of Lancaster **8**:1118, 1119, 1122
Edward the Confessor **6**:816, **8**:1046–1047, *1048*
Edward the Elder **6**:816, 820
Einhard **6**:798, 802, 803, 806–807, *808*
Elagabalus **5**:*595,* 596, *596*–597
El Bekri **9**:1270
El Cid **8**:*1021,* 1021
Eleanor of Aquitaine **8**:1049, 1052, *1054,* 1054, 1056
Eliezer **2**:225
Elizabeth I **10**:1380, 1387
Elizabeth of York **8**:1125
Ellac **5**:651
Emmelia **5**:695
Enheduanna **1**:61
Enmebaragesi **1**:57
Epaminondas **3**:382, 383
Epicurus **3**:412–413, *413*
Erasistratus **3**:411
Erasmus, Desiderius **10**:1397
Eratosthenes **3**:380
Eratosthenes of Cyrene **3**:410
Eric II of Norway **8**:1098
Eric of Pomerania **8**:1099–1100
Erigena, John Scotus **6**:820
Eriksson, Leif **9**:1206, *1207,* 1207
Erik the Red **9**:1206
Ertugrul **9**:1242
Esarhaddon **1**:109, **2**:220
Esau **2**:226
Es Saheli **9**:1271
Este, Beatrice d' **10**:1404
Euclid **3**:407, *408,* **10**:1390
Eudoxia (wife of Arcadius) **5**:666, 668
Eudoxia (wife of Valentinian III) **5**:653
Eugenius **5**:615, *635*
Eugenius III **8**:1037–1038, *1039,* 1040, **9**:1190
Eugenius IV **8**:1093
Eunomius **5**:695
Euric **5**:645
Euripides **3**:324–325, *325,* 349, 356, 378
Eusebius **5**:629–630
Eusebius of Nicomedia **5**:630
Eustochium **5**:697

Eutropius **5**:666, 668
Evans, Arthur **2**:170, 172, 174, 179
Ezana **9**:1266, 1269

F

Fabius, Quintus Maximus Verrucosus **4**:472
Fatima **6**:751, 756, 758
Ferdinand I (Aragon) **8**:*1020*
Ferdinand I (Austria) **9**:1252
Ferdinand I (Castile) **8**:1016–1017, 1021
Ferdinand II (Aragon) **8**:1019, 1133
Ferdinand II (Spain) **10**:1372, 1374, *1376*
Ferdinand III (Castile) **8**:*1019*
Fernández de Quirós, Pedro **7**:988
Ficino, Marsilio **10**:1401
Firdawsi **6**:732
Firuz II **6**:734
Flaminius, Gaius **4**:471
Florus **4**:556
Fra Angelico **10**:1401
Francis I of France **10**:1379, 1409
Francis of Assisi **5**:*693,* **8**:1042, *1042*
Francis Xavier **7**:917
Frederick I (Barbarossa) **8**:1039, 1040, 1058, *1059,* 1060–1064, *1061,* **9**:1192
Frederick II **8**:1064–1065, 1069, 1070, 1072–1073, 1078, 1096, **9**:1191, 1193, 1195
Frederick III **8**:1094, 1130–1131, 1132, **9**:1216
Frobisher, Martin **10**:1378
Fu Hao **7**:876

G

Gainas **5**:668
Gaiseric **5**:652, 653, 654
Gaius (son of Agrippa) **4**:515
Galahad **5**:*663*
Galaup, Jean-François de **7**:986
Galba, Sulpicius **4**:529, 532, *535*
Galen **10**:1390
Galerius **5**:607, 610, 611
Galla Placidia **5**:643
Gallienus **5**:601, 602
Gama, Vasco da **10**:1370, *1371*
Gandhi, Mohandas **7**:923
Gaozu (Li Yuan) **7**:901
Gaumata **2**:236, 243
Gelasius II **6**:844
Gelimer **5**:671, 673
Gemellus, Tiberius **4**:519
Genghis Khan **6**:775, **7**:*905,* **9**:1218, *1219,* 1220–1224, *1222*
  Islamic world and **9**:1235
  Japan and **7**:916
  Kiev and **9**:1214
  Polo, Marco, and **9**:1225
  Song dynasty and **7**:904
Geoffrey II **8**:1054

Geoffrey Plantagenet **8**:1051
George of Clarence **8**:1120, 1122–1123
Germanicus **4**:518
Germanos I **6**:761
Germanus I **9**:1166
Geta **5**:595
Gézo **9**:1275
Ghazan Khan **9**:1229, 1238
Ghiberti, Lorenzo **10**:1401
Ghiyath-al-Din Tughluq **7**:970
Giordano, Luca **4**:*529*
Giorgione **10**:1406
Giotto **10**:1402
Go-Daigo **7**:916
Godfrey of Bouillon **9**:*1187,* 1187, 1188, 1189
Godigisel **5**:652
Godwin, Earl **8**:1047
Gonçalves, Nuño **10**:*1366*
Gordian I **5**:598
Gordian II **5**:598
Gordian III **5**:598, 599
Gorgias **3**:362
Go-Sanjo **7**:913
Gozzoli, Benozzo **10**:1401
Gracchus, Gaius Sempronius **4**:*479,* 480, 481–482, 549
Gracchus, Tiberius Sempronius **4**:479–481
Gratian **5**:614–615, 634, 636, 643
Gregory I **6**:820
Gregory II **6**:761, 800, **9**:1167
Gregory III **6**:800, **9**:1167
Gregory IV **6**:812
Gregory V **6**:834
Gregory VI **6**:837, 839
Gregory VII **6**:838, 839, 841–843, *842,* **8**:1058, 1086
Gregory VIII **6**:844, 845, **9**:1192
Gregory IX **8**:*1073,* 1073, **9**:1193
Gregory XI **8**:1088–1089, *1089*
Gregory XII **8**:1092
Gregory XIII **10**:1408
Gregory of Nazianzus **5**:695, 696–697
Gregory of Tours **5**:657
Grey, Thomas **8**:1123
Gudea **1**:62–63, *64,* 64
Guesclin, Bertrand du **8**:1107, 1108
Gunderic **5**:652
Gundobad **5**:652
Gutenberg, Johannes **10**:1391, *1392,* 1392
Guthrum **9**:1198
Guy de Lusignan **9**:1191
Gylippus **3**:376

H

Haakon VI **8**:1099
Hadewig **8**:1044
Hadrian **4**:*533,* 540, 541, 542–543, **5**:585
Hadrian IV **8**:1039, 1040, 1060, 1061
Hakim, Al- **6**:775

Halfdan **9**:1196, 1198
Hamilcar Barca **4**:468, 469
Hammurabi **1**:62, 110–111, 114, 120, **2**:210
Han Fei **7**:891, 893
Hannibal **4**:*469*, 469, 470–475, 478
Hanno **2**:201–202, 205
Harald Finehair **9**:1204
Harald Hardrada **8**:1047–1048
Hardecnut **8**:1046
Harihara Raya I **7**:971
Harmodius **3**:*305*, 305
Harold Bluetooth **6**:816
Harold of Wessex **8**:1047
Harsa of Kanauj **7**:963
Harun al-Rashid **6**:*771*, 772, *772*, 781, 787
Hasdrubal (brother-in-law of Hannibal) **4**:469
Hasdrubal (brother of Hannibal) **4**:473, 474
Hassan ben Ali **6**:751, *756*, 757, 764
Hastings, William **8**:1123, 1125
Hatshepsut **1**:92, 96, 98, 99
Hattusilis I **2**:150, 154
Hattusilis III **2**:153
Hekanakhte **1**:86
Henry I (Capetian dynasty) **6**:827–828, *828*
Henry I (England) **8**:1049, 1051
Henry I (Germany) **9**:1176
Henry I (Henry the Fowler) **6**:*829*, 829, 832
Henry II (Bavaria) **6**:832
Henry II (England) **8**:1049, 1051, *1052*, 1052, 1053, 1056
Henry II (Germany) **6**:835–836, *837*
Henry III (England) **8**:1067, 1076
Henry III (Holy Roman emperor) **6**:837, 839, *841*
Henry IV (England) **8**:1108
Henry IV (Holy Roman emperor) **6**:839, 841–843, *843*, *844*
Henry V (England) **8**:1110, 1111, 1114, 1126
Henry V (Holy Roman emperor) **6**:843–845, *845*, **8**:1051, 1058
Henry VI (England) **8**:1110, 1113, 1114, 1116–1117, 1118, 1119, 1120, 1121, 1122, 1125
Henry VI (Holy Roman emperor) **8**:1056, 1063, 1064, *1065*
Henry VII (England) **8**:1124, 1125, **10**:1378
Henry VIII (England) **8**:1124, **10**:1397, 1409
Henry of Germany **8**:1070
Henry the Lion **8**:*1063*, 1063
Henry the Navigator **8**:1093, **10**:1364, *1366*, 1366–1367, 1369, 1370
Hephaestion **3**:393, *394*
Heraclitus **3**:355, 362

Heraclius **6**:735, 752, **9**:*1163*, 1165
Herihor **1**:107
Herjolfsson, Bjarni **9**:1206
Herodotus **3**:*335*, 335, **4**:445
  Croesus and **3**:328
  First Persian War and **3**:330
  Greece and **3**:298, 299, 300–301, 349
  Medes and **2**:232
  Persians and **2**:236, 244, 245, **3**:331
  Phoenicians and **2**:201, 202
Herod the Great **1**:13
Hero of Alexandria **3**:408, *409*, **10**:1390
Herophilus **3**:411
Hesiod **2**:256, *257*, **3**:313
Hiero **4**:464, *464*–465, 473
Hildebrand of Soana *see* Gregory VII
Hipparchus **3**:305
Hippias **3**:301–302, 304, 305, 329
Hippocrates **3**:352, 410–411, **10**:1390
Hippodamas **3**:349
Hiram **2**:199, 231
Holbein, Hans **10**:1409
Homer **2**:182, 193, 194, 256, **3**:313, **4**:557, **6**:732
Hong-wu (Zhu Yuanzhang) **7**:905
Honorius **5**:640–641, 642, 643, 666, **9**:1158
Honorius III **8**:1072, 1073
Horace **4**:510, *511*, 511, 557
Horatius **4**:456
Horemheb **1**:104, 105
Hormizd II **6**:733
Huascar **10**:1347
Huayna Capac **10**:*1339*, 1339, 1347
Hugh Capet **6**:827, **8**:1044
Hugh Magnus **6**:827
Hugh of Vermandois **9**:1185
Hugh the Great **8**:1044
Hui **7**:890
Hulagu Khan **6**:*775*, 775, **9**:1222, 1228, 1228–1229, 1235–1236
Hunneric **5**:653
Hunyadi, János **9**:1246
Hus, Jan **8**:*1090*, 1090
Husayn ibn Al **6**:775
Hussein **6**:751, *757*, 757, 767
Hussein, Muzahim Mahmoud **2**:219
Hypatia **5**:*639*, 639
Hypatius **5**:671, **9**:1164

Ibbi-Sin **1**:65–66
Ibn Battuta **9**:1271–1272
Ibn Hisham **6**:739
Ibn Ishaq **6**:739

Ibn Ruhd **6**:783
Ibn Sina **6**:*783*, 783
Idris Alooma **9**:1274
Igor **9**:1203, 1210
Imhotep **1**:73, 75
Ingebord **8**:1066, 1067
Ingres, Jean-Auguste-Dominique **8**:*1113*
Innocent II **8**:1040, 1058
Innocent III **8**:1025, 1039, 1042, *1064*, 1064, 1065–1067, 1068, 1069, **9**:1191, 1192, 1194
Innocent IV **8**:1078
Irenaeus **5**:678
Irene **6**:802, 811, **9**:1168, *1170*, 1170
Irnerius **10**:1384
Isaac **2**:226, **6**:748
Isabella of Angoulême **8**:1054
Isabella of Hainault **8**:1054, 1066
Isabella of Jerusalem **8**:1073
Isabella of Spain **8**:1019, 1133, **10**:1372, 1374
Ishmael **2**:225, 226, **6**:742, 748
Ishme-Dagan I **2**:210
Ishtupilum **1**:*119*
Isidorus of Miletus **5**:672
Ismael I **9**:1240, **10**:1418
Ivan I **9**:1215
Ivan III (the Great) **8**:1101, **9**:1215, 1217, *1217*, 1217
Ivan IV (the Terrible) **9**:1217
Ivar the Boneless **9**:1196, 1198

J
Jacob **2**:226–227
Jacoba of Bavaria **8**:1128
Jacques **10**:*1421*
Jadwiga **8**:1100
Jagiello **8**:1100
Jalal-ud-Din Firuz **7**:970
Jatavarman Sundara Pandyan **7**:966
Jayavarman IV **7**:979
Jayavarman VII **7**:*979*, 979
Jerome **5**:696–697, *698*
Jesus Christ **4**:530, **5**:*681*, **6**:748, 749
Jimmu **7**:908, *910*
Joanna (Juana) of Castile **8**:1133
Joan of Arc **8**:1110, 1112–1113, *1113*
John I (Portugal) **10**:1364
John I Tzimisces **6**:832, **9**:1175–1176, 1177
John II (France) **8**:1105, 1107
John II (Portugal) **10**:1369, 1372, *1375*
John V **9**:1244, 1245
John VI **9**:1244
John XV **6**:834
John XIX **6**:836
John XXII **8**:1092
John Chrysostom **5**:668

John Comnenus **9**:1181
John of Bohemia **8**:1106
John of England **8**:1054, 1055, 1056, 1067, *1069*, 1076
John of Gaunt **8**:1109, 1114
John Sigismund **9**:1252
John the Fearless **8**:1108, 1110, 1126, *1129*
Josephus Flavius **4**:*521*
Joshua **2**:227, 229
Jovian **5**:613, 634
Judas Maccabaeus **3**:400, *402*
Judith **6**:812
Julia (daughter of Augustus Caesar) **4**:*510*, 510, 511, 515
Julia (daughter of Julius Caesar) **4**:493–494, 496
Julian the Apostate **5**:612–613, 632, 633, *636*, 654
Julianus, Didius **5**:592
Julius II **10**:*1400*, *1404*, 1406
Julius Caesar **1**:46, **4**:488, *489*, 492, 493–496, *494*, 497, 498–501
Julius Civilis **4**:535
Julius Vindex **4**:529
Junayad **7**:968
Justin (emperor) **5**:669, 674
Justin (saint) **5**:681
Justinian I **5**:639, 654, **666–677**, *667*, *673*, **6**:735, **9**:1163–1164, 1165
Juvenal **4**:548

K
Kalidasa **7**:961, 963
Kamil, Al- **9**:1195
Kammu **7**:912
Kamose **1**:91, 92
Kanishka **7**:931
Kavadh I **5**:670, **6**:734
Khadijah **6**:741, 743, 744, 756
Kharavela **7**:929
Khayr al-Din **9**:*1253*, 1253
Khizr Khan **7**:970
Khosrow I **5**:670–671, **6**:726, *734*, 734–735
Khosrow II **6**:*735*, 735, 752
Khwarizmi, Mohammed ibn Musa al- **6**:783, 784
Köckert, Julius **6**:*772*
Kongolo **9**:1276
Kotoku **7**:910
Kremer, Gerhard **10**:1368
Krum **9**:1171, 1177
Kubja Vishnuvardhana **7**:966
Kublai Khan **7**:904, 916, **9**:1224, *1226*, 1226–1227
Kujula Kadphises **7**:931

L
Labarnas *see* Hattusilis I
Langton, Stephen **8**:1067
Lao-tzu **7**:877, 886, *888*, 888, *889*, 889, 890
Lars Porsena **4**:456, *459*

Lasso, Orlando di **10**:1407, 1408
Layard, Austen Henry **2**:208, 213
Leah **2**:226, 227
Le Maire, Jakob **7**:989
Leo I (emperor) **5**:626, 653, 669
Leo I (pope) **5**:625, 651, 653, **9**:1163
Leo II (emperor) **5**:669
Leo III (emperor) **6**:761, 763, 800, 811, **9**:1165–1166, 1168
Leo III (pope) **6**:802, 802–803, 811, **9**:1170
Leo IV (emperor) **9**:1168
Leo IV (pope) **8**:1022
Leo V (emperor) **9**:1171
Leo VI (emperor) **9**:1174
Leo IX (pope) **6**:838, 840
Leonardo da Vinci **8**:1096, **10**:1403, 1404, 1405, 1405, 1406
Leonidas **2**:264, **3**:333
Leopold III **8**:1096
Leopold of Austria **8**:1056
Leotychides **3**:336, 339
Lepidus **4**:502, 503
Leucippus **3**:361
Licinius **5**:611, 628
Lionel of Clarence **8**:1114, 1116
Li Si **7**:891, 893
Liu Bang **7**:881, 893, 894
Livia **4**:509, 510
Livy **4**:438, 510, 524
Li Yuan see Gaozu
Lodhi, Bahlul Khan **7**:970
Lothair I **6**:805, 806, 812, 813, **8**:1128, 1129
Lothair II (emperor) **8**:1058
Lothair III of Saxony **6**:845
Lothair of France **6**:827, 832
Louis (son of Louis the Stammerer) **6**:818
Louis I de Valois **8**:1108, 1126
Louis II (emperor) **8**:1022
Louis II (Hungary) **9**:1252
Louis II de Nevers **8**:1106
Louis IV (the Overseas) **6**:827
Louis V **6**:827
Louis VII **8**:1052, **9**:1190
Louis VIII **8**:1078
Louis IX **8**:1071, 1078, **9**:1195, 1222, 1236
Louis XI **8**:1114, 1130, 1131, 1131
Louis of Bavaria **8**:1092, 1094
Louis the Child **6**:828
Louis the German **6**:812, 812, 813
Louis the Pious **6**:802, 803, 811–812, 813
Louis the Stammerer **6**:818
Lucullus, Lucius **4**:489, 490
Lugalzaggisi **1**:58–59
Luther, Martin **10**:1393, 1395, 1415
Lycurgus **2**:262, 263

Lysander **3**:378, 379, 379
Lysias **3**:380, 380
Lysimachus **3**:399

M
Machiavelli, Niccolò **10**:1396, 1396, 1397
Macrinus, Marcus Opellius **5**:596
Madhva **7**:964
Magellan, Ferdinand **7**:988, 988, **10**:1376–1377, 1379, 1421
Magnus IV **8**:1098
Magnus Erickson **8**:1098, 1099
Mahabalipuram **7**:965
Mahavira **7**:927, 931, 948
Mahdi, Al- **6**:787
Mahendra **7**:958
Mahendravarman I **7**:965
Mahmud **9**:1232
Mahmud II **9**:1255
Mahmud of Ghazna **6**:732, **7**:968, 968
Mahudel, Nicholas **1**:45
Maiano, Benedetto da **8**:1020
Makeda **9**:1268
Malik Shah **9**:1232
Mamun, Al- **6**:772, 782, 787
Manco Capac **10**:1337, 1347
Manetho **1**:78
Manfred of Sicily **8**:1073, 1074, 1074
Mangu Khan **7**:904, **9**:1223–1224, 1228
Mani **5**:682, **6**:730–731, 731, 733
Mansa Maghan **9**:1272
Mansa Musa **9**:1271, 1272
Mansa Süleyman **9**:1272
Mansur, Al- **6**:771–772, 785, 787
Manu **7**:940–941
Manuel Comnenus **9**:1181
Manutius, Aldus **10**:1393
Marcel, Étienne **8**:1105, 1107, 1108
Marcian **5**:651, 666, 669
Marcus Antonius **4**:489, 490
Marcus Aurelius **4**:484, 543, 544–546, 545, 546, 557, **5**:590, 593
Marcus Aurelius (Caracalla) see Caracalla
Mardonius **3**:336, 337
Margaret of Anjou **8**:1114, 1116, 1116, 1117, 1119, 1120, 1122
Margaret of Denmark **8**:1098–1099
Margaret of Flanders **8**:1126
Mari Jata see Sundiata Keita
Marius, Gaius **4**:483, 483, 484, 485, 486
Mark Antony **4**:497, 500, 501, 502–503, 503, 510
Martin IV **8**:1078
Martin V **8**:1092–1093, 1093, **10**:1406
Martin of Tours **5**:696, 697
Marwan II **6**:769

Mary of Burgundy **8**:1131, 1132–1133, 1133
Masaccio, Tommaso **10**:1401, 1403–1404
Masolino **10**:1403
Masudi, Al- **6**:781
Matilda **8**:1049, 1051, 1051, 1063
Matthias Corvinus **9**:1216
Maurice **9**:1165
Mauricius **6**:735
Maxentius **5**:611, 628
Maximian **5**:607, 610
Maximilian I **8**:1131, 1132–1133
Maximinus **5**:598
Maximus, Magnus **5**:614, 615
Medici, Cosimo de' **10**:1401
Medici, Lorenzo de' **8**:1096, **10**:1396, 1401, 1403
Mehmed I **9**:1246
Mehmed II **9**:1246, 1247, 1249, 1250
Menander **3**:325, 407, 407, **4**:557
Mencius **7**:887, 890, 891
Mendaña, Álvaro de **7**:988
Menelik I **9**:1269
Menkaure **1**:71
Mentuhotep II **1**:81, 82, 82
Mentuhotep III **1**:82
Mercator **10**:1368
Merneptah **1**:106, **2**:225, 229
Merodach-baladan **1**:122
Merodach-baladan II **2**:217, 218–219
Messalina **4**:523
Metellus, Caecilius **4**:483
Metellus, Quintus Caecilius **4**:478
Metellus Pius **4**:488
Michael I **6**:803, **9**:1171, 1172
Michael II **9**:1171–1172
Michael III **9**:1173, 1177
Michael IV **9**:1178
Michael V **9**:1178
Michael VII **9**:1179
Michael VIII **9**:1181, 1193
Michael Cerularius **6**:840
Michael Paleologus **8**:1068
Michelangelo **8**:1096, **10**:1402, 1403, 1404, 1406
Michelozzo **10**:1401
Mihirakula **7**:962–963
Milos **2**:167, 169
Miltiades **3**:330
Mimar Sinan **9**:1255
Minamoto Yoritomo **7**:914, 916
Mirandola, Pico della **10**:1401, 403
Mithridates VI **4**:485, 486, 487, 488–489, 490
Mohammad ibn Tughluq **7**:969, 971
Mohammed **6**:736–751, 737, 741, 746, 750, 764, 769
Mohammed Shah **9**:1223
Mohesh **9**:1277
Molay, Jacques de **8**:1080

Monteverdi, Claudio **10**:1407, 1407
Montezuma I **10**:1334
Montezuma II **10**:1334, 1335
Montfort, Simon de **8**:1025, 1076, 1077
More, Anthony **10**:1381
More, Thomas **8**:1124, **10**:1397
Moses **2**:228, 228, 229, **3**:297, **6**:748, 749
Mpande **9**:1277
Mstislav **9**:1211
Mu'awiyah **6**:756–757, 758, 764, 776
Muhammad of Ghur **7**:968, 970
Murad I **9**:1245, 1245, 1246, 1255
Murad II **9**:1246, 1249
Murasaki Shikibu **7**:913
Mursilis I **1**:120, **2**:150, 152
Mursilis II **2**:152–153
Mustansir, Al- **6**:775
Mu'tasim, Al- **6**:786
Mutawakkil, Al- **6**:786
Muwatallis **2**:153
Mzilikazi Kumalo **9**:1277

N
Nabis **3**:403
Nabonidus **1**:125, **2**:234
Nabu-nasir **1**:122, **2**:216
Naram-Sin **1**:60–61, 61–62, 63
Narasimhavarman I **7**:965
Narmer **1**:73
Narses **5**:675, 676
Nawfal, Waraqah ibn **6**:741
Nebuchadnezzar I **1**:121
Nebuchadnezzar II **1**:124, **2**:231
Necho **2**:201
Nefertiti **1**:103
Nero **4**:516, 517, 524–525, 527, 527–529, 531, **5**:678
Nero, Gaius Claudius **4**:474
Nero, Tiberius Claudius **4**:510
Nerva, Marcus Cocceius **4**:538
Nestorius **5**:678, 680, **6**:734, **9**:1163
Neville, Anne **8**:1120
Neville, Richard (earl of Salisbury) **8**:1116, 1117, 1118
Neville, Richard (earl of Warwick) **8**:1116, 1117, 1118, 1119–1122, 1122
Nicephorus I **9**:1170–1171
Nicephorus Phocas **9**:1175
Nicholas of Cusa **10**:1398
Nicias **3**:373, 374, 376
Nogaret, Guillaume de **8**:1081
Numa Pompilius **4**:440, 446, 549
Numerian **5**:606
Nur ad-Din **9**:1191

O
Oba Ozolua **9**:1274–1275
Octavia **4**:527
Octavian **4**:497, 499, 501–502, 503
Octavius, Marcus **4**:480

Odoacer **5**:646, *647*, 647, **9**:1163
Odo of Aquitaine **6**:761, 792
Odo of Cluny **6**:826
Odo of France **6**:827
Odo of Metz **6**:807
Ogotai **9**:1214, 1223, 1227
Olaf IV **8**:1099
Oleg **9**:1201, 1203, 1210, *1211*, 1211
Olga **9**:1203, 1210
Olympias **3**:384, 386
Omar bin Khattab **6**:752, 754, 755, 758, 764
Oppert, Jules **1**:67
Orhan **9**:1242, 1244
Orsini, Latino **8**:*1020*
Osman I **9**:1241, *1243*
Othman ibn Affan **6**:743–744, 755–756, 758, 764
Otho, Marcus Salvio **4**:527, 532, *536*
Otto I **6**:830, *831*, 831, 832, **8**:1022
Otto II **6**:832, *835*, 836, **9**:1176
Otto III **6**:832, 834–835, *836*
Otto IV **8**:1055, *1057*, 1065, *1066*
Otto of Brunswick *see* Otto IV
Ovid **4**:510–511, *512*, 526

P

Pacal **10**:*1316*, 1322
Pachacuti Inca Yupanqui **10**:*1338*–1339
Pachomius **5**:691–692
Padmasambhava **7**:959
Palestrina **10**:1407
Panehsi **1**:107
Papinian **5**:594
Parmenides **3**:355, 358, 360, 362–363
Parrot, André **1**:114
Paschal II **6**:843–844
Patinier, Joachim **4**:*526*
Paul **4**:530, **5**:683, 686
Paula **5**:697
Paul of Thebes **5**:688, *689*
Paulus, Lucius Aemilius **4**:472
Pausanias **3**:337, 379
Peisistratus **3**:300–301
Pelagius (monk) **5**:685
Pelagius (pope) **5**:*687*
Pépin (mayor) **6**:791–792
Pépin (son of Charlemagne) **6**:802
Pépin of Aquitaine **6**:812
Pépin the Short **6**:794, 795, **8**:1020
Pepy I **1**:78
Pepy II **1**:78
Perdiccas **3**:386, 396
Peri, Jacopo **10**:1407
Periander **3**:*295*, 296, 298, 299
Pericles **3**:340, *341*, 342, 345, 346–347, 356, 370, 371
Perseus **4**:478
Pertinax, Helvius **5**:592

Pescennius Niger **5**:*592*, 592, 616
Peter **4**:530, **5**:609, **6**:840
Peter III of Aragon **8**:1075
Peter the Cruel **8**:1107
Peter the Hermit **9**:1185
Petrarch **8**:1088
Phidias **3**:349, 351
Philip I (France) **9**:1185
Philip I (Philip the Arabian) **5**:*598*, 599
Philip I (West Francia) **6**:828
Philip II (Macedonia) **3**:*383*, 383, 384, *386*
Philip II Augustus (France) **8**:*1055*, *1057*, *1067*, **9**:1192
development of France and **8**:1044, 1052, 1054–1055, 1057
marriages of **8**:1066–1067
Otto of Brunswick and **8**:1065
Richard I (the Lionheart) and **8**:1056
Philip III (Burgundy) **8**:*1127*
Philip III (France) **8**:1078–1079
Philip III (Macedonia) **3**:396
Philip IV (France) **8**:1079, 1080, 1081, 1087, 1133
Philip V (Macedonia) **4**:476, *478*, 478
Philip VI (France) **8**:1102, 1106
Philip of Swabia **8**:1065
Philip the Bold **8**:1126
Philip the Good **8**:1110, 1113, 1126, 1128–1129, 1130
Phocas **9**:1165
Phraortes **2**:232
Phrynichus **3**:321–322
Pilate, Pontius **4**:507–508, 530
Piso, Gaius Calpurnius **4**:529
Piso Licinianus **4**:532
Pizarro, Francisco **10**:*1347*, 1347, 1421
Plato **3**:*353*, **10**:*1388*
Academy and **3**:365, 367
democracy and **3**:347–348
Heracles and **3**:355
humanism and **10**:1393, 1395
Islamic world and **6**:782, 783
Neoplatonism **5**:684
preserving knowledge of **5**:661
Renaissance and **10**:1404
Socrates and **3**:362, 364, 365
Sophists and **3**:361, 412
Sparta and **2**:264
Pliny the Elder **4**:536
Pliny the Younger **4**:536, 556
Pocahontas **10**:*1382*, 1382
Politian **10**:1403
Polo, Marco **8**:*1098*, **9**:*1179*, 1224, *1225*, 1225, 1226, **10**:1362, *1363*
Polycrates **3**:356
Pompeius, Gnaeus *see* Pompey

Pompeius, Gnaeus (son of Pompey) **4**:499
Pompeius, Sextus **4**:499, 502–503
Pompey **4**:*490*
Augustus Caesar and **4**:506
Cicero and **4**:490–491
Egypt and **4**:496, 497, 498
first triumvirate and **4**:493–494, 495–496
Parthia and **5**:585
Roman republic and **4**:488, 499
Seleucid Empire and **5**:586
theater and **4**:555
Pomponius, Marcus **4**:471
Poppaea Sabina **4**:525, 527
Postumas, Marcus **5**:601
Powhatan **10**:1356, 1382
Prempeh I **9**:1275
Prester John **9**:1225, **10**:1360
Priam **2**:193, 194
Protagoras **3**:349, 352
Prusias II **4**:475
Psamtik I **1**:109
Ptolemy I **3**:396, *398*, 398, 404, **4**:497
Ptolemy II **3**:398, 404
Ptolemy XII Auletes **4**:497
Ptolemy XIII **4**:497, 498
Ptolemy of Alexandria **3**:*405*, 409–410, **10**:1368, 1372, 1390–1391, *1391*, 1397
Publius Aelius Hadrianus *see* Hadrian
Pulakesin I **7**:966
Pulakesin II **7**:966
Pulcheria **5**:666, *669*
Pushyamitra Shunga **7**:929
Pyrrhon of Elis **3**:412
Pyrrhus **4**:461–462, *463*
Pythagoras **3**:356–357, *358*, *359*

Q

Qasim, Muhammad ibn **7**:966
Qutb-ud-Din Aybak **7**:968–969, 970

R

Rachel **2**:226, 227
Radha **7**:945
Rajaraja I **7**:966
Rajendra I **7**:966
Raleigh, Walter **10**:1380, *1381*
Ramses I **1**:105
Ramses II **1**:106, **2**:153, 229
Ramses III **1**:106–107, *107*
Raphael **10**:1404, 1406
Raven Floki **9**:1204
Raymond IV of Toulouse **9**:1185, 1187, 1188–1189
Raymond VI of Toulouse **8**:1025
Rea Silvia **4**:438, *443*
Redjedef **1**:74
Rekhmire **1**:99
Rembrandt van Rijn **10**:1409
Remus **4**:438, 438–439, *439*

Rib-Addi **1**:101
Richard I (the Lionheart) **8**:1054, *1056*, 1056, 1076, **9**:1192
Richard II **8**:1108, 1109, 1114
Richard III **8**:1120, 1123, 1124, *1125*, 1125
Richard of Gloucester *see* Richard III
Richard of York **8**:1116–1118, 1123, 1124
Richard the Kingmaker *see* Neville, Richard (earl of Warwick)
Robert I **6**:827
Robert Guiscard **8**:1023, *1024*, 1024
Robert of Flanders **9**:1185
Robert of Gloucester **8**:1051
Robert of Normandy **6**:*828*
Robert the Bruce **8**:1077
Robert the Pious **6**:827
Robert the Strong **6**:827
Roderick **6**:760
Roger I **8**:*1023*, 1023, 1025
Roger II **8**:1025
Roggeveen, Jacob **7**:986, 989
Roland **6**:798, *801*
Rolfe, John **10**:1382
Rollo **6**:*817*, 819, **8**:1023
Romanus II **9**:*1169*, 1175
Romanus III **9**:1178
Romanus IV **9**:1178–1179
Romanus Lecapenus **9**:1174, 1175
Romulus **4**:438, 438–439, *439*, 439–440
Romulus Augustulus **5**:*647*, 647, **9**:1163
Roxana **3**:396
Rudolf of Burgandy **6**:827
Rudolf of Swabia **6**:843, *844*
Rufinus **5**:666, 668
Rurik **9**:1200, 1201, 1208, *1210*, 1210
Rutilus, Marcius **4**:453–454

S

Saladin **6**:774, **8**:1056, 1068, **9**:*1191*, 1191, *1192*, 1234, *1235*, 1236
Samsu-ilina **1**:120
Samu-abu **1**:110
Samudra Gupta **7**:960
Samuel **2**:230
Samuel of Bulgaria **9**:1176, 1178
Sancho II **8**:1017, 1021
Sancho III **8**:1016
Sangallo, Giuliano da **10**:1403
Sappho **2**:*250*
Sarai (Sarah) **2**:225, 226
Sargon **1**:59–61, 114
Sargon II **2**:155, 217–218, 231
Saturnius **4**:537, 538
Saud, Abdul Aziz ibn **6**:775
Saul **2**:230
Scaevola, Mucius **4**:456, *459*
Scheffer, Ary **6**:*800*

Schliemann, Heinrich **2**:163, 182–183, 184, 185, 186, 192–193, 195
Scipio, Ganaeus Cornelius **4**:474
Scipio, Publius Cornelius **4**:471, 473–474
Scipio, Quintus Metellus **4**:496, 498
Scipio Aemilianus **4**:481, *482*, 482
Scipio Africanus **4**:*470*, *472*, 474, 475, 480
Sebastian **5**:*610*
Sebetwane **9**:1277
Sei Shonagon **7**:913
Sejanus **4**:517–518
Seleucus I **3**:*391*, 398, 399, *401*, 401, **5**:586, **7**:928
Seleucus IV **5**:586
Selim I **9**:1249–1252
Selim II **9**:1255
Sempronius Longus **4**:471
Senebtyfy **1**:*84*
Seneca **4**:524, 525, 527, *529*, 529, 555
Sennacherib **2**:217, 218, *231*, 231
Seqenenre **1**:91, 92
Sergius III **6**:826
Sertorius, Quintus **4**:488
Servius Tullius **4**:442
Sesostris I **1**:*79*, 83–84, 87
Sesostris II **1**:87
Sesostris III **1**:87, *89*
Seti I **1**:96, 105–106
Setnakht **1**:106
Severus **5**:610, 611
Severus, Septimius **5**:585, 592–595, *593*, 616, *618*
Severus, Sulpicius **5**:696
Sforza, Ludovico **10**:1404, *1405*, 1405
Shabaka **1**:109, **9**:1266
Shahryar **6**:781
Shaka **9**:*1277*, 1277
Shakespeare, William **3**:407
Shalmaneser I **2**:210
Shalmaneser III **2**:207, 213, 215–216
Shalmaneser V **2**:217
Shamshi-Adad I **1**:115, **2**:208, 210
Shang Yang **7**:877
Shankara **7**:964
Shapur (brother of Ardashir I) **6**:726
Shapur I **5**:*600*, 601, **6**:726, *729*, 729, *730*, 730, 731, 733, **7**:931
Shapur II **5**:613, **6**:*733*, 733
Sharkalisharri **1**:62
Sheshonk **1**:109
Shi Huang Di **7**:877, *879*, 879
Shomu **7**:912
Shotoku **7**:910
Shulgi **1**:63, 65
Shutruk-Nahhunte I **1**:121
Sichelgaita **8**:1024
Siddharta Gautama *see* Buddha

Sigismund of Hungary **9**:*1248*, 1248
Silius, Gaius **4**:523
Sima Qian **7**:886, 899
Sima Yan **7**:900
Simeon of Bulgaria **9**:1177
Simeon Stylites **5**:*695*, 695
Simpson, James H. **10**:1351
Skanda Gupta **7**:962
Smendes **1**:107
Smenkhkare **1**:104
Smith, John **10**:1381, *1382*, 1382, *1383*
Snefru **1**:74, 83
Sobhuza **9**:1277
Socrates **3**:348, 356, 361, 361–365, *362*, *363*, 366, 373
Solomon **2**:198, 199, *223*, 231
Solon **2**:*267*, 267, 269, **3**:294, 298, *328*, 328
Somerset, duke of **8**:1116
Sophocles **3**:323–324, 349
Soshangane **9**:1277
Spartacus **4**:489–490, *492*
Statilia Messalina **4**:527
Stauracius **9**:1171
Stefan Dusan **9**:1245
Stephen **5**:678, *687*
Stephen I (Hungary) **6**:837
Stephen II (pope) **6**:794, 795
Stephen III (pope) **6**:796, *798*
Stephen of Blois **8**:1051
Steuben, Charles **6**:762
Stilicho, Flavius **5**:*637*, 642, 654, 666
Strabo **9**:1266
Suffolk, duke of **8**:1116
Süleyman (son of Orhan) **9**:1244–1245
Süleyman I **9**:*1250*, *1252*, 1252, 1253, 1255, **10**:*1419*
Sulla, Lucius Cornelius **4**:483, *486*, 486–487, 488
Sulpicianus **5**:592
Sulpicius, Publius **4**:486
Sundiata Keita **9**:1271
Sunni Ali **9**:1272
Suppiluliumas I **1**:104–105, **2**:152
Svyatopolk the Accursed **9**:1212
Svyatoslav **9**:1203, 1210
Sweyn Forkbeard **6**:816, 819, **8**:1046, **9**:1198–1199
Sylvester I **5**:*630*, **9**:*1161*
Sylvester II **6**:834
Sylvester III **6**:837
Symmachus **5**:636, 683

T

Tacitus **4**:516, 525, **5**:582, 606, 660, *662*, **6**:808
Takauji **7**:916–917
Talha **6**:743–744
Tamerlane **7**:969, 970, **8**:1082, **9**:*1228*, *1229*, 1229, 1238, 1240, 1245–1246
Tanaquil **4**:441, 442

Tarasius **9**:1168
Tariq ibn-Ziyad **6**:759
Tarquinius Priscus, Lucius **4**:441–442
Tarquin the Proud **4**:438, 442, *447*
Tarunza **2**:*152*
Tasman, Abel **7**:989
Tassilo III **6**:796, 797
Tavarone, Lazzaro **10**:*1376*
Tefnakhte **1**:109
Tenzin Gyatso *see* Dalai Lama
Tertullian **5**:680–681, *682*, 682
Tetricus **5**:601
Thales of Miletus **3**:352, *354*
Themistocles **3**:331, 334
Theocritus **3**:406–407, **4**:512
Theodemir **5**:645
Theodora **5**:670, 671, *674*, 674, **9**:1172–1173, 1244
Theodoric I **5**:645
Theodoric the Great **5**:645–646, 647, 648, 650–651, 660, 661, 669, 673
Theodosius I **5**:*615*, *635*, *637*, *638*
   Christianity and **5**:630, 632
   division of the Roman Empire and **5**:666
   massacre and **5**:637, 639
   military leadership and **5**:614–615
   paganism and **5**:636–637
   Roman Empire and **9**:1158, 1160
   Visigoths and **5**:640, 643
Theodosius II **5**:618, 649, 666, 668, *680*, **6**:763, **9**:1161–1162
Theodosius III **9**:1165
Theodosius the Elder **5**:614
Theophano **9**:1175, 1176
Theophanu **6**:832
Theophilus **9**:1172, *1174*
Theseus **2**:*171*, 176, 264
Thespis **3**:318, 321
Thomas Aquinas **10**:*1388*, *1389*, 1389–1390
Thomas the Slav **9**:1171–1172
Thomsen, Christian **1**:42, 45
Thrasybulus **3**:299, 379
Thucydides **3**:352, 371, 372, *377*, 377
Thutmose I **1**:*95*, 96, 98
Thutmose II **1**:96, 98
Thutmose III **1**:92, 98, 98–99
Thutmose IV **1**:99
Tiberius **4**:513, 515, 516–519, *518*, 519
Tigellinus **4**:527
Tiglath-pileser I **2**:210, 216–217, 219
Tiglath-pileser III **1**:122
Tijing **7**:967
Timur the Lame *see* Tamerlane
Tintoretto **10**:1406
Titian **10**: *1406*, 1406
Titus **4**:535
Titus Aelius Antoninus *see* Antoninus Pius

Titus Flavius Vespasianus *see* Vespasian
Titus Tatius **4**:439
Tizoc **10**:1334
Toramana **7**:962
Torres, Luis Váez de **7**:988–989
Toscanelli, Paolo **10**:1395, 1397
Tosar **6**:730
Totila **5**:675, 676
Trajan **4**:538–540, *539*, **5**:582, 585, **6**:728, 736
Trebonian **5**:677
Tudor, Henry *see* Henry VII (England)
Tukulti-Ninurta I **1**:120–121, **2**:210, 211
Tukulti-Ninurta II **2**:212
Tullus Hostilius **4**:440
Tupac Amaru **10**:1347
Tutankhamen **1**:92, 104, *105*, 106, **9**:*1268*
Tyler, Wat **8**:1108, *1109*, 1109
Tyrell, James **8**:1124
Tyrtaeus **2**:258

U

Ubayd Allah **6**:774
Ubbi **9**:1196, 1198
Ulfsson, Gunnbjörn **9**:1204, 1206
Umako **7**:910
Umma **1**:58
Unas **1**:74
Urban II **9**:1182, *1183*, 1184, *1187*, 1187
Urban VI **8**:1089, 1091
Ur-Nammu **1**:63, 111
Urqon **10**:1338
Uruinimgina **1**:58
Utuhegal **1**:63

V

Vacarius, Roger **10**:1384
Valens **5**:614, 620, 630, 631, 640, 643
Valentinian I **5**:613–614, 634
Valentinian II **5**:614, 615, 634, 636
Valentinian III **5**:650, 653
Valerian **5**:601, **6**:726, 729, *730*
Valerius Laevinus **4**:478
Vallabha **7**:964
Vardhamana *see* Mahavira
Varro, Gaius Terentius **4**:472
Vasari, Giorgio **10**:1402, 1403
Vasily II **9**:1215
Vasily III **9**:1217
Vasnetsov, Victor **9**:*1211*
Vega, Lope de **8**:1021
Veronese **10**:1406
Verrazzano, Giovanni da **10**:1379
Verrocchio, Andrea del **10**:1403
Verus, Lucius **4**:543, 544, **6**:728
Vespasian **4**:529, 533–535, 541
Vespucci, Amerigo **10**:1375–1376
Vibius Pansa **4**:502
Victor IV **8**:1062

Vijaya **7**:929
Vima Kadphises **7**:931
Viracocha **10**:1336
Virgil **2**:200, **3**:406–407, **4**:438, 510, 512, 526, 557
Vitellius, Aulus **4**:532–533
Vladimir Monomachus **9**:1211, 1213
Vladimir the Great **9**:1203, 1210, 1212–1213
Vladislav of Lithuania **8**:1100

W

Wai Wang **9**:1222
Waldemar IV **8**:1098–1099
Waldseemüller, Martin **10**:1376
Walid, Al- **6**:768
Wallia **5**:643, 645
Wallis, Samuel **7**:989
Wang Mang **7**:897–898
Waqidi, Al- **6**:739
Widukind **6**:797, *800*

William I (England) **8**:*1045*, 1047, 1047–1048, *1049*, 1050
William II Rufus **8**:1049
William of Aquitaine **6**:826
William of Bavaria **8**:1128
William of Normandy *see* William I (England)
Willigis **6**:834, 835
Winthrop, John **10**:1383
Wladyslaw I **8**:1100
Wladyslaw II **8**:1100, **9**:1216
Wladyslaw III **9**:1246
Woodville, Anthony **8**:1123
Woodville, Elizabeth **8**:1120, 1122, 1123, 1124, 1125
Woolley, Leonard **1**:57, *67*
Wu Ding **7**:876
Wu Ti **7**:895–897, *897*, 899

X

Xanthippus **3**:340, **4**:467–468

Xenophanes **3**:355, *357*
Xenophon **3**:303, 362
Xerxes I **2**:237, 239, 240, **3**:330–331, 331–332, 334, 336, 390
Xunzi **7**:891, 894

Y

Yabahya **2**:219
Yang Jian **7**:900–901
Yaroslav the Wise **9**:1211, 1212
Yavuz the Grim *see* Selim I
Yazdegerd I **6**:734
Yazdegerd III **6**:735, 755
Yazid I **6**:*757*, 757, 764, 767
Yung-lo **10**:1420
Yu the Great **7**:873

Z

Zachary **6**:794, 795
Zamasp **6**:734

Zangi, Imad ad-Din **9**:1189, 1190
Zannanza **1**:105
Zápolya, John **9**:1252
Zarco, João Gonçalves **10**:1366, *1367*
Zeno **5**:*626*, 626, 645–646, 647, 653, 669, **9**:1162, 1165
Zenobia **5**:*602*, 602, 603
Zeno of Citium **3**:413, **4**:557
Zeno of Elea **3**:360, 362–363
Zhang Qian **7**:895
Zhao Kuangyin **7**:902
Zhuangzi **7**:889
Zhu Yuanzhang **7**:905
Zimrilim **1**:114, **2**:224
Zoe (daughter of Constantine VIII) **9**:*1178*, 1178
Zoe (mother of Constantine VII) **9**:1174
Zoroaster **2**:241–243
Zurbarán, Francisco de **9**:*1187*

RELIGION

Page numbers in *italics* refer to illustrations. Page numbers in **bold** refer to entire chapters.

A

Abraham 2:225–226, *226*, 5:*679*, 6:742, 748, 749
action, Taoism and 7:888, 890
Adam and Eve 5:*685*, 685, 6:742
Adrian I 6:796
Adrian II 9:1177
afterlife 1:84–85, 117, 3:413, 4:526, 7:*881*, 10:1322
Ahura Mazda 2:241, 242, 242–243, 6:726
Akkadians 1:61–62
Albigensian Crusade 8:1025, 9:1182, 1191, *1194*, 1194
Alexander III 8:1061–1062, 1062–1063
Allah 6:743, 748–749
altars 2:*160*, 244, 244, 3:312, 4:550, 5:*684*
Ambrose 5:636, *638*, 683, *684*
Amon 1:82, 95, 101
Amon-Re 1:82, 3:391, 393, 403
Anastasius 9:1166
ancestor worship 7:873, 979, 10:1309, 1340–1341
angels 5:*679*, 680, 6:741, 748
animals, religious beliefs and 10:1355
animism, Melanesia and 7:987
Anthony of Egypt 5:688, *690*, 690, 691, 692
antipopes 8:1062, 1089, 1091–1093
Aphrodite 3:310, 314, 316–317
Apollo 2:164, 167, 3:310, *311*, 313, 314, 315, 412
arhats (saints) 7:956, 957
Arianism 5:630, 631, 632, 633
    Athanasius of Alexandria and 5:695–696
    Basil of Caesarea and 5:693, 694–695
    Byzantine Empire and 9:1162–1163
    Germanic peoples and 5:645, 648, 653–654, 657, 658, 660, 671, 6:788
    Nicaea, Council of, and 5:*624*, 624–625, 628–630
Arius 5:624, 629–630, 631
Ark of the Covenant 2:229, *230*
Artemis 2:167, 190, 3:314, *346*
Aryan people 7:926
asceticism 3:366
    Black Death and 8:1086
    Buddha and 7:948

Cathars and 9:1194
Christianity and 5:691, 693, 696, 697
Jainism and 7:948
religious orders and 8:1035
Sufis and 9:1233
ashramas (goals of life) 7:942
Assyrians 2:211, 218
atheism 3:316–317, 352
Athena 2:190, *259*, 269, 3:314, *344*
    Athena Promachos (statue) 2:*259*
    Athens and 3:301, 312, 351
    Etruscans and 4:445
    Sanctuary of Athena Pronaia 3:*316*
    Temple of Athena Nike 3:*347*
Augustine 5:633, 680, 682–685, *684*, *686*, 686, 687, 696, 9:*1166*
Aztecs 10:1329–1331, 1334

B

Baal 2:*229*, 229, 3:403, 5:593, *595*, 596–597
Babylonians 1:117, 119
baptism 5:680–681, 685
barbarian invaders 5:658, 660
Basil of Caesarea 5:*692*, 692–695, *694*
Bedouin nomads
    Islam and 6:735, 747, 751, 752, 785
    Mohammed and 6:740
Benedict 5:688, 697, *699*, 699–701, *701*, 6:*824*, 826, 8:1035
Benedict VII 6:835
Benedict VIII 8:1023
Benedict IX 6:837
Benedict XI 8:1087
Benedict XIII 8:*1091*, 1091, 1092
Benedictine Rule 5:699–701, 6:*824*, 825
Bible
    Babylon and 1:124
    Benedict of Nursia and 5:700
    Canaanites and 2:222
    Egypt and 1:91
    Islam and 6:749
    Israelites and 2:225, 227, 228
    Jericho and 1:13
    Jerome and 5:697
    printing press and 10:1392, 1393
    study of 6:806
bishops 5:609, 628, 629, 632, 695
    see also popes
bodhisattvas (enlightened person) 7:957
Bogomil Christians 9:1249
Boniface 6:794, 797
Boniface VIII 8:*1081*, 1081, 1087

Brahma 7:938, *939*, 939–940, *940*, 948
brahman (divine consciousness) 7:936–937, 938
brahmins (priests) 7:925, 927, 946
Bronze Age 1:38–39
Buddha 7:*911*, 942, **946–959**, *947*, *952*, *956*, *958*
    Great Renunciation 7:*949*, 949
    life of 7:948, 949, 950
    Mahayana Buddhism and 7:956–957
    teachings of 7:950–954
Buddhism 6:730, 7:889, *903*, **946–959**, 967
    China and 7:892, 901, 902, 904
    Hepthalites and 7:962–963
    India and 7:928, 928–929, 930, 931, 963
    Japan and 7:909–910
    Mongols and 9:1226, 1238
    Southeast Asia and 7:975, 979
burial mounds
    Bronze Age and 1:39
    China and 7:879, 881
    dolmens and 1:24–25
    funnel-beaker culture and 1:22
    Hallstatt culture and 1:48
    Japan and 7:909
    Scythian people and 1:49, 51
    West Kennet Long Barrow 1:27–28, *28*
burial practices
    Assyrians and 2:219
    Babylonians and 1:117
    Bronze Age and 1:38, 39
    Celtic people and 1:46, 52, 2:257
    Cycladic people and 2:165, 166–167
    Dark Age Greece and 2:246
    Egypt and 1:73–74, *75*, 75, 77, 82, 84–85, 95–96, *97*
    funnel-beaker culture and 1:22, 24, 24–25
    Hallstatt culture and 1:48
    India and 7:927
    Japan and 7:909
    Latium and 4:443
    Maya and 10:1322
    Mycenaeans and 2:185–187, 188, 190
    Natufian culture and 1:11
    Persians and 2:244
    Roman Empire and 4:550
    Rössen culture and 1:18, *21*
    Scythian people and 1:51
    Sumerian people and 1:57–58
    Urnfield culture and 1:39–40

Byzantine Empire 5:670
    Christianity and 5:628–634, 636–637, 639, 6:761, 799–800, 811, 839, 840
    crusades and 8:1068, 9:1182, 1184, 1185, 1187, 1190
    Islam and 6:754, 755, 757, 763, 768, 776, 8:1014, 10:1360

C

capacochas (sacrifices) 10:1343
Cappadocian Fathers 5:695
Carthusian Order 8:1035
Celestine III 8:1065
celibacy, Christianity and 5:635, 692, 6:838, 840
Celtic people 1:46, 52
Ch'an Buddhism 7:958
charity, Islam and 6:749
children, Christianity and 5:635, 680
China 7:873, 892, 893, 904
    Buddhism and 7:958, 959
    Indian missionaries and 7:967
Christian expansion 8:**1014–1025**
Christianity
    Africa and 9:1266, 1268, 1269
    Arabia and 6:736
    Bulgarian Empire and 9:1177
    Byzantine Empire and 5:618, 626, 9:1158, 1166–1167
    Carolingian Empire and 6:804
    Constantine and 5:611, 611–612
    doctrinal disputes and 5:624–625, 627, 6:733, 761, 766–767, 839, 840, 9:1162–1163, 10:1415
    early Christian churches 5:*609*
    Franks and 5:654, 656, 657
    Germanic peoples and 5:645
    Islam and 6:736, 743, 748, 749, 759
    Japan and 7:917
    monasticism and 5:**688–701**
    North American peoples and 10:1382
    Pacific islands and 7:987
    Persians and 6:730, 733–734
    religious tolerance and 9:1160
    rise of 5:**628–639**
    Roman emperors and 5:599, 601, 610, 613
    Russia and 9:1203, 1210, 1212
    Southeast Asia and 7:981
    spread of 5:609
    theology of 5:**678–687**
    Vikings and 6:819, 9:1198, 1200, 1204
    see also crusades; Roman Catholic Church
Christians 4:*528*, 528, 530, 552, 6:766–767, 780

Christian theology, development of 5:678–687
church reform movements
crusades and 9:1187
Henry II of Germany and 6:835–836
Holy Roman Empire and 6:837, 838, 841
investiture controversy and 6:839, 841–842, 843–844, 845
monasteries and 6:826
popes and antipopes 8:1086, 1089, 1090, 1091–1093
Reformation and 8:1094
see also Roman Catholic Church
Cistercian Order 8:1029, 1035, 1035
Clement II 6:837, 841
Clement III 6:843, 8:1063
Clement V 8:1080, 1081, 1087–1088
Clement VII 8:1089
clergy 6:806, 821–822, 825, 830–831, 835, 838, 841, 845
Clermont, Council of 9:1182, 1183, 1184
Cluny, abbey at 6:826, 826, 838, 838, 8:1017
comos (religious procession) 3:320
Confessions (Augustine) 5:683, 686, 687
Confucianism 7:884–886, 887, 890, 910, 975
Buddhism and 7:892, 902
China and 7:877, 881, 882, 893, 901
legalism and 7:891, 893
Taoism and 7:888, 889
Confucius 7:877, 882, 883, 884, 884–886, 886, 889, 894
Constance, Council of 8:1090, 1092
Constantine I
Christianity and 5:625, 628, 680
Hagia Sophia and 5:672
Nicaea, Council of, and 5:628–630, 631
Roman Catholic Church and 6:800, 802
convents 5:697, 10:1344
see also monasteries
conversions
to Buddhism 7:950
to Christianity 5:628, 657, 686, 6:788, 791, 9:1158, 1177, 1198, 1200, 1203, 1210, 1212
to Islam 6:743–744, 746, 757, 759, 768, 774
Coptic Christians 6:759
corruption, Roman Catholic Church and 6:837, 838, 8:1086–1087, 1088, 1090, 1093, 9:1194

council theory, western schism and 8:1091–1093
creation, Buddhism and 7:954
creation stories 1:117, 2:243–244, 7:934, 936, 939–940, 10:1322, 1329, 1354
crusades 9:1182–1195, 1184
Constantinople and 5:618, 672, 8:1082, 9:1168, 1179, 1181
Frederick I (Barbarossa) and 8:1063
Frederick II and 8:1073
Islamic world and 10:1360
Knights Templar and 8:1080
Louis IX and 8:1078
Mamluk dynasty and 9:1237
Nicopolis, Battle of, and 9:1248
Richard I (the Lionheart) and 8:1056
Roman Catholic Church and 8:1014, 1067, 1068, 1069
Teutonic Knights and 8:1101
cults, secret 3:315

D

Dalai Lama 7:959, 959
deification, Roman emperors and 4:511, 520, 523, 525, 535, 537, 538, 540, 544, 5:608
Delphi, oracle at 2:234, 3:313, 315, 331
dharma, Buddhism and 7:950–954
disciples, Buddha and 7:948, 950
divination 3:315, 4:445, 7:872, 873, 876, 877, 887, 887, 889
divinity
Buddha and 7:951, 956
of Christ 5:624–625, 627
kings and 7:979
see also deification
doctrinal disputes
Augustine and 5:684–685
Buddhism and 7:955–957
Christianity and 5:633, 681, 6:734, 766–767, 811, 840, 9:1160, 1162–1163
crusades and 9:1182, 1187, 1191, 1194
Donatism 5:685
iconoclasm 9:1166–1167, 1168
Islam and 6:756, 772–773, 774, 9:1233
Manichaeism and 5:682
Monophysitism 5:626, 627, 670
Nicaea, Council of, and 5:628–630
religious beliefs and 10:1415
Roman Catholic Church and 8:1025, 1090, 1112–1113
Socrates and 3:364–365
see also Arianism
Dominican Order 8:1042
dominium mundi (sovereignty over the world) 8:1064, 1067, 1075, 1081

Donation of Constantine 6:800, 802
duties, Islam and 6:749, 766

E

Edict of Milan 5:611, 628, 635
Egypt 1:74, 75, 84, 95, 100, 101–102, 104
Christianity and 5:625, 688, 690, 691–692
crusades and 9:1191, 1193, 1195
Islam and 6:745, 755, 757, 774, 775
elect, Manichaeism and 6:731, 733
Eleusinian Mysteries 3:315–316, 5:633
Ephesus, Council of 5:678, 680, 680
Epistles (St. Augustine) 5:687
Etruscans 4:445
Eucharist 5:632, 681, 683
Eugenius III 8:1037–1038, 1039, 1040, 9:1190
Eugenius IV 8:1093
Europe, Islam and 6:759–762, 793, 9:1230
European settlers 10:1381, 1383
excommunication 5:682, 6:840, 841–842, 844, 8:1039, 1066–1067, 1073
Exodus (from Egypt) 2:227, 228, 229

F

fasting, Islam and 6:749
Fatima 6:751, 756, 758
fertility cults 1:28, 39, 7:909, 920, 945
Fifth Crusade 9:1193
First Crusade 6:823, 9:1182, 1184–1189, 1234
Fourth Crusade 8:1068, 1068, 9:1181, 1191, 1192–1193, 1193, 1213
Francis of Assisi 5:693, 8:1042, 1042
free will, original sin and 5:685, 687
funnel-beaker culture 1:19, 24

G

Germanic peoples 5:648, 654
Arianism and 5:630, 632
gods and goddesses and 5:651
Gnosticism 6:730
God, biblical 2:225–226, 227, 228
gods and goddesses
Akkadians and 1:61, 61–62
Alexander the Great and 3:391, 393
Assyrians and 2:219
Baal 5:595, 596
Babylonians and 1:112–113, 117
Buddhism and 7:952
Celtic people and 1:52
Christianity and 5:632–634

Cycladic people and 2:166
Diocletian and 5:608, 610
drama and 3:323
Egyptians and 1:73, 74, 81–82, 93, 95, 100
Franks and 5:654
Germanic tribes and 5:651
Greeks and 2:167, 3:301, 310–312, 314, 352, 376, 412
Hellenism and 3:402–403
Hinduism and 7:936, 938–943, 945, 961
Hittites and 2:151, 155, 158, 159–160
Hyksos kings and 1:90
India and 7:920, 923, 927, 928, 937
Japan and 7:909, 912
literature and 3:313
Mari and 1:114
Minoans and 2:176–177
Mycenaeans and 2:190, 190
Persians and 2:234, 241, 6:726
philosophy and 3:355, 413
Phoenicians and 2:206
pre-Columbian cultures and 10:1308, 1310, 1320, 1322, 1322, 1329–1330, 1341, 1343, 1354
pre-Islamic Arabia and 6:736, 739, 742–743
Rome and 4:448, 449, 550, 552, 7:934
Sumerians and 1:56, 64, 66, 69
Syrian 5:597
Vedic religion and 7:932, 934
Vikings and 9:1205
grace, God's 5:685, 686
Great Renunciation 7:949, 949
Great Schism 6:839, 840
Greek Orthodox Christianity 6:839
Greek religion 3:310–317
Gregory I 6:820
Gregory II 6:761, 800, 9:1167
Gregory III 6:800, 9:1167
Gregory IV 6:812
Gregory V 6:834
Gregory VI 6:837, 839
Gregory VII 6:838, 839, 841–843, 842, 8:1058, 1086
Gregory VIII 6:844, 845, 9:1192
Gregory IX 8:1073, 1073, 9:1193
Gregory XI 8:1088–1089, 1089
Gregory XII 8:1092
Gregory XIII 10:1408
Gregory of Nazianzus 5:695, 696–697
Gregory of Tours 5:657

H

Hadrian IV 8:1039, 1040, 1060, 1061
Hagia Sophia 5:621, 668, 672, 672
Constantine I and 5:621
Macedonian Renaissance and 9:1180

mosaics and 9:*1159, 1178, 1180*
Nika Revolt and 5:671
Ottoman Turks and 9:1247
hagiography 5:688, 690, 691
heresy *see* doctrinal disputes
hermits 5:688, 690, 691, 693, 695
Hinduism 6:731, 7:*932–945*
Gangetic civilization and 7:927
Gupta dynasty and 7:960–961
India and 7:928, 931, 948, 959
Indian missionaries and 7:967
Islam and 7:969
Southeast Asia and 7:975, 979,
981
historical sources, Mohammed and
6:739–740
Hittites 2:159–160
Holy Spirit 5:633, 6:840
holy wars *see* crusades; jihad
Honorius III 8:1072, 1073
household gods and goddesses
3:312
household shrines 4:448, *449*
human sacrifice
Aztecs and 10:1320, 1329–1331,
1331, 1334
Chibcha people and 10:1310
Egyptians and 1:73
Incas and 10:1343, 1344
Maya and 10:1317, 1322
Minoans and 2:180
Phoenicians and 2:206
Rome and 4:551
Scythian people and 1:51
Sumerian people and 1:58
Teotihuacán and 10:1308
Toltec people and 10:1309

I

I Ching (Book of Changes) 7:*887*,
887, 892
iconoclasm 6:761, 800, 811, 9:*1166*,
1166–1167, 1168, 1172, 1173,
1180
idols 6:742, 742–743, 747, 811
ignorance, Buddhism and 7:951,
953
imams 6:758
impermanence, Buddhism and
7:952–953
Incas 10:1340–1341, 1343, 1344
India 7:920, 925, 931, 967
Buddhism and 7:892, **946–
959**
Hinduism and 7:**932–945**
Lao-tzu and 7:889
Manichaeism and 6:731
Zoroastrianism and 6:731
indulgences, sale of 8:1090
Innocent II 8:1040, 1058
Innocent III 8:*1064*, 9:1191, 1192,
1194
crusades and 8:1025, 1068, 1069
Francis of Assisi and 8:1042
political power of 8:1039, 1064,
1065–1067

Innocent IV 8:1078
Inquisition 8:1019–1020, 9:1194
Irenaeus 5:678
Ishtar 1:59, 61, 62, 114, 117, *120*,
2:159, 228, 3:310
Islam
Africa and 9:1269, 1270, 1271,
1272–1273, 1274
Christian Europe and 10:1360,
1362, 1415
crusades and 9:1182–1195
Frederick II and 8:1070
India and 7:959, 966, 968–971
Islamic culture 6:**776–787**
Judaism and 2:226
Mohammed and 6:**736–751**
Mongols and 9:1229, 1238,
1240
Ottoman Turks and 9:1250
Persians and 6:735
Reconquista and 8:1014,
1016–1018, 1021
Southeast Asia and 7:981
spread of 6:**752–763**, *754*, 768,
793, 9:1165, 1230
Sufis and 9:1233
Zoroastrianism and 6:731
Israelites 2:225–226, 227, 228,
229

J

Jainism 7:927, *931*, 948
Japan 7:909–910, 911
Jerome 5:696–697, *698*
Jerusalem
Christianity and 5:632, 678
crusades and 6:*823*, 8:1014,
1068, 1069, 9:1182, 1188–
1189, 1195
Dome of the Rock 6:768, 769
Jesus Christ 4:530, 5:*681*, 6:748,
749
see also Christianity
jihad 6:744
John XV 6:834
John XIX 6:836
John XXII 8:1092
Judaism
Arabia and 6:736
baptism and 5:680
Christianity and 5:678
Islam and 6:736, 742, 743, 745,
748
Jacob and 2:226
Mohammed and 6:745
Persians and 6:730, 733
Seleucid dynasty and 3:400
Temple Mount 6:769
"just war," concept of 8:1018

K

Kali 7:945, 963
karma 7:937–938, 953
Koran 6:739, *748*, 748–749, 751,
772, 9:1233
Krishna 7:942, 944

L

laity 6:838, 839, 7:956, 8:1058
Lao-tzu 7:877, 886, *888*, 888, *889*,
889, 890
Leo I 5:625, 651, 653, 9:1163
Leo III 6:*802*, 802–803, 811,
9:1170
Leo IV 8:1022
Leo IX 6:838, 840
liturgy, Roman Catholic Church
and 6:807
Luther, Martin 10:1393, *1395*, 1415

M

Mahabharata 7:943, *944*, 944
Mahayana Buddhism 7:892, 956,
956–957, 958, 959, 981
Mani 5:682, 6:730–731, *731*, 733
Manichaeism 5:682, 683, 684–685,
6:730–731, 733
Martin IV 8:1078
Martin V 8:1092–1093, *1093*,
10:1406
Martin of Tours 5:696, *697*
martyrs 5:609, 610, 678
Mary, veneration of 5:678, 680, *681*
Maya 10:1317, 1320, 1322
Mecca
Adb al-Malik and 6:767, 768
Africa and 9:1271
Islam and 6:*740*, 749
Mohammed and 6:736, 746, 747
pre-Islamic Arabia and 6:738–739
meditation 7:948, 951
megaliths 1:18–31, 38–39, 10:1307
mendicant friars 8:1042
Minoans 2:176–177, *178*, 180
miracles, Christianity and 5:690,
696
missionaries 6:791, 7:929, 930, 957–
958, 967, 9:1230, 1233
Mohammed 6:**736–751**, *737*, *741*,
746, *750*, 764, 769
monasteries
Basil of Caesarea and 5:693, *694*
Benedict of Nursia and
5:699–701
Buddhism and 7:*892*, 902, 946,
954–955, 956, 959
Byzantine Empire and 9:1175
education and 6:804, 10:1387
India and 7:*964*
medieval Europe and 6:814, 816,
825, *826*, 826, 838, 8:1035,
9:1196, 1201
Pachomius and 5:692
preserving knowledge and 5:661,
665
Sufism and 9:*1233*
see also convents
monasticism, appeal of 5:**688–701**
monastic rules 5:692, 693–694,
699–701, 6:825, 826, 7:954
monks, Buddhist 7:*954*
Monophysitism 5:625, 626, 627,
670, 6:766–767, 9:1163

monotheism 1:*100*, 101–102,
2:228, 241–242, 10:1354
morality, Buddhism and 7:953
mortification 5:695
mosques
Abu Dulaf Mosque 6:*786*
Africa and 9:*1270*
Dome of the Rock 6:*768*, 768,
769
Hagia Sophia and 5:672
Medina and 6:745, 746
in Mesopotamia 6:755
Mosque of Ahmed ibn Tulun
6:*774*
Mosque of Mohammed Ali 6:*745*
Ottoman Turks and 9:1247, 1255
in Persia 6:*753*
Qarawuyin Mosque 9:*1241*
Southeast Asia and 7:*981*
Umayyad Mosque 6:765, 767
muezzins 6:743, *744*
Muslims *see* Islam
Mycenaeans 2:190
mystery religions 3:315–316, 5:680
mysticism 5:684

N

nature deities 2:160
Neolithic period 1:26, 27–28, 29
Nestorianism 6:734
Nestorius 5:678, 680, 6:734, 9:1163
Newgrange burial mound 1:*25*,
25, *26*
Nicaea, Council of 5:*624*, 625,
628–630, *631*, 631, 633,
9:1162, 1168
Nicaea, Seventh Council of 6:811
Nicene Creed 5:629, 630, 6:840
nirvana 7:953–954
Noah's Ark 2:224
"non-doing," Taoism and 7:888
non-Muslims, Islam and 6:746, 747,
754, 766–767, 773
North American peoples
10:1354–1355, 1358

O

obedience, monasteries and 5:694
offerings, religious 1:19, 24, 25, 85,
3:312
On the Holy Spirit and Moralia (Basil
of Caesarea) 5:695
oracle bones *see* divination
oracles 2:255, 3:297, 313, 315, 331
original sin 5:685, 687
orphans, Islam and 6:740
orthodox Christianity
Athanasius of Alexandria and
5:695–696
barbarian invaders and 5:658, 660
Justinian I and 5:670
Russia and 9:1212, 1215
Vandals and 5:653–654
see also Christianity
Orthodoxy, Council of 6:811,
9:1173

P

Pacific islands **7:**987, 988
paganism
  Africa and **9:**1269, 1270
  Augustine and **5:**687
  Christianity and **5:**632–634, 635, 636, 691
  crusades and **9:**1182
  Europe and **8:**1082, **9:**1182, 1196, 1204, 1216
  Iceland and **9:**1204
  Lithuania and **8:**1100, **9:**1216
  northern Europe and **6:**839, **8:**1025, 1101
  pre-Islamic Arabia and **6:**736, 739, 742–743
  Saxons and **6:**796
  Theodosius I and **5:**636–637
  Vikings and **6:**809, **9:**1196
  see also gods and goddesses
Papal States **8:**1064, 1065, 1072, 1096
Paschal II **6:**843–844
patriarchs **5:**632
Paul **4:**530, **5:**683, 686
Paula **5:**697
Paul of Thebes **5:**688, *689*
peace of God **8:**1018
Pelagius (monk) **5:**685
Pelagius (pope) **5:***687*
penance **5:**639, 682, **6:**842–843, *843*, 845
People's Crusade **9:**1184
persecution
  Christianity and **5:**609, 610, 628, 635, 678
  hermits and **5:**688
  of pagans **5:**636–637, 639
Persians **2:**241–244
Peter **4:**530, **5:**609, **6:**840
Peter the Hermit **9:**1185
Phoenicians **2:**206
Pilate, Pontius **4:**507–508, 530
pilgrimages
  Buddhism and **7:**955
  crusades and **9:**1182
  Islam and **6:**742, 746, 747, 749, 769, 786, **9:**1271
pillars, Buddhist **7:**928, *929, 930,* 930, 958
political power
  Buddhist monasteries and **7:**955
  Inquisition and **8:**1019–1020
  religious beliefs and **10:**1415
  Roman Catholic Church and **6:**824–825, 835, **8:**1058, 1061, 1064, 1075, 1081, 1086, **9:**1170, 1191
  western schism and **8:**1089
polytheism *see* gods and goddesses
popes
  Byzantine Empire and **6:**799–800, 802, **9:**1167, 1170
  Carolingian dynasty and **6:**794, 794–795
  Constantine I and **5:**628

development of the church and **5:**632
  emperors and **8:1058–1069**
  Frederick II and **8:**1072–1073
  Holy Roman Empire and **6:**834, 837, 839, 841–845
  Renaissance and **10:**1406
  Rome and **8:**1037–1038
  Tordesillas, Treaty of, and **10:**1375–1376
  western schism and **8:**1082, 1089, 1091–1093
  see also crusades; Roman Catholic Church; specific popes
Poseidon **2:**167, 176, 190, **3:**314
prayer
  Benedict of Nursia and **5:**700
  Cycladic people and **2:**166
  Greece and **3:**312
  Hittites and **2:**159
  Islam and **6:**742, *743,* 749
  monasteries and **5:**693, 694, 6:824, 826
  muezzins and **6:**743
pre-Columbian cultures **10:**1302, 1309, *1311*
pre-Islamic Arabia **6:**736, 741
priestesses, Rome and **4:**441
priests
  Assyrians and **2:**217, 218
  Aztecs and **10:**1326, *1327,* 1328, 1331
  Babylonians and **1:**119
  brahmins **7:**925, 927, 946
  Bronze Age and **1:**38, 39
  Chibcha people and **10:**1310
  China and **7:**873
  Christian **5:**609, 685
  Egyptians and **1:**74, 85, 100, 107
  Greece and **3:**312, 313, 315
  Hittites and **2:**159, 160
  Incas and **10:**1345
  India and **7:**924
  Maya and **10:**1318–1319, 1323
  Mycenaeans and **2:**190
  North American peoples and **10:**1354
  pagan **5:**596–597
  Persians and **2:**244
  Sumerians and **1:**65
prophets **6:**741, 748
Protestant Reformation **8:**1094, **10:**1393, *1415,* 1415
Pyramid of the Moon **10:***1308*
Pyramid of the Sun **10:***1308,* 1308

R

Ramadan **6:**749
Re **1:**74, 101–102
reform movements, Roman Catholic Church and *see* church reform movements
reincarnation **5:**682, 685, **7:**937–938, 946, **9:**1194
relics, Christian **5:***695,* **6:**735

religious festivals **3:**301, 312, 315, 318, 320
religious law, Ottoman Turks and **9:**1250
religious orders
  agricultural improvements and **8:**1029
  education and **10:**1384
  Henry the Navigator and **10:**1366
  medieval Europe and **8:**1035
  mendicant friars and **8:**1042
  military forces and **8:**1014, 1025, *1080,* 1080, **9:**1190
  Safavid Empire and **10:**1418
  Sufis and **9:**1233
  see also monasteries
religious rituals
  mystery religions and **3:**315–316
  pre-Columbian cultures and **10:**1343, *1345,* 1353, 1354
  Vedas and **7:**935
religious sects **3:**356–357
religious tolerance
  Buddhism and **7:**930
  Byzantine Empire and **5:**613, 614, **9:**1160, 1166–1167, 1172
  Charlemagne and **6:**810
  Christianity and **9:**1160
  Frederick II and **8:**1070
  iconoclasm and **9:**1166–1167, 1172
  Islamic world and **6:**747, 766–767, **9:**1238
  Kushan India and **7:**931
  Mongols and **9:**1226
  Normans and **8:**1023, 1025
  Ottoman Turks and **9:**1245, 1249, 1250, **10:**1418
  Persians and **6:**733–734
  Southeast Asia and **7:**979
religious visions **6:**741–742, **8:**1112, **9:**1188
reliquaries **6:***789,* **9:***1171*
Renaissance **10:**1326, 1403–1404
Roman Catholic Church
  Arnold of Brescia and **8:**1040
  Becket, Thomas, and **8:**1053
  Burgundy and **8:**1129
  Charlemagne and **6:**788, 807
  crisis in **8:**1086–1089, 1090, 1091–1093
  eastern Europe and **9:**1216
  education and **10:**1387, 1388
  feudalism and **6:**822, 823–824, 826
  Franks and **5:**656, 657, **6:**791–792
  Greek philosophers and **10:**1389
  Holy Roman Empire and **6:**835
  humanism and **10:**1397, 1400
  Inquisition and **8:**1019–1020
  Japan and **7:**917
  landownership and **6:**790, 792
  mendicant friars and **8:**1042

moneylending and **8:**1033
music and **10:**1407
Ostrogoths and **5:**648
Otto the Great and **6:**830–831
political power and **6:**824–825, 835, **8:**1058, 1061, 1064, 1075, 1081, 1086, **9:**1170, 1191
Protestant Reformation and **10:**1415
Renaissance and **8:**1099
Rome and **8:**1037
taxation and **8:**1079, 1081
Vandals and **5:**653–654, 671
Visigoths and **5:**645
Vulgate Bible and **5:**697
warfare and **8:**1018
western schism and **8:**1089, 1091–1093
see also church reform movements; crusades; orthodox Christianity; popes
Rome **4:**493, 511, **5:**596–597, 599, 601

S

sacrifices
  Aryan people and **7:**926, 932, 934
  Christianity and **5:**635
  Greece and **3:**312, *313*
  Vedic religion and **7:**936, 946
  see also human sacrifice
sacrilege, Alcibiades and **3:**376
sadhu (holy man) **7:***938*
saints
  Buddhism and **7:**956, 957
  Byzantine Empire and **9:**1175, 1180
  Christianity and **5:**656, 678, 688, 690, 691–695, 696–697, 699–701
Scholasticism **10:**1384, 1386–1390
scriptures
  Buddhism and **7:***953,* 957
  Vedas and **7:**932, 935, 936–937, 937–938, 940, 945, 946
  see also Bible
Scythians **1:**51
Second Crusade **9:**1189–1191, *1190*
self-denial, monasteries and **5:**693, 695
Semi-Arianism **5:**630, 631
Sergius III **6:**826
Seventh Crusade **9:**1236
shamans, Africa and **9:**1262
Shi'ite Islam **6:**757, *758,* 758, 767, 769, 773, 786, **10:**1415
Shintoism **7:**910
Shiva **7:**920, *937, 938, 939, 940, 943,* 943, 945, 963, 966
Shravakayana Buddhism **7:**956
shrines
  Buddhist **7:**930, 950, *951, 955*
  household **4:***449*
  Incas and **10:**1343
  Mycenaeans and **2:**190

Siddharta Gautama *see* Buddha
Simeon Stylites 5:*695*, 695
simony 6:838, 839, 8:1086–1087, 1088
sins, forgiveness of 5:678, 681–682, 685
Sirat Rasul Allah (The Life of God's Prophet) 6:739
souls 7:952–953, 964
Southeast Asia 7:975, 979, 981
Sparta 2:264
spirits, Greek 3:310–311
standing stones 1:*20*, *24*, 25–27, *27*, *29*, 29
Stephen 5:678, *687*
Stephen II 6:794, 795
Stephen III 6:796, *798*
stone circles 1:26–27, 29
Stonehenge 1:26, *29*, 29
stupas 7:950, *951*, *955*
suffering, Buddhism and 7:950–951, 953
Sufis 9:1230, 1233
Sumerians 1:56, 62, 64, 65, 66, 69
Summa Theologiae (Aquinas) 10:*1389*, 1389
Sunni Islam 6:758, 764, 766, 767, 772, 10:1415
sun worship 1:39, *100*, 101–102
Sylvester I 5:*630*, 9:*1161*
Sylvester II 6:834
Sylvester III 6:837

T

Tantric Buddhism 7:959
Tao 7:884, 885, 886, 888
Taoism 7:877, 886, 888, 889, 890, 892, 901, 902, 975
Taoist societies 7:899
Tao Te Ching (Lao-tzu) 7:886, 888, 889, 892
temples
　Angkor Wat 7:977, *978*
　Assyrians and 2:216, 217
　Byzantine Empire and 5:618, 636–637
　Egyptians and 1:75, 81–82, 87, 95, 98, 100, 101, 104, 106
　Greece and 3:311–312
　Hittites and 2:154
　India and 7:*933*, *941*, *945*, *950*, 961, *965*, 965, 966, *967*, 968, *969*
　Israelites and 2:229, 231
　Maya and 10:1315
　Minoans and 2:180
　Mycenaeans and 2:190
　Persians and 2:234, 236
　Phoenicians and 2:206
　pre-Columbian cultures and 10:1302, *1303*, 1310, *1313*, 1315, 1316, 1318, *1319*, *1331*, 1335, *1341*, 1342, 1346, 1350

Rome and 4:451, *487*, 511, 520, 555, 5:597, *613*
　Southeast Asia and 7:*973*, *980*
　Sumerian 1:56, 64, 66
Ten Commandments 2:227, 228, 229
theocracy, Tibet and 7:959
Theogony (Birth of the Gods) (Hesiod) 3:313
theology
　Christian 5:678–687, 696
　Islamic 6:782–783
Theravada Buddhism 7:956, 957, 958, 981
Third Crusade 8:1063, 9:1192
Thomas Aquinas 10:*1388*, *1389*, 1389–1390
transmigration of souls 5:685
Trinity 5:628–629, 631, *633*, 633

U

Ulama ball game 10:*1317*, 1317, 1318
Urban II 9:1182, *1183*, 1184, *1187*, 1187
Urban VI 8:1089, 1091

V

Vajrayana Buddhism *see* Tantric Buddhism

Valhalla 9:*1204*
Vedas 7:927, 932, 935, 936–937, 937–938, 940, 945, 946
Vedic religion 7:932, 934, 938–939, 945, 946, 952, 967
　see also Hinduism
Vesta 4:441, 5:597
Vestal Virgins 4:438, 441
Victor IV 8:1062
Vishnu 7:938–939, *940*, 940–942, *941*, 960, *965*, 975
votive figures 2:166
Vulgate Bible 5:697

W

Wailing Wall 4:535
warfare, religious beliefs and 10:1414–1415
western schism 8:1089, 1091–1093
Wise Men 5:*681*
witchcraft, Germanic peoples and 5:662

Z

Zachary 6:794, 795
Zen Buddhism 7:958–959
Zeus 2:167, 190, 3:*301*, 310, 313, 314, 393, 403, 412
Zoroaster 2:241–243
Zoroastrianism 6:726, 730, 731, 733, 734, 735

TECHNOLOGY

Page numbers in *italics* refer to illustrations. Page numbers in **bold** refer to entire chapters.

A

About Nature (Anaximander) **3**:354
accounting systems **6**:784, **10**:1341, *1343*
agriculture
  Africa and **9**:1256, 1258–1259, 1265, 1271
  Arabia and **6**:738
  Assyrians and **2**:211
  Aztecs and **10**:1324, 1333
  Byzantine Empire and **9**:1175
  China and **7**:870–871, 873, 875, 877, 878, 897
  Cistercian Order and **8**:1035
  climate change and **8**:1084
  Crete and **2**:172
  Cycladic people and **2**:164–165
  development of states and **10**:1414
  early humans and **1**:6, 11, 14–15
  in Egypt **1**:70, 78, 86, 87, 101
  Etruscans and **4**:444
  in Europe **8**:*1030*, **10**:1416
  European settlers and **10**:1381, 1383
  feudal Europe and **6**:*821*, 821, *822*, 823, **8**:1026, *1027*, 1028–1029, *1029, 1030*
  funnel-beaker culture and **1**:19
  Germanic people and **5**:665
  Greece and **2**:162, 258, 260, 261, 266, **3**:*302*, 302–303, *306*, 370
  Greek colonies and **2**:256
  Hittites and **2**:156, 158
  Incas and **10**:1340, 1342
  India and **7**:918
  Islamic world and **9**:1238, 1240
  Japan and **7**:906, 911
  Linearbandkeramik culture and **1**:17
  Maya and **10**:1312, 1314, 1323
  Mesopotamia and **1**:54
  Minoans and **2**:175–176
  Mycenaeans and **2**:189
  Neolithic period and **1**:12, 13, 14–15, 16, 18
  North American peoples and **10**:1350, 1352, 1357
  pre-Columbian cultures and **10**:1304, 1311
  religious rituals and **10**:1354–1355
  Roman Empire and **4**:466, 476, *477*, **5**:606
  Southeast Asia and **7**:972, 974–975, 976–977

Sumerian people and **1**:65
  tools and **1**:21–22, 42
  Vikings and **9**:1205
alchemy **10**:*1385*, 1391
algorism **6**:784
alloys **1**:32–33, 35
Almagest (Ptolemy) **10**:1390–1391
Al-Qanan fi at-tibb (Ibn Sina) **6**:783, *784*
anatomy, study of **3**:411
Anaxagoras **3**:356, *358*
Anaximander **3**:354
Anaximenes **3**:354–355
ancient knowledge, rediscovery of **10**:*1390*
aqueducts **2**:220, **5**:619, *620*, 620, *670*, 675, 676
Arabic numerals **6**:783–784, **7**:926
Archimedes **3**:408, *410*, **10**:1390
architecture
  Africa and **9**:*1270*
  Assyrian **2**:213, 215, 220
  Byzantine Empire and **5**:672, **9**:1180
  Greece and **3**:298, 311–312, 349, 351
  India and **7**:960, 961, **10**:*1364*, 1419
  Islamic world and **6**:*763*, 767, 769
  mathematics and **3**:407
  Minoan **2**:173, 174
  Mycenaean **2**:187
  Norman **8**:*1022*
  Ottoman Turks and **9**:1255
  Palatine Chapel and **6**:807
  pre-Columbian cultures and **10**:1302, 1304, 1309, 1315, 1333, 1342, 1345–1347
  Renaissance and **10**:1401, 1402, 1406, *1409*, 1409
  Spain and **6**:*763*
Aristarchus of Samos **3**:409
armor *see* weapons and armor
astrolabes **3**:410, **10**:*1365*, 1365, 1391
astrology **10**:1391
astronomy **10**:1318, 1365, 1390–1391, *1393*
  Babylonian Empire and **1**:119
  Bronze Age and **1**:39
  Egypt and **1**:77
  Greek philosophy and **3**:352, 354, 356, 358, 409–410
  India and **7**:961, 962
  Islamic world and **6**:784
  Neolithic period and **1**:25, 26, 28
atlases **10**:1368
atomic theory **3**:361, 412–413
Averroës **6**:783
axes **1**:6, 7, *17*, **7**:*875*, 906, **9**:*1263*

B

baths **4**:*524*, 553, *554*, **7**:920
Bessarion, Basilius **10**:*1390*, 1390–1391
boats **1**:9, 10, *91*
  see also ships and shipbuilding
bone for tools **1**:7, 9
Book of Adding and Subtracting by Indian Methods (Khwarizmi) **6**:784
bridges, Incas and **10**:1347
bronze **1**:32–33, 35, 90, 94, **2**:156, 188
building materials
  Assyrians and **2**:213
  Constantinople and **5**:619
  Egyptians and **1**:73
  Etruscans and **4**:445
  Greece and **2**:162
  Indus Valley civilization and **7**:920
  Mycenae and **2**:184
  Neolithic period and **1**:30
  Persians and **2**:240
  Phoenicians and **2**:198
  pre-Columbian cultures and **10**:1305, 1307, 1315, 1332, 1345–1346, 1348
  Sumerians and **1**:67
building programs
  Africa and **9**:1271
  Baghdad and **6**:787
  barbarian invaders of Rome and **5**:648
  China and **7**:877, 901
  Constantinople and **5**:616, **9**:1172
  Maya and **10**:1318
  Mongols and **9**:1226
  Ottoman Turks and **9**:1244, 1249, 1255
  Persians and **6**:726, 729
  Roman Empire and **4**:498–499, 504, 508, 522, 528, 534, 539, **5**:595
  Roman provinces and **4**:547
  Tarquinius Priscus, Lucius, and **4**:442

C

calendars **2**:211, **4**:500, 502, **10**:1302, 1320, *1330*, 1330
calendar stone **10**:1329
canoes **1**:9, 10, **7**:985
cartography *see* mapmaking
chariots **1**:46, 90, *98*, **2**:157, 210, 214, **7**:875, 876
circumnavigation of the globe **10**:1377, 1379
compasses **10**:1363–1364, 1365, 1391
Copernicus, Nicolaus **3**:*410*
copper **1**:31, 32, 33, 35, 94, **2**:165

crafts and craftspeople
  Anasazi people and **10**:1350
  Aztecs and **10**:1327, 1333
  Celtic people and **1**:46, 50
  copper and **1**:32
  Egypt and **1**:86
  Etruscans and **4**:445
  Franks and **6**:*793*
  Goths and **5**:*645*
  Greece and **3**:302–303
  Hallstatt culture and **1**:45, 47
  Hittites and **2**:156
  Huns and **5**:*649*
  Iberian people and **1**:50
  India and **7**:920, 925
  Islamic world and **6**:*779*, 780–781
  Maya and **10**:1314, 1316, 1319
  medieval Europe and **8**:1041, 1043, 1086
  Mixtec people and **10**:1310
  Mycenaeans and **2**:189
  Neolithic period and **1**:15
  Phoenicians and **2**:198, 200
  pre-Columbian cultures and **10**:1302, 1304, 1305, 1305–1306
  Renaissance and **10**:1403
  Rome and **4**:466, 548
  Tarascan people and **10**:1310
crop rotations **3**:302, **6**:823, **8**:1028

D

dams, Persians and **6**:729
decimal notation **6**:784
drainage projects **4**:442

E

Earth, circumference of **3**:410
earthenware pots *see* pottery
Elements (Euclid) **3**:407, *408*
elements, primary **3**:354, 355, 356, 358
embalming **1**:96
Euclid **3**:407, *408*, **10**:1390
European exploration **10**:1421

F

firearms, Japan and **7**:917
fishing **1**:7, **7**:975, 988, **10**:1358
flint daggers **1**:*23*
flint mining **1**:19, 23

G

Galen **10**:1390
Geography (Ptolemy) **3**:410, **6**:784, **10**:1368, 1397
geometry **3**:354, 358, 407, 409, **7**:926
  see also mathematics
glass lamps, Mamluk **9**:*1240*

glassware, Phoenicians and **2**:200
Grand Canal **7**:901
Great Pyramid of Giza **1**:74, *76*
Great Pyramid of Tenochtitlán
   10:1329, 1331, *1332*, 1332,
   1335
Great Wall of China **7**:879, *880*,
   901, 904, **9**:1222
Greek fire **6**:762, 763
Gregorian calendar **4**:502
Gutenberg, Johannes **10**:1391,
   1392, 1392

H
hand grenades **9**:*1181*
Harmonica (Ptolemy) **3**:410
Hero of Alexandria **3**:408, *409*,
   10:*1390*
Herophilus **3**:411
Hippocrates **3**:352, 410–411,
   10:*1390*
hunting
   early humans and **1**:6, 8–10
   Egypt's New Kingdom and **1**:*98*
   funnel-beaker culture and **1**:19
   North American peoples and
      10:1352–1353, *1354*, 1354,
      1355, *1356*, 1358
   Persians and **6**:734, *735*

I
Ibn Ruhd **6**:783
Ibn Sina **6**:*783*, 783, *784*
"indivisibility of being" theory
   3:358, 360
inventors **3**:408, *409*, 410, **4**:473,
   6:780
iron **2**:156, **9**:1266
iron tools **1**:*43*, 47
irrigation
   Arabia and **5**:587
   Assyrians and **2**:211
   China and **7**:877
   Egypt and **1**:80–81
   Latium and **4**:444
   Mesopotamia and **1**:54
   Persians and **2**:245
   pre-Columbian cultures and
      10:1310, 1311, 1312, 1333,
      1350
   see also aqueducts

J
Julian calendar **4**:500, 502

K
Kamares ware **2**:173, 180
Khwarizmi, Mohammed ibn Musa
   al- **6**:783, 784
Kitab ash-shifa (Ibn Sina) **6**:783

L
Leonardo da Vinci **10**:1403, 1404,
   1405, 1406
Leucippus **3**:361
levers and fulcrums **3**:408

Library of Alexandria **3**:392, 398,
   406, 407
Long Count calendar **10**:1320
longitude and latitude **3**:410
longships, Viking **6**:*809*, **9**:1196,
   1202, 1202, *1204*
looms **8**:1030, *1031*
lost-wax process **10**:1310

M
mapmaking **3**:354, 410, **10**:1367,
   1368, 1395, 1397
mathematics
   Alexandria and **3**:404, 407–408
   astronomy and **3**:409, 410
   Babylonians and **1**:119
   Byzantine Empire and
      9:1174–1175
   Greek philosophy and **3**:361
   India and **7**:926, 961–962
   Islamic world and **6**:782, 783–
      784
   medieval Europe and **10**:1390,
      1391
   Pythagoras and **3**:357, 358
   Sumerians and **1**:69
medicine
   Alexander the Great and **3**:384
   Alexandria and **3**:410–411
   Athens and **3**:372
   Babylonians and **1**:119
   Black Death and **8**:1085
   Hippocrates **3**:352
   India and **7**:926
   Islamic world and **6**:783
   medieval Europe and **10**:1390,
      1391
megaliths **1**:**18–31**, 38–39, **10**:1307
metals, sources of **2**:164
metalwork
   Africa and **9**:1261, 1263, 1265,
      1266
   Akkadian **1**:*61*
   Celtic **1**:50
   Greece and **2**:162, 172
   Hallstatt culture and **1**:45, 47
   Hittites and **2**:156, 158
   Iberian **1**:49–50
   pre-Columbian cultures and
      10:1305–1306, *1310*, 1310
   Southeast Asia and **7**:972, 974
   Sumerian **1**:65
minerals, sources of **2**:164
mining
   Anatolia and **3**:328
   Athens and **3**:331, 348
   Bronze Age and **1**:37
   copper **1**:94
   flint **1**:19, 23
   Hittites and **2**:156
   Phoenicians and **2**:200
   salt **1**:45
   Teotihuacán and **10**:1308
   tin **1**:*36*
molds, copper tools and **1**:32, 35
mowing tools **1**:11

mud-brick architecture **9**:*1270*
Museum of Alexandria **3**:392, 398,
   404, 406–407, *411*

N
navigation
   medieval Europe and **10**:1363–
      1364, 1365, 1367, 1391
   Phoenicians and **2**:200–201,
      202
   Polynesia and **7**:985
   Vikings and **9**:1202
Neolithic Revolution **1**:14, **7**:871

O
observatories, Toltecs and **10**:1318
obsidian **2**:167, **10**:1308
On Nature (Anaxagoras) **3**:356
Optics (Ptolemy) **3**:410
origins of the world, Greek
   philosophers and **3**:354, 355,
   356

P
paper **7**:899, **10**:1319, 1328
papyrus **1**:88
Parts of the Universe, The **6**:784
plows **1**:21, **3**:302, **8**:1026, 1028
plumbing and water supplies
   aqueducts **5**:*620*, *670*, 675, 676
   Constantinople and **5**:619, 620
   Cycladic culture and **2**:169
   Hittites and **2**:154
   India and **7**:918
   Khmer people and **7**:976–977
   Minoans and **2**:174, 175
   Mycenae and **2**:184
   Persians and **6**:735
   pre-Columbian cultures and
      10:1316, 1332
   Rome and **5**:675, 676
   Saint Anthony's Monastery and
      5:*691*
   see also irrigation
pottery
   African **9**:1259, *1262*
   bell-beaker culture and **1**:*19*, 31
   Bükk culture and **1**:*16*
   China and **7**:870, 871–872
   corded-ware culture and **1**:31
   Crete and **2**:172
   funnel-beaker culture and
      1:18–19, 21
   Greece and **3**:296, *298*, 301, *308*
   Hallstatt culture and **1**:47
   India and **7**:924, 927
   Japan and **7**:906, *909*
   Minoans and **2**:170, 173, 180
   Minyan people and **2**:163
   Neolithic period and **1**:16–17
   Pacific islands and **7**:984, 987
   pre-Columbian cultures and
      10:1305, 1310, 1311, 1314,
      1315, *1323*, *1350*, 1350, *1352*
   Rössen and Michelsburg cultures
      and **1**:18

Sumerian people and **1**:65
   Thera and **2**:168
pottery wheels **7**:872, 906
printing, Tang dynasty and **7**:901
printing presses **10**:1391–1392,
   1408
Ptolemy of Alexandria **3**:*405*,
   409–410, **10**:1368, 1372,
   1390–1391, *1391*, 1397
pueblos **10**:1348, 1350, *1351*, 1351
pyramids
   Egyptian **1**:73–74, *75*, 75, 77, 78
   Nubia and **5**:*585*, **9**:*1269*
   pre-Columbian cultures and
      10:1305, 1307, *1308*, 1308,
      1333
   see also ziggurats
Pythagoras **3**:356–357, *358*, *359*

Q
quadrants **10**:1365
quipus (accounting system) **10**:1341,
   1343

R
Regimen in Acute Diseases
   (Hippocrates) **3**:411
roads **1**:21, **2**:177, 245, **3**:301, **4**:508,
   10:1346, 1347
Roman baths *see* baths

S
sails, medieval ships and **10**:1369
salt mining **1**:45
School of Miletus **3**:352, 354
sciences
   Babylonians and **1**:119
   Byzantine Empire and
      9:1174–1175
   Egyptians and **1**:77
   Europe and **10**:1390–1391, 1395,
      1398
   Greeks and **3**:361, 404, 407–
      408
   India and **7**:961–962
   Islamic culture and **6**:782, 783
   see also astronomy; mathematics;
      medicine
ships and shipbuilding
   China and **10**:1419, 1420
   European conquests and **10**:1421
   Islamic world and **6**:777, 779–
      780
   longships, Viking **6**:*809*, **9**:1196,
      1202, 1202, *1204*
   medieval Europe and **6**:809,
      814, 817, **10**:1363, 1367,
      1369
   Minoans and **2**:172
   Phoenicians and **2**:198, *201*,
      205
   Rome and **4**:465, 466, 467
   Vandals and **5**:652
ships' logs **2**:202, 205
slash-and-burn agriculture **1**:16,
   19, **10**:1312

sleds, Neolithic period and
  1:21
smelting **1**:32, 37, 41
smiths **1**:36–37, **6**:780–781
solar calendars **10**:1320
solar eclipses **3**:354, *356*
specific gravity **3**:408, *410*
steam turbines **3**:408, *409*
stonemasons **2**:158
stone tools **9**:1256
sundials **3**:354, 410

T
technology
  agriculture and **8**:1026,
    1028–1029
  barbarians and **5**:658
  Egypt and **1**:90
  European conquests and
    10:1421
  Leonardo da Vinci and
    10:1405
  mathematics and **3**:407–408
  navigation and **10**:*1365*, 1365
  pre-Columbian cultures and
    10:1302, 1345
  textiles and **8**:1030
  warfare and **10**:1419
terraces, agriculture and **10**:1304
Tetrabiblos (Ptolemy) **3**:410

textiles
  Africa and **9**:1271
  China and **7**:874
  Greece and **3**:302
  Islamic world and **6**:781, **9**:*1231*
  Japan and **7**:906
  medieval Europe and
    8:1029–1030, *1031*
  Mycenaeans and **2**:189
  Pacific islands and **7**:987
  Phoenicians and **2**:198, 202
  pre-Columbian cultures and
    10:1306, 1310, 1311, 1314,
    1323, 1345
Thales of Miletus **3**:352, *354*
tin **1**:32–33, 35, *36*, **2**:200
tools
  Africa and **9**:1256, *1263*,
    1263
  for agriculture **1**:12, 21–22
  bronze **1**:*37*, *40*, **2**:167, 172
  China and **7**:870, 871, 877
  copper **1**:32, 34
  early humans and **1**:9–10, *11*
  flint **1**:*23*, 23
  iron **1**:42, *43*, *44*, 47
  Japan and **7**:906
  metal **1**:31
  Natufian culture and **1**:11
  Neolithic period and **1**:15, *17*

Pacific islands and **7**:985, 986,
  987
for pottery **1**:21
pre-Columbian cultures and
  10:1304, 1308, 1315,
  1331
Southeast Asia and **7**:972, 974
transportation **1**:37, **10**:1316,
  1327
trigonometry **3**:410

V
Valens Aqueduct **5**:619, *620*, 620

W
warships **3**:331, 334, *339*, 339, *371*
water supplies *see* plumbing and
  water supplies
weapons and armor
  Africa and **9**:*1274*
  Berber peoples and **9**:1235
  breastplates **4**:*465*, **9**:*1274*
  Bronze Age and **1**:38
  Carthaginian **4**:*465*
  Celtic people and **1**:46, **4**:*460*
  Charlemagne and **6**:799
  Copper Age and **1**:32, 34
  early 16th century CE and
    10:1419
  Egyptian **1**:90

European conquests and **10**:1419,
  1421
Frankish **5**:*657*
gladiators and **4**:*531*, *552*
Greek **2**:265
Greek fire **6**:762
hand grenades **9**:*1181*
Iron Age and **1**:42
Islamic Spain and **6**:780–781
Japan and **7**:909, 917,
  10:*1416*
Macedon and **3**:387
medieval Europe and **8**:1105,
  1106
Mongols and **9**:1220–1221
Parthians and **6**:728
pre-Columbian cultures and
  10:1329, *1353*
Rome and **4**:449, 462, 484
Vikings and **9**:*1197*
Villanovan **4**:*457*
weaving *see* textiles
weights and measures **1**:119, **2**:212,
  238, **7**:879
wheels **1**:21–22, 65, **7**:874,
  10:1304–1305, 1333
windmills **6**:780, **8**:1028

Z
ziggurats **1**:56, *58*, 124, **2**:*209*

TRADE AND ECONOMY

Page numbers in *italics* refer to illustrations. Page numbers in **bold** refer to entire chapters.

A

accounting systems **6**:784, **10**:1341, *1343*
Africa **9**:1266, 1269, 1271, 1272, 1273, 1274, 1276, **10**:1367
agriculture
  Africa and **9**:1256, 1258–1259, 1265, 1271
  Arabia and **6**:738
  Assyrians and **2**:211
  Aztecs and **10**:1324, 1333
  Byzantine Empire and **9**:1175
  China and **7**:870–871, 873, 875, 877, 878, 897
  Cistercian Order and **8**:1035
  climate change and **8**:1084
  Crete and **2**:172
  Cycladic people and **2**:164–165
  development of states and **10**:1414
  early humans and **1**:6, 11, 14–15
  Egypt and **1**:70, 78, 86, 87, 101
  Etruscans and **4**:444
  Europe and **8**:*1030*, **10**:1416
  European settlers and **10**:1381, 1383
  feudal Europe and **6**:*821*, 821, *822*, 823, **8**:1026, *1027*, 1028–1029, *1029, 1030*
  funnel-beaker culture and **1**:19
  Germanic people and **5**:665
  Greece and **2**:162, 258, 260, 261, 266, **3**:*302*, 302–303, *306, 370*
  Greek colonies and **2**:256
  Hittites and **2**:156, 158
  Incas and **10**:1340, 1342
  India and **7**:918
  Islamic world and **9**:1238, 1240
  Japan and **7**:906, 911
  Linearbandkeramik culture and **1**:17
  Maya and **10**:1312, 1314, 1323
  Mesopotamia and **1**:54
  Minoans and **2**:175–176
  Mycenaeans and **2**:189
  Neolithic period and **1**:12, 13, 14–15, 16, 18
  North American peoples and **10**:1350, 1352, 1357
  pre-Columbian cultures and **10**:1304, 1311
  religious rituals and **10**:1354–1355
  Roman Empire and **4**:466, 476, *477*, **5**:606

Southeast Asia and **7**:972, 974–975, 976–977
Sumerian people and **1**:65
tools and **1**:21–22, 42
Vikings and **9**:1205
Akkadian Empire **1**:59–60
Alexandria **3**:392
apprentices **8**:1043
Arabia **5**:587
aristocracy, luxury goods and **8**:1033
Assyrians **2**:208, 211
Athens **3**:301
awilu (free) class, Code of Hammurabi and **1**:113, 115
ayllu (family unit) **10**:1340

B

Baghdad **6**:776
banking **4**:466, **6**:784, **8**:1031, 1032–1033, 1079, 1080
barbarian rulers **5**:665
be (communities of workers) **7**:909
Bedouin nomads **6**:738
bills of exchange **6**:784, **8**:1032
Black Death **8**:1084–1086
blood money **5**:662, 664
Bronze Age **1**:33, 36, 37
Byzantine Empire **5**:618–619, **9**:1162, 1164

C

caravans **6**:740–741, *749*, 776
caravels **10**:1367, 1369
carracks **10**:1367, 1369
Carthage **2**:200, 257, **4**:464
charters, cities and **8**:1034, 1039, 1041
China **5**:589, **6**:776, **7**:898, 899, 901, 903, **10**:1371, 1420
cities and towns **8**:1033–1034, 1036–1039, 1086, 1094
coins
  Athens and **3**:*304*
  Byzantine Empire and **9**:*1165, 1170, 1185*
  Egypt and **3**:*398*
  English **8**:*1034*
  Franks and **6**:*792*
  Greece and **3**:303, *312*
  India and **7**:931, *963*
  Islamic world and **6**:*769*, **9**:*1235, 1236*
  Lydia and **3**:328, *330*
  Macedonia and **3**:*383, 391*
  Persians and **6**:727
  Phoenicians and **3**:303
  Roman Empire and **4**:*494, 527, 535, 538*, **5**:*606, 611, 629, 635*
  Vikings and **9**:1200
  see also currency

Constantinople **9**:1160–1161
Corinth **3**:295–296, 298, 342
crafts and craftspeople
  Anasazi people and **10**:1350
  Aztecs and **10**:1327, 1333
  Celtic people and **1**:46, 50
  copper and **1**:32
  Egypt and **1**:86
  Etruscans and **4**:445
  Franks and **6**:*793*
  Goths and **5**:*645*
  Greece and **3**:302–303
  Hallstatt culture and **1**:45, 47
  Hittites and **2**:156
  Huns and **5**:*649*
  Iberian people and **1**:50
  India and **7**:920, 925
  Islamic world and **6**:*779*, 780–781
  Maya and **10**:1314, 1316, 1319
  medieval Europe and **8**:1041, 1043, 1086
  Mixtec people and **10**:1310
  Mycenaeans and **2**:189
  Neolithic period and **1**:15
  Phoenicians and **2**:198, 200
  pre-Columbian cultures and **10**:1302, 1304, 1305, 1305–1306
  Renaissance and **10**:1403
  Rome and **4**:466, 548
  Tarascan people and **10**:1310
crop rotations **3**:302, **6**:823, **8**:1028
currency
  banking and **8**:1032–1033
  barbarian rulers and **5**:665
  Bronze Age and **1**:37
  Byzantine Empire and **9**:1158, *1165*
  China and **7**:877, 879, 901
  Egypt and **1**:97
  Hittites and **2**:156
  India and **7**:946
  Persians and **2**:238
  pre-Columbian cultures and **10**:1314, 1345
  Roman Empire and **5**:595–596, 603, 604, 612
  see also coins
Cycladic people **2**:167, 169

D

Damascus **6**:776, 781
debts **2**:266–267, **3**:294, 298, 403, **4**:450, 455, 493, **5**:664
desert trade routes **6**:776, 778, 779
disintegration of the Roman Empire **5**:604
dowries **1**:118, **3**:350, **10**:1323
Dutch **10**:1371

E

economy
  annual fairs and **8**:1030–1032
  Arabic culture and **6**:784
  Black Death and **8**:1086
  China and **7**:877, 894, 901, 903
  coinage and **2**:303
  Constantinople and **9**:1160–1161
  Egypt and **1**:97, 99
  Hundred Years' War and **8**:1102
  Roman Empire and **5**:604, 608
  see also finances, Roman Empire and; trade
education **10**:1384
Edward III of England, banking and **8**:1033
Egypt **1**:87, 101, **5**:587, 589
employment
  actors **3**:321
  cities and towns and **10**:1416
  crafts and craftspeople **3**:302–303
  Egypt and **1**:108
  guilds and **8**:1043
  Hittites and **2**:158
  Hundred Years' War and **8**:1102
  mercenaries **3**:388–389
  Peasants' Revolt (England) and **8**:1109
  pre-Columbian cultures and **10**:1319, 1327, 1344
  Rome and **4**:548, 549
  shoemakers **4**:*550*
  Socrates and **3**:362
  Sophists and **3**:361
  temples and **7**:966
  see also agriculture; labor; work specialization
Etruscans **4**:445
Europe **2**:257, **8**:1026, 1028–1034
European exploration, trade routes and **10**:1362–1364

F

fairs, annual **8**:1030–1032, *1032, 1033*
famine **5**:622, **8**:1084, **10**:1381
farming *see* agriculture
feudal Europe **6**:**814–831**
feudalism
  Carolingian Empire and **6**:808
  China and **7**:882, 900
  cities and towns and **8**:1034, 1041
  crusades and **9**:1182
  daily life and **6**:823
  England and **8**:1048–1049
  Franks and **6**:793
  Hittites and **2**:155–156
  Holy Roman Empire and **6**:831, **8**:1058, 1060, 1063
  leagues and alliances and **8**:1094
  Peasants' Revolt (England) and **8**:1109

feudalism (*continued*)
Philip II Augustus and **8**:1054, 1057
primogeniture and **6**:828
religion and **6**:823–824, 825
rise of **6**:819, 821
Roman Catholic Church and **8**:1014, 1061
social classes and **6**:821–822
warfare and **6**:822–823
feudal manors, daily life in **6**:823
finances, Roman Empire and **5**:592, 595–596, 603, 604
flint mining **1**:19, 23
food
Africa and **9**:1256, 1262
agricultural improvements and **8**:1028–1029
China and **7**:895, 911
crusades and **9**:1187
distribution of **5**:603, 612, 616, 621–622
Mongols and **9**:1220
Pacific islands and **7**:987
pre-Columbian cultures and **10**:1312, 1314, 1316, 1331, 1333
religious offerings of **3**:312
Rome and **4**:482, 490, 498
freemen **6**:821, **7**:911

G
glassware, Phoenicians and **2**:200
gold
Africa and **9**:1269, 1270, 1271, **10**:1367
Bronze Age and **1**:37–38
Chibcha people and **10**:1310
Constantinople and **9**:1160–1161
Egypt and **1**:101
Iron Age and **1**:49–50
Neolithic period and **1**:31
Phoenicians and **2**:202–203
Spanish conquistadores and **10**:1335
government spending **4**:516–517, 520, 531, 532–533, 534, 539
grain **1**:11, 12, **4**:481–482, 508, 548–549, **5**:586, 621–622
Greece **1**:49, **2**:162, 248, 253–254, **3**:302, 304
Greek colonies **2**:257
guilds **8**:1041, *1041*, 1043, *1087*
Black Death and **8**:1086
cities and towns and **8**:1037, 1041, 1043
education and **10**:1387
Hundred Years' War and **8**:1102, 1104

H
Hallstatt culture **1**:45, 47
Hanseatic League **8**:1033–1034, 1094, *1095*, *1097*, 1097, 1098, 1100, **9**:1213

helots (serfs) **2**:258, 260
Henry the Navigator **8**:1093, **10**:*1364*, *1366*, 1366–1367, 1369, 1370
horses **1**:49, **2**:211, 251, **9**:1220, 1221, **10**:1358

I
Iberian people **1**:49
India **5**:589, **7**:918, 920, 921, 931, 946, 966
industry **8**:1030, 1032–1033
inflation **5**:604, 608
inheritance rights **5**:664–665, **6**:809, 828, 830, **9**:1212, 1255
interest rates **1**:116, **4**:466
Iron Age **1**:44
irrigation
Arabia and **5**:587
Assyrians and **2**:211
China and **7**:877
Egypt and **1**:80–81
Latium and **4**:444
Mesopotamia and **1**:54
Persians and **2**:245
pre-Columbian cultures and **10**:1310, 1311, 1312, 1333, 1350
Islamic world **6**:767, 774, 776, 784, 787, **9**:1230
Israelites **2**:231
Italy **3**:296

J
Jamestown Colony **10**:1380–1381
Japan **7**:917
Jewish people **4**:534, **6**:780, **8**:1033
journeymen, guilds and **8**:1043

K
Kiev **9**:1208

L
labor
Black Death and **8**:1086
Buddhism and **7**:954–955
Egypt and **1**:86, 97, 99, 100
Incas and **10**:1341
India and **7**:924–925
monasteries and **5**:692, 693, 694, 700, **6**:824, 826
pyramids and **1**:73–74
see also employment; work specialization
landownership
Akkadian Empire and **1**:61
barbarians and **5**:660
Buddhist monasteries and **7**:955
Capetian dynasty and **6**:828
Carolingian Empire and **6**:811, 813
Charles Martel and **6**:792–793
China and **7**:875, 879, 897, 899, 900, 901–902
Christians and **5**:628

Egypt and **1**:86, 94, 107
feudalism and **6**:808, 819, 821, 823
Franks and **6**:788, 790
Greece and **2**:255–256, 266, **3**:301, 403
Hittites and **2**:155–156
Japan and **7**:910, 911, 913, 917
Merovingian dynasty and **6**:790
monasteries and **8**:1035
Ottoman Turks and **9**:1255
pre-Columbian cultures and **10**:1328, 1340
Roman Catholic Church and **6**:790
Roman Empire and **4**:513, **5**:606
Rome and **4**:476, 479–481, 484
Vikings and **6**:809
land reforms **4**:479–481
latifundia (estates) **4**:476, *477*
leagues and alliances **8**:**1094–1101**
learning and knowledge **10**:1416, 1418
legal systems, Hanseatic League and **8**:*1097*
London Company **10**:1380
luxury goods **8**:1033
Lydia **3**:328

M
manufacturing industries **7**:911
Mari **1**:114
Mecca **6**:739
merchants **2**:175, **8**:*1087*, **10**:*1327–1328*
metals, sources of **2**:164
minerals, sources of **2**:164
mining
Anatolia and **3**:328
Athens and **3**:331, 348
Bronze Age and **1**:37
copper **1**:94
flint **1**:19, 23
Hittites and **2**:156
Phoenicians and **2**:200
salt **1**:45
Teotihuacán and **10**:1308
tin **1**:*36*
Minoans **2**:175
Mohammed **6**:740–741
money *see* currency
moneychanging **8**:1031, 1032–1033
moneylending **4**:466, **6**:784, **8**:1033
Mongols **9**:1224, 1225
Morocco **10**:1366
Mycenaeans **2**:191

N
Neolithic period **1**:15
Northern Passage **10**:1378
Novgorod **9**:1208

P
patrons, Renaissance and **10**:1400–1401, 1403, 1404, 1405, 1406

payments **2**:202–203
perfume makers **6**:*779*
Persian Empire, taxation and **6**:779
Philip IV (France), fiscal problems of **8**:1079
Phoenicians **1**:49, **2**:196, 198, 198–199, 202–203, 222
piracy **4**:464, 489, 490, **6**:779, 780
Piraeus **3**:349, 370, 371, *372*
political power, trade guilds and **4**:550
Polo, Marco **8**:*1098*, **9**:*1179*, 1224, *1225*, 1225, 1226, **10**:*1362*, *1363*
Portugal **10**:1364, 1366, 1370–1371, *1417*, 1418
poverty
Athens and **3**:298, 300
Constantinople and **5**:621, 622
Dark Age Greece and **2**:246, 248
Rome and **4**:481–482, 548
pre-Columbian cultures and **10**:1308, 1309, 1316, 1327–1328
professions, Sumerians and **1**:69
see also labor
property rights
Athens and **2**:267, 269
Babylonians and **1**:113
early Byzantine Empire and **9**:1165
monasteries and **5**:694, 700
Rome and **4**:449, 453, 550
serfs and **6**:823
women and **5**:664
see also landownership

Q
quipus (accounting system) **10**:1341, *1343*

R
Raleigh, Walter **10**:1380
ransoms **8**:1056, 1111
Rome **4**:466, 489, 546, 548
Russia **9**:1208, 1210, 1213

S
salt mining **1**:45
Samarra **6**:786
seafaring
Athens and **2**:264
Corinth and **3**:295, 296
Dong Son civilization and **7**:974
Pacific islands and **7**:985, 987
Phoenicians and **2**:196, 198–199, 200–202
Southeast Asia and **7**:972, 976
trade and **3**:304
see also ships and shipbuilding
seagoing traders **6**:779–780
serfs **5**:606, **6**:819, 821, 822, 823, **8**:1041
ships and shipbuilding
China and **10**:1419, 1420
European conquests and **10**:1421

Islamic world and **6**:777, 779–780
longships, Viking **6**:809, **9**:1196, *1202*, 1202, *1204*
medieval Europe and **6**:809, 814, 817, **10**:1363, 1367, 1369
Minoans and **2**:172
Phoenicians and **2**:198, *201, 205*
Rome and **4**:465, 466, 467
Vandals and **5**:652
shoemakers **2**:*266*, **3**:*303*, **4**:*550*
shopkeepers **4**:*480*
shudras **7**:925, 927, 946
Silk Road **5**:589, **7**:898, 899
silver mining **4**:466
Sima Qian **7**:886, 899
simony **6**:838, 839, **8**:1086–1087, 1088
slash-and-burn agriculture **1**:16, 19, **10**:1312
slavery
 Africa and **9**:1272, 1274–1275
 agriculture and **4**:476
 Assyrians and **2**:214
 Babylonians and **1**:115
 Carthage and **4**:469
 Celtic people and **1**:50
 China and **7**:877
 Christianity and **5**:635
 debts and **4**:453, 455
 Egyptians and **1**:86
 Germanic peoples and **5**:664
 Greece and **2**:253, 255, 266–267, **3**:308, 347, 403
 Islam and **6**:743
 Japan and **7**:911
 Macedonia and **3**:388
 Mycenaeans and **2**:189
 Peloponnesian War and **3**:376
 Portuguese traders and **10**:1367
 pre-Columbian cultures and **10**:1326–1327, 1358
 Punic Wars and **4**:481
 Rome and **4**:446, **5**:606
 Spartacus and **4**:489–490
 Sumerians and **1**:57
 Vikings and **9**:1196, 1205
slave trade **9**:1274–1275
smiths **1**:36–37, **6**:780–781
Southeast Asia **7**:975, 976, 977, 978, 980, 980–981
spending, government **4**:516–517, 520, 531, 532–533, 534, 539, **5**:595
spice trade **7**:931, 980–981, **10**:1362–1363, 1370–1371

T
tailors **8**:*1036*
taxation
 Africa and **9**:1271
 Assyrians and **2**:216, 217

barbarians and **5**:658
Byzantine Empire and **5**:608, 612, 676, **9**:1161, 1164, 1170, 1175
China and **7**:877, 879, 894, 895, 896, 897, 901–902, 904
cities and towns and **8**:1034, 1039
Egypt and **1**:77, 86, 105
England and **8**:1050, 1056, 1067, 1109, 1116
France and **8**:1079, 1081
Greece and **3**:301
Hittites and **2**:158
Holy Roman Empire and **8**:1072
Incas and **10**:1341
India and **7**:928
Islamic world and **6**:746, 759, 768
Japan and **7**:911, 913
Kievan Rus and **9**:1211
Mongols and **9**:1220, 1222, 1226
Ottoman Turks and **9**:1249, 1250
Persians and **2**:238, 245, **6**:735
Roman Empire and **4**:476, 479, 508, 525, 534, 546, **5**:595, 596, 604
tax collectors **5**:604
tenant farmers **5**:606, 608
textiles
 Africa and **9**:1271
 China and **7**:874
 Greece and **3**:302
 Islamic world and **6**:781, **9**:*1231*
 Japan and **7**:906
 medieval Europe and **8**:1029–1030, *1031*
 Mycenaeans and **2**:189
 Pacific islands and **7**:987
 Phoenicians and **2**:198, 202
 pre-Columbian cultures and **10**:1306, 1310, 1311, 1314, 1323, 1345
thetes (laborers) **2**:266, 267, **3**:304, 344
tolls, desert trade routes and **6**:779
trade
 Africa and **9**:1266, 1269, 1271, 1272, 1273, 1274, 1276, **10**:1367
 Akkadian Empire and **1**:59–60
 Alexandria and **3**:392
 annual fairs and **8**:1030–1032
 Arabia and **5**:587
 Assyrians and **2**:208, 211
 Athens and **3**:301
 barbarian rulers and **5**:665
 Bedouin nomads and **6**:738
 Bronze Age and **1**:33, 36, 37
 Byzantine Empire and **5**:618–619, **9**:1162, 1164
 Carthage and **2**:200, **4**:464

China and **5**:589, **7**:898, 899, 901, 903, **10**:1420
cities and towns and **8**:1034
Corinth and **3**:295–296, 298, 342
Cycladic people and **2**:167, 169
desert routes and **6**:776, 778, 779
Dutch and **10**:1371
education and **10**:1384
Egypt and **1**:87, 101
Etruscans and **4**:445
Greece and **2**:162, 248, 253–254, **3**:302, 304
Greek colonies and **2**:257
guilds and **8**:1041, 1043
Hallstatt culture and **1**:45, 47
Hanseatic League and **8**:1094, *1095*, 1097
Iberian people and **1**:49
India and **5**:589, **7**:918, 920, 921, 931, 946, 966
Iron Age and **1**:44
Islamic world and **6**:767, 774, 776, 784, 787, **9**:1230
Israelites and **2**:231
Japan and **7**:917
learning and knowledge and **10**:1416, 1418
Lydia and **3**:328
Mari and **1**:114
Mecca and **6**:739
Minoans and **2**:175
Mohammed and **6**:740–741
Mongols and **9**:1224, 1225
Mycenaeans and **2**:191
Neolithic period and **1**:15
networks **8**:1033–1034
Phoenicians and **2**:196, 198, 198–199, 202–203, 222
Portugal and **10**:1364, 1366, 1370–1371, *1417*
pre-Columbian cultures and **10**:1308, 1309, 1316, 1327–1328
Rome and **4**:466, 489, 546, 548
Russia and **9**:1208, 1210, 1213
Samarra and **6**:786
seagoing traders and **6**:779–780
slaves and **9**:1274–1275
Southeast Asia and **7**:975, 976, 977, 978, 980, 980–981
Troy and **2**:192, 195
Vikings and **9**:1196, 1200, 1201, 1203
Wars of the Roses and **8**:1117
trade caravans *see* caravans
trade guilds **4**:548, 550
trade laws **1**:116
trade networks **8**:1033–1034
trade routes, European expansion and **10**:1362–1364

trading posts **2**:199, 208, 253–254, **8**:1097, **10**:1367
tribute
 Byzantine Empire and **5**:671
 Charlemagne and **6**:798
 China and **7**:903
 England and **8**:1046
 Greece and **3**:341, 381
 Huns and **5**:651, **9**:1161–1162
 India and **7**:960
 Islamic Spain and **8**:1016
 medieval Europe and **6**:830
 Mongols and **8**:1101, **9**:1215, 1222, 1228, 1235
 Ottoman Turks and **9**:1245
 Persians and **6**:726
 pre-Columbian cultures and **10**:1324, 1327, *1328*, 1334, 1356
 Rome and **4**:469, 478, 497, 508
 Saracens and **8**:1022
 Seljuk Turks and **9**:1179
 Vikings and **6**:818–819, **9**:1201
Troy **2**:192, 195

U
urban Europe, growth of **8**:**1026–1043**
urban planning **5**:618–619, **7**:918, 920–921, **10**:1307–1308, 1315–1416

V
vaishyas (farmers and traders) **7**:925, 946
Venice
 Polo, Marco, and **8**:*1098*, **9**:1225, **10**:*1363*
 spice trade and **10**:1362–1363
Vikings **9**:1196, 1200, 1201, 1203

W
wages **1**:116, **8**:1086, 1109
war booty **3**:304, 390, **4**:459, 466, **5**:604, **6**:729, 755, 814
Wars of the Roses **8**:1117
wealth
 Assyrians and **2**:208
 Athens and **3**:348
 Greeks and **2**:251, 269
 Minoans and **2**:180
 Rome and **4**:446, 449, 450, 507, 548
weights and measures **1**:119, **2**:212, 238, **7**:879
wool **8**:1102
work specialization **1**:36–37, 38, 70
 see also employment

Z
zeugitai (farmers) **2**:266, 267, **3**:304, 344

WARS AND BATTLES

Page numbers in *italics* refer to illustrations. Page numbers in **bold** refer to entire chapters.

A

Abrittus, Battle of **5**:*599*
Actium, Battle of **4**:512, **5**:586
Adrianople, Battle of **5**:614, 640, 643, **9**:1160
Aegates Islands, Battle of **4**:468–469
Africa **9**:1277
Agincourt, Battle of **8**:1110, *1111*, 1111
Ain Jalut, Battle of **9**:1228, 1236–1237
Akkadians **1**:60, 62
Albigensian Crusade **8**:1025, **9**:1182, 1191, *1194*, 1194
Allia, Battle of **4**:462
alliances
    Achaean League **3**:403
    Athens and **3**:340
    Corinthian League **3**:385
    Delian League **3**:341, 342, 368, 370
    Peloponnesian League **3**:368, 370, 373
    Peloponnesian War and **3**:368
    Rome and **4**:458, 463
    Spartan Confederacy **3**:342
al-Qadisiyah, Battle of **6**:755
Ankara, Battle of **9**:1246
Antioch, siege of **9**:1187, *1188*
archers **6**:*728*, 728, **9**:1220–1221
armies *see* military forces
armor *see* weapons and armor
Arsuf, Battle of **8**:1056
Artemisium, Battle of **3**:332–333
Asculum, Battle of **4**:462
Assyrians **2**:210, 212–213, 216, 221
Athens
    First Persian War and **3**:329–330
    Lamian War and **3**:401–402
    Peloponnesian War and **2**:239, 250, 254, **3**:342, 344, 362, **368–383**
    Second Persian War and **3**:331, 333–334, 336, 337, *339*

B

Babylonians **1**:110
Badr, Battle of **6**:*746*, 746
Baecula, Battle of **4**:474
Baghdad, siege of **6**:772, *775*
Bagradas, Battle of **4**:467–468
Barnet, Battle of **8**:1121–1122, *1122*
Bedouin nomads **6**:738

Belgrade, siege of **9**:*1254*
Benevento, Battle of **8**:*1074*, 1074
Borylaeum, Battle of **9**:1187
Bosworth Field, Battle of **8**:1125
Bouvines, Battle of **8**:1055, *1057*, 1065, 1067
breastplates **4**:*465*, **9**:*1274*
Bronze Age **1**:40
Burgundy **8**:1108, 1110, 1112, 1113, 1120, 1121, 1130–1133
Byzantine Empire
    civil strife **5**:626, 627, 669, 670, 671, **9**:1164, 1178
    crusades and **8**:1068, **9**:1182, 1184, 1185, 1187, 1190
    piracy and **6**:779–780

C

Cade's Rebellion **8**:1116, *1117*
Cannae, Battle of **4**:*471*, 472–473
Cape Mycale, Battle of **3**:336, 339, 340
Capitoline Hill, Battle of **4**:459
Carchemish, Battle of **2**:152
Carolingian Empire **6**:812
Carrhae, Battle of **4**:496, **6**:728
Carthage **4**:462, **464–475**, *465*, 469, 481
Catalaunian Plains, Battle of **5**:645, *650*, 650–651, *652*
cataphracts (cavalry troops) **6**:728
cavalry
    Agincourt, Battle of, and **8**:1111
    Alexander the Great and **3**:*385*, 389
    Assyrians and **2**:213
    Berber peoples and **9**:1235
    feudalism and **6**:822
    Franks and **6**:792, 799, 830
    Mongols and **9**:1221
    Parthians and **6**:728
    Rome and **4**:462
    see also knights
Celtic people **1**:50
Chaeronea, Battle of **3**:383, 384
Chaldiran, Battle of **10**:1418, 1419
chariots **1**:46, 90, *98*, **2**:157, 210, 214, **7**:875, 876
children, military forces and **9**:1230, 1236, 1255
China **7**:877, 881, 882, 898, **9**:1226–1227
Ciompi Rebellion **8**:1086
cities and towns **8**:1041
civil strife
    Africa and **9**:1277
    Assyrians and **2**:216, 221
    Black Death and **8**:1086
    Byzantine Empire and **5**:626, 627, 669, 670, 671, **9**:1164, 1178

Carolingian Empire and **6**:812
Carthage and **4**:469
China and **7**:877, 881, 882, 898, **9**:1226–1227
Constantinople and **5**:624
dynastic succession and **4**:516, 518–519, 529, 537, **5**:598, 599, 611
England and **8**:1051, 1076–1077, 1109, 1114–1125
foederati (allies) and **5**:588
France and **8**:1130
Francia and **8**:1044
Greece and **3**:294, 296, 300, 378–379
Holy Roman Empire and **6**:835, **8**:1058
Hundred Years' War and **8**:1108
India and **7**:969, 971
Islamic world and **6**:756–757, 768–769, 773, 785
Janissaries and **9**:1255
Japan and **7**:916–917
Macedonian Empire and **3**:396
Persians and **2**:236, 239
pre-Columbian cultures and **10**:1338, 1340, 1347
Renaissance and **10**:1398
Rome and **4**:442, 482, 485–487, 496, 502, 532
Salian dynasty and **6**:837, 843–844
Sicilian Vespers and **8**:1074–1075
Thomas the Slav and **9**:1171–1172
conquered peoples
    Alexander the Great and **3**:388, 391
    crusades and **9**:1189, 1191
    Islamic world and **6**:752
    Italian cities and **4**:463
    Jerusalem and **4**:541
    Macedonian Wars and **4**:478
    Mongols and **9**:1221–1222, 1223, 1227, 1228, 1229, 1240
    Ottoman Turks and **9**:1247
    Peloponnesian War and **3**:376, 378–379
    Persians and **2**:239, 245, **3**:327
    pre-Columbian cultures and **10**:1334
    Punic Wars and **4**:469, 475, 481
    Trajan and **4**:539–540
    Vikings and **9**:1201
conscription, military forces and **2**:214, 216
Constantinople **5**:624, **6**:762, 763, **9**:1172, 1247
Corinth **3**:342, 368, 370, 382
Corinthian League **3**:385
Corinthian War **3**:382

Corupedium, Battle of **3**:399
coups d'état **3**:294, 300, 301, **4**:518, **9**:1171, 1175
    see also civil strife
Crannon, Battle of **3**:401
Crécy, Battle of **8**:1105, *1106*, 1106
crusades **9**:**1182–1195**, *1184*
    Constantinople and **5**:618, 672, **8**:1082, **9**:1168, 1179, 1181
    Frederick I and **8**:1063
    Frederick II and **8**:1073
    Islamic world and **10**:1360
    Knights Templar and **8**:1080
    Louis IX and **8**:1078
    Mamluk dynasty and **9**:1237
    Nicopolis, Battle of, and **9**:1248
    Richard I (the Lionheart) and **8**:1056
    Roman Catholic Church and **8**:1014, 1067, 1068, 1069
    Teutonic Knights and **8**:1101
Cynoscephalae, Battle of **4**:476, 478

D

Damascus **9**:*1190*, 1190–1191
Dorylaeum, Battle of **9**:1190
Durazzo, Battle of **8**:1024
dynastic succession **4**:516, 518–519, 529, 537, **5**:598, 599, 611, **10**:1415–1416

E

Edessa, Battle of **6**:729
Edgecote Moor, Battle of **8**:1120
Edington, Battle of **6**:820
Egypt
    crusades and **9**:1191, 1193, 1195
    warfare and **1**:77, 87, 92, 94, 98, 99, 105, 106, 107, 109, **2**:225
England
    civil strife and **8**:1051, 1076–1077, 1109, 1114–1125
    Hundred Years' War **8**:1085, **1102–1113**, 1126
    Wars of the Roses **8**:**1114–1125**
Eurymedon River, battle near **3**:341
Evesham, Battle of **8**:1076

F

feudalism **6**:822–823
Fifth Crusade **9**:1193
firearms, Japan and **7**:917
First Crusade **6**:*823*, **9**:1182, 1184–1189, 1234
First Macedonian War **4**:478
First Persian War **3**:329–330
First Punic War **4**:464, 464–465, 467–470
foederati (allies) **5**:588, 643, 645, 652, 654, 660

Fontenay, Battle of **6**:813
fortifications
    Athens and **2**:264, **3**:370, 371
    Bronze Age and **1**:40
    castles and **6**:823
    China and **7**:875, 877, 879, *880*,
        896, **9**:1222
    Constantinople and **5**:618, *619*,
        622, **9**:1161, 1165, 1179, 1247
    Cycladic people and **2**:167
    Egyptian **1**:87
    Great Zimbabwe **9**:*1275*
    Hittites and **2**:152–153, 154
    India and **7**:918, 927
    Japan and **7**:916
    Krak des Chevaliers **9**:*1189*
    Mycenaeans and **2**:183–184, 187,
        191
    Nimrud and **2**:213
    Novgorod and **9**:*1214*
    Persepolis and **2**:240
    pre-Columbian cultures and
        10:1311, 1357
    Rhodes and **9**:*1195*
    Rome and **4**:442, 459
    Troy and **2**:193, 195
Fourth Crusade **8**:*1068*, 1068,
    9:1181, 1191, 1192–1193,
    1193, 1213
France
    civil strife and **8**:1130
    crusades and **9**:1182, 1185, 1187
    Hundred Years' War **8**:1085,
        1102–1113
    Wars of the Roses and **8**:1117,
        1120, 1125
Francia **8**:1044
Frigidus River, Battle of **5**:615

G

Gallic Wars **4**:494–495
Gascony, Hundred Years' War and
    8:1102, 1108
Gaugamela, Battle of **3**:393
Germanic people **1**:53
ghazi warriors **9**:1240–1241, 1242
Grandson, Battle of **8**:1132
Granicus River, Battle of **3**:389–390
Great Army **9**:1198
Great Plains, Battle of **4**:474
Great Zab River, Battle of **6**:769
Greece **2**:258, **3**:302, 303, **4**:456
    civil strife and **3**:294, 296, 300,
        378–379
    Peloponnesian War **2**:239, 250,
        254, **3**:342, 344, 362, **368–383**
    Persian Wars **2**:264, **3**:326–339,
        329
Greek fire **6**:762, 763
Guadalete, Battle of **6**:760, *761*
guerrilla warfare **6**:797, **8**:1113

H

Hallstatt culture **1**:47
hand grenades **9**:*1181*
Hanseatic League **8**:1097, 1098

Hastings, Battle of **8**:1047–1048,
    1049
Hastings, William **8**:1123, 1125
Hattin, Battle of **9**:1191
Heiji Disturbance **7**:*914*, 914
helmets, Corinthian **2**:265
Heraclea, Battle of **4**:462
Hittites **2**:150, 152, 153, 157
Holy Roman Empire **6**:835,
    8:1058, 1073
holy wars *see* crusades; jihad
Homs, Battle of **9**:1238
hoplites **2**:*265*, 265, **3**:304, 330,
    336, 337, *369*, *376*, 382–383
Hormuz, Battle of **6**:726
Hundred Years' War **8**:1085, 1088,
    1102–1113, *1103*, *1104*, 1108,
    1126
Hydaspes, Battle of **3**:394

I

Illipa, Battle of **4**:474
infantry **2**:157, 214
Ionian rebellion **3**:326–327
Islam **6**:744, 746, 751, 752, 754,
    755–757, 768
Islamic world **6**:756–757, 768–769,
    773, 785
Israelites **2**:230, 231
Issus, Battle of **3**:*389*, 390–391

J

Jalowaz, Battle of **9**:1246
Janissaries **9**:1230, 1245, 1247,
    1249, 1255
Japan **7**:916–917
Jerusalem
    crusades and **6**:*823*, **8**:1014,
        1068, 1069, **9**:1182, 1188–
        1189, 1195
    military forces of **9**:1189–
        1190
    siege of **9**:1189
jihad **6**:744
"just war," concept of **8**:1018

K

Kadesh, Battle of **1**:106, **2**:153
Kalka River, Battle of **9**:1223
Karbala, Battle of **6**:*757*, 757, 767
knights **6**:822–823, *823*, **8**:1014,
    1018
Knights Hospitaller **8**:1014, 1101,
    9:1190, 1247, 1249, 1252, 1255
Knights Templar **8**:1014, 1018,
    1079, 1079, *1080*, 1080, **9**:1190
Konya, Battle of **9**:1245
Kosedagh, Battle of **9**:1235
Kozelsk, siege of **9**:*1215*
Kulikovo, Battle of **9**:1215, *1216*

L

Lake Peipus, Battle of **9**:1217
Lamian War **3**:401–402
Las Navas de Tolosa, Battle of
    8:1017, *1018*, **9**:1235

Latin League **4**:458, 460
Lechfeld, Battle of **6**:*831*, 831
Legnano, Battle of **8**:*1062*, 1062
Lepanto, Battle of **9**:1253
Leuctra, Battle of **3**:382
Lewes, Battle of **8**:1076
Liegnitz, Battle of **8**:1101, **9**:*1227*,
    1227
longbowmen, English **8**:1105, 1106,
    1111
longships, Viking **6**:*809*, **9**:1196,
    1202, 1202, *1204*
Lonkoping, Battle of **8**:1099
Ludford Bridge, Battle of **8**:1117
Lupia River, Battle of **4**:514

M

Macedonia **3**:396, **4**:476
Macedonian Wars **4**:478
Magnesia, Battle of **4**:475, 476
Mamertines **4**:464
Mamluk armies **9**:1236
Mantinea, Battle of (418 BCE)
    3:373
Mantinea, Battle of (362 BCE)
    3:383
Manzikert, Battle of **9**:1168,
    1178–1179, 1182, 1232, 1240
maps **3**:*329*, **8**:*1104*, **9**:*1184*
Marathon, Battle of **2**:238, **3**:305,
    327, 329–330, *333*
Marj Dabiq, Battle of **9**:1252
massacres **2**:213, 214, 216, **4**:502,
    529, **5**:643
mawali, rebellion of **6**:768
Medes **2**:232
mercenaries
    Alexander the Great and
        3:388–389
    Egypt and **1**:107
    Fatimid dynasty and **6**:774
    Greece and **3**:294, 303
    Greek colonies and **4**:461
    Hittites and **2**:157
    Hundred Years' War and **8**:1107
    Italian city-states and **8**:1096
    Tang dynasty and **7**:902
Metcaurus River, Battle of **4**:474
military coups *see* coups d'etat
military forces
    Africa and **9**:*1268*, 1270, *1273*,
        1274, *1277*
    Agincourt, Battle of, and **8**:1111
    Alexander the Great and **3**:*385*,
        388–389, 394
    archers **6**:*728*, 728, **9**:1220–1221
    Aryan people and **7**:924
    Assyrians and **2**:210–211, 213,
        214, 214, 216
    Athens and **3**:306, 331
    barbarians and **5**:658
    Bedouin nomads and **6**:751
    Berber peoples and **9**:1235
    Britain and **5**:663, *664*
    Bulgar people and **9**:1176, *1177*,
        1178

Byzantine Empire and
    5:612–613, 625, 671, 673,
    9:1163, 1165, 1168, 1170, 1171,
    1174, 1175, 1176, 1178–1179
Carthage and **4**:464
cavalry **4**:462
Charlemagne and **6**:*799*, 799
Charles Martel and **6**:792
children and **9**:1230, 1236, 1255
China and **7**:875, 877, *881*, 881,
    902, 903
Crécy, Battle of, and **8**:1106
crusades and **9**:1184–1185, *1187*,
    1187
cultural influence in Roman
    provinces **4**:547
early Rome and **4**:446, 449–550,
    454, 456–463, 484
Egypt's New Kingdom and
    1:99–100, 105, 107
equestrians **5**:601
First Persian War and **3**:329–330
Germanic peoples and **4**:*547*,
    5:641–642, 643, 645–646, 653,
    660, *665*, **6**:808
Hittites and **2**:*157*, 157, 158
hoplites **2**:265, **3**:304, 330, *336*,
    369, *376*, 382–383
Huns and **9**:1161
India and **7**:928
Ionian rebellion and **3**:326–327
Islamic culture and **6**:785
Italian rebels and **4**:485–486
Janissaries **9**:1230, 1245, 1247,
    1249, 1255
Japan and **7**:911, 912, 913–914,
    916
Jewish people and **4**:*541*
Khosrow I and **6**:735
Kiev and **9**:1211
Knights Hospitaller **8**:1014, 1101
Knights Templar **8**:1014, 1018,
    1079, 1079, *1080*, 1080
Macedonia and **3**:383, 386, *387*,
    387, **4**:478
Mamluk dynasty and **9**:1236,
    1238, 1251–1252
Mari and **1**:115
Medes and **2**:232
mercenaries **3**:294, 303, 388–389
Mongols and **7**:904, **9**:1215,
    1219, 1220–1222, 1223, *1227*,
    1237, 1238, 1240
Mycenaeans and **2**:189, 191
Normans and **8**:1023
Ottoman Turks and **9**:1250,
    1254
Otto the Great and **6**:831
Parthians and **6**:*728*, 728
Persians and **2**:*237*, 237, **3**:332
Praetorian Guard **4**:517, 519–520,
    521, 521, 532
pre-Columbian cultures and
    10:1324, 1327, 1328–1329,
    1329, 1341, *1349*
Reconquista and **8**:1017–1018

military forces (*continued*)
  religious orders and **8**:1014, 1025
  Roman emperors and **4**:493, 494,
    504, 506, 511–513, 520–521,
    536, 537–538, 539–540,
    542–543
  Roman Empire and **5**:582,
    593–594, 604, *605*, 607, 608
  Rome and **4**:*484*
  Samites and **4**:*461*
  Second Persian War and **3**:336,
    337, 339
  Seljuk Turks and **9**:*1234*, 1240–
    1241
  Sparta and **2**:258, 260, 261, 263
  succession of Roman leadership
    and **4**:532–533, 538, **5**:592–593
  Thebes and **3**:382–383
  tyranny and **3**:294
  Vikings and **9**:1198
  see also warfare
Milvian Bridge, Battle of **5**:628
Mohács, Battle of **9**:1252, **10**:1418
Mongols **9**:1222
Morat, Battle of **8**:*1132*, 1132
Mount Uhud, Battle of **6**:746
Mughal Empire **10**:*1418*
Munda, Battle of **4**:499
Mutina, Battle of **4**:502
mutinies **3**:394
Mylae, Battle of **4**:467, *468*

N

Nahavand, Battle of **6**:755
Nancy, siege of **8**:1132
naval power
  Antony and Cleopatra and **4**:503
  Athens and **3**:331, 340
  blood games and **4**:552
  Byzantine Empire and **9**:1176,
    1181
  China and **7**:904
  Delian League and **3**:341
  India and **7**:966
  Islamic world and **6**:763
  Italian city-states and **8**:1025,
    1034, 1036
  medieval Europe and **6**:814, 817,
    10:1365
  Mylae, Battle of **4**:*468*
  Ottoman Turks and **9**:1244, 1247,
    1249, *1251*, 1253, 1255,
    10:1418
  Peloponnesian War and **3**:368,
    370, 376, 378
  piracy and **4**:489
  Portugal and **10**:1364, 1366–
    1367, 1369–1371
  Punic Wars and **4**:465, 467, 468–
    469, 470, 473
  Salamis, Battle of **3**:334, 336
  Second Persian War and **3**:332–
    333
  Thucydides and **3**:377
  triremes (warships) **3**:331, 334,
    339, 339

Vandals and **5**:652, 653
Vikings and **9**:1196, 1201, *1202*,
  1202
Nedao, Battle of **5**:651
Nicopolis, Battle of **9**:1245, *1248*,
  1248
Nika Revolt **5**:670, 671, 672, 674,
  9:1164
Northampton, Battle of **8**:1117

O

Onin War **7**:917
Orléans, siege of **8**:1110, *1112*,
  1112

P

palisades **10**:1357
Pallene, Battle of **3**:301
Panipat, Battle of **7**:970
Paris, siege of **6**:832, **9**:1199–1200,
  1201
Peasants' Revolt (England) **8**:1108,
  1109, 1109
peasants' revolts **8**:1086, 1107, 1116
Peloponnesian War **2**:239, 250, 254,
  3:342, 344, 362, **368–383**
Period of the Warring States
  (China) **7**:877, *885*, 906
Period of the Warring States
  (Japan) **7**:917
Persians **2**:232, 233–234, 238–
  239, **3**:381–382, **6**:726, 729,
  733, 735
Persian Wars **2**:264, **3**:**326–339**, *329*
phalanxes **3**:386, *387*, 387, 389,
  4:478
Pharsalus, Battle of **4**:496
Philippi, Battle of **4**:502
piracy **4**:464, 489, 490, **6**:779, 780
Plataea, Battle of **2**:239, **3**:336, *337*,
  337, 340
Poitiers, Battle of **8**:1105
Praetorian Guard
  Caligula and **4**:519–520, *521*, 521
  Caracalla and **5**:596
  Elagabalus and **5**:597
  Galba, Sulpicius, and **4**:532
  Pertinax, Helvius, and **5**:592
  Postumas, Marcus, and **5**:601
  Severus, Septimius, and **5**:594
  Tiberius and **4**:517
pre-Columbian cultures **10**:1308,
  1318, 1324, 1328–1329, 1334,
  1336, 1338–1339, 1340, 1347,
  1356
Preveza, Battle of **9**:1253, 1255
prisoners of war, Aztecs and
  10:1328, 1329, 1330
Punic Wars **4**:**464–475**
Pydna, Battle of **4**:478
Pylos, Battle of **3**:371

R

ramming, naval warfare and **3**:339,
  4:467
Raydaniyya, Battle of **9**:1252

rebellions
  China and **7**:890, 894, 897, 898,
    899, 905
  in Italian cities **4**:485–486
  Jewish people and **4**:541
  provinces and **4**:534–535
  Roman emperors and **4**:528–
    529, 531, 537, 540
  Spartacus and **4**:489–490
  see also civil strife
Reconquista **6**:762, 770,
  8:**1014–1025**, 1082, **9**:1235,
  10:1364
religious beliefs **8**:1018, **10**:1414–
  1415
Renaissance **10**:1398
Rhodes, siege of **9**:1255
Riade, Battle of **6**:830
River Garonne, Battle of **6**:761, 792
Rome
  civil strife and **4**:442, 482,
    485–487, 496, 502, 532
  early wars and conquests of
    4:**456–463**
  Punic Wars and **4**:**464–475**
Roncesvalles, Battle of **6**:798–799,
  801, 801

S

Salamis, Battle of **2**:239, **3**:*334*, 334,
  336, 339, 340
samurai **7**:913–914, 916
Saxons **6**:797
Scythian people **1**:49
Second Crusade **9**:1189–1191,
  1190
Second Macedonian War **4**:476, 478
Second Persian War **3**:330–339
Second Punic War **4**:470–475, 476,
  478
Sempach, Battle of **8**:*1096*
Seventh Crusade **9**:1236
Seville, siege of **6**:760
shoguns (chief military
  commanders) **7**:914, 916–917
sieges **3**:386, 391
  of Antioch **9**:1187, *1188*
  of Baghdad **6**:772, *775*
  of Belgrade **9**:*1254*
  Carthage and **4**:481
  of Constantinople **6**:762, 763,
    9:1172, 1247
  of Damascus **9**:*1190*
  of Jerusalem **9**:1189
  Mongols and **9**:1222
  of Nancy **8**:1132
  of Orléans **8**:1110, *1112*, 1112
  of Paris **6**:832, **9**:1199–1200,
    1201
  of Rhodes **9**:1255
  Rome and **5**:675
  of Seville **6**:760
Siffin, Battle of **6**:756
Sluys, Battle of **8**:*1103*, 1104
Soissons, Battle of **5**:*659*
Spanish Wars **4**:479

Sparta
  First Persian War and **3**:329, 330
  Peloponnesian War and **2**:239,
    250, 254, **3**:342, 344, 362,
    368–383
  Plataea, Battle of, and **3**:337
  Second Persian War and **3**:331,
    334, 336
  Thermopylae, Battle of, and
    3:333
Spartan Confederacy **3**:342, 344
spearthrowers **1**:7
spear-tips **7**:872
strategoi (commanders-in-chief)
  3:345, 373, 377
Sumerian people **1**:57, 58–59,
  65–66
supplies **3**:374, 394–395

T

Tannenberg, Battle of **8**:*1100*,
  1100–1101, **9**:1217
technology **10**:1419
Testry, Battle of **6**:791
Teutoburg Forest, Battle of **4**:514
Teutonic Knights **8**:1025, 1100,
  1101, **9**:1216, 1217
Tewksbury, Battle of **8**:1122, *1123*
Thermopylae, Battle of **2**:264,
  3:332, 333
Thessalonica, massacre at **5**:637,
  639
Third Crusade **8**:1063, **9**:1192
Third Macedonian War **4**:478
Third Punic War **4**:479, 481
Tolbiac, Battle of **5**:*655*
Tours, Battle of **6**:761–762, *762*,
  768, 792, 793, *795*
Towton Field, Battle of **8**:1119
Trasimene, Battle of **4**:471–472
Trebia River, Battle of **4**:471
tribunes **4**:453
tribute
  Byzantine Empire and **5**:671
  Charlemagne and **6**:798
  China and **7**:903
  England and **8**:1046
  Greece and **3**:341, 381
  Huns and **5**:651, **9**:1161–1162
  India and **7**:960
  Islamic Spain and **8**:1016
  medieval Europe and **6**:830
  Mongols and **8**:1101, **9**:1215,
    1222, 1228, 1235
  Ottoman Turks and **9**:1245
  Persians and **6**:726
  pre-Columbian cultures and
    10:1324, 1327, *1328*, 1334,
    1356
  Rome and **4**:469, 478, 497, 508
  Saracens and **8**:1022
  Seljuk Turks and **9**:1179
  Vikings and **6**:818–819, **9**:1201
triremes (warships) **3**:331, 334,
  339, 339

Troy **2**:194, 195

V

Varna, Battle of **9**:1246
Versinicia, Battle of **9**:1171

W

Wakefield, Battle of **8**:1118–
1119
war booty **3**:304, 390, **4**:459,
466, **5**:604, **6**:729, 755,
814
warfare
Akkadians and **1**:60, 62
Alexander the Great and
3:384–391, 393–395
Alfred the Great and **6**:820
Assyrians and **2**:210, 212–213
Babylonians and **1**:110
Bedouin nomads and **6**:738
Bronze Age and **1**:40
Burgundy and **8**:1130–1133
Celtic people and **1**:50
cities and towns and **8**:1041
dynastic succession and
10:1415–1416
Egypt and **1**:77, 87, 92, 94, 98, 99,
105, 106, 107, 109, **2**:225
feudalism and **6**:822–823

France and **8**:1079
Germanic people and **1**:53
Greece and **2**:258, **3**:302, 303,
4:456
guerrilla warfare **6**:797, **8**:1113
Hallstatt culture and **1**:47
Hanseatic League and **8**:1097,
1098
Hittites and **2**:150, 152, 153, 157
Holy Roman Empire and **8**:1073
Islam and **6**:744, 746, 751, 752,
754, 755–757, 768
Israelites and **2**:230, 231
Macedonia and **4**:476
Medes and **2**:232
Mughal Empire and **10**:*1418*
Persians and **2**:232, 233–234,
238–239, **3**:381–382, **6**:726,
729, 733, 735
pre-Columbian cultures and
10:1308, 1318, 1324,
1328–1329, 1334, 1336,
1338–1339, 1356
religious beliefs and **8**:1018,
10:1414–1415
Rome and **4**:456–463, 488–489
Saxons and **6**:797

Scythian people and **1**:49
sieges **3**:386, 391, **6**:760, 762, 763,
772, *775*, 832
Sumerian people and **1**:57,
58–59, 65–66
supplies and **3**:374, 394–395
technology and **10**:1419
Troy and **2**:194, 195
war booty and **3**:304, 390, **4**:459,
466
see also military forces; naval
power
warships **3**:331, 334, *339*, 339,
371
Wars of the Roses **8**:**1114–1125**
weapons and armor
Africa and **9**:*1274*
Berber peoples and **9**:1235
breastplates **4**:*465*, **9**:*1274*
Bronze Age and **1**:38
Carthaginian **4**:*465*
Celtic people and **1**:46, **4**:*460*
Charlemagne and **6**:799
Copper Age and **1**:32, 34
early 16th century CE and
10:1419
Egyptian **1**:90

European conquests and **10**:1419,
1421
Frankish **5**:*657*
gladiators and **4**:*531, 552*
Greek **2**:265
Greek fire **6**:762
hand grenades **9**:*1181*
Iron Age and **1**:42
Islamic Spain and **6**:780–781
Japan and **7**:909, 917, **10**:*1416*
Macedon and **3**:387
medieval Europe and **8**:1105,
1106
Mongols and **9**:1220–1221
Parthians and **6**:728
pre-Columbian cultures and
10:1329, *1353*
Rome and **4**:449, 462, 484
Vikings and **9**:*1197*
Villanovan **4**:*457*
see also military forces

Y

Yarmuk River, Battle of **6**:755

Z

Zama, Battle of **4**:*475*, 475

COMPREHENSIVE INDEX

Page numbers in *italics* refer to illustrations. Page numbers in **bold** refer to entire chapters.

A

Aachen 6:807
Abbasid caliphate 6:769, 770, 771–773, 775, 785, 786, 9:1228, 1230, 1236
Abd ar-Rahman 6:770, 771, 798
Abd ar-Rahman III 6:770
Abderrahman 6:743–744
Abelard, Peter 8:1040, 10:1384
About Nature (Anaximander) 3:354
Abraham 2:225–226, *226*, 5:*679*, 6:742, 748, 749
Abrittus, Battle of 5:*599*
absolute monarchies 8:1057, 1072, 1094, 1114, 10:1416
Abu al-Abbas 6:769, 770, 771, 785
Abu Bakr 6:743, *750*, 751, 752, 758
Abu Dulaf Mosque 6:*786*
Abu Hureyra 1:12
Abu-Lu'lu'ah 6:755
Abu Muslim 6:769, 771
Abu Simbel, temple at 1:106, *108*
Abu Talib 6:740, 744
abutya (impermanence) 7:952–953
Academy, Plato's 3:365, 367, 413, 5:633, *634*, 639
accounting, development of 6:784
accounting systems, Incas and 10:1341
Achaean League 3:403
Achaemenid dynasty 2:233, 6:726, 728, 732
Acharnians (Aristophanes) 3:378
Achilles 2:194, *251*
Achilles and the Turtle (paradox) 3:360
acllas (chosen women) 10:1344
Acre 8:1080, 9:1192, 1195, 1237
Acropolis 2:264, *269*, 3:*300, 309*, 342, *347*, 349
action, Taoism and 7:888, 890
Actium, Battle of 4:512, 5:586
actors 2:318, 321, 322, 323, 5:*674*
Adad 1:114
Adad-nirari I 2:210
Adad-nirari II 2:212
Adam and Eve 5:*685*, 685, 6:742
Adb-Allah 6:739–740
Adb al-Malik 6:767–768, 769
Adhemar of Le Puy 9:1184, 1187
Aditi 7:945
Adonis 3:314

Adrian I 6:796
Adrian II 9:1177
Adrianople, Battle of 5:614, 640, 643, 9:1160
Adrianopole, Ottomon Turks and 9:1245
adultery, punishments for 5:635
Advaita Vedanta 7:964
aedile (temple functionaries) 4:451, 474
Aegates Islands, Battle of 4:468–469
Aegean Sea 2:246, 254, 3:341, 6:780
Aelfgifu 8:*1047*
Aeneas 4:*44*, 438, *441, 513*
Aeneid (Virgil) 2:200, 4:438, 512
Aeolic dialect 2:246, 248, 250
Aeschines 3:383
Aeschylus 3:318, 322, 322–323, 349
Aethelred I 6:820
Aethelred the Unready 6:816, 8:1046, 9:1198–1199
Aethelstan 8:*1046*, 1046
Aethelwulf 6:820
Aetius, Flavius 5:650, 651
Aetolian League 3:401
Afghanistan, Persians and 6:733
Africa 9:1256–1265, *1258*, **1266–1277**, 10:1364, 1410, 1416, 1420
Berber peoples and 9:1234–1235
Bronze Age and 1:45
Byzantine Empire and 9:1163
early humans and 1:6, 9
Greeks and 2:254–255
Islam and 6:759, 773, 774, 9:1230
Ottoman Turks and 9:1242, 1255
Phoenicians and 2:201, 202–203, 205
Portuguese exploration of 10:1366–1367, 1369–1370
Roman Empire and 4:474–475, 483, 498, 502, 503, 5:588–589, 671, 673
temples in 5:*613*
trade and 10:1366, 1367, 1371, 1418
Vandals and 5:652–653
Africanus the Elder *see* Scipio Africanus
Afro-Asiatic languages 9:1258, 1264
afterlife 1:84–85, 117, 3:413, 4:526, 7:*881*, 10:1322
Against Eunomius (Basil of Caesarea) 5:695
Agaja 9:1275

Agamemnon 2:182, 183, 194
Agamemnon (Aeschylus) 3:*322*, 322
Agesilaus II 3:*381*, 381–382
Agincourt, Battle of 8:1110, *1111*, 1111
Agnes of Meran 8:1067
Agni 7:*928*, 936, 939
agriculture
Africa and 9:1256, 1258–1259, 1265, 1271
Arabia and 6:738
Assyrians and 2:211
Aztecs and 10:1324, 1333
Byzantine Empire and 9:1175
China and 7:870–871, 873, 875, 877, 878, 897
Cistercian Order and 8:1035
climate change and 8:1084
Crete and 2:172
Cycladic people and 2:164–165
development of states and 10:1414
early humans and 1:6, 11, 14–15
in Egypt 1:70, 78, 86, 87, 101
Etruscans and 4:444
in Europe 8:*1030*, 10:1416
European settlers and 10:1381, 1383
feudal Europe and 6:*821*, 821, *822*, 823, 8:1026, *1027*, 1028–1029, *1029, 1030*
funnel-beaker culture and 1:19
Germanic people and 5:665
Greece and 2:162, 258, 260, 261, 266, 3:*302*, 302–303, *306*, 370
Greek colonies and 2:256
Hittites and 2:156, 158
Incas and 10:1340, 1342
India and 7:918
Islamic world and 9:1238, 1240
Japan and 7:906, 911
Linearbandkeramik culture and 1:17
Maya and 10:1312, 1314, 1323
Mesopotamia and 1:54
Minoans and 2:175–176
Mycenaeans and 2:189
Neolithic period and 1:12, 13, 14–15, 16, 18
North American peoples and 10:1350, 1352, 1357
pre-Columbian cultures and 10:1304, 1311
religious rituals and 10:1354–1355
Roman Empire and 4:466, 476, *477*, 5:606
Southeast Asia and 7:972, 974–975, 976–977

Sumerian people and 1:65
tools and 1:21–22, 42
Vikings and 9:1205
Agrigentum 4:465, *467*
Agrippa 4:503, 515
Agrippina 4:523–524, *525*, 525
Agum II 1:120
Ahenobarbus, Domitius 4:524
Ahmad Baba 9:1273
Ahmose I 1:91, 92, 94–95
Ahuitzotl 10:1334
Ahura Mazda 2:241, 242, 242–243, 6:726
Ain Jalut, Battle of 9:1228, 1236–1237
Aisha 6:756
Ajanta cave sculptures 7:*961*, 961, *964*
Ajax 2:*251*
Ajax (Sophocles) 3:323
Akhenaton 1:92, *100*, 101, *102*, 102–103, 103–104
Akhetaton 1:101, 103
Akhtal, Al- 6:766
Akhthoes 1:80
Akkad 1:59
Akkadian Empire 1:59–62, 114, 117
Akkadian language 2:161
Akkadians 2:208, 222
Akrotiri 2:167, 169
Aksum 9:1266, 1268–1269
Alans 5:649
Al-Aqsa Mosque 6:769
Alaric I 5:*641*, 641–643, *644*, 660, 666
Alaric II 5:645, 657
Alaskan tribes 10:1358
Ala-ud-Din Bahman Shah 7:971
Ala-ud-Din Khalji 7:970
Alba Longa 4:438, 440
Albert of Mecklenburg 8:1099
Albigensian Crusade 8:1025, 9:1182, 1191, *1194*, 1194
Albinus, Clodius 5:592–593, 594
Albrecht of Bavaria 10:1408
alchemy 10:*1385*, 1391
Alcibiades 3:*373*, 373–374, *374*, 376
Alcmaeonidae family 3:300, 302, 304
alcohol 5:700, 6:766
Alcuin 6:804, *806*, 806, 807
Alemanni 5:603, 654, 657, 6:792, 797
Aleppo 2:150, 9:1190, 1228, 1238, *1239*
Aleuts 10:1358
Alexander (finance minister) 5:675
Alexander, Severus 5:597–598

Alexander III 8:1061–1062,
1062–1063
Alexander IV 3:396
Alexander VI 10:1375
Alexander Cuts the Gordian Knot
(Berhtélemy) 3:*390*
Alexander Nevsky 8:*1101*, 1101,
9:*1214*, 1217
Alexander sarcophagus 3:*395*
Alexander the Great 3:*384–395*,
396
in artworks 3:*385, 389, 390, 391,
394*
Chaeronea, Battle of, and 3:383
Egypt and 1:109, 4:497
Hellenism and 3:402
India and 7:928
Persepolis and 2:240
Persians and 2:232, 239, 240, 241,
6:731
Phoenicians and 2:207
Alexandria 3:*392*, 392, 4:*507*
Alexander the Great and 3:391
Christianity and 5:632, 636–
637
cultural influence of 3:404,
406–407
philosophy and 3:411–413
Pompey's Pillar 3:*400*
Ptolemy I and 3:398
sciences and 3:407–411
Alexius III 8:1068
Alexius IV 8:1068
Alexius V 8:1068
Alexius Comnenus 9:1179, 1181,
1182, *1185*, 1185, 1187
Alfonso I 8:*1015*, 1020
Alfonso III 8:1020
Alfonso VI 8:1017, 1021
Alfred the Great 6:816, *820*, 820,
9:1198
al-Ghaba 9:1270
Algonquian peoples 10:1356–1357
algorism 6:784
Ali 6:*741*, 743, 756, 758, 769
Ali Dunamami 9:1274
Ali Gaji 9:1274
alignments, standing stones and
1:26, 29
Allah 6:743, 748–749
Allia, Battle of 4:462
alliances
Achaean League 3:403
Athens and 3:340
Corinthian League 3:385
Delian League 3:341, 342, 368,
370
Peloponnesian League 3:368, 370,
373
Peloponnesian War and 3:368
Rome and 4:458, 463
Spartan Confederacy 3:342
see also foederati (allies)
alloys 1:32–33, 35
Almagest (Ptolemy) 10:1390–1391
Almeria culture 1:36

Almohad dynasty 8:1017, 9:1235,
1238
Almoravid dynasty 8:1017,
9:1234–1235, 1271
Alp Arslan 9:1179, 1232
alphabets
Africa and 9:1264
Cyrillic 9:1177, 1212
Greek 2:207, 248–249, 252
Linear B script 2:*252*
Phoenicians and 2:203–204, 207
see also writing
al-Qadisiyah, Battle of 6:755
Al-Qanan fi at-tibb (Ibn Sina) 6:783,
784
altars 2:*160*, 244, *244*, 3:312, 4:550,
5:*684*
Althing 9:1204
Alypius 5:695
Amarna Letters 1:101, 103–104,
2:230–231
Amarna period 1:101–103
Amaterasu 7:909, 912
Ambedkar, Bhimrao Ramji
7:959
Ambrose 5:636, *638*, 683, *684*
Amelekites 2:230
Amenemhet I 1:82–83
Amenemhet II 1:87
Amenemhet III 1:87, 89, *90*
Amenhotep I 1:95
Amenhotep II 1:99
Amenhotep III 1:99, 101
Amenhotep IV *see* Akhenaton
American Samoa 7:*985*
Amhara people 9:1268
Amidism 7:959
Amin, Al- 6:772
Ammit 1:*85*
Ammonites 2:230
Amon 1:82, 95, 101
Amon-Re 1:82, 3:391, 393, 403
Amorites 1:62, 110, 2:208, 210
Amphipolis 3:371, 373, 377
amphitheaters 4:*466*, 551
amphora, Egyptian 1:*99*
Amsterdam 10:1371
amulet, Viking 9:*1203*
Amyntas 3:386
Anagni 8:1081, 1089
anarchy, democracy and 3:347–
348
Anasazi people 10:1348, 1350,
1358
Anastasius (patriarch) 9:1166
Anastasius I 5:625, *627*, 627, 669,
9:1162
Anatolia
Alexander the Great and
3:384–385, 389–390
Byzantine Empire and 9:1165,
1171–1172, 1178–1179, 1181
Constantinople and 5:618
Etruscans and 4:445
First Crusade and 9:1184, 1185,
1187–1188

Greek settlers and 2:246, 254
Hittites and 2:150
Ionian rebellion 3:326–327
Mongols and 9:1229, 1235
Ottoman Turks and 9:1241, 1245,
1245–1246, 1252
Palmyra and 5:602
Persians and 3:309, 326, 381–
382
Rome and 4:482, 488–489,
513, 529, 538, 5:586
Seleucid dynasty and 3:401
Seljuk Turks and 9:1232, 1234,
1240–1241
Troy and 2:192–195
anatomy, study of 3:411
Anaxagoras 3:348, 356, *358*, 362
Anaximander 3:354
Anaximenes 3:354–355, *355*
ancestor worship 7:873, 979,
10:1309, 1340–1341
Anchises 4:*442, 513*
ancient knowlege, rediscovery of
10:*1390*, 1398
Ancus Marcius 4:440–441, 442
Andrew Bogolyubsky 9:1211
angels 5:*679*, 680, 6:741, 748
Angkor Wat 7:977, *978*
Angles 5:663
Anglo-Saxon Chronicle, The 6:820
Anglo-Saxons 6:791, 792, 819,
8:1046–1049
Angra Mainyu 2:242, 243
animals, domesticated 8:1026, 1028,
10:1304, 1312, 1352
Africa and 9:1258
Crete and 2:172
early humans and 1:9, 13, 14
funnel-beaker culture and 1:19,
21
Greece and 2:162
medieval Europe and 8:1026,
1028
Pacific islands and 7:987
Persians and 2:243–244
Polynesia and 7:988
Scythian people and 1:49
single-grave culture and 1:31
animals, religious beliefs and
10:1355
animism, Melanesia and 7:987
Anjou 6:826
Ankara 9:1229
Ankara, Battle of 9:1246
Ankhesenaten 1:104
Anna 9:1203, 1212
Anthony of Egypt 5:688, *690*, 690,
691, 692
antibarbarian party, Rome 5:643
Antigone (Sophocles) 3:323, 324
Antigonid dynasty 3:398–399,
402
Antigonus Gonatas 3:*397*, 399,
401–402
Antigonus Monophthalmos 3:398
Antinous 4:543

Antioch 3:399, 5:632, 6:729, 735,
9:1187, 1187–1188, *1188*,
1189
Antioch III 4:475, 476
Antiochus I 3:401
Antiochus III 5:586
Antipater 3:388, 401
antipopes 8:1062, 1089, 1091–1093
Antisthenes 3:366
Antonine emperors 4:538–540,
542–547, 5:590, 593
Antonine Wall 5:663
Antoninus Pius 4:543–544, *544*
Anu 1:66, 117
Anubis 1:*85*
Anyang, excavation of 7:876
Apache people 10:1359
Aphrodite 3:310, 314, 316–317
Apollo 2:164, 167, 3:310, *311*, 313,
314, 315, 412
Apology (Plato) 3:364
Apophis 1:92
Apotheosis of Claudius, The (cameo)
4:*523*
Appius Claudius 4:462
apprentices 8:1043
aqueducts 2:220, 5:619, *620*, 620,
670, 675, 676
Aquitaine 6:760, 768, 792, 812,
8:1107, 1113
Aquitania 5:643, 645
Arabia 10:1410, 1414, 1420
before Islam 6:736, 738–739
Ottoman Turks and 9:1242,
1252
Roman Empire and 4:540,
5:587, 588, 677
Arabic language 6:773
Arabic numerals 6:783–784,
7:926
Arabs 9:1165, 1170, 1203, 1268,
1275
see also Islamic world
Aragon 8:1016, 1017, 1018–1019
Aramaeans 1:121, 2:210, 212–213,
215, 216, 217
Ara Pacis Augustae 4:*514, 515*
Aratus of Sicyon 3:403
Arcadia, poetry and 3:406–407
Arcadius 5:641, 642, 666, 668,
9:1158
archaeology 1:67, 4:536
Archaic period, Greece 2:248–249,
251, 3:294–296, 298–302, 310
archers 6:*728*, 728, 9:1220–1221
Archidamus II 3:370
Archilochus 2:257
Archimedes 3:408, *410*, 4:*473*, 473,
10:1390
architecture
Africa and 9:*1270*
Assyrian 2:213, 215, 220
Byzantine Empire and 5:672,
9:1180
Greece and 3:298, 311–312, 349,
351

architecture (*continued*)
  India and 7:960, 961, 10:*1364*, 1419
  Islamic world and 6:*763*, 767, 769
  mathematics and 3:407
  Minoan 2:173, 174
  Mycenaean 2:187
  Norman 8:*1022*
  Ottoman Turks and 9:1255
  Palatine Chapel and 6:807
  pre-Columbian cultures and 10:1302, 1304, 1309, 1315, 1333, 1342, 1345–1347
  Renaissance and 10:1401, 1402, 1406, *1409,* 1409
  Spain and 6:*763*
archives, Hittites and 2:159, 161
archons (magistrates) 2:266, 269, 3:320, 344, 344–345
Ardashir I 6:726, *727,* 730
Arduin of Ivrea 6:835
Areopagus 3:344
Ares 3:314
Ares Borghese 3:*314*
Argiletum 4:548
Argos 2:251, 3:373, 382
arhats (saints) 7:956, 957
Ariadne 5:626, 669, 9:1162
Arianism 5:630, 631, 632, 633
  Athanasius of Alexandria and 5:695–696
  Basil of Caesarea and 5:693, 694–695
  Byzantine Empire and 9:1162–1163
  Germanic peoples and 5:645, 648, 653–654, 657, 658, 660, 671, 6:788
  Nicaea, Council of, and 5:*624,* 624–625, 628–630
Aristarchus of Samos 3:409
Aristides 3:341
aristocracy
  Burgundy and 8:1128
  Carolingian dynasty and 6:795, 804, 811, 826–827
  Charlemagne and 6:808, 810
  Charles Martel and 6:793
  China and 7:875, 877, 879
  Confucianism and 7:885
  democracy and 3:304
  England and 8:1048–1049
  France and 8:1079
  Greece and 3:296, 298, 299, 300–301
  India and 7:924, 925
  Japan and 7:911
  luxury goods and 8:1033
  Merovingian dynasty and 6:788, 790–791
  Middle Ages and 8:1094, 1131
  Salian dynasty and 6:837, 843, 844, 844–845

social classes and 6:822
  tyranny and 3:294, 295
  see also nobility
Aristogeiton 3:*305,* 305
Aristophanes 3:325, 349, 364, *378,* 378
Aristotle 3:*353, 367,* 367, 10:*1388,* 1389, 1391, 1404
  Alexander the Great and 3:384
  Islamic world and 6:782, 783
  preserving knowledge of 5:661
  Sophists and 3:361, 412
  Thales of Miletus and 3:354
Arius 5:624, 629, 629–630, 631
  see also Arianism
Ark of the Covenant 2:229, *230*
Armenia 4:513, 529, 540, 9:1176, 1228, 1229
armies *see* military forces
armor *see* weapons and armor
Arnold of Brescia 8:1038, 1039, 1040
Arnulf 6:818
Árpád 6:*818*
Arras, Treaty of 8:1113, 1126, 1128
Arsuf, Battle of 8:1056
Artabanus V 6:726
Artaphernes 3:327
Artaxerxes 3:390
Artemis 2:167, 190, 3:314, *346*
Artemisium, Battle of 3:332–333
Artevelde, Jacob van 8:1102, 1104
Arthur 5:*663,* 663
Arthur of Brittany 8:1054
artists, Renaissance and 10:1402, 1403
arts
  Africa and 9:1259, 1262, 1263, *1267*
  Assyrians and 2:215, 216, 220
  Babylonian 1:*111*
  Byzantine Empire and 9:1166–1167, 1174–1175
  Celtic 1:46, *52*
  China and 7:903
  Cycladic people and 2:165–166, 169
  early humans and 1:7, 11, *12*
  Egypt and 1:*71,* 77, 92, 103
  Hittites and 2:156, 158–159
  India and 7:940, 942, 960, 961, 965, 966
  Islamic culture and 6:766, 767, 772
  Japan and 7:906
  Macedonian Renaissance and 9:1180
  Mari and 1:*114*
  medieval Europe and 8:1093, 1096, 1099
  Minoans and 2:170, 178–180
  Neolithic period and 1:14–15, *15*
  Ottoman Turks and 9:1255
  Pacific islands and 7:987, 988
  Persians and 2:240

pre-Columbian cultures and 10:1305, 1319, 1333
  Renaissance and 10:1398, 1400–1401, 1402, 1403–1404, 1406–1407
  Roman Empire and 4:525, 527
  Southeast Asia and 7:978
  see also crafts and craftspeople
Aryabhata 7:962
Aryan peoples
  Bronze Age and 1:40, 41
  Hinduism and 7:932
  India and 7:923–925, 926, 927
  Iron Age and 1:42
  Persians and 2:232, 6:728, 731
Asarhaddon 1:109
asceticism 3:366
  Black Death and 8:1086
  Buddha and 7:948
  Cathars and 9:1194
  Christianity and 5:691, 693, 696, 697
  Jainism and 7:948
  religious orders and 8:1035
  Sufis and 9:1233
Asculum, Battle of 4:462
Ashanti people 9:*1267, 1274,* 1275
Ashikaga family 7:916, 917
Ashoka 7:928–929, 930, 958, 960, 963
ashramas (goals of life) 7:942
Ashur 2:208, 210, 221
Ashura 6:757
Ashurbanipal 2:220–221, *221*
Ashurnasirpal II 2:212–213
Ashur-uballit I 2:210
Ashur-uballit II 2:221
Asia 10:1302, 1304, 1348, 1416
  Alexander the Great and 3:388–389, 393–394
  Iron Age and 1:42
  Persians and 6:729
  Rome and 4:486, 5:589
  spread of Islam and 6:763
  see also specific countries
Askia Muhammad I 9:*1272,* 1272, 1273
Askold 9:1201, 1210
assemblies of the three orders 8:1131
Asser 6:820
assimilation policy, Incas and 10:1343
Assyria 1:101, 109, 120–121, 122, 2:*211,* 5:586
Assyrians 2:208–221, *211*
  Africa and 9:1261
  Egypt and 9:1266
  Hittites and 2:150, 153
  Israelites and 2:227, 231
  Medes and 2:232
  Neo-Hittites and 2:155
  Phoenicians and 2:207
Astarte 2:206, 3:310
astrolabes 3:410, 10:*1365,* 1365, 1391

astrology 10:1391
astronomy 10:1318, 1365, 1390–1391, *1393*
  Babylonian Empire and 1:119
  Bronze Age and 1:39
  Egypt and 1:77
  Greek philosophy and 3:352, 354, 356, 358, 409–410
  India and 7:961, 962
  Islamic world and 6:784
  Neolithic period and 1:25, 26, 28
Astyages 2:233, *233*–234
Aswan 9:1266
Atahuallpa 10:1347
Ataulf 5:643
Athanasius of Alexandria 5:629, 630, 688, 690, 691, 695–696
atheism 3:316–317, 352
Athena 2:190, *259,* 269, 3:314, *344*
  Athena Promachos (statue) 2:*259*
  Athens and 3:301, 312, 351
  Etruscans and 4:445
  Sanctuary of Athena Pronaia 3:*316*
  Temple of Athena Nike 3:*347*
Athens 2:264–269, 3:**340–351**
  Acropolis 3:*300, 309,* 342, *347,* 349
  Alaric I in 5:*644*
  architecture and 3:349, 351
  Athena and 3:301, 312, 351
  citizenship and 2:253
  coins and 3:303, *304*
  colonization and 2:251
  Corinth and 3:298, 382
  First Persian War and 3:329–330
  government and 3:298, 300–302, 304, 306–309
  Lamian War and 3:401–402
  Macedon and 3:383
  marriage and 3:350
  Mycenaeans and 2:182
  Peloponnesian War and 3:342, 344, **368–383**
  Persians and 2:239, 3:326, 327
  philosophy and 3:356, 361
  Second Persian War and 3:331, 333–334, 336, 337, *339*
  Sparta and 2:**258–268**
  see also Sparta
Atlantis, legend of 2:169
atlases 10:1368
atman (self) 7:936–937
atomic theory 3:361, 412–413
Aton (Aten) 1:*100, 102,* 102–103, 104
Atreus 2:188
Attica 2:264, 3:300, 333–334, 336, 344
Attila 5:649–651, *650, 652*
auditors, Manichaeism and 6:733
Augustaion 5:621

Augustine 5:633, 680, 682–685, *684, 686*, 686, 687, 696, 9:*1166*

Augustus Caesar 4:**504–515**, *505, 506, 508*, 5:582, 586, 588

Aulus Hirtius 4:502

Aurelian 5:601, 602, 603, *606*

Aurelian Wall 5:*603*

Aurelius Carus 5:606

Aureolus 5:601

Australopithecus 1:9, 9:*1256*

Austrasia 6:791

Austria, Middle Ages and 8:1094
see also Holy Roman Empire

Austroasiatic languages 7:972

Ava dynasty 7:977

Avar people 6:797–798, 9:1165, 1208

Avebury, stone circle at 1:*20*, 26–27, 28

Averroës 6:783

Avers 5:677

Avesta 2:242–244, 6:730, 731

Avicenna see Ibn Sina

Avidius Cassius 4:544, 545–546

Avignon 8:*1083*, 1087–1088, *1088*, 1089, 1091

awilu (free) class, Code of Hammurabi and 1:113, 115

Axayacatl 10:1334

axes 1:*17*, 7:*875*, 906

Aya 1:104, 105

ayllu (family unit) 10:1340

Aymara Indians 10:1311

Ayurveda (life knowledge) 7:926

Ayutthaya dynasty 7:977

Ayyubids 9:*1232*, 1234, *1236*, 1236

Azores 10:1366, 1367

Aztec culture, Easter Island and 7:986

Aztecs 10:1302, 1304, 1320, **1324–1335**, *1326*, 1421

B

Baal 2:229, *229*, 3:403, 5:593, *595*, 596–597

Babak 6:726

Babur 7:970, *971*, 9:1229, 1232, 10:*1411*, 1418

Babylon 1:101, **110–125**, 3:310, 399, 5:586
Alexander the Great and 3:393, 395
Assyrians and 2:210, 211–212, 216–217, 218–219, 220–221
Greek philosophy and 3:352, 354
Hittites and 1:42, 2:150, 153
Israelites and 2:227, 231
Judaism and 6:730
Medes and 2:232
Persians and 2:234, 239, 3:326
Phoenicians and 2:199, 207

Babylonian Captivity 8:1087–1088

Babylonian language 2:243

Babylonians 1:**110–125**

Bacchiad family 3:296, 297

Bachwezi dynasty 9:1275, 1276

Bactria 3:401, 5:585, 586, 7:895, 929, 931

Badami 7:966

Badr, Battle of 6:*746*, 746

Baecula, Battle of 4:474

Baghdad
Islamic world and 6:771, 782, 786
Mongols and 9:1228, 1229, 1236, *1237*, 1240
Seljuk Turks and 9:1232
siege of 6:772, *775*
Tigris River and 6:787, *787*
trade and 6:776

Bagradas, Battle of 4:467–468

Bahamas 10:1374

Bahmani Sultanate 7:971

Bahram I 6:733

Bahram V 6:734

bailiffs, Philip II Augustus and 8:1057

Baldwin I (Constantinople) 9:1192

Baldwin I (Jerusalem) 9:1188, 1189

Baldwin II (Constantinople) 9:1192–1193

Baldwin Iron-Arm 6:809

Baldwin of Flanders 8:1068

Balearic Islands 8:1025

Bali (god) 7:942

Bali (island) 7:967

Balkans 4:513–514, 5:649, 651, 9:1165, 1181, 1245, 1248, 1252, 10:1360

Baltic countries 8:1025, 1029, 1082, 1101, 9:1200–1201, 1203

Baluchistan 7:918

Bamberg 6:835

Bamberg Cathedral 6:*840*

bamboo fan, Japanese 7:*915*

Ban Chiang 1:35

banking 4:466, 6:784, 8:1031, 1032–1033, 1079, 1080

Bantu people 9:1262, 1263, 1264, *1265*, 1265, 1275, 1277

baptism 5:680–681, 685

barbarian invaders, Rome and 5:**640–657, 658–665**
see also Germanic peoples

barbarian kingdoms, maps of 5:*642*

Barbarossa (admiral) see Khayr al-Din

Barcelona 8:1016

Barents, Willem 10:1378

Bar Kochba 4:541, 542

Barnet, Battle of 8:1121–1122, *1122*

barons, French 8:1108

Basil (father of Basil of Caesare) 5:695

Basil I 6:817, 9:1173–1174

Basil II 9:*1176*, 1176, 1178, 1203, 1210, 1212

Basilica of Maxentius and Constantine 5:*612*

Basilica of San Isidoro 8:1017

Basilica of Sant'Apollinare Nuovo 5:*667*

Basilica of San Vitale 5:*673, 674*

Basiliscus 5:626

Basil of Caesarea 5:*692*, 692–695, *694*

Basque people 6:798

Bassianus see Elagabalus

Bastetani people 1:49

Batavians 1:53, 4:534–535

Bath 4:*524*

baths 4:*524*, 553, *554*, 7:920

Baths of Caracalla 4:553, *554*, 5:*594*, 595

Battersea Shield 1:*50*

Batu Khan 9:1214, *1215*, 1227, 1228

Bavaria 6:812, 819, 829, 832, 8:1094

Bavarians 6:792, 797

Bayon Temple 7:*973*

Baybars I 6:775, 8:1082

Bayeux Tapestry 8:*1049*

Bayezid I 9:1245–1246, *1247*, 1248

Bayezid II 9:1249

Bayt al-Hikma (House of Wisdom) 6:782

Beaufort, Margaret 8:1125

Beaufort Sea 10:*1378*

Becket, Thomas 8:*1053*, 1053

be (communities) 7:909

Bedouin nomads 6:*738, 739*
camels and 6:778, 778
Islam and 6:735, 747, 751, 752, 785
Mohammed and 6:740
pre-Islamic Arabia and 6:736, 738–739

beehive tombs see *tholos* tombs

Béhanzin 9:1275

Behistun Inscription 2:236, 243

Bela IV 9:1227

Belém Tower 10:*1370*

Belgium, Africa and 9:1276, 1277

Belgrade 9:1252, *1254*

Belisarius 5:654, 670, 671, 673, 675, *676*, 9:1163, 1164

bell-beaker people 1:31

bell-beaker pottery 1:*19*

Belshazzar 1:125

Benedict (saint) 5:688, 697, *699*, 699–701, *701*, 6:*824*, 826, 8:1035

Benedict VII 6:835

Benedict VIII 8:1023

Benedict IX 6:837

Benedict XI 8:1087

Benedict XIII 8:*1091*, 1091, 1092

Benedictine Rule 5:699–701, 6:*824*, 825

Benevento, Battle of 8:*1074*, 1074

Benin 9:1274, 1275

Berber people 5:589, 6:759, 768, 8:1016, 9:1234–1235, 1264

Berengar II 6:*830*

Berno 6:826

Bessarion, Basilius 10:*1390*, 1390–1391

Bhagavad Gita 7:*935*, 944

Bhairava 7:945

Bible
Babylon and 1:124
Benedict of Nursia and 5:700
Canaanites and 2:222
Egypt and 1:91
Islam and 6:749
Israelites and 2:225, 227, 228
Jericho and 1:13
Jerome and 5:697
printing press and 10:*1392*, 1393
study of 6:806

Bilal 6:743

bills of exchange 6:784, 8:1032

Bimbisara 7:927

Bindusara 7:928

Bingham, Hiram 10:*1342*

Bini people 9:*1273*, 1274–1275

Bishapur 6:729

bishops 5:609, 628, 629, 632, 695
see also popes

Bismarck, Otto von 6:845

Bismark Archipelago 7:982

Bithynia 4:475, 488–489

Black Death 8:*1084*, 1084–1086, *1085, 1086*, 1105, 1108, 1109

Blackfeet people 10:1356, *1357*

black-figure pottery 3:301, *308*

Black Obelisk 2:213, 216, *217*

Black Sheep Turks 9:1240

Black Stone of Mecca 6:742

Blanche of Castile 8:1078

blood games 4:551–552

blood money 5:662, 664

Blore Heath, Battle of 8:1117, *1119*

Blues 5:623–624, 627, 671

boats 1:9, 10, *91*

Bocchoris 1:109

Bocchus I 4:483

bodhisattvas (enlightened person) 7:957

Boethius 5:661, 6:820

Bogomil Christians 9:1249

Bohemia 6:835, 837, 8:1094, 1100

Bohemond of Taranto 9:1187, 1188

Bokhara 7:895

Boleslav I 6:835

bone, tools and 1:7, 9

Boniface 6:794, 797
Boniface VIII 8:*1081*, 1081, 1087
Bonifacius 5:652
Book of Adding and Subtracting by Indian Methods (Khwarizmi) 6:784
Book of Kings, The 6:*732*, 732
Book of Roads and Kingdoms, The (El Bekri) 9:1270
books 10:1387, 1391–1392, 1392–1393, 1394
border regions, Roman Empire and 5:**582–589**, 601, 604, 614, 640–641
Boris I 9:1177
Boris II 9:1177
Borneo 7:967
Bornu 9:1273–1274
Borobudur, temple complex at 7:967, 979
Borylaeum, Battle of 9:1187
Bosworth Field, Battle of 8:1125
Botticelli, Sandro 10:1403
Boudicca 4:528–529, *530*
Bougainville, Louis-Antoine de 7:989
Bourdin, Maurice 6:844
Bouvines, Battle of 8:1055, *1057*, 1065, 1067
Brackenbury, Robert 8:1124
Brahma 7:938, *939*, 939–940, *940*, 948
brahman (divine consciousness) 7:936–937, 938
brahmins (priests) 7:925, 927, 946
Bramante, Donato 10:1406
Brancacci, Felice 10:1403
"bread and circuses" 4:531, 548–553
breastplates 4:*465*, 9:*1274*
Bretigny, Treaty of 8:1107–1108
bridges, Incas and 10:1347
Brihadishvara Temple 7:966, *967*
Britain 4:*524*
    Africa and 9:1275, 1277
    barbarian invaders and 5:663
    Pacific islands and 7:989
    Phoenicians and 2:200
    Roman Empire and 4:522–523, 528–529, 537–538, 542, *543*, 544, 5:582, 595, 663
    Southeast Asia and 7:981
    Vikings and 6:816, 819
    see also England
Britannicus 4:524, 525
Brittany 5:663
Bronocice pot 1:22
bronze 1:32–33, 35, 90, 94, 2:156, 188
Bronze Age 1:31, **32–41**, 45
    Africa and 9:1261
    China and 7:872–873, 875, 876, 877
    Crete and 2:172

Greece and 2:**162–169**, *164–165*
    India and 7:918
bronze artifacts
    Akkadian 1:*62*
    Bronze Age and 1:*35, 37, 40*
    Celtic 1:*51*
    China and 1:*33*, 7:*871*
    Greek 3:*301*
    Hallstatt culture and 1:*39*
    Persian 2:*242*
    Phoenician 2:*216*
    Southeast Asia and 7:*974, 975*
    statuettes 7:*896, 898, 903, 966*
Bronze Gates of Balawat 2:216
brooch, Roman 5:*598*
Bruges 8:1039
Brunelleschi, Filippo 10:*1399*, 1401, 1404
Bruno of Cologne 8:1035
Brutus, Lucius Junius 4:442
Brutus, Marcus Junius 4:*498*, 500–501, 502
Bubnov, Alexander 9:*1216*
Buckingham, duke of 8:1124, 1125
Buddha 7:*911*, 942, **946–959**, *947, 952, 956, 958*
    Great Renunciation 7:*949*, 949
    life of 7:948, 949, 950
    Mahayana Buddhism and 7:956–957
    teachings of 7:950–954
Buddhism 6:730, 7:889, *903*, **946–959**, 967
    China and 7:892, 901, 902, 904
    Hepthalites and 7:962–963
    India and 7:928, 928–929, 930, 931, 963
    Japan and 7:909–910
    Mongols and 9:1226, 1238
    Southeast Asia and 7:975, 979
building materials
    Assyrians and 2:213
    Constantinople and 5:619
    Egyptians and 1:73
    Etruscans and 4:445
    Greece and 2:162
    Indus Valley civilization and 7:920
    Mycenae and 2:184
    Neolithic period and 1:30
    Persians and 2:240
    Phoenicians and 2:198
    pre-Columbian cultures and 10:1305, 1307, 1315, 1332, 1345–1346, 1348
    Sumerians and 1:67
building programs
    Africa and 9:1271
    Baghdad and 6:787
    barbarian invaders of Rome and 5:648

China and 7:877, 901
    Constantinople and 5:616, 9:1172
    Maya and 10:1318
    Mongols and 9:1226
    Ottoman Turks and 9:1244, 1249, 1255
    Persians and 6:726, 729
    Roman Empire and 4:498–499, 504, 508, 522, 528, 534, 539, 5:595
    Roman provinces and 4:547
    Tarquinius Priscus, Lucius, and 4:442
Bukka Raya I 7:971
Bükk culture 1:17
Bulala people 9:1273
Bulgaria 6:763, 9:1175, 1177, 1181, 1193, 1245, 1248
Bulgar people 9:1165, 1170, 1171, 1172, *1176*, 1176, 1201
bulls 1:*111*, 2:*176, 177*, 177, 7:*934*
bureaucracy *see* government
Burgundy 8:**1126–1133**, *1128*
    cultural achievements of 8:1093, 1094
    Franks and 6:826, 836
    Hundred Years' War and 8:1108, 1110, 1112, 1113
    Vikings and 9:1200
    Wars of the Roses and 8:1120, 1121
burial mounds
    Bronze Age and 1:39
    China and 7:879, 881
    dolmens and 1:24–25
    funnel-beaker culture and 1:22
    Hallstatt culture and 1:48
    Japan and 7:909
    Scythian people and 1:49, 51
    West Kennet Long Barrow 1:27–28, *28*
burial practices
    Assyrians and 2:219
    Babylonians and 1:117
    Bronze Age and 1:38, 39
    Celtic people and 1:46, 52, 2:257
    Cycladic people and 2:165, 166–167
    Dark Age Greece and 2:246
    Egypt and 1:73, 73–74, *75*, 75, 77, 82, 84–85, 95–96, *97*
    funnel-beaker culture and 1:22, 24, 24–25
    Hallstatt culture and 1:48
    India and 7:927
    Japan and 7:909
    Latium and 4:443
    Maya and 10:1322
    Mycenaeans and 2:185–187, 188, 190
    Natufian culture and 1:11
    Persians and 2:244
    Roman Empire and 4:550
    Rössen culture and 1:18, *21*
    Scythian people and 1:51
    Sumerian people and 1:57–58

Urnfield culture and 1:39–40
    see also religious beliefs
Buridan, Jean 10:1391
Burma *see* Myanmar
Burrus, Afranius 4:524, 525, 527
Bursa 9:1242, 1244
Bututsi people 9:1276
Buyids 6:773
Byblos 1:77, 101, 2:196
Byland Abbey 8:*1035*
Byron, John 7:989
Byzantine Empire 9:**1158–1167**, **1168–1181**
    Africa and 9:1269
    Charlemagne and 6:802, 803
    Christianity and 5:628–634, 636–637, 639, 6:761, 799–800, 811, 839, 840
    crusades and 8:1068, 9:1182, 1184, 1185, 1187, 1190
    European scholarship and 10:1390
    Germanic peoples and 5:665
    Holy Roman Empire and 6:832
    Islam and 6:754, 755, 757, 763, 768, 776, 8:1014, 10:1360
    Italy and 6:794, 795, 817, 8:1020, 1022, 1024
    Justinian I and 5:**666–677**
    naval power of 6:779–780
    Ottoman Turks and 9:1242, 1244, 1246, 1246–1247, 1248
    Persians and 6:734, 735, 752
    Russia and 9:1203, 1210, 1215
    Seljuk Turks and 9:1232, *1234*, 1234, 1240, 1241
Byzantium *see* Constantinople

C
Cabot, John 10:1378
Cabral, Pedro Álvares 10:1375, *1377*
cacao 10:1314
Cadamosto, Alvise 10:1367
Cade's Rebellion 8:1116, *1117*
Caernarfon Castle 8:*1077*
Caesar, Lucius 4:515
Caesarion 4:497, 498, 503
Cahokia 10:1350
Cairo 6:774, 776, 786
Calais 8:1105, 1113
Caledonia 5:584
calendars 2:211, 4:500, 502, 10:1302, 1320, *1330*, 1330
calendar stone 10:1329
California tribes 10:1359
Caligula 4:516, 519–521, *520, 521*
caliphate 6:**764–775**, 776, 778, 779–780, 780–781, 781–783, 784, 785, 787
caliphs
    Abu al-Abbas 6:769, 771
    Abu Bakr 6:751, 752
    Adb al-Malik 6:767–768
    Ali 6:756–757

Córdoba and 6:770
Harun al-Rashid 6:787
Mahdi, Al- 6:787
Mamun, Al- 6:787
Mansur, Al- 6:771–772
Mu'awiyah 6:757
Mu'tasim, Al- 6:786
Mutawakkil, Al- 6:786
Omar bin Khattab 6:752,
754
Shi'ite Muslims and 6:773,
758, 774
Sunni Muslims 6:758
Walid, Al- 6:768
Calixtus 6:844
Callixus 5:682
calpullis 10:1327
camayo (social ranking) 10:1344
Cambodia 7:967, 976–977, 978,
979
Cambyses I 2:233
Cambyses II 1:109, 2:235–236, 244,
3:309, 326
camels 6:778, 778, 779
cameos 4:523, 6:730
Camphausen, Wilhelm 6:844
Canaan 2:196, 222, 225–226,
229
Canaanites 2:229, 230
Cannae, Battle of 4:471, 472–473
Cano, Juan Sebastian del 10:1377,
1379
canoes 1:9, 10, 7:985
Canossa, Henry IV and 6:842–843,
843, 845
Canterbury Tales, The (Chaucer)
10:1394
Canuleian Law 4:451
Canute see Cnut
Cão, Diogo 10:1369
Cao Cao 7:899
capacochas (sacrifices) 10:1343
Capac Yupanqui 10:1339
Cape Bojador 10:1366
Cape Mycale, Battle of 3:336, 339,
340
Cape of Good Hope 10:1369,
1369–1370
Capetian dynasty 6:826–828
Capitoline Hill, Battle of 4:459
Capitoline Wolf 4:439
capitularies, Charlemagne and
6:810
Cappadocian Fathers 5:695
Capri 4:518, 519
Captain of the Mediterranean,
The (Phoenician manual)
2:202
Capture of Miletus, The (Phrynichus)
3:322
Capua 4:460, 466, 473
Caracalla 5:593, 595–596
Caractacus 4:522
caravans, trade and 6:740–741, 749,
776
caravels 10:1367, 1369

Carchemish 2:155, 217
Carchemish, Battle of 2:152
Carinus 5:606, 607
Carl of Durazzo 8:1091
Carloman (son of Charles Martel)
6:794
Carloman (son of Louis the
Stammerer) 6:818
Carloman (son of Pépin I) 6:795,
796
Carnac menhir alignment 1:26, 27
Carnarvon, Lord 1:104
Caroline Islands 7:984
Carolingian dynasty 6:791,
794–799, 802–803, 827
Carolingian Empire 6:804–813,
817–818, 818–819, 828, 832,
8:1026
Carolingian miniscule script 6:806
Carolingian Renaissance 6:806–
807
Carolingian warrior 6:799
carpets 6:781, 9:1231
carracks 10:1367, 1369
Carrhae, Battle of 4:496, 6:728
Carter, Howard 1:104, 105
Carteret, Philip 7:989
Carthage 2:203, 5:653
  Cato the Elder and 4:479
  Etruscans and 4:456
  Latium and 4:444
  Phoenicians and 2:196, 199–200,
  222
  Punic Wars and 4:464–475, 481
  Pyrrhus and 4:462
  Roman Empire and 5:588–589
  trade and 2:257
  Vandals and 5:653, 671, 673
  weapons and armor of 4:465
Carthusian Order 8:1035
Cartier, Jacques 10:1379–1380
cartography see mapmaking
Cassander 3:401
Cassian, John 5:696
Cassiodorus 5:661, 661
Cassius 4:500–501, 502
Castagno, Andrea de 10:1401
caste system, India and 7:923,
924–925, 927, 946
Castile 8:1016, 1017, 1018
Castile-León 8:1018
castles 6:822, 823, 8:1048, 1050,
1077, 9:1189
catacombs 5:683
Catalan people 8:1018–1019
Catalaunian Plains, Battle of 5:645,
650, 650–651, 652
Çatalhüyük settlement 1:14–15, 30
cataphracts (cavalry troops) 6:728
Cathars 8:1025, 9:1194
Cathedral of Pisa 8:1037
Cathedral School of York 6:804
Catilina, Lucius Sergius 4:492, 493
Cato the Elder 4:458, 479, 492,
498, 499
Cato the Younger 4:557

Cauchon, Pierre 8:1113
cauldron, Hunnish 5:649
cavalry
  Agincourt, Battle of, and 8:1111
  Alexander the Great and 3:385,
  389
  Assyrians and 2:213
  Berber peoples and 9:1235
  feudalism and 6:822
  Franks and 6:792, 799, 830
  Mongols and 9:1221
  Parthians and 6:728
  Rome and 4:462
  see also knights
cave paintings 1:7, 11, 12, 10:1307
Caxton, William 10:1394
Çayönü settlement 1:14–15
Cayuga people 10:1356
Celestine III 8:1065
celibacy, Christianity and 5:635,
692, 6:838, 840
Celtic people
  arts and crafts and 1:46, 46, 51,
  52
  Carthage and 4:469
  Christianity and 5:636
  Germanic people and 1:53
  Hallstatt culture and 1:45
  La Tène culture 1:50, 52
  Rome and 4:458–460, 482,
  5:584
  trade and 2:257
  weapons and armor of 4:460
censors 4:454, 506, 522, 533–
534
census, Domesday Book and
8:1050
central African kingdoms
9:1276–1277
Central America 1:14, 10:1302
Central Andean region 10:1304,
1305
Central and Southern Plateau
region 9:1260
central Asian peoples, Zhou dynasty
and 7:875, 877
ceramic artifacts 1:99, 10:1315,
1320, 1322, 1340
Cetshwayo 9:1277
Ceuta 10:1366
Ceylon 7:929, 958, 965, 10:1371
Chabiru people 1:101
Chaco Culture National Historical
Park 10:1351
Chaeronea, Battle of 3:383, 384
Chalcedon, Council of 5:625
Chaldeans 1:121–122, 2:217
Chaldiran, Battle of 10:1418,
1419
chalice, Byzantine 9:1169
Chalice of Tassilo 6:803
chalk circles 1:27, 28
Chalukya dynasty 7:966
Champagne region 8:1031, 1032
Cham people 7:977–978
Ch'an Buddhism 7:958

Chancas people 10:1336, 1338,
1339
Chan Chan 10:1311
Chandragupta I 7:960
Chandragupta II 7:960
Chandragupta Maurya 7:928
Chang'an 7:901
chansons de geste (songs of heroic
deeds) 6:801, 10:1394
chapels 10:1403
character, Roman 4:457–458
chariot races 4:552–553, 553
chariots 1:46, 90, 98, 2:157, 210,
214, 7:875, 876
Chariots of the Gods (Däniken)
7:986
charity, Islam and 6:749
Charlemagne 6:772, 788–803, 789,
796, 800, 802, 806, 808, 810
  Abbasid caliphate and 6:772
  Byzantine Empire and 9:1170,
  1171
  Carolingian Empire and
  6:804
  government of 6:807–808,
  810–811
  iconoclasm and 6:811
  intellectual pursuits and 6:806
  Italy and 8:1020
  Roman Empire and 6:836
  throne of 6:807
  Vikings and 6:809, 9:1199
  see also Carolingian Empire
Charlemagne Shrine 6:807
Charles II (Alençon) 8:1106
Charles II (Navarre) 8:1107
Charles IV (France) 6:827,
8:1102
Charles IV (Holy Roman emperor)
8:1110
Charles V (France) 8:1107, 1108,
1110, 1126
Charles V (Holy Roman emperor)
8:1133, 9:1253
Charles V (Spain) 10:1376, 1377
Charles VI (France) 8:1108, 1110,
1126
Charles VII (France) 8:1110, 1112,
1113, 1114, 1126, 1128
Charles Martel 6:760, 761, 768,
791, 792–793, 794, 795, 804
Charles of Anjou 8:1074,
1074–1075
Charles of Lorraine 6:827
Charles the Bald 6:812, 813, 813,
814, 815, 821, 8:1044
Charles the Bold of Burgundy
8:1120, 1129–1132, 1130
Charles the Fat 6:818, 819, 9:1200
Charles the Simple 6:818, 818–819,
827, 8:1046, 9:1200
Charon 4:526, 526
charters, cities and 8:1034, 1039,
1041
chaski runners 10:1346, 1347
Chaucer, Geoffrey 10:1394

Cheng Ho 10:*1420*, 1420

Cheops 1:74

Cheyenne people 10:*1354*

Chiang Mai dynasty 7:977

Chibcha people 10:1302, *1310*, 1310

Chichén Itzá 10:1309, 1315, 1316, 1317, 1318, *1319, 1321*

chiefs, North American peoples and 10:1355

Childeric I 5:654

Childeric III 6:794

children
    Christianity and 5:635, 680
    Germanic peoples and 5:664–665
    Greece and 2:263, 268, 3:350
    military forces and 9:1230, 1236, 1255
    Minoans and 2:180
    Phoenicians and 2:206
    pre-Columbian cultures and 10:1331, 1343, 1353
    Rome and 4:551
    see also family life

Chimú people 10:1311, 1339

China 7:870–881, *872*, 882–893, **894–905**, 10:*1414*
    agriculture in 1:14
    Black Death and 8:1084
    Bronze Age and 1:33, 35
    Buddhism and 7:958, 959
    European knowledge of 10:1360
    exploration and 10:1420
    Indian missionaries and 7:967
    Iron Age and 1:41
    Japan and 7:915
    Ming dynasty and 10:1419, 1421
    Mongols and 9:1222, 1223, 1224, 1226
    Roman Empire and 5:589
    Southeast Asia and 7:975, 978, 980
    technology and 10:1365, 1391
    trade and 6:776, 10:1371
    warfare and 10:1416

chinampas (artificial islands) 10:1324

Chippewa people 10:1354

Chittor 10:*1418*

chivalry 6:734, 799, 823, 8:1018

Choerilus 3:321

Chola dynasty 7:965–966

Chopán 10:1315

chorus, Greek drama and 3:318, 320–321

Christendom *see* Europe

Christian expansion 8:**1014–1025**

Christianity 5:628–639, 678–687, **688–701**, 9:*1159*
    Africa and 9:1266, 1268, 1269
    Arabia and 6:736
    Bulgarian Empire and 9:1177
    Byzantine Empire and 5:618, 626, 9:1158, 1166–1167

Carolingian Empire and 6:804
    Constantine and 5:611, 611–612
    doctrinal disputes and 5:624–625, 627, 6:733, 761, 766–767, 839, 840, 9:1162–1163, 10:1415
    early churches 5:*609*
    Franks and 5:654, 656, 657
    Germanic peoples and 5:645
    Islam and 6:736, 743, 748, 749, 759
    Japan and 7:917
    North American peoples and 10:1382
    Pacific islands and 7:987
    Persians and 6:730, 733–734
    religious tolerance and 9:1160
    Roman emperors and 5:599, 601, 610, 613
    Russia and 9:1203, 1210, 1212
    Southeast Asia and 7:981
    spread of 5:609
    Vikings and 6:819, 9:1198, 1200, 1204
    see also crusades; Roman Catholic Church

Christians 4:*528*, 528, 530, 552, 6:766–767, 780

Christian theology, development of 5:**678–687**

Chronicle of England, The 8:*1121*

Chronicle of the Famous and Invincible Knight, Cid Ruy Diaz 8:*1021*

Chrysippus 3:413

Chu Hsi 7:887

church reform movements
    crusades and 9:1187
    Henry II (Germany) and 6:835–836
    Holy Roman Empire and 6:837, 838, 841
    investiture controversy and 6:839, 841–842, 843–844, 845
    monasteries and 6:826
    popes and 8:1086, 1089, 1090, 1091–1093
    Reformation and 8:1094

Cicero, Marcus Tullius 3:335, 5:683 4:491–492, *492*, 494–495, 501, 502

Cimbrians 4:483, 485

Cimon 3:341, 341–342

Ciompi Rebellion 8:1086

circumnavigation of the globe 10:1377, 1379

Circus Maximus 4:454, 552, 5:676

Cistercian Order 8:1029, *1035*, 1035

cities and towns
    Africa and 9:1270
    Arabia and 6:736
    Babylon 1:124
    early 16th century CE and 10:1416

East Francia and 6:830
    feudalism and 6:822
    government and 8:1131
    India and 7:918, 927, 971
    Latium and 4:443–444
    leagues and alliances 8:1094
    medieval Europe and 8:1033–1034, 1036–1039, 1086
    pre-Columbian cultures and 10:1306–1307, 1315–1316, 1318, 1332, 1342, 1350
    Roman provinces and 4:547
    Rome and 4:508
    social classes and 8:1086
    Southeast Asia and 7:978, 980
    spread of Islam and 6:755
    Sumerian people and 1:54, 55
    Swabian League of Cities 8:1094
    see also towns and villages

citizenship
    Athens and 2:266, 269, 3:307–309, 346, 350
    Christians and 4:530
    Constantinople and 9:1161
    Greek poleis and 2:253
    Italian cities and 4:485, 486, 490
    medieval Europe and 8:1041, 10:1397
    military forces and 4:512
    Rome and 4:460, 463, 499, 508, 522, 5:595
    Sparta and 2:258, 260, 260–261, 262, 3:403

city-states
    Africa and 9:1274
    Assyrian 2:208
    Crete and 2:181
    Flemish 8:1102, 1104
    Greece and 2:249, 251, 258, 260–264, 264–269, 3:294, 312
    Italian 8:1025, 1060, 1061–1063, 1064, 1065, 1073, 1096
    Latium and 4:444
    medieval Europe and 8:1039, 1041
    Mycenaeans and 2:182
    Phoenicians and 2:196–197, 197–198
    pre-Columbian cultures and 10:1307, 1314–1315, 1318, 1323
    Renaissance and 10:1398
    Russia and 9:1212–1213
    Sumerian people and 1:57, 58–59
    see also specific cities

civil rights, Roman allies and 4:482

civil servants 1:100, 4:476, 479, 8:1063
    see also government

civil service exams 7:887, 893, 894–895, 901, 911

civil strife
    Africa and 9:1277
    Assyrians and 2:216, 221

Black Death and 8:1086

Byzantine Empire and 5:626, 627, 669, 670, 671, 9:1164, 1178

Carolingian Empire and 6:812

Carthage and 4:469

Catilina, Lucius Sergius, and 4:492

China and 7:877, 881, 882, 898, 9:1226–1227

Constantinople and 5:624

dynastic succession and 4:516, 518–519, 529, 537, 5:598, 599, 611

England and 8:1051, 1076–1077, 1109, 1114–1125

foederati (allies) and 5:588

France and 8:1130

Francia and 8:1044

Greece and 3:294, 296, 300, 378–379

Holy Roman Empire and 6:835, 8:1058

Hundred Years' War and 8:1108

India and 7:969, 971

Islamic world and 6:756–757, 768–769, 773, 785

Janissaries and 9:1255

Japan and 7:916–917

Macedonian Empire and 3:396

Persians and 2:236, 239

pre-Columbian cultures and 10:1338, 1340, 1347

Renaissance and 10:1398

Rome and 4:442, 482, 485–487, 496, 502, 532

Salian dynasty and 6:837, 843–844

Sicilian Vespers and 8:1074–1075

Thomas the Slav and 9:1171–1172

clans 5:660, 664, 10:1353

Clarendon Constitution 8:1053

classical antiquity, arts and 10:1404

Classic period, pre-Columbian cultures and 10:1304, 1307–1309, 1315

Claudian Aqueduct 5:*670*

Claudius, Appius Pulcher 4:480

Claudius I 4:516, 521–524, *522, 523*

Claudius II 5:601

clay bowl, Nubian 9:*1262*

Cleanthes 3:413

Cleisthenes 3:304, 309

Clement II 6:837, *841*

Clement III 6:843, 8:1063

Clement V 8:1080, 1081, 1087–1088

Clement VII 8:1089

Cleomenes III 3:403

Cleon 3:371, 373, 378

Cleopatra 4:*497*, 497, 498, *499, 501*, 503, 5:586

clergy 6:806, 821–822, 825,
830–831, 835, 838, 841, 845
Clermont, Council of 9:1182,
1183, 1184
client system 4:447
climate 2:162, 7:921, 923, 8:1026,
1084, 9:1256, 1258–1259,
10:1352
Cloaca Maxima 4:442
Clodia Pulchra 4:510
Clodius, Publius Pulcher
4:494–495, 496, 549
cloisoinné brooch, Viking 9:*1206*
cloth *see* textiles
clothing 2:156, 179, 212
Celtic people and 1:46
Copper Age and 1:34
Mari and 1:115
pre-Columbian cultures and
10:1323, 1329, 1331,
1344–1345, 1353
Clotilda 5:654, *656*, 656
Clouds (Aristophanes) 3:364, 378
Clovis I 5:645, *646*, 654, *655*, 656,
657, *659*, 6:788, *791*
clubs, Hippodrome and 5:623–624,
627
Cluny, abbey at 6:*826*, 826, *838*,
838, 8:1017
Cnut 6:816, 8:1046, *1047*, 9:1199,
1200
Cnut IV of Denmark 8:1066
coats of arms, guilds and
8:*1041*
Code of Hammurabi 1:111–117
codices 10:1319, 1328
coffin texts 1:84
coins
Athens and 3:*304*
Byzantine Empire and 9:*1165,
1170, 1185*
Egypt and 3:*398*
English 8:*1034*
Franks and 6:*792*
Greece and 3:303, *312*
India and 7:931, *963*
Islamic world and 6:*769*, 9:*1235,
1236*
Lydia and 3:328, *330*
Macedonia and 3:*383, 391*
Persians and 6:*727*
Phoenicians and 3:303
Roman Empire and 4:*494,
527, 535, 538*, 5:*606, 611,
629, 635*
Vikings and 9:1200
see also currency
Colima culture 10:1307
colonies
Athens and 3:349, 373
Corinth and 3:296, 368, 370
Croton 3:356–357
European 7:981, 10:1379–1381,
1382, 1383, 1421
Greece and 2:251, 253, 253–257,
255, 3:294, 4:456, 461–463

Phoenicians and 2:199–200
Roman 4:482, 498–499, 508,
512, 513
Colonna, Sciarra 8:*1081*, 1081
Colosseum 4:534
Columbus, Christopher 10:*1372,
1373*, 1374–1375, 1395,
1397
comedy 3:318, 320, 325, 378,
407
comitatus (companionship) 6:808
comitia centuriata 4:449–450, 453
comitia curiata 4:449
comitia tributa 4:451–452
Commodus 4:546, 5:590, 592
Commodus, Lucius Ceonius
4:543
common people 10:1324, 1331,
1332, 1340, 1344, 1358, 1397
see also plebians
communes 8:1034, 1036–1039,
1060
see also cities and towns
comos (religious procession)
3:320
compasses 10:1363–1364, 1365,
1391
competition, Greece and 3:308,
318, 320, 323
concilium plebis (council of the
plebians) 4:451, 455, 480
Concordat of Worms 8:1058, 1060
Conferences of the Egyptian Monks
(Cassian) 5:696
Confessions (Augustine) 5:683, 686,
687
Confucianism 7:884–886, 887, 890,
910, 975
Buddhism and 7:892, 902
China and 7:877, 881, 882, 893,
901
legalism and 7:891, 893
Taoism and 7:888, 889
Confucius 7:877, 882, *883, 884*,
884–886, *886*, 889, 894
Congo River Basin 9:1256, *1260*,
1260
conquered peoples
Alexander the Great and 3:388,
391
crusades and 9:1189, 1191
Islamic world and 6:752
Italian cities and 4:463
Jerusalem and 4:541
Macedonian Wars and 4:478
Mongols and 9:1221–1222, 1223,
1227, 1228, 1229, 1240
Ottoman Turks and 9:1247
Peloponnesian War and 3:376,
378–379
Persians and 2:239, 245, 3:327
pre-Columbian cultures and
10:1334
Punic Wars and 4:469, 475, 481
Trajan and 4:539–540
Vikings and 9:1201

Conrad II 6:836, *839*
Conrad III 9:1190
Conrad IV 8:1073
Conradin 8:1073, 1074
Conrad of Franconia 6:828–829
Conrad of Hohenstaufen 8:1058
conscription, military forces and
2:214, 216
Consolation of Philosophy, The
(Boethius) 5:661, 6:820
Constance, Council of 8:1090,
1092
Constance of Sicily 8:1063
Constans I 5:632–633
Constantine I 5:*611, 629, 630, 632*,
9:*1161*
Christianity and 5:625, 628,
680
Constantinople and 5:616
Hagia Sophia and 5:672
Nicaea, Council of, and
5:628–630, *631*
Roman Catholic Church and
6:800, 802
Roman Empire and 5:610–612,
9:1158
Constantine IV 6:762
Constantine V 6:811, 9:1168
Constantine VI 9:1168, 1170
Constantine VII 9:1174–1175,
1175
Constantine VIII 9:1176, 1178
Constantine IX 9:1178
Constantine XI 9:1181, 1247
Constantinople 5:*616–627, 617,
619, 622, 623, 625*, 9:*1162,
1164, 1179*
Arcadius and 5:666
attacks on 9:1165, 1172
Christianity and 5:632, 6:839,
840
Constantine I and 5:611
crusades and 8:*1068*, 1068, 1082,
9:1168, 1179, 1181, 1187, 1192,
1193, 1213
early 16th century CE and
10:1418
economy of 9:1160–1161
Germanic peoples and 5:649,
651, 653, 665
Islamic world and 6:762, 763,
10:1360
Moscow and 9:1215
Ottoman Turks and 9:1245,
1246–1247, *1250*
Persians and 6:734
Vikings and 9:1201, 1203,
1210
see also Byzantine Empire
Constantius 5:607, 610
Constantius II 5:612–613, 625, 630,
631, 633
constitutions 2:262–263, 3:304,
344, 7:910
consuls 4:448, 453, 458, 474, 492,
493, 504, 8:1036

convents 5:697, 10:1344
see also monasteries
conversions
to Buddhism 7:950
to Christianity 5:628, 657, 686,
6:788, 791, 9:1158, 1177,
1198, 1200, 1203, 1210,
1212
to Islam 6:743–744, 746, 757,
759, 768, 774
Cook, James 7:986, 987, 989
Cook Islands 7:982
Copernicus, Nicolaus 3:*410*
copper 1:31, 32, 33, 35, 94,
2:165
Copper Age 1:32–33
Coptic Christians 6:759
Coptic language 9:1258
Corbulo 4:529
corded-ware culture 1:28, 31
Córdoba 6:*770*, 770, *773*, 8:1016,
1017
Corfu 3:368, *370*, 370
Corinth 2:253, 254, 3:*297, 345*
Corinthian War 3:382
Peloponnesian War and 3:342,
368, 370
Temple of Apollo and 3:*299*
tyranny and 3:294, 295–296,
298
Corinthian League 3:385
Corinthian War 3:382
Corneille, Pierre 8:1021
Coronation of Poppea (Monteverdi)
10:*1407*, 1407
Corpus Juris Civilis 5:*677*, 677
corruption
caliphate and 6:764
England and 8:1116
government 4:476, 479, 491–
492, 9:1163, 1164, 1166
Roman Catholic Church and
6:837, 838, 8:1086–1087, 1088,
1090, 1093, 9:1194
Corsica 4:469, 470, 5:653,
8:1025
Cortés, Hernán 10:1333, 1334,
1335, 1335, 1419
Corupedium, Battle of 3:399
Council of 500 3:304, 306,
307–308, 344
council theory, western schism and
8:1091–1093
counts, Carolingian Empire and
6:808, 810, 811, 812–813
coups d'etat 3:294, 300, 301, 4:518,
9:1171, 1175
see also civil strife
court life
Burgundy and 8:1129
Carolingian Empire and 6:805,
806, 807
Islamic world and 6:785
Mali and 9:1272
Mongols and 9:1224, 1225,
1226

crafts and craftspeople
  Anasazi people and 10:1350
  Aztecs and 10:1327, 1333
  Celtic people and 1:46, 50
  copper and 1:32
  Egypt and 1:86
  Etruscans and 4:445
  Franks and 6:*793*
  Goths and 5:*645*
  Greece and 3:302–303
  Hallstatt culture and 1:45, 47
  Hittites and 2:156
  Huns and 5:*649*
  Iberian people and 1:50
  India and 7:920, 925
  Islamic world and 6:*779*,
    780–781
  Maya and 10:1314, 1316,
    1319
  medieval Europe and 8:1041,
    1043, 1086
  Mixtec people and 10:1310
  Mycenaeans and 2:189
  Neolithic period and 1:15
  Phoenicians and 2:198, 200
  pre-Columbian cultures and
    10:1302, 1304, 1305,
    1305–1306
  Renaissance and 10:1403
  Rome and 4:466, 548
  Tarascan people and 10:1310
  see also arts
Crannon, Battle of 3:401
Crassus, Marcus Licinius 4:490,
  493–494, 496
creation goddess, India 7:*927*
creation stories 1:117, 2:243–244,
  7:934, 936, 939–940, 954,
  10:1322, 1329, 1354
Crécy, Battle of 8:1105, *1106,*
  1106
cremation 1:39–40
Crete 2:167, 168, 170, 182, 204,
  246, 3:310
Crimea 8:1084, 9:1214, 1217,
  1228
crises in the Middle Ages
  8:1082–1093
Croesus 2:234, 244, 3:*328*, 328
crop rotations 3:302, 6:823, 8:1028
Croton 3:356–357
crusades 9:1182–1195, *1184*
  Constantinople and 5:618, 672,
    8:1082, 9:1168, 1179, 1181
  Frederick I and 8:1063
  Frederick II and 8:1073
  Islamic world and 10:1360
  Knights Templar and 8:1080
  Louis IX and 8:1078
  Mamluk dynasty and 9:1237
  Nicopolis, Battle of, and 9:1248
  Richard I (the Lionheart) and
    8:1056
  Roman Catholic Church and
    8:1014, 1067, 1068, 1069
  Teutonic Knights and 8:1101

Ctesiphon 5:585, *586*, 6:726
Cuba 10:1374
Cubells, Salvador Martínez
  6:*761*
cults, secret 3:315
cultural changes, Greek expansion
  and 2:256–257
cultural influences
  African kingdoms and 9:1275
  Alexander the Great and 3:395
  Bulgarian Empire and 9:1177
  Byzantine Empire and 9:1167
  England and 8:1048–1049
  Germanic peoples and 5:658,
    665
  Greek culture and 3:352,
    402–403, 404–413
  Kushan India and 7:931
  Latium and 4:444
  Mongols and 9:1238, 1240
  Pacific islands and 7:985
  Roman Empire and 4:504,
    546–547
  Russia and 9:1212
  Seleucid dynasty and 3:401
  Sicily and 8:1023, 1025
  Southeast Asia and 7:975, 978
cultures of the Pacific 7:982–989
cuneiform writing
  Akkadian 1:60–61
  Assyrians and 2:208
  Babylonians and 1:119
  Greeks and 2:252
  Hittites and 2:150, 161
  Mesopotamians and 2:204
  Sumerian 1:67, *68*, 68, 69
Curia 4:*455*
Curiatii 4:457–458
currency
  banking and 8:1032–1033
  barbarian rulers and 5:665
  Bronze Age and 1:37
  Byzantine Empire and 9:1158,
    1165
  China and 7:877, 879, 901
  Egypt and 1:97
  Hittites and 2:156
  India and 7:946
  Persians and 2:238
  pre-Columbian cultures and
    10:1314, 1345
  Roman Empire and 5:595–596,
    603, 604, 612
  see also coins
curses, Assyrians and 2:219
Cusco 10:*1346*
Cuzco 10:1302, 1336, 1340, 1343,
  1346, *1346*
Cyaxares 2:232
Cycladic people 2:164–169, 172
Cyclopean masonry 2:184
cylinder seal, Babylonian 1:*121*
Cynics 3:366, 413
Cynoscephalae, Battle of 4:476, 478
Cyprus 2:246, 250, 3:327, 339, 396,
  6:763

Cypselus 3:294, 296, 297
Cyrus the Great 1:125, 2:207,
  233–234, *236*, *238*, 3:326, 328

D
Dacia 5:599, 601, 603
Dacians 4:538, 539–540
Daedalus 2:176
Dafne (Peri) 10:*1407*
Dagan 1:114, 117
dagger, Chinese 7:*890*
Dahomey 9:1275
Daia, Maximinus 5:610, 611
daily life
  barbarian rulers and 5:658–665
  Cycladic people and 2:169
  Egypt and 1:86, 97, 108
  feudalism and 6:823
  Hittites and 2:154, 159
  Minoans and 2:174
  Persians and 2:244–245
  pre-Columbian cultures and
    10:1322–1323, 1328, 1331,
    1333, 1354
  Renaissance and 10:1394, 1398
  Roman Empire and 4:520, 536,
    546–547, 548–557
  Sparta and 2:263–264
  Vikings and 9:1205
  Zhou dynasty and 7:877
Dai Viet dynasty 7:977
Dalai Lama 7:*959*, 959
dalits see untouchables
Damascus
  Assyrians and 2:216
  crusades and 9:*1190*, 1190–
    1191
  Islamic world and 6:754, 764,
    767
  Mongols and 9:1228
  Persians and 6:735
  trade and 6:776
  weaving and 6:781
Damasus I 5:697
Damietta 9:1193, 1195
damnatio memoriae (damned in
  memory) 4:531, 537, 5:590
Damasus I 3:348
Dampier, William 7:989
dams, Persians and 6:729
dance see music and dance
Dance of Apollo with the Muses
  (Peruzzi) 3:*411*
Danegeld 6:816, 8:1046
Danelaw 6:820, 9:1198
Daniel Nevsky 9:1215
Däniken, Erich von 7:986
Danishmend emirate 9:1234, 1241
Dante, Alighieri 10:1394
Dante Pyramid 10:1316
Darius I 2:240, 243, 3:305, 6:726
  government and 2:236, 237
  Persian Wars and 3:326, 329, 330,
    332, 393
  territorial expansion and
    2:238–239

Darius III 2:239, 241, 3:*389*,
  390–391, 393–394, 395
Dark Age, Greek expansion and
  2:192, **246–257**
Daulatabd 7:969
David 2:230, 231
David (Michelangelo) 10:1404
Davis, John 10:1378
death mask, Mycenaean 2:*183*
Death of Seneca, The (Giordano)
  4:*529*
Death of Socrates, The (David)
  3:*363*
debts 2:266–267, 3:294, 298,
  403, 4:450, 455, 493,
  5:664
Decebalus 4:538, 539
decemvirate 4:452–453
decimal notation 6:784
Decius 5:*599*, 599, 601
De civitate Dei (Augustine) 5:687
decline of Rome 5:590–603
De Germania (Tacitus) 6:808
deification, Roman emperors and
  4:511, 520, *523*, 525, 535, 537,
  538, 540, 544, 5:608
Deioces 2:232
delatores (informers) 4:518–519,
  537
Delhi 9:1229, 1232
Delhi Sultanate 7:963, 968–970,
  10:1418
Delian League 3:341, 342, 368,
  370
Delos 2:164, 167
Delphi, oracle at 2:234, 3:313, 315,
  331
Demaratus 3:329, 4:441
Demeter 3:314, 316, 5:601
Demetrius Poliorcetes 3:398
demigods 3:310, 314
democracy, Greece and 3:304,
  306–309, 344, 346–348,
  378–379, 380
Democritus 3:317, 361
demon mask, Japanese 7:*907*
demons, Hinduism and 7:941, 942,
  945
demos (common people) 3:304
Demosthenes 3:371, *382*, 383, 386,
  401
demotic writing 1:88
Dengizich 5:651
Denmark 8:1097, 1098, 1098–1099,
  1100, 9:1199, 1205
deportations, Assyrians and 2:213,
  219
desert trade routes 6:776, 778,
  779
Desiderius 6:796
Devi 7:930
Dhammayangyi Temple 7:*980*
dharma, Buddhism and 7:950–
  954
diadochs 3:396, 398, 399, 401
Diagoras of Melos 3:317, 352

dialects *see* languages
Dias, Bartolomeu 10:1369–1370
Diaz de Vivar, Rodrigo *see* El Cid
dice set, Roman 4:*549*
dictators, Rome and 4:453–454, 461–462, 472, 487, 498–500
Dijon 8:1129
Dingane 9:1277
Diocletian 5:606–608, *607*, 610, *611*, 628, 9:1158
Diodorus 1:46
Diodorus Siculus 2:206
Diogenes 3:*353, 365, 366*, 366
Dionysius of Halicarnassus 4:456
Dionysus 3:*319, 321, 403*
  cults and 3:402
  Greeks and 3:310, 311, 314
  Mycenaeans and 2:190
  religious festivals and 3:318, 320
Dir 9:1201, 1210
disciples, Buddha and 7:948, 950
diseases
  Black Death and 8:*1084*, 1084–1086, *1085, 1086*
  disintegration of the Roman Empire and 5:604, 606
  European conquests and 10:1421
  European settlers and 10:1381
  pre-Columbian cultures and 10:1311, 1335, 1347
  Roman Empire and 4:544
disintegration of the Roman Empire 5:604–615
disputations, education and 10:1387
dithyramb (poem) 3:318, 320
divination 3:315, 4:445, 7:872, 873, 876, *877, 887*, 887, 889
Divine Comedy, The (Dante) 4:*459*, 10:1394
divinity
  Buddha and 7:951, 956
  of Christ 5:624–625, 627
  kings and 7:979
  see also deification, Roman emperors and
divisions, Roman Empire and 5:607–608, 613–614, 615, 616, 632, 666
  see also Byzantine Empire; Roman Empire
divorce 1:118, 2:161, 3:350, 4:510, 5:674
Djefai-Hapi 1:85
Djenné 9:*1270*, 1272
Djoser 1:73, 75
Dmitry Donskoy 9:1215
Dnieper River 9:1202, 1208, *1212*, 1223
doctrinal disputes
  Augustine and 5:684–685
  Buddhism and 7:955–957

Christianity and 5:633, 681, 6:734, 766–767, 811, 840, 9:1160, 1162–1163
  crusades and 9:1182, 1187, 1191, 1194
  Donatism 5:685
  iconoclasm 9:1166–1167, 1168
  Islam and 6:756, 772–773, 774, 9:1233
  Manichaeism and 5:682
  Monophysitism 5:626, 627, 670
  Nicaea, Council of, and 5:628–630
  religious beliefs and 10:1415
  Roman Catholic Church and 8:1025, 1090, 1112–1113
  Socrates and 3:364–365
  see also Arianism
dogs 1:9, 2:243–244
Dolmen of Menga 1:25
dolmens 1:*22*, 24–25
Dome of the Rock 6:*768*, 768, 769
Domesday Book 8:1026, 1050
Dominican Order 8:1042
dominium mundi (sovereignty over the world) 8:1064, 1067, 1075, 1081
Domitian 4:535–538, *538*, 5:678
Domna, Julia 5:593, 595, 596, 597
Donatello 10:1401
Donation of Constantine 6:800, 802
Donatism 5:685
Dong Son civilization 7:972, 974–975, *975*
Dorian people 1:41, 44, 2:169, 191, 246, 250, 258, 3:310
Dorylaeum, Battle of 9:1190
Dougga, ruins of 5:*588*
dowries 1:118, 3:350, 10:1323
drainage projects 4:442
drama 3:318–325, 378, 384, 407, 7:*907*, 963, 8:1021
dramatists 3:321–322, *322*–325, 407
Dravidian peoples 7:920
drinking vessel, Minoan 2:*176*
dromos (tomb entrance) 2:187, *188*, 188
Drusus, Marcus Livius 4:485
Drusus, Nero Claudius 4:514
dualism, Aztecs and 10:1329
Duilius 4:467
dukedoms 6:819, 828–830, 837
duma (council) 9:1211
Duomo 10:*1399*
Durazzo, Battle of 8:1024
Dürer, Albrecht 10:*1408*, 1408–1409
Durga 7:945, 960
Dur Sharrukin 2:208, 218
duties, Islam and 6:749, 766
dyes, Phoenicians and 2:202

dynastic succession *see* succession
dynasties, Egyptian 1:76, 82, 89, 92
Dyophysitism 9:1163

E

early Byzantine Empire 9:**1158–1167**, *1160*
Early Cycladic period 2:166–167
Early Dynastic period, Egypt 1:73, 76
Early Dynastic period, Sumer 1:57–59
early humans 1:**6–17**, 7:870, 906, 972, 984, 9:1256
Early Minoan period 2:172
early Rome 4:**438–455**
earrings, silver 6:*793*
Earth, circumference of 3:410
earthenware pots *see* pottery
earth mounds 1:27–28, *31*, 10:1350
earthquakes, Constantinople and 5:619, 672
east African kingdoms 9:1275–1276
East Anglia 9:1196, 1198
Easter Island 7:982, 985, 986, *986*
eastern border, Roman Empire and 5:584–585
Eastern Highland region 9:1260
eastern Roman Empire *see* Byzantine Empire
East Francia 6:813, 828–830
Eboracum 9:1196, 1198
ecclesia (public assembly) *see* public assembly
Ecloga 6:761, 9:1165–1166
Ecnomus, Battle of 4:467
Ecologues (Virgil) 4:512
economy
  annual fairs and 8:1030–1032
  Arabic culture and 6:784
  Black Death and 8:1086
  China and 7:877, 894, 901, 903
  coinage and 3:303
  Constantinople and 9:1160–1161
  Egypt and 1:97, 99
  Hundred Years' War and 8:1102
  Roman Empire and 5:604, 608
  see also finances, Roman Empire and; trade
Edessa 9:1188, 1189, 1190, 1191
Edessa, Battle of 6:729
Edgecote Moor, Battle of 8:1120
Edict of Milan 5:611, 628, 635
Edington, Battle of 6:820
Edmund Langley 8:1114, 1116
Edmund of Rutland 8:1118
education
  Abbasid caliphate and 6:772
  Alexander the Great and 3:384
  Alfred the Great and 6:820

Aristotle and 3:367
  Babylonians and 1:119
  Bulgarian Empire and 9:1177
  Carolingian Empire and 6:804, 806
  China and 7:882, 887, 894–895, 903
  Confucianism and 7:884–885
  Egyptians and 1:108
  Frederick II and 8:1070
  gladiators and 4:551
  Greek philosophy and 3:356, 361, 364, 367, 411
  humanism and 10:1400
  Jerome and 5:696
  Laws of the Twelve Tables and 4:453
  Mali and 9:1271
  medieval Europe and 8:1043, 10:1366, 1384, 1400
  military training and 10:1328
  Museum of Alexandria and 3:404, 406–407
  Persians and 2:244
  Plato's Academy and 3:365, 367
  pre-Columbian cultures and 10:1327, 1328, 1331, 1353
  Rome and 4:556–557
  Scholasticism and 10:1384, 1386–1390
  Sparta and 2:263
  Sumerians and 1:65, 69
  Taoism and 7:888
Edward (Black Prince) 8:1105, 1107
Edward I 8:*1076*, 1076, 1077–1078, 1081
Edward III 8:*1034*
  banking and 8:1033
  Bretigny, Treaty of, and 8:1107, 1108
  Crécy, Battle of, and 8:1106
  Hundred Years' War and 8:1102, 1104, 1105
  Richard III and 8:1125
  Wars of the Roses and 8:1114, 1116
Edward IV 8:1117, 1118, 1119–1222
Edward V 8:1123, 1124
Edward VI 10:1387
Edward of Lancaster (son of Henry VI) 8:1118, 1119, 1122
Edward of York *see* Edward IV
Edward the Confessor 6:816, 8:1046–1047, *1048*
Edward the Elder 6:816, 820
Eflatun Pinar sanctuary 2:*156*
Egypt 1:**70–77, 78–91, 92–109**
  Africa and 9:1261, 1266, *1268*, 1268, 1274
  Alexander the Great and 3:391, 392, 393
  Alexandria and 3:404, 406–407
  Assyrians and 2:220

Egypt (*continued*)
astronomy and 3:354
Ayyubid Empire and 9:1234
Babylon and 1:124
Byzantine Empire and 9:1163, 1165
Christianity and 5:625, 688, 690, 691–692
crusades and 9:1191, 1193, 1195
Cycladic people and 2:167
Fatimid dynasty and 9:1188–1189
Hittites and 2:150, 152, 153
Indus Valley civilization and 7:920
Islam and 6:*745*, 755, 757, 774, 775
Israelites and 2:225, 226–227, 228, 229
Mamluk dynasty and 8:1082, 9:1195, 1236, 1236–1238
Minoans and 2:170, 179
Neolithic period and 1:16
Nile River 5:*587*
Ottoman Turks and 9:1242, 1251–1252, 10:1418
Palmyra and 5:602
Persians and 2:235–236, 238–239, 3:326
Phoenicians and 2:196, 198, 199, 201
Ptolemies and 3:396, 398, 402
Roman Empire and 4:543, 5:582, 586
Rome and 4:496, 497, 498, 503, 508
Sea Peoples and 2:192
Seljuk Turks and 9:1232, 1234
trade and 5:587, 589
writing and 2:204
Egyptian language 9:1264
Eightfold Path 7:948, 951–952
Einhard 6:798, 802, 803, 806–807, *808*
Elagabalus 5:*595*, 596, 596–597
Elam 1:60, 65–66, 110, 112, 121
Elamite language 2:243
Elamites 2:219, 220–221
El Argar culture 1:36
El Bekri 9:1270
El cantar de mío Cid (The Song of the Cid) 8:1021
El Castillo 10:1318
El Cid 8:*1021*, 1021
El Dorado, legend of 10:1310
Eleanor of Aquitaine 8:1049, 1052, *1054*, 1054, 1056
elect, Manichaeism and 6:731, 733
elections 3:306, 4:448, 449, 450, 9:1218, 1224
Electra (Sophocles) 3:323
Elements (Euclid) 3:407, *408*
elements, primary 3:354, 355, 356, 358

Eleusinian Mysteries 3:315–316, 5:633
El-Gabal 5:596
Elis 3:373
Elizabeth I 10:1380, 1387
Elizabeth of York 8:1125
Ellac 5:651
El Mirador 10:1316
El Tigre 10:1316
Elysian Fields 4:526
embalming 1:96
emperors
Charlemagne as 6:799–800, 802–803
China and 7:870, 877, 895–897, 897–898, 902
Henry II of Germany 6:835
Japan and 7:908, 909, 910–911, 912, 916–917
Otto II and 6:832
Otto III and 6:834
Otto the Great and 6:831
popes and 6:839, 841–842, 843–845, 8:**1058–1069**
see also Carolingian Empire; emperors, Byzantine; emperors, Roman; Holy Roman Empire; kings
emperors, Byzantine
Anastasius I 5:625, *627*, 627, 669
Arcadius 5:641, 642, 666, 668
Constantius II 5:612–613, 625, 630, 631, 633
government of 5:624
Hippodrome and 5:622, 624
Jovian 5:613, 634
Justin 5:669, 674
Justinian I 5:639, 654, **666–677**, *667*, *673*
Leo I 5:626, 653, 669
Theodosius II 5:618, 649, 666, 668, *680*
Valens 5:614, 620, 630, 631, 640, 643
Zeno 5:*626*, 626, 645–646, 647, 653, 669
see also Constantine I; Theodosius I
emperors, Roman
Alexander, Severus 5:597–598
Antoninus Pius 4:543–544
Augustus Caesar 4:**504–515**, *505*, *506*, *508*
Byzantine Empire and 9:1158
Caligula 4:516, 519–521
Caracalla 5:595–596
chariot races and 4:552, 553
Claudius I 4:516, 521–524
Commodus 5:590, 592
Constantine 5:610–612, *611*
Domitian 4:535–538
Galba, Sulpicius 4:529, 532, *535*
Gratian 5:614–615, 634, 636, 643
Hadrian 4:*533*, 540, 542–543
Illyrian emperors 5:601, 603, 606–607

Julian the Apostate 5:612–613, 632, 633, *636*, 654
Julius Caesar 4:488, *489*, 492, 493–496, *494*, 497, 498–501
Macrinus, Marcus Opellius 5:596
Marcus Aurelius 4:544–546
Maximinus 5:598
Nero 4:516, *517*, 524–525, 527–529, 531
Nerva, Marcus Cocceius 4:538
purchase of the emperorship 5:592
Severus, Septimius 5:592–595
soldier emperors 5:599, 601
tetrarchy and 5:607–608, 610–611
Tiberius 4:516–519
Titus 4:535
Trajan 4:538–540
Vespasian 4:533–535
Vitellus, Aulus 4:532–533, 532–533
Empire of Charlemagne, map of 6:*790*
Empire of the Golden Horde *see* Mongols
empires and unions 10:1356, 1418–1419, 1421
employment
actors 3:321
cities and towns and 10:1416
crafts and craftspeople 3:302–303
Egypt and 1:108
guilds and 8:1043
Hittites and 2:158
Hundred Years' War and 8:1102
mercenaries 3:388–389
Peasants' Revolt 8:1109
pre-Columbian cultures and 10:1319, 1327, 1344
Rome and 4:548, 549
shoemakers 4:*550*
Socrates and 3:362
Sophists and 3:361
temples and 7:966
see also agriculture; labor; work specialization
enamel plaque, French 9:*1163*
England
Christianity and 8:1025
France and 8:**1044–1057**, 1079
government and 8:1057, 1067, 1094, 1131
Hundred Years' War and 8:1085, 1102–1113, 1126
North America and 10:1378, 1380–1381, 1382, 1383
population growth in 8:1026
pre-Conquest 8:1046–1047
rulers of 6:820, 8:1067, 1076–1078
Vikings and 9:1196, 1198–1199, 1200

Wars of the Roses 8:**1114–1125**
see also Britain
Enheduanna 1:61
Eninnu temple 1:64
Enki 1:66
Enlil 1:66, 117
Enmebaragesi 1:57
entertainment 4:531, 548, 548–553, 548–553, 8:1031, 1043
see also drama; music and dance
Epaminondas 3:382, 383
Ephesus 3:303
Ephesus, Council of 5:678, 680, *680*
Epic of Gilgamesh (Babylonian) 1:123
Epicureanism 3:412–413
Epicurus 3:412–413, *413*
Epiphany (Giotto) 10:1402
Epistles (Augustine) 5:687
Epistula de litteris colendis (Alcuin) 6:806
equality, Stoicism and 3:413
equestrians 4:481, 488, 507, 542, 543, 5:594, 596, 601
Erasistratus 3:411
Erasmus, Desiderius 10:1397
Eratosthenes 3:380
Eratosthenes of Cyrene 3:410
Erechtheion 3:*309*, 349
Eric II of Norway 8:1098
Eric of Pomerania 8:1099–1100
Erigena, John Scotus 6:820
Eriksson, Leif 9:1206, *1207*, 1207
Erik the Red 9:1206
Eritria 3:327, 329
Erlitou culture 1:35
Ertugrul 9:1242
Esarhaddon 2:220
Esau 2:226
Eshnunna 1:110, 111
Es Saheli 9:1271
Estates General 8:1079, 1105, 1107, 1131, 1132
Este, Beatrice d' 10:1404
Estonia 8:1101
ethics 3:362–363, 411, 412, 7:886
Etruscans 4:*445*, 445, *452*, *551*, 551
early Rome and 4:446
Greeks and 4:456
Latium and 4:444
Rome and 4:441–442, 456–458
Eucharist 5:632, 681, *683*
Euclid 3:407, *408*, 10:1390
Eudoxia (wife of Arcadius) 5:666, 668
Eudoxia (wife of Valentinian III) 5:653
Eugenius (of Rome) 5:615, *635*
Eugenius III 8:1037–1038, *1039*, 1040, 9:1190
Eugenius IV 8:1093
Eumenides (Aeschylus) 3:323
Eunomius 5:695
Euric 5:645

Euridice (Peri) **10**:1407

Euripides **3**:324–325, *325*, 349, 356, 378

Europe **6**:814–831, **8**:*1016*, **1026–1043**, *1028*
  agriculture in **1**:15
  Arabic learning and **6**:783, 784
  Bronze Age and **1**:33
  Greek literature and **6**:783
  Iron Age and **1**:41, 44–45
  Islam and **6**:759–762, 793, **9**:1230
  Japan and **7**:917
  Mesolithic period and **1**:9, 10, 14
  Mongols and **9**:1227–1228
  Neolithic period and **1**:18
  Ottoman Turks and **9**:1242, 1245
  raiders on **6**:814, 816, 819, 822–823, 832
  Roman Empire and **5**:582, 584
  Southeast Asia and **7**:980–981
  trade and **2**:257

European expansion **10**:1360–1371

European exploration **10**:1360–1371, **1372–1383**, *1374*
  humanism and **10**:1395, 1397
  North American peoples and **10**:1359
  Pacific islands and **7**:986, 988–989
  Portugal and **8**:1093
  pre-Columbian cultures and **10**:1309, 1311, 1332
  technology and **10**:1421

European settlers **10**:1375, 1379–1381, 1382, 1383, 1421

Eurymedon River, battle near **3**:341

Eusebius **5**:629–630

Eustochium **5**:697

Eutropius **5**:666, 668

Evans, Arthur **2**:170, 172, 174, 179

Eve **5**:678, 685

Evesham, Battle of **8**:1076

excommunication **5**:682, **6**:840, 841–842, 844, **8**:1039, 1066–1067, 1073

Exodus (from Egypt) **2**:227, *228*, 229

expansion
  China and **7**:879, 895–896, 901
  European **10**:1360–1371
  Greek **2**:253–257
  India and **7**:930, 960
  Roman Empire and **4**:532–547

exploration
  China and **10**:1419, 1420
  Greeks and **2**:248
  Phoenicians and **2**:200–201, 205
  see also European exploration

Ezana **9**:1266, 1269

Ezo **7**:912

F

Fabius, Quintus Maximus Verrucosus **4**:472

fairs, annual **8**:1030–1032, *1032*, *1033*

Faiyum oasis **1**:87

family law **1**:113

family life
  Augustus and **4**:509–510
  Christianity and **5**:635
  early Rome and **4**:446
  Germanic peoples and **5**:664–665
  legal system and **4**:453
  military forces and **4**:513
  pre-Columbian cultures and **10**:1312, 1322–1323, 1340, 1346–1347, 1353
  Roman character and **4**:458
  Roman emperors and **4**:516, 518, 523–524, 525, 527

famine **5**:622, **8**:1084, **10**:1381
  see also food

farming *see* agriculture

fasces (king's symbol) **4**:446, *454*

fasting, Islam and **6**:749

Fatima **6**:751, 756, 758

Fatimid dynasty **6**:774, 786, 814, **9**:1188–1189, 1232

Federated States of Micronesia **7**:982

Ferdinand I (Aragon) **8**:*1020*

Ferdinand I (Austria) **9**:1252

Ferdinand I (Castile) **8**:1016–1017, 1021

Ferdinand II (Aragon) **8**:1019, 1133

Ferdinand II (Spain) **10**:1372, 1374, *1376*

Ferdinand III (Castile) **8**:*1019*

Ferghana **7**:895

Fernández de Quirós, Pedro **7**:988

Fertile Crescent **1**:12, 14, 18
  see also Mesopotamia

fertility **2**:244

fertility cults **1**:28, 39, **7**:909, 920, 945

festivals **4**:511, 527, 549–550

feudal Europe **6**:814–831

feudalism
  Carolingian Empire and **6**:808
  China and **7**:882, 900
  cities and towns and **8**:1034, 1041
  crusades and **9**:1182
  daily life and **6**:823
  England and **8**:1048–1049
  Franks and **6**:793
  Hittites and **2**:155–156
  Holy Roman Empire and **6**:831, **8**:1058, 1060, 1063
  leagues and alliances and **8**:1094
  Peasants' Revolt and **8**:1109
  Philip II Augustus and **8**:1054, 1057
  primogeniture and **6**:828
  religion and **6**:823–824, 825
  rise of **6**:819, 821

Roman Catholic Church and **8**:1014, 1061
  social classes and **6**:821–822
  warfare and **6**:822–823

feudal manors, daily life in **6**:823

Ficino, Marsilio **10**:1401

Fifth Crusade **9**:1193

Fiji **7**:982

finances, Roman Empire and **5**:592, 595–596, 603, 604

fines, Germanic peoples and **5**:662, 664

Firdawsi **6**:732

firearms, Japan and **7**:917

fires, cities and **4**:527–528, 535, 548, **5**:619

First Crusade **6**:*823*, **9**:1182, 1184–1189, 1234

First Intermediate period, Egypt **1**:78, 80–81

First Macedonian War **4**:478

First Persian War **3**:329–330

First Punic War **4**:464, 464–465, 467–470

first triumvirate **4**:493–496

Firuz II **6**:734

fiscal problems, Philip IV (France) and **8**:1079

fishing **1**:7, **7**:975, 988, **10**:1358

Five Chariots **7**:965

Five Classics **7**:887

Five Pecks of Rice Society **7**:899

Flaminius, Gaius **4**:471

Flanders **8**:*1027*, 1102, 1104, 1130, **10**:1408

Flavian emperors **4**:533–538

flint daggers **1**:*23*

flint mining **1**:19, 23

flooding, Nile River and **1**:70

Florence **8**:1036, 1085, 1086, 1096, **10**:1398, *1399*, 1400, 1402

flower wars, Aztecs and **10**:1329

foederati (allies) **5**:588, 643, 645, 652, 654, 660

Fontainebleu, architecture of **10**:*1409*

Fontenay, Battle of **6**:813

food
  Africa and **9**:1256, 1262
  agricultural improvements and **8**:1028–1029
  China and **7**:895, 911
  crusades and **9**:1187
  distribution of **5**:603, 612, 616, 621–622
  Mongols and **9**:1220
  Pacific islands and **7**:987
  pre-Columbian cultures and **10**:1312, 1314, 1316, 1331, 1333
  religious offerings of **3**:312
  Rome and **4**:482, 490, 498

foreign expeditions, Egyptian **1**:77, 82, 98

foreign relations
  Amarna Letters and **1**:101, 103–104
  Babylonians and **1**:110
  Egypt and **1**:72, 77, 98, 99
  Mycenaeans and **2**:191
  Phoenicians and **2**:199
  see also warfare

forests, early humans and **1**:8

Forms, Plato and **3**:367

fortifications
  Athens and **2**:264, **3**:370, 371
  Bronze Age and **1**:40
  castles and **6**:823
  China and **7**:875, 877, 879, *880*, 896, **9**:1222
  Constantinople and **5**:618, *619*, *622*, **9**:1161, 1165, 1179, 1247
  Cycladic people and **2**:167
  Egyptian **1**:87
  Great Zimbabwe **9**:*1275*
  Hittites and **2**:152–153, 154
  India and **7**:918, 927
  Japan and **7**:916
  Krak des Chevaliers **9**:*1189*
  Mycenaeans and **2**:183–184, 187, 191
  Nimrud and **2**:213
  Novgorod and **9**:*1214*
  Persepolis and **2**:240
  pre-Columbian cultures and **10**:1311, 1357
  Rhodes and **9**:*1195*
  Rome and **4**:442, 459
  Troy and **2**:193, 195

forum **4**:508, **5**:*675*

Four Books **7**:887

Four Noble Truths **7**:948, 950–951

Fourth Crusade **8**:*1068*, 1068, **9**:1181, 1191, 1192–1193, *1193*, 1213

Fra Angelico **10**:1401

France
  Africa and **9**:1275
  Avignon popes and **8**:1087–1088, 1091
  Burgundy and **8**:1126–1133
  crusades and **9**:1182, 1185, 1187
  England and **8**:1044–1057, 1076
  exploration and **10**:1379–1380
  feudal territories of **6**:813
  Franks and **5**:657
  government and **8**:1057, 1114, 1131
  Greek colonies and **2**:254
  Holy Roman Empire and **6**:832
  Hundred Years' War and **8**:1085, 1102–1113
  leagues and alliances and **8**:1094
  Renaissance and **10**:1409
  rulers of **8**:1066–1067, 1078–1079, 1081
  Southeast Asia and **7**:981

France (*continued*)
Vikings and 9:1199–1200
Wars of the Roses and 8:1117, 1120, 1125
see also Carolingian Empire; West Francia
Francis I of France 10:1379, 1409
Francis of Assisi 5:*693*, 8:*1042*, 1042
Francis Xavier 7:917
Franconia 6:819
Frankfurt 8:1039, *1040*
Franks
Charlemagne and 6:788, 790–793
Christianity and 5:654, 656, 657
coins and 6:*792*
crafts and 5:*657*
Huns and 5:649–650
Islamic world and 6:760–762, 768, 776
Italy and 8:1020
legal system of 5:662, 664
military forces of 5:*665*
Roman Catholic Church and 5:660
Vandals and 5:652
Visigoths and 5:645
Frederick I (Barbarossa) 8:1039, 1040, 1058, *1059*, 1060–1064, *1061*, 9:1192
Frederick II 8:1064–1065, 1069, 1070, 1072–1073, 1078, 1096, 9:1191, 1193, 1195
Frederick III 8:1094, 1130–1131, 1132, 9:1216
freedom of thought 10:1388, 1390
freemen 6:821, 7:911
free will, original sin and 5:685, 687
frescos
chariot races in 4:*553*
Cycladic people and 2:*169*, 169
Italian 3:*311*, 5:*687*
Mani and 6:*731*
Minoans and 2:*177*, 178, *179*, 179, *181*
music and dance in 4:*557*
Pompeii and 4:*537*
Renaissance and 10:*1401*, 1403–1404
Roman 4:*509*, 9:*1161*
Freya 5:*651*
frieze, Persian 2:*237*
Frigidus River, Battle of 5:615
Frisians 6:791, 797
Frobisher, Martin 10:1378
Frogs (Aristophanes) 3:325
Fu Hao 7:876
Fujiwara period 7:912–913
Funan, kingdom of 7:975
funerals *see* burial practices
funnel-beaker culture 1:18–19, 21, 22, 24

G
Gabriel 6:*737*, 741
Gades 2:196, 200
Gainas 5:668
Gaiseric 5:652, 653, 654
Gaius *see* Caligula
Gaius (son of Agrippa) 4:515
Galahad 5:*663*
Galaup, Jean-François de 7:986
Galba, Sulpicius 4:529, 532, *535*
Galen 10:1390
Galerius 5:607, 610, 611
Gallic Wars 4:494–495
Gallienus 5:601, 602
Gama, Vasco da 10:1370, *1371*
games
Maya and 10:*1317*, 1317, 1318
Rome and 4:*500*, 511, *549*, 549–550, 551–552, *552*–553
Gandhi, Mohandas 7:923
Ganesh 7:944, *945*, *976*
Ganges 7:945
Gangetic civilization 7:*926*, 927
Gao 9:1271, *1272*, 1272
Gaozu (Li Yuan) 7:901
Gascony, Hundred Years' War and 8:1102, 1108
Gathas 6:731
Gaugamela, Battle of 3:393
Gaul
Franks and 6:776
Gallic Wars 4:494–495
Germanic peoples and 5:*643*, 652, 654, 657
Huns and 5:649–650
monasteries and 5:696
rebellion in 4:529, 531
Roman Empire and 4:496, 520–521, 5:601, 603, 606, 607, 612–613
Rome and 4:459–460, 462
trade and 2:257
Gaumata 2:236, 243
Gaza Empire 9:1277
Gelasius II 6:844
Gelimer 5:671, 673
Gemellus, Tiberius 4:519
gender roles, pre-Columbian cultures and 10:1323, 1331, 1352, 1353, 1355
genealogy 9:1259, 1261, 10:1319
general assembly, Charlemagne and 6:807–808
Genghis Khan 7:*905*, 9:1218, *1219*, 1220–1224, *1222*
Islamic world and 6:775, 9:1235
Japan and 7:916
Kiev and 9:1214
Polo, Marco, and 9:1225
Song dynasty and 7:904
Genoa 8:1025, 1036, *1038*
Geoffrey II 8:1054
Geoffrey Plantagenet 8:1051

geography
Africa and 9:1258–1259, 1260
European knowledge of 10:1360, 1368, 1372, 1379
Inca Empire and 10:1336
Russia and 9:1208
Geography (Ptolemy) 3:410, 6:784, 10:1368, 1397
geometry 3:354, 358, 407, 409, 7:926
George of Clarence 8:1120, 1122–1123
Georgia 9:1228, 1229
Georgics (Virgil) 4:512
Germanic peoples 5:**640–657**, **658–665**
Arianism and 5:630, 632
Charlemagne and 6:797–798, 808
Franks and 5:654, 656, 657
gods and 5:*651*
Huns and 5:651
Iron Age and 1:52–53
Justinian I and 5:670, 677
Odoacer and 5:647
Ostrogoths and 5:645–646, 648
Roman Empire and 4:514, 545, 546, *547*, 5:582, 584, 598, 599, 607
Rome and 4:483, 485
Vandals and 5:652–654
Visigoths and 5:640–645
Germanicus 4:518
Germanos I 6:761
Germanus I 9:1166
Germany
Burgundy and 8:1128, 1129
Carolingian Empire and 6:813
government and 8:1131
leagues and alliances and 8:1094, 1097
Poland and 8:1100
Roman Empire and 4:504, 514, 532, 538, 542, 544
see also East Francia; Holy Roman Empire
Geta 5:595
Gézo 9:1275
Ghana 9:1269, 1270, 1271
Ghazan Khan 9:1229, 1238
ghazi warriors 9:1240–1241, 1242
Ghaznavid Empire 9:1232
Ghent 8:1039, 1102, *1105*
Ghiberti, Lorenzo 10:1401
Ghiyath-al-Din Tughluq 7:970
Ghurid dynasty 9:1232
Ghuzz Turks 9:1232
Gibraltar 6:759, *760*
gift giving, caste system and 7:925, 927
Gilgamesh 1:57, 123, *123*
Gilgamesh and Agga of Kish (Sumerian poem) 1:57
Giorgione 10:1406
Giotto 10:1402
Gla 2:182, 191

gladiators 4:*500*, *531*, *551*, 551–552, *552*, 5:590, *591*, 635
glass lamps, Mamluk 9:*1240*
glassware, Phoenicians and 2:200
Gnosticism 6:730
God, biblical 2:225–226, 227, 228
Go-Daigo 7:916
Godfrey of Bouillon 9:*1187*, 1187, 1188, 1189
Godigisel 5:652
gods and goddesses
Akkadians and 1:61, 61–62
Alexander the Great and 3:391, 393
Assyrians and 2:219
Baal 5:*595*, 596
Babylonians and 1:112–113, 117
Buddhism and 7:952
Celtic people and 1:52
Christianity and 5:632–634
Cycladic people and 2:166
Diocletian and 5:608, 610
drama and 3:323
Egyptians and 1:73, 74, 81–82, *93*, 95, 100
Franks and 5:654
Germanic tribes and 5:*651*
Greeks and 2:167, 3:301, 310–312, 314, 352, 376, 412
Hellenism and 3:402–403
Hinduism and 7:936, 938–943, 945, 961
Hittites and 2:*151*, 155, 158, 159–160
Hyksos kings and 1:90
India and 7:920, *923*, *927*, *928*, *937*
Japan and 7:909, 912
literature and 3:313
Mari and 1:114
Minoans and 2:176–177
Mycenaeans and 2:*190*, 190
Persians and 2:234, 241, 6:726
philosophy and 3:355, 413
Phoenicians and 2:206
pre-Columbian cultures and 10:1308, 1310, 1320, *1322*, 1322, 1329–1330, 1341, 1343, 1354
pre-Islamic Arabia and 6:736, 739, 742–743
Rome and 4:448, *449*, 550, 552, 7:*934*
Sumerians and 1:56, 64, 66, 69
Syrian 5:*597*
Vedic religion and 7:932, 934
Vikings and 9:1205
see also religious beliefs; specific gods and goddesses
Godwin, Earl 8:1047
gold
Africa and 9:1269, 1270, 1271, 10:1367
Bronze Age and 1:37–38

Chibcha people and 10:1310
Constantinople and 9:1160–1161
Egypt and 1:101
Iron Age and 1:49–50
Neolithic period and 1:31
Phoenicians and 2:202–203
Silk Road and 7:898
Spanish conquistadores and 10:1335
gold artifacts
  Africa and 9:*1267*
  Akkadian 1:*61*
  Byzantine 9:*1173*
  Celtic 1:*46*
  Greece and 2:*164, 166*
  Hallstatt culture and 1:*45*
  Mycenaean 2:*183*
  Phoenician 2:*207*
  pre-Columbian cultures and 10:*1305, 1310*
  Scythian 1:*48, 49*
  Sumerian 1:*69*
golden age, Southeast Asia and 7:977–978
golden age of exploration **10:1372–1383**
Golden Horde 9:1227–1228, 1229, 1237, 1238
  see also Mongols
Golden Horn 5:*625*
Gonçalves, Nuño 10:*1366*
Gordian I 5:598
Gordian II 5:598
Gordian III 5:598, 599
Gordian knot 3:*390*, 390
Gordium 3:390
Go-Sanjo 7:913
Goths
  Adrianople, Battle of, and 5:614
  Constantinople and 5:666
  eastern Roman Empire and 5:675–676
  Roman Empire and 5:598, 599, 601, 640, 9:1160
  Theodosius I 5:615
Gournia 2:177, *178*
government
  Abbasid caliphate and 6:772–773
  absolute monarchies 8:1057, 1072, 1094, 1114
  Africa and 9:1259, 1270, 1272
  Akkadian Empire and 1:61
  Aristotle and 3:367
  Assyrians and 2:213, 217
  Athens and 2:266, 267, 269, 3:307–308, 344–348, 378–380
  Aztecs and 10:1326, 1334
  barbarian invaders and 5:658, 660
  Bedouin nomads and 6:738
  Burgundy and 8:1128, 1129
  Byzantine Empire and 9:1163–1164, 1167, 1174, 1175

caliphs and 6:751, 755–756, 764, 776, 785, 787
Carolingian Empire and 6:807–808, 810–811
Chibcha people and 10:1310
cities and towns and 8:1034, 1036–1037, 1039, 1041, 1096
Confucianism and 7:882, 884, 885–886, 887, 890
Constantine and 5:612
Constantinople and 5:619, 624
corruption and 4:476, 479
democracy 3:304, 306–309
development of states 10:1414
dictators, Rome and 4:453–454, 461–462, 472, 487, 498–500
early Rome and 4:440–442, 444, 446
Egypt and 1:73, 77, 83, 86, 87, 89, 3:398
Egypt's Middle Kingdom and 1:86, 87, 89
Egypt's New Kingdom and 1:94, 97, 99
Egypt's Old Kingdom and 1:77
England and 8:1049, 1052, 1076, 1077–1078, 1119
English parliament and 8:1076, 1077, 1108, 1118, 1131
Estates General 8:1079, 1105, 1107, 1131, 1132
Etruscans and 4:445
Europe and 10:1384, 1393, 1396, 1397
feudalism and 6:793
France and 8:1044, 1057, 1078, 1079, 1114
Greece and 2:262–263
Greek poleis and 2:249, 251, 253
Han dynasty and 7:893, 894–895, 896–897
Hittites and 2:155, 158
Holy Roman Empire and 8:1061, 1063, 1072
Hundred Years' War and 8:1105, 1107
Iceland and 9:1204
Incas and 10:1339–1340, 1343, 1346
India and 7:928, 931
Japan and 7:910, 910–911, 914, 917
Julian and 5:613
Khosrow I and 6:735
League of the Iroquois 10:1356
legalism and 7:891, 893
Magna Carta and 8:1067
Maya and 10:1312, 1314, 1315
Mayflower Compact 10:1381, 1383
Merovingian dynasty and 6:790–791
Mohammed and 6:747–748
Mongols and 9:1218, 1220, 1222, 1224, 1238, 1240

Mycenaeans and 2:189
North American peoples and 10:1353, 1355
oligarchy 3:298, 348, 378–380, 8:1036–1037
Ottoman Turks and 9:1245, 1249, 1250, 1255
Pacific islands and 7:987
Persians and 2:236, 238, 245
Phoenicians and 2:197
Plato and 3:367
popes and 8:1088
provinces and 4:470, 507–508, 546
Qin dynasty and 7:877, 879, 894
reforms and 4:479–481, 481–482, 490, 498–499
religious beliefs and 10:1322
Renaissance and 8:1099
Roman character and 4:458
Roman republic and 4:447–455, **488–503**
Rome and 8:1037–1039, 1060
Russia and 9:1211, 1215, 1217
second triumvirate 4:502–503
Seljuk Turks and 9:1241
Severus, Septimius, and 5:594
Song dynasty and 7:903
Southeast Asia and 7:975–976
Sparta and 2:261–263
spending and 4:516–517, 520, 531, 532–533, 534, 539
Sui dynasty 7:901
Sulla, Lucius Cornelius, and 4:487
Tang dynasty and 7:901
Taoism and 7:888
Teotihuacán and 10:1308
tetrarchy 5:607–608, 610
Theodoric the Great and 5:646, 648
Tibet and 7:959
tyranny and 3:294–296, 298–302, 305
Valentinian I and 5:614
Xin dynasty and 7:898
Yuan dynasty and 7:904
Zhou dynasty and 7:875, 877
see also emperors, Byzantine; emperors, Roman; kings; ruling classes
governors, provincial 4:507–508, 546
Gozzoli, Benozzo 10:1401
Gracchus, Gaius Sempronius 4:*479*, 480, 481–482, 549
Gracchus, Tiberius Sempronius 4:479–481
grace, God's 5:685, 686
Graces 3:412
grain 1:11, 12, 4:481–482, 508, 548–549, 5:586, 621–622
grammar schools 10:1387
Granada 6:770
Grand Canal 7:901
Grand Menhir, Locmariaquer, France 1:*24*, 26

Grand Shrine 7:912
Grandson, Battle of 8:1132
Granicus River, Battle of 3:389–390
Gratian 5:614–615, 634, 636, 643
grave goods
  Bronze Age and 1:38
  Celtic people and 2:257
  China and 7:873, 874, 876, *881*, 881
  Cycladic people and 2:166–167
  Egyptian 1:*74*, 75, 84–85, *87*
  Hallstatt culture and 1:48
  Japan and 7:909
  Mycenaeans and 2:186, 190
  pre-Columbian cultures and 10:*1305*, 1309
  Scythian 1:49
  Sumerian 1:57–58, *69*
  see also burial practices
grave robbery 1:96, 104
Great Army 9:1198
Great Britain *see* Britain
Great Migration 10:1383
Great Plains, Battle of 4:474
Great Pyramid of Giza 1:74, *76*
Great Pyramid of Tenochtitlán 10:1329, 1331, *1332*, 1332, 1335
Great Renunciation 7:*949*, 949
Great Rift Valley 9:1260, *1264*
Great Schism 6:839, 840
Great Swabian League 8:1094
Great Wall of China 7:879, *880*, 901, 904, 9:1222
Great Yasa 9:1220
Great Zab River, Battle of 6:769
Great Zimbabwe 9:*1275*, 1276
Greece
  Africa and 9:1266, 1269
  Alexander the Great and 3:384–395
  alphabet and 2:207
  Bronze Age and 1:33, 40–41, **2:162–169**
  Celtic people and 1:50
  Christianity and 5:609
  Constantinople and 5:616
  cultural influence of 3:**404–413**
  Cycladic people and 2:167
  Dark Age and expansion of 2:**246–257**
  drama and 3:**318–325**
  Egypt and 1:109, 3:396, 398
  great philosophers and 3:**352–367**
  Hellenism 3:402–403
  Iron Age and 1:44
  Julius Caesar and 4:496
  Lamian War and 3:401–402
  maps of 2:*248–249*, 3:*296, 329, 388, 399*
  Mycenaeans and 2:182–192
  Peloponnesian War 3:**368–383**
  Pericles and 3:**340–351**

Greece (continued)
    Persians and 2:238, 239
    Persian Wars and 3:326–339
    Phoenicians and 2:202
    Scythian people and 1:48–49
    trade and 1:49
    Troy and 2:195
    tyranny and democracy in
        3:294–309
    Vandals and 5:653
    Visigoths and 5:642, 644
Greek drama 3:318–325, 349,
    407
Greek fire 6:762, 763
Greek language 2:186
Greek legacy 3:404–413
Greek myths 1:69
Greek Orthodox Christianity
    6:839
Greek philosophy 3:352–367,
    6:781–782, 9:1273, 10:1389,
    1404
Greek religion 3:310–317
Greeks
    Byzantine Empire and 9:1193
    Constantinople and 5:618, 621
    preserving knowledge of 5:661
    Rome and 4:444, 445, 456,
        461–463, 464
Greenland 8:1026, 9:1204, 1206
Greens 5:623–624, 627, 671
Gregorian calendar 4:502
Gregorian chant 5:700
Gregorian Reform 6:839
Gregory I 6:820
Gregory II 6:761, 800, 9:1167
Gregory III 6:800, 9:1167
Gregory IV 6:812
Gregory V 6:834
Gregory VI 6:837, 839
Gregory VII 6:838, 839, 841–843,
    842, 8:1058, 1086
Gregory VIII 6:844, 845, 9:1192
Gregory IX 8:1073, 1073,
    9:1193
Gregory XI 8:1088–1089, 1089
Gregory XII 8:1092
Gregory XIII 10:1408
Gregory of Nazianzus 5:695,
    696–697
Gregory of Tours 5:657
Grey, Thomas 8:1123
griffin, statue of (Persian) 2:245
griots (singer-poets) 9:1271
Guadalete, Battle of 6:760, 761
Guangzhou 7:901
Gudea 1:62–63, 64, 64
Guerrero culture 10:1307
guerrilla warfare 6:797, 8:1113
Guesclin, Bertrand du 8:1107, 1108
Guide to Northern Antiquities, A
    (Thomsen) 1:45
guilds 8:1041, 1087
    Black Death and 8:1086
    cities and towns and 8:1037,
        1041, 1043

education and 10:1387
    Hundred Years' War and 8:1102,
        1104
Gunderic 5:652
Gundestrup Cauldron 1:52
Gupta dynasty 7:960–963
Gupta Empire, map of 7:962
Gutenberg, Johannes 10:1391,
    1392, 1392
Guthrum 9:1198
Gutians 1:62–63
Guy de Lusignan 9:1191
Gylippus 3:376

H
Haakon VI 8:1099
Hades 3:314, 317
Hadewig 8:1044
Hadrian 4:533, 540, 541, 542–543,
    5:585
Hadrian IV 8:1039, 1040, 1060,
    1061
Hadrian's Wall 4:542, 543, 5:583,
    584, 595, 663
Hagia Sophia 5:621, 668, 672,
    672
    Constantine I and 5:621
    Macedonian Renaissance and
        9:1180
    mosaics and 9:1159, 1178,
        1180
    Nika Revolt and 5:671
    Ottoman Turks and 9:1247
hagiography 5:688, 690, 691
Haiman 7:896
Hajex region 6:768, 769
Hakata Bay 7:916
Hakim, Al- 6:775
Halfdan 9:1196, 1198
Hall of the Ambassador, Ugarit
    2:206
Hallstatt culture 1:39, 44–45, 45,
    47–48
Hamburg 8:1095
Hamilcar Barca 4:468, 469
Hammurabi 1:62, 110–111, 114,
    120, 2:210
    see also Code of Hammurabi
Hammurabi's palace, ruins of
    1:118
hand axes 1:6, 7, 9:1263
hand grenades 9:1181
Han dynasty 7:881, 893, 894–897,
    896, 898–899
Han Fei 7:891, 893
Hanging Gardens of Babylon
    1:124–125, 125
Hanging Monastery of Shanxi
    7:892
haniwa (terra-cotta sculptures)
    7:909, 912
Han-li Academy 7:901
Hannahanna 2:160
Hannibal 4:469, 469, 470–475,
    478
Hanno 2:201–202, 205

Hanseatic League 8:1033–1034,
    1094, 1095, 1097, 1097, 1098,
    1100, 9:1213
Hanuman 7:942, 944
Hapsburg dynasty 8:1133
Harald Finehair 9:1204
Harald Hardrada 8:1047–1048
Harappa 7:918, 920–921, 921
Hardecnut 8:1046
Harihara Raya I 7:971
Harmodius 3:305, 305
Harmonica (Ptolemy) 3:410
harness ring, Persian 2:242
Harold Bluetooth 6:816
Harold of Wessex 8:1047
harp, Sumerian 1:55
Harran 2:221, 225, 226
Harsa of Kanauj 7:963
Harun al-Rashid 6:771, 772, 772,
    781, 787
Hasdrubal (brother-in-law of
    Hannibal) 4:469
Hasdrubal (brother of Hannibal)
    4:473, 474
Hassan ben Ali 6:751, 756, 757,
    764
Hastings, Battle of 8:1047–1048,
    1049
Hastings, William 8:1123, 1125
Hatshepsut 1:92, 96, 98, 99
Hattin, Battle of 9:1191
Hattushash 2:150, 153, 154, 154,
    155, 159, 161
Hattusilis I 2:150, 154
Hattusilis III 2:153
Hausa people 9:1274
Hawaiian Islands 7:982, 985
headband, Greek 2:166
Hebrews see Israelites
hegira 6:745–746
Heiji Disturbance 7:914, 914
Heijo 7:911–912
Hekanakhte 1:86
Hekau-chasut (desert kings) 1:89–
    90
Helios 3:312, 357
Helladic people 2:162, 172
Hellenism 3:402–403
    see also Greece
helmets, Corinthian 2:265
helots (serfs) 2:258, 260
Henotikon letter 5:626
Henry I (Capetian dynasty)
    6:827–828, 828
Henry I (England) 8:1049, 1051
Henry I (Germany) 9:1176
Henry I (Henry the Fowler) 6:829,
    829, 832
Henry II (Bavaria) 6:832
Henry II (England) 8:1049,
    1051, 1052, 1052, 1053,
    1056
Henry II (Germany) 6:835–836,
    837
Henry III (England) 8:1067,
    1076

Henry III (Holy Roman emperor)
    6:837, 839, 841
Henry IV (England) 8:1108
Henry IV (Holy Roman emperor)
    6:839, 841–843, 843, 844
Henry V (England) 8:1110, 1111,
    1114, 1126
Henry V (Holy Roman emperor)
    6:843–845, 845, 8:1051, 1058
Henry VI (England) 8:1110, 1113,
    1114, 1116–1117, 1118, 1119,
    1120, 1121, 1122, 1125
Henry VI (Holy Roman emperor)
    8:1056, 1063, 1064, 1065
Henry VII (England) 8:1124, 1125,
    10:1378
Henry VIII (England) 8:1124,
    10:1397, 1409
Henry of Germany 8:1070
Henry the Lion 8:1063, 1063
Henry the Navigator 8:1093,
    10:1364, 1366, 1366–1367,
    1369, 1370
Hephaestion 3:393, 394
Hephthalites 6:734, 7:962–963
Hera 3:310
Heraclea, Battle of 4:462
Heracles 3:317
Heraclitus 3:355, 362
Heraclius 6:735, 752, 9:1163,
    1165
Herakleopolis 1:80–81
Herculaneum 4:535, 536
herding 1:31
hereditary rule, tyranny and
    3:294–295
heresy see doctrinal disputes
Herihor 1:107
Herjolfsson, Bjarni 9:1206
Hermes 3:310
hermits 5:688, 690, 691, 693,
    695
Herodotus 3:335, 335, 4:445
    Croesus and 3:328
    First Persian War and 3:330
    Greece and 3:298, 299, 300–301,
        349
    Medes and 2:232
    Persians and 2:236, 244, 245,
        3:331
    Phoenicians and 2:201, 202
Herod the Great 1:13
heroes 3:310, 4:456–458
Hero of Alexandria 3:408, 409,
    10:1390
Herophilus 3:411
Hesiod 2:256, 257, 3:313
hetairoi (Companions), Alexander
    the Great and 3:388, 389, 395
hieratic writing 1:88
Hiero 4:464, 464–465, 473
hieroglyphic writing
    Africa and 9:1264
    Egyptians and 1:72–73, 88, 2:204,
        252
    Hittites and 2:160–161, 203–204

Minoans and 2:179, 180
Phoenicians and 2:203
pre-Columbian cultures and
10:1305, 1319
Hildebrand of Soana *see*
Gregory VII
Hinduism 6:731, **7:932–945**
Gangetic civilization and 7:927
Gupta dynasty and 7:960–961
India and 7:928, 931, 948, 959
Indian missionaries and 7:967
Islam and 7:969
Southeast Asia and 7:975, 979,
981
Hipparchus 3:305
hippei (horsemen) 2:266, 267
Hippias 3:301–302, 304, 305, 329
Hippocrates 3:352, 410–411,
10:1390
Hippodamas 3:349
Hippodrome 5:621, 622–624, 627,
671
Hippolytus (Euripides) 3:325
Hiram 2:199, 231
Hispaniola 10:1374, 1375
Hissarlik, Troy and 2:192, 193, 195
historians 3:*335*, 335, 352, 377,
4:456, 516, 524, 531, 7:886, 899
Historia Roderici (History of
Rodrigo) 8:1021
historical eras, labels for 10:1398,
1400
historical sources, Mohammed and
6:739–740
History (Herodotus) 3:335
History of King Richard III (More)
8:1124
History of the Jewish People, The
(Flavius) 4:*521*
History of the Peloponnesian War
(Thucydides) 3:377
Hittites **2:150–161**, *158*
Assyrians and 2:210
Babylonian Empire and 1:120
Egypt and 1:101, 104–105, 106
Greeks and 3:310
iron weapons and 1:*41*, 42
Israelites and 2:229, 230
Mycenaeans and 2:192
Phoenicians and 2:196, 199
writing and 2:203–204
Hoabinhian Age 7:972
Holbein, Hans 10:1409
Holy Roman Empire 6:772,
832–845, *834*
Italy and 8:1022, 1023, 1039
Middle Ages and 8:1094
Philip II Augustus and 8:1055
popes and 8:1058, 1060–1065
rulers of 8:1058, 1060–1065,
1070, 1072–1073
Holy Spirit 5:633, 6:840
holy wars *see* crusades; jihad
Homer 2:182, 193, 194, 256, 3:313,
4:557, 6:732
Homeric Hymns (Homer) 3:313

Homo erectus 7:870, 9:1256, *1259*
Homo habilis 1:6, 9, 9:1256
Homo neanderthalensis 1:9
Homo sapiens 1:9, 9:1256
Homs, Battle of 9:1238
Hong-wu (Zhu Yuanzhang) 7:905
Honorius 5:640–641, 642, 643,
666, 9:1158
Honorius III 8:1072, 1073
Honshu 7:912
hoplites 2:*265*, 265, 3:304, 330,
336, 337, *369*, *376*, 382–383
Horace 4:510, *511*, 511, 557
Horatii 4:456–458
Horatius 4:456
Horemheb 1:104, 105
Hormizd II 6:733
Hormuz, Battle of 6:726
horse racing 5:622, 623, 624
horses 1:49, 2:211, 251, 9:1220,
1221, 10:1358
Horus 1:*93*
hospitium (visitor's rights) 5:658
hostages 5:643, 653
household gods and goddesses
3:312
household shrines 4:448, *449*
House of the Frescos 2:178
House of the Poseidoniasts 3:*343*
House of Tiles 2:162
housing
Anasazi people and 10:1348,
1350, 1351
Aztecs and 10:1331, 1332
Babylonian Empire and 1:115
barbarian invaders and 5:658
China and 7:870, 872
Crete and 2:172
Cycladic people and 2:169
Egyptian 1:86, 97
funnel-beaker culture and 1:19
Greece and 2:162
Hittites and 2:154
Incas and 10:1342, 1346
India and 7:918, 920
Japan and 7:906
Latium and 4:443–444,
445
Linearbandkeramik culture and
1:17
Maya and 10:1312, 1316,
1323
Minoans and 2:173, 177
Minyan people and 2:163, 164
Mongols and 9:*1223*
Mycenae and 2:184
Neolithic period and 1:13, 14–15
North American peoples and
10:1352, 1353, 1357, 1358
Rome and 4:548, *556*
Rössen and Michelsburg cultures
and 1:18
serfs and 6:823
Skara Brae and 1:30
students and 10:1386
Sumerian people and 1:65

Teotihuacán and 10:1308–1309
Vikings and 9:1205, 1207
Hsai dynasty 9:1222
Huascar 10:1347
Huayna Capac 10:*1339*, 1339,
1347
Hugh Capet 6:*827*, 8:1044
Hugh Magnus 6:827
Hugh of Vermandois 9:1185
Hugh the Great 8:1044
Hui 7:890
Huitzilopochtli 10:1329, 1332,
1334
Hulagu Khan 6:*775*, 775,
9:1222, 1228, 1228–1229,
1235–1236
humanism 10:**1384–1397**, 1398,
1400
humans, early *see* early humans
human sacrifice
Aztecs and 10:1320, 1329–1331,
1331, 1334
Chibcha people and 10:1310
Egyptians and 1:73
Incas and 10:1343, 1344
Maya and 10:1317, 1322
Minoans and 2:180
Phoenicians and 2:206
Rome and 4:551
Scythian people and 1:51
Sumerian people and 1:58
Teotihuacán and 10:1308
Toltec people and 10:1309
Hundred Years' War 8:1085, 1088,
1102–1113, *1103*, *1104*, 1126
Hungary
Byzantine Empire and 9:1181
Conrad II and 6:837
crusades and 9:1185, 1187,
1192
Mongols and 8:1084, 9:1214,
1227
Ottoman Turks and 9:1245,
1252
Poland and 8:1100
Russia and 9:1213, 1216
Hunneric 5:653
Huns 5:*648*, 648–651, *649*
Byzantine Empire and 9:1158,
1161–1162
China and 7:895
Constantinople and 5:625, 666
Ostrogoths and 5:645
Visigoths and 5:614, 640, 645
hunter-gatherers 7:871, 906,
9:1256, 1259, 10:1312, 1350,
1359
hunting
early humans and 1:6, 8–10
Egypt's New Kingdom and 1:98
funnel-beaker culture and 1:19
North American peoples and
10:1352–1353, *1354*, 1354,
1355, *1356*, 1358
Persians and 6:734, *735*
Hunyadi, János 9:1246

Huron people 10:*1349*, 1353,
1356
Hurrians 1:120, 2:150, 152, 159,
210
Hus, Jan 8:*1090*, 1090
Husayn ibn Al 6:775
Hussein 6:751, *757*, 757, 767
Hussein, Muzahim Mahmoud
2:219
Hydaspes, Battle of 3:394
Hyksos kings 1:90–91, 92, 98, 2:227
Hypatia 5:639, *639*
Hypatius 5:671; 9:1164

I

Ibbi-Sin 1:65–66
Iberian people 1:49–50
Ibn Battuta 9:1271–1272
Ibn Hisham 6:739
Ibn Ishaq 6:739
Ibn Ruhd 6:783
Ibn Sina 6:*783*, 783, *784*
ice ages 1:7–8
Iceland 8:1098, 9:1203–1204,
1205
Iceni 4:528–529
I Ching (Book of Changes) 7:*887*,
887, 892
iconoclasm 6:761, 800, 811, 9:*1166*,
1166–1167, 1168, 1172, 1173,
1180
idealism, Plato and 3:367, 412
"ideal world," philosophy of
3:358
idols 6:742, 742–743, 747, 811
Idris Alooma 9:1274
ignorance, Buddhism and 7:951,
953
Igor 9:1203, 1210
Iliad (Homer) 2:182, 192,
194, 248–249, 256, 3:313,
404, 6:732
Il-Khanate 9:1228–1229,
1235–1236, 1238
Illapa 10:1343
Illipa, Battle of 4:474
Illium 2:195
Illyrian emperors 5:601, 603,
606–607
Illyrians 3:385–386
Il Milione (Polo) 9:*1225*, 1225, 1226
imams 6:758
Imhotep 1:73, 75
immigration
Athens and 3:308
Constantinople and 5:616, 618,
621, 666
Egypt and 1:89
Immortals 2:237
imperial dynasties, China
7:894–905
imperial orb and sword, German
6:*833*, 835
imperial provinces, Roman
4:507–508

impermanence, Buddhism and 7:952–953
imports and exports *see* trade
Incas 10:1302, 1304, **1336–1347**, *1338*, 1419, 1421
incense 5:587
incense burners 7:*899*, 10:*1334*
India
  Aksum and 9:1269
  Alexander the Great and 3:394
  Bronze Age and 1:33, 40
  Buddhism and 7:892, **946–959**
  Chinese exploration and 10:1420
  colonial period and 10:*1364*
  European knowledge of 10:1360
  first civilizations of **7:918–931**
  Hinduism **7:932–945**
  Islamic world and 6:763, 780, 783–784, 9:1232
  Lao-tzu and 7:889
  Manichaeism and 6:731
  Middle Ages and **7:960–971**
  Mongols and 9:1223
  Mughal Empire and 10:1418
  Persians and 2:232, 6:726
  Portugal and 10:1370, *1371*, 1371
  Roman Empire and 5:589
  Southeast Asia and 7:975
  Tamerlane and 9:1229
  trade and 5:587, 6:776
  Zoroastrianism and 6:731
Indies 10:1372, 1375
indigenous peoples 7:915, 982, 984
"indivisibility of being" theory 3:358, 360
Indochina Peninsula 7:972, 974
Indo-European languages 2:160, 4:443
Indonesia 7:979, 980, 984, 9:1230
Indra 7:936, 939
indulgences, sale of 8:1090
Indus River 3:394, 7:*922*, 928
industry 8:1030, 1032–1033
  see also trade
Indus Valley civilization 7:918, *920*, 920–921, 923–924, 932, *934*
infanticide 2:263, 268
infantry 2:157, 214
inflation 5:604, 608
Ingapirca, temple at 10:*1341*
Ingeborg 8:1066, 1067
Ingres, Jean-Auguste-Dominique 8:*1113*
inheritance rights 5:664–665, 6:809, 828, 830, 9:1212, 1255
Innocent II 8:1040, 1058
Innocent III 8:*1064*, 9:1191, 1192, 1194
  crusades and 8:1025, 1068, 1069
  Francis of Assisi and 8:1042
  political power of 8:1039, 1064, 1065–1067

Innocent IV 8:1078
In Praise of Folly (Erasmus) 10:1397
Inquisition 8:1019–1020, 9:1194
Institutes of the Monastic Life (Cassian) 5:696
Institutiones (Justinian) 9:1164
insults 5:662, 664
interest rates 1:116, 4:466
interglacial periods 1:8
Intermediate region 10:1304
Inti 10:1341, 1343
Intiwatana temples 10:1342
Inuit 10:1358, 1378
inventors 3:408, *409*, 410, 4:473, 6:780
investiture controversy 6:839, 841–842, 843–844, 845, 8:1058, 1064
Ionian people 2:167, 169, 248, 250
Ionian philosophy 3:352, 354–355
Ionian rebellion 3:326–327
Iran *see* Persia
Iraq *see* Mesopotamia
Ireland, Vikings and 6:816
Irenaeus 5:678
Irene 6:802, 811, 9:1168, *1170*, 1170
Irnerius 10:1384
iron 2:156, 9:1266
Iron Age 1:41, *42–53*, 7:877, 908, 927, 9:1261, 1263
iron tools 1:*43*, 47
Iroquois peoples 10:1356–1357
irrigation
  Arabia and 5:587
  Assyrians and 2:211
  China and 7:877
  Egypt and 1:80–81
  Latium and 4:444
  Mesopotamia and 1:54
  Persians and 2:245
  pre-Columbian cultures and 10:1310, 1311, 1312, 1333, 1350
Isaac 2:226, 6:748
Isabella of Angoulême 8:1054
Isabella of Hainault 8:1054, 1066
Isabella of Jerusalem 8:1073
Isabella of Spain 8:1019, 1133, 10:1372, 1374
Isaurian dynasty 6:761, 800, 9:1165
Isaurians 5:625, 626, 9:1162
Ishmael 2:225, 226, 6:742, 748
Ishme-Dagan I 2:210
Ishtar 1:59, 61, 62, 114, 117, *120*, 2:159, 228, 3:310
Ishtar Gate 1:*122*, 124
Ishtupilum 1:*119*
Isidorus of Miletus 5:672
Isin, Second Dynasty of 1:121
Islam
  Africa and 9:1269, 1270, 1271, 1272–1273, 1274
  Christian Europe and 10:1360, 1362, 1415
  crusades and 9:1182–1195

culture of **6:776–787**
Frederick II and 8:1070
India and 7:959, 966, 968–971
Judaism and 2:226
Mohammed and **6:736–751**
Mongols and 9:1229, 1238, 1240
Ottoman Turks and 9:1250
Persians and 6:735
Reconquista and 8:1014, 1016–1018, 1021
Southeast Asia and 7:981
spread of **6:752–763**, *754*, 768, 793, 9:1165, 1230
Sufis and 9:1233
Zoroastrianism and 6:731
Islamic Spain 8:1016–1020, 1021, 1082, 1099
Islamic world 6:766, 8:1082, 10:1390, 1418–1419
  Byzantine Empire and 9:1174, 1175–1176
  Khoresm Empire and 9:1223
  Mongols and 9:1228–1229
  Spain and 9:1182, 1235, 1238
  Turkish empires and 9:1230–1241
  Visigoths and 5:645
islands, Greek 2:164–169
Ismael I 9:1240, 10:1418
Israel
  kingdom of 2:224, 227, 231
  Ottoman Turks and 9:1242
  tribes of 2:227
  see also Palestine
Israelites 1:91, 101, 2:196, 216, 217, 222, **222–231**, 234
Issus, Battle of 3:*389*, 390–391
Istanbul *see* Constantinople
Italian cities 4:485–486, 490
Italy
  Byzantine Empire and 6:800, 802, 9:1163, 1165, 1167, 1174, 1178, 1181
  Carolingian Empire and 6:813
  city-states and 8:1039, 1041
  Constantinople and 5:618
  culture and 8:1093
  Greek colonies and 2:254, *255*, 256
  Holy Roman Empire and 6:831, 832, 834–835, 836, 837, 8:1060–1063, 1073
  Huns and 5:651
  Islamic world and 6:817
  Justinian I and 5:673, 675–676
  leagues and alliances and 8:1096
  Lombards and 6:794–795
  Middle Ages and 8:1020, 1022, 1094
  monasteries and 5:696
  Renaissance and 8:1099, 10:1398, 1400–1404, 1405, 1406–1408
  Theodoric the Great and 5:646, 648

trade and 3:296
see also Roman Empire; Rome
Ivan I 9:1215
Ivan III (the Great) 8:1101, 9:1215, *1217*, 1217
Ivan IV (the Terrible) 9:1217
Ivar the Boneless 9:1196, 1198
ivory carving, Byzantine 9:*1167*
ivory figurine, Minoan 2:*172*

J
Jacob 2:226–227
Jacoba of Bavaria 8:1128
Jacques 10:*1421*
jade artifacts 7:872, *875*, 989, 10:*1304, 1316*
Jadwiga 8:1100
Jagiello 8:1100
Jainism 7:927, *931*, 948
Jalal-ud-Din Firuz 7:970
Jalisco culture 10:1307
Jalowaz, Battle of 9:1246
Jamestown Colony 10:1380–1381, 1382, *1383*
Janissaries 9:1230, 1245, 1247, 1249, 1255
Japan 7:879, 901, **906–917**, *908*, 958–959, 10:*1416*, 1416, *1417*
Japanese language 7:912, 915
jar, Mycenaean 2:*191*
Jatavarman Sundara Pandyan 7:966
Java 7:*956*, 967, 975, 977, 979
Jayavarman IV 7:979
Jayavarman VII 7:*979*, 979
Jebusites 2:231
Jerome 5:696–697, *698*
Jerusalem
  Alexander the Great and 3:391
  Assyrians and 2:219
  Christianity and 5:632, 678
  crusades and 6:*823*, 8:1014, 1068, 1069, 9:1182, 1188–1189, 1195
  destruction of 4:535
  Dome of the Rock 6:768, 769
  Frederick II and 8:1073
  geography and 10:1360, *1361*, 1368
  Israelites and 2:230–231
  Judas Maccabaeus and 3:400, *402*
  medieval maps and 10:1368
  military forces of 9:1189–1190
  Persians and 6:735
  Phoenicians and 2:198
  Roman Empire and 4:491, 520, 529, 541
  Saladin and 9:1191, *1192*
  Seljuk Turks and 9:1234
Jesus Christ 4:530, 5:*681*, 6:748, 749
  see also Christianity
jewelry 1:*60*, 2:156, 179, 180, *207*, *251*, 10:*1358*

Jewish people
  Black Death and 8:1085
  Christianity and 5:678
  crusades and 9:1185
  Islamic world and 6:739, 746,
    9:1238
  moneylending and 8:1033
  Philip IV of France and 8:1079
  Roman Empire and 4:491, 520,
    541
  taxation and 4:534
  trade and 6:780
  see also Israelites
jihad 6:744
Jimmu 7:908, *910*
Jin dynasty 7:900, 903, 904,
  9:1223
Joanna (Juana) of Castile 8:1133
Joan of Arc 8:1110, 1112–1113,
  1113
John I (Portugal) 10:1364
John I Tzimisces 6:832,
  9:1175–1176, 1177
John II (France) 8:1105, 1107
John II (Portugal) 10:1369, 1372,
  1375
John V 9:1244, 1245
John VI 9:1244
John XV 6:834
John XIX 6:836
John XXII 8:1092
John Chrysostom 5:668
John Comnenus 9:1181
John of Bohemia 8:1106
John of England 8:1054, 1055,
  1056, 1067, *1069*, 1076
John of Gaunt 8:1109, 1114
John Sigismund 9:1252
John the Fearless 8:1108, 1110,
  1126, *1129*
Jomon period 7:906, *909*, 909
Josephus Flavius 4:*521*
Joshua 2:227, 229
journeymen, guilds and 8:1043
Jovian 5:613, 634
Judaea 4:508, 520, 529, 533, 538,
  541, 542
Judah 1:124, 2:231
Judaism
  Arabia and 6:736
  baptism and 5:680
  Christianity and 5:678
  Islam and 6:736, 742, 743, 745,
    748
  Jacob and 2:226
  Mohammed and 6:745
  Persians and 6:730, 733
  Seleucid dynasty and 3:400
  Temple Mount and 6:769
  see also Israelites; Jewish people
Judas Maccabaeus 3:400, *402*
judicial systems *see* legal systems
Judith 6:812
jug, Athenian 3:*349*
Julia (daughter of Augustus Caesar)
  4:*510*, 510, 511, 515

Julia (daughter of Julius Caesar)
  4:493–494, 496
Julian calendar 4:500, 502
Julian the Apostate 5:612–613, 632,
  633, *636*, 654
Julianus, Didius 5:592
Julio-Claudian emperors **4:516–
  531**
Julius II 10:1400, *1404*, 1406
Julius Caesar 1:46, 4:488, *489*, 492,
  493–496, *494*, 497, 498–501
Julius Civilis 4:535
Julius Vindex 4:529
Jumièges Abbey 6:*825*
Junayad 7:968
Justin (emperor) 5:669, 674
Justin (saint) 5:681
Justinian I 5:639, 654, **666–677**,
  667, *673*, 6:735, 9:1163–1164,
  1165
"just war," concept of 8:1018
Jutes 5:663
Juvenal 4:548

K

Kaaba 6:738–739, 741, *742*, 742,
  746, 747
Kadesh, Battle of 1:106, 2:153
Kalahari Desert 9:1260, 1262
Kali 7:945, 963
Kalidasa 7:961, 963
Kalinga 7:929, 930, 958
Kalka River, Battle of 9:1223
Kalyani 7:966
Kamares ware 2:173, 180
Kamil, Al- 9:1195
Kammu 7:912
Kamose 1:91, 92
Kampung Kling mosque 7:*981*
Kanem 9:1273–1274
Kanesh 2:150, 208
Kanishka 7:931
Kano 9:1272, 1273, 1274
Kanun Nameh 9:1249
Karanga people 9:1276
Karbala, Battle of 6:*757*, 757, 767
karma 7:937–938, 953
Karnak, temple at 1:82, *83*, 100,
  106, 107
Kassites 1:120–121
Kausambi 7:927
Kavadh I 5:670, 6:734
Kazakhstan 7:874, 895
Kazembe 9:1276
Keftiu people 2:170
Kenilworth Castle 8:*1050*
Kennet Way 1:27
Kephala *see* Knossos
Khadijah 6:741, 743, 744, 756
Khalji dynasty 7:970
Khan-balik 7:904
Kharavela 7:929
Khartoum 9:1266
Khayr al-Din 9:*1253*, 1253
Khazar people 9:1201, 1203,
  1208

Khitan Mongols 7:902
Khizr Khan 7:970
Khmer state 7:976–977
Khoikhoi people 9:1256, 1264,
  1265, 1277
Khoisan languages 9:1264, 1265
Khoresm Empire 9:1223, 1234,
  1235
Khosrow I 5:670–671, 6:726, *734*,
  734–735
Khosrow II 6:*735*, 735, 752
Khwarizmi, Mohammed ibn
  Musa al- 6:783, 784
Ki 1:66
Kiev **9:1208–1217**
  Hungary and 9:1216
  Mongols and 8:1101, 9:1227
  trade and 9:1208
  Vikings and 9:1201, 1202, 1203
Kievan Rus 9:1201, 1210, 1211
kingdoms
  Africa and 9:1263, 1266–1277
  India and 7:927, 963, 965–966
  Southeast Asia and 7:975–976
  Spain and 8:1016, 1017,
    1018–1019
  see also specific kingdoms
kings
  Assyrians and 2:215
  China and 7:875, 890
  early Rome and 4:440–442
  feudal Europe and 6:821,
    826–827
  Francia and 8:1044
  Germanic tribes and 5:582, 660
  Greece and 2:253, 258, 262, 263
  Hekau-chasut (desert kings)
    1:89–90
  Hittites and 2:155, 157, 159, 160
  Israelites and 2:230
  Julius Caesar and 4:500
  Minoans and 2:173, 174, 175
  Mycenaeans and 2:188, 189
  Phoenicians and 2:197
  pre-Columbian cultures and
    10:1326, 1340, 1340–1341,
    1343, 1344
  Rome and 4:444, 446, 458
  Sumerian people and 1:56–57
  see also emperors, Byzantine;
    emperors, Roman; pharaohs;
    specific kings
Kiribati 7:982
Kirtimukha gargoyle 7:*977*
Kish 1:57
Kitab ash-shifa (Ibn Sina) 6:783
kivas 10:1351, 1358
knights 6:822–823, *823*, 8:1014,
  1018
Knights (Aristophanes) 3:325, 378
Knights Hospitaller 8:1014, 1101,
  9:1190, 1247, 1249, 1252,
  1255
Knights Templar 8:1014, 1018,
  1079, 1079, *1080*, 1080,
  9:1190

Knossos 2:170, 172, 173, *174*, 174,
  175, 175, 182
knowledge *see* learning and
  knowledge
Köckert, Julius 6:*772*
Kojiki (Records of Ancient Matters)
  7:908
Kokin-shu (poetry collection)
  7:912
Kololo people 9:1277
Kongo 9:1276
Kongolo 9:1276
Konya, Battle of 9:1245
Koran 6:739, *748*, 748–749, 751,
  772, 9:1233
Korean Peninsula 7:896, 901, 906,
  909
Kosedagh, Battle of 9:1235
Kosovo 8:1082, 9:1245, 1246
Kossak, Wojciech 8:*1100*
Kotoku 7:910
Kozelsk, siege of 9:*1215*
Krak des Chevaliers 9:*1189*
Kremer, Gerhard 10:1368
Krishna 7:942, 944
Krum 9:1171, 1177
kshatriyas (aristocracy) 7:925,
  927, 946
Kubja Vishnuvardhana 7:966
Kublai Khan 7:904, 916, 9:1224,
  1226, 1226–1227, 1228–
  1229
Kujula Kadphises 7:931
Kulikovo, Battle of 9:1215,
  1216
kurgans (burial mounds) 1:49, 51
kurultai (tribal council) 9:1218
Kush *see* Nubia
Kushan India 7:929, 931, 960
Kyrgyzstan 7:874

L

Labarnas *see* Hattusilis I
labor
  Black Death and 8:1086
  Buddhism and 7:954–955
  Egypt and 1:86, 97, 99, 100
  Incas and 10:1341
  India and 7:924–925
  monasteries and 5:692, 693, 694,
    700, 6:824, 826
  pyramids and 1:73–74
  see also employment; work
    specialization
labyrinth 2:170, 176
La Casa de las Monjas 10:1318
Lady with an Ermine (da Vinci)
  10:*1405*
Lagash 1:58, 62
laity 6:838, 839, 7:956, 8:1058
Lake Peipus, Battle of 9:1217
Lake Texcoco 10:1324
Lakota people 10:1354
Lakshmi 7:941, 945
Lamian War 3:401–402
Lancaster, house of 8:1114

landownership
  Akkadian Empire and 1:61
  barbarian invaders and 5:660
  Buddhist monasteries and 7:955
  Capetian dynasty and 6:828
  Carolingian Empire and 6:811,
    813
  Charles Martel and 6:792–793
  China and 7:875, 879, 897, 899,
    900, 901–902
  Christians and 5:628
  Egypt and 1:86, 94, 107
  feudalism and 6:808, 819, 821,
    823
  Franks and 6:788, 790
  Greece and 2:255–256, 266,
    3:301, 403
  Hittites and 2:155–156
  Japan and 7:910, 911, 913, 917
  Merovingian dynasty and
    6:790
  monasteries and 8:1035
  Ottoman Turks and 9:1255
  pre-Columbian cultures and
    10:1328, 1340
  Roman Catholic Church and
    6:790
  Roman Empire and 4:513,
    5:606
  Rome and 4:476, 479–481, 484
  Vikings and 6:809
land reforms 4:479–481
Langton, Stephen 8:1067
languages
  Africa and 9:1258, 1259, 1263,
    1264, 1265
  Amarna Letters and 1:101
  Assyrians and 2:216
  Behistun Inscription and 2:243
  Bulgar people and 9:1177
  Byzantine Empire and 9:1167
  Carolingian Empire and 6:804,
    806
  Chinese 7:873
  Egypt and 1:88, 103
  England and 8:1049
  Etruscans and 4:445
  Europe and 10:1387–1388, 1393,
    1394
  Germanic peoples and 5:665
  Ghazan Khan and 9:1238
  Greece and 2:163, 246, 248, 250,
    3:402
  Hittites and 2:160
  India and 7:940, 971
  Islamic world and 6:759, 771,
    773
  Japanese 7:912, 915
  Latium and 4:443
  Mycenaeans and 2:186
  Pacific islands and 7:988
  pre-Columbian cultures and
    10:1335, 1336, 1348,
    1353–1354
  Roman Empire and 4:540,
    546–547

Semitic people and 2:222
Southeast Asia and 7:972
Sumerian people and 1:54
Lao-tzu 7:877, 886, 888, 888, 889,
  889, 890
Lapita culture 7:984
Lares 4:448
Lars Porsena 4:456, 459
Lascaux, France, cave paintings at
  1:11, 12
Las Navas de Tolosa, Battle of
  8:1017, 1018, 9:1235
Lasso, Orlando di 10:1407, 1408
Lasta 9:1269
Last Supper, The (da Vinci) 10:1404,
  1405
Late Egyptian language 1:103
Late Minoan period 2:172
La Tène culture 1:46, 50, 52
Late period, Egypt 1:109
Later Le dynasty 7:977
latifundia (estates) 4:476, 477
Latin 5:665, 10:1394
Latin League 4:458, 460
Latium 4:443–444, 458, 460,
  463
Latvia 8:1101
La Venta 10:1306, 1307
law enforcement, Incas and 10:
  1347
laws see legal systems
Laws, The (Plato) 3:367
Laws of Manu 7:939–940
Laws of the Twelve Tables 4:453
Layard, Austen Henry 2:208, 213
leaders, North American peoples
  and 10:1355, 1356
League of the Iroquois 10:1356
leagues and alliances 8:1094–1101
learning and knowledge
  Il-Khanate and 9:1238
  medieval Europe and 10:1360,
    1362, 1367, 1384–1397, 1418
  Ottoman Turks and 9:1249, 1255
  Plato and 3:367
  preservation of 5:661, 665, 701
  Skeptics and 3:412
  Socrates and 3:362, 363–364
  Songhai and 9:1272–1273
Lebanon 2:196, 5:602
Lechfeld, Battle of 6:831, 831
Lefkandi Centaur 2:248
legalism, philosophy of 7:877, 879,
  881, 891, 893
legal systems
  Africa and 9:1272, 1273
  Assyrians and 2:212
  Athens and 2:267, 269
  Byzantine Empire and 5:674,
    9:1163–1164, 1165–1166, 1174
  China and 7:877, 898, 901
  Christianity and 5:635
  Christians and 4:530
  cities and towns and 8:1034, 1041
  Code of Hammurabi 1:111–117

comitia centuriata and 4:450
education and 10:1384
Egyptian 1:105
England and 8:1049, 1052
feudal Europe and 6:820, 8:1031
France and 8:1078
Germanic peoples and 5:660,
  662, 664–665
Greece and 2:253, 261–262,
  3:294, 298, 301, 364–365, 380
Hanseatic League and 8:1097
Hittites and 2:161
India and 7:928
Islamic world and 6:761, 766
Justinian I and 5:676–677, 677
Mongols and 9:1220
morality laws 4:510
Ottoman Turks and 9:1249, 1250,
  1255
Persians and 2:238, 239
plebians and 4:451, 452, 452–454,
  455
Pompey and 4:496
quaestors and 4:451
reform movements and 4:481
Roman Empire and 4:518–519
Russia and 9:1211, 1212
Severus, Septimius and 5:594
Stoicism and 4:557
Sumerian 1:63, 111
Verres, trial of, and 4:491–
  492
Legend of Saint Anthony, The 5:690
legends, Corinth and 3:297
Legnano, Battle of 8:1062, 1062
Le Maire, Jakob 7:989
Leo I (emperor) 5:626, 653, 669
Leo I (pope) 5:625, 651, 653,
  9:1163
Leo II (emperor) 5:669
Leo III (emperor) 6:761, 763, 800,
  811, 9:1165–1166, 1168
Leo III (pope) 6:802, 802–803, 811,
  9:1170
Leo IV (emperor) 9:1168
Leo IV (pope) 8:1022
Leo V (emperor) 9:1171
Leo VI (emperor) 9:1174
Leo IX (pope) 6:838, 840
León 8:1016, 1017, 1018
Leonardo da Vinci 8:1096, 10:1403,
  1404, 1405, 1405, 1406
Leonidas 2:264, 3:333
Leopold III 8:1096
Leopold of Austria 8:1056
Leotychides 3:336, 339
Lepanto, Battle of 9:1253
Lepidus 4:502, 503
Leptis Magna 5:593, 593
Lesson of Amenemhet (Egyptian text)
  1:84
Letter of Tosar, The 6:730
Leucippus 3:361
Leuctra, Battle of 3:382
levers and fulcrums 3:408
Lewes, Battle of 8:1076

Liao dynasty 7:902, 903
Libation Bearers (Aeschylus)
  3:323
liberal arts, study of 6:804, 806
libraries 2:221, 4:553, 5:693, 701,
  6:782, 10:1392, 1401
Library of Alexandria 3:392, 398,
  406, 407
Libri Carolini (Charlemagne)
  6:811
Libya 1:106, 107, 109
Licinian-Sextian Laws 4:452–455
Licinius 5:611, 628
Liegnitz, Battle of 8:1101, 9:1227,
  1227
Life of Charlemagne (Einhard)
  6:806, 808
Life of Saint Anthony, The
  (Athanasius) 5:696
lifestyle see daily life
Lindisfarne 6:816, 816, 9:1196,
  1198
Linear A script 2:179, 181, 186
Linearbandkeramik culture
  1:16–17, 18
Linear B script 2:186, 252
Lionel of Clarence 8:1114, 1116
Lion Gate, Mycenae 2:184
lion sculpture, Hittite 2:159
Lisbon 10:1370, 1371
Li Si 7:891, 893
literacy, medieval Europe and
  10:1387, 1393, 1394
literature and writings
  Africa and 9:1264, 1273
  Alexander the Great and 3:384
  Alfred the Great and 6:820
  Assyrians and 2:211
  Athens and 2:267, 3:301, 305,
    349
  Augustine and 5:686, 687
  Babylonian 1:123
  Buddhism and 7:953
  chansons de geste (songs of heroic
    deeds) 6:801, 10:1394
  China and 7:879, 882, 893,
    901
  Confucianism and 7:884, 887
  Constantine VII and 9:1174–
    1175
  Egypt's Middle Kingdom and
    1:81, 82–83, 83–84, 88
  Egypt's New Kingdom and 1:97,
    101, 103–104
  El Cid and 8:1021
  Greece and 2:194, 248–249, 256,
    257
  Greek drama 3:318–325
  Greek literature 6:782, 783
  Greek religion and 3:313
  hagiography 5:688, 690, 691
  Hinduism and 7:943, 944
  India and 7:927, 961, 963
  Japan and 7:908–909, 912–913,
    915
  Kublai Khan and 9:1226

Mari Letters 1:115
medieval Europe and 10:1394, 1397
Museum of Alexandria and 3:404
Mycenaeans and 2:182
navigation and 2:202
One Thousand and One Nights 6:781
Ottoman Turks and 9:1255
Persians and 2:242–244, 6:730, 731, 732, 735
Polynesia and 7:988
preservation of 5:661, 701
Roman Empire and 4:510–511, 512, 524, 555–556, 557
Russia and 9:1212
Sparta and 2:258, 264
Sumerian 1:57
Theocritus and 3:406–407
Vedas and 7:935
Vikings and 9:1205
Lithuania 8:1082, 1084, 1100–1101, 9:1215, 1216, 1217
liturgy, Roman Catholic Church and 6:807
Liu Bang 7:881, 893, 894
Liutitians 6:836
Lives of the Artists, The (Vasari) 10:1402, 1403
Livia 4:*509*, 510
Livy 4:438, 510, 524
Li Yuan *see* Gaozu
Lodhi, Bahlul Khan 7:970
Lodhi dynasty 7:970
logic, Aristotle and 3:367
logograms 10:1305
Logos 3:355, 413
lokapala 7:*903*
Lombard League 8:1062, 1070
Lombards
　Byzantine Empire and 5:677, 6:794–795, 9:1165
　Charlemagne and 6:796
　Holy Roman Empire and 6:831, 834
　Italy and 8:1020, 1022
　legal system of 5:662, 664
　territory of 5:660
Lombard warrior 5:*660*
Lombardy 8:1061, 1096
London 8:1039, 1117, 1118–1119
London Company 10:1380
longbowmen, English 8:1105, 1106, 1111
Long Count calendar 10:1320
longhouses 10:1357
longitude and latitude 3:410
Long-Shan culture 7:871–872
longships, Viking 6:*809*, 9:1196, *1202*, 1202, *1204*
Long Walls 3:370, 371
Lonkoping, Battle of 8:1099
looms 8:1030, *1031*
Lorraine 6:819, 832, 837
"lost tribes of Israel" 2:227
lost-wax process 10:1310

Lothair I 6:*805*, 806, 812, 813, 8:1128, 1129
Lothair II 8:1058
Lothair III (Saxony) 6:845
Lothair of France 6:827, 832
Lotharingia 6:829–830
Lothal 7:920
Louis (son of Louis the Stammerer) 6:818
Louis I de Valois 8:1108, 1126
Louis II (emperor) 8:1022
Louis II (Hungary) 9:1252
Louis II de Nevers 8:1106
Louis IV (the Overseas) 6:827
Louis V 6:827
Louis VII 8:1052, 9:1190
Louis VIII 8:1078
Louis IX 8:*1071*, *1078*, 9:1195, 1222, 1236
Louis XI 8:1114, 1130, *1131*, 1131
Louis of Bavaria 8:1092, 1094
Louis the Child 6:828
Louis the German 6:*812*, 812, 813
Louis the Pious 6:802, 803, 811–812, 813
Louis the Stammerer 6:818
Low Countries 8:1128–1129
Lower Egypt 1:72
Lu 7:884
Luba people 9:*1276*, 1276
Lucanians 4:461
Lucifer 5:680
Lucullus, Lucius 4:489, 490
Ludford Bridge, Battle of 8:1117
ludi magni (big games) 4:549–550
ludi saeculares (secular games) 4:511
lugal (king) 1:56–57
Lugalzaggisi 1:58–59
Lunda Empire 9:1276–1277
Lun Yu (Sayings of Confucius) 7:884
Luo people 9:1275–1276
Lupia River, Battle of 4:514
Luther, Martin 10:1393, *1395*, 1415
Luxor *see* Thebes
luxury goods, trade and 8:1033
Lyceum 3:367, 413
Lycia 4:522
Lycurgan Constitution 2:262–263
Lycurgus 2:262, *263*
Lydia 3:303, 326, 328, 336, 339
Lysander 3:378, *379*, 379
Lysias 3:*380*, 380
Lysimachus 3:399
Lysistrata (Aristophanes) 3:378

M

Macedonia 3:384–395, *388*, 4:476
　after Alexander the Great 3:396–403
　Macedonian Empire 5:586
　Ottoman Turks and 9:1244
　Persians and 3:326
　Philip II and 3:383

Phoenicians and 2:207
　Spartan Confederacy and 3:342
Macedonian dynasty 9:1173–1176, 1178, 1180
Macedonian Renaissance 9:1180
Macedonian Wars 4:478
Machiavelli, Niccolò 10:*1396*, 1396, 1397
Machu Pichu 10:1302, *1342*, 1342
Macrinus, Marcus Opellius 5:596
Madeira 10:1366, 1367
Madhva 7:964
madrigals 10:1407
Magadha 7:927, 928, 929, 960
Magdalenian people 1:11
Magellan, Ferdinand 7:*988*, 988, 10:1376–1377, *1379*, 1421
Magellan, Strait of 10:1377, *1380*
Magi 2:244
magistrates 4:450, 451, 452, 546
Magna Carta 8:1067, 1076
Magnanimity of Scipio Africanus, The (Fungai) 4:*472*
Magnesia, Battle of 4:475, 476
Magnus IV 8:1098
Magnus Erickson 8:1098, *1099*
Magyars 6:814, *818*, 819, 828, 830, 831
Mahabalipuram 7:965
Mahabharata 7:943, *944*, 944
mahajanapadas (great realms) 7:927
Mahasanghikas (Great Assembly) 7:956
Mahavira 7:927, 931, 948
Mahayana Buddhism 7:892, 956, 956–957, 958, 959, 981
Mahdi, Al- 6:787
Mahendra 7:958
Mahendravarman I 7:965
Mahmud 9:1232
Mahmud II 9:1255
Mahmud of Ghazna 6:732, 7:*968*, 968
Mahudel, Nicholas 1:45
Maiano, Benedetto da 8:*1020*
Maijiayao culture 1:35
major domus (chief official) 5:660
major palatii (mayor of the palace) *see* mayors, Merovingian dynasty and
Makeda 9:1268
Malacca 7:980, *981*, 981
Malacca, Straits of 7:976
Malacca dynasty 7:977
Malayo-Polynesian languages 7:972
Malay Peninsula 7:975, 977
Mali 9:*1271*, 1271–1272
Malik Shah 9:1232
Malinke people 9:1271
Mamertines 4:464
Mamluk armies 9:1236
Mamluk dynasty (Egypt) 9:*1231*, 1236, *1240*
　crusaders and 9:1195
　Islamic world and 6:775

Mongols and 9:1228, 1230, 1236–1237
　Ottoman Turks and 9:1251–1252, 10:1418, 1419
　rulers of 8:1082
　warfare and 9:1240
Mamluk dynasty (India) 7:969, 970
Mamun, Al- 6:772, 782, 787
Manchu people 9:1222, 10:1414
Manchuria 7:896, 901, 902
Manco Capac (king) 10:*1337*, 1347
Manco Capac (mythical leader) 10:1336
mandalas 7:959, 975–976
manes (spirits) 4:526
Manetho 1:78
Manfred of Sicily 8:1073, *1074*, 1074
Mangu Khan 7:904, 9:1223–1224, 1228
Mani 5:682, 6:730–731, *731*, 733
Manichaeism 5:682, 683, 684–685, 6:730–731, 733
manners, Aztecs and 10:1331
Mansa Maghan 9:1272
Mansa Musa 9:1271, 1272
Mansa Süleyman 9:1272
Mansur, Al- 6:771–772, 785, 787
Mantinea 3:373
Mantinea, Battle of (418 BCE) 3:373
Mantinea, Battle of (362 BCE) 3:383
Mantrapureeswarar Temple 7:*933*
mantras 7:959
Mantua 8:1096
Manu 7:940–941
Manuel Comnenus 9:1181
manufacturing industries 7:911
manuscripts 5:661, *677*, 693
Manutius, Aldus 10:1393
Manzikert, Battle of 9:1168, 1178–1179, 1182, 1232, 1240
Maori people 7:988
mapmaking 10:1367, 1368, 1395, 1397
maps
　Africa 9:*1258*
　Americas and 10:1376
　Assyrian Empire 2:*211*
　Babylonian Empire 1:*112*
　barbarian kingdoms 5:*642*
　China 7:*872*, 900
　Constantinople 9:*1179*
　crusades 9:*1184*
　development of 3:354, 410
　early Byzantine Empire 9:*1160*
　Egypt 1:*72*, 80, 94
　Empire of Charlemagne 6:*790*
　European cities 8:*1028*
　European exploration and 10:*1362*, *1374*, 1378
　Greece and Greek world 2:*164–165*, *248–249*, 261, 3:*296*, 354, 399

maps (continued)
Hittite Empire 2:153
Holy Roman Empire 6:834
Hundred Years' War 8:1104
India 7:920, 962
Islamic world 6:754, 766, 782
Israel 2:224
Japan 7:908
Macedonian Empire 3:388
medieval 10:1361, 1368
Minoan world 2:173
Mongol Empire 9:1220
Mycenaean civilization 2:185
Ottoman Empire 9:1244
Pacific islands 7:984
Persian Empire 2:235
Persian Wars 3:329
Phoenician world 2:198–199
pre-Columbian cultures and 10:1314, 1326, 1338
Ptolemy of Alexandria and 3:410
Roman Empire 4:491, 534, 5:584
Roman world 4:440
Southeast Asia 7:974
southern Europe 8:1016
Sumerian world 1:56
Viking world 9:1199
world circa 1530 CE 10:1412–1413
Maqurrah 9:1238
Marathon, Battle of 2:238, 3:305, 327, 329–330, 333
marathon races 3:330
Marcel, Étienne 8:1105, 1107, 1108
Marcian 5:651, 666, 669
Marco 4:519–520
Marcus Antonius 4:489, 490
Marcus Aurelius 4:484, 543, 544–546, 545, 546, 557, 5:590, 593
Marcus Aurelius (Caracalla) see Caracalla
Mardonius 3:336, 337
Marduk 1:117, 120, 121, 124, 2:211, 219, 220, 239
Margaret of Anjou 8:1114, 1116, 1116, 1117, 1119, 1120, 1122
Margaret of Denmark 8:1098–1099
Margaret of Flanders 8:1126
Margus, Treaty of 5:649
Mari 1:110, 111, 114, 2:210
Mariana Islands 10:1377
Mari Jata see Sundiata Keita
Mari Letters 1:115, 2:224
Marius, Gaius 4:483, 483, 484, 485, 486
Marj Dabiq, Battle of 9:1252
Mark Antony 4:497, 500, 501, 502–503, 503, 510
Marmoutier 5:696
Marquesas Islands 7:982
marriage
Athens and 2:268, 3:350
Augustus Caesar and 4:510

Buddha and 7:948
Byzantine Empire and 9:1165–1166, 1170
Charlemagne and 6:796
Code of Hammurabi and 1:113, 118
Constantine I and 5:635
early Africa and 9:1261
of Edward IV 8:1120
Egypt's New Kingdom and 1:108
Germanic peoples and 5:664, 665
Hittites and 2:158, 161
Khosrow I and 6:735
of Mohammed 6:740–741
Mongols and 9:1220
Philip II Augustus and 8:1066–1067
pre-Columbian cultures and 10:1323, 1340, 1344
Rome and 4:441, 453
social classes and 4:447, 451
Sparta and 2:263
Mars 4:438, 440
Marshall Islands 7:982, 984–985
Martin IV 8:1078
Martin V 8:1092–1093, 1093, 10:1406
Martin of Tours 5:696, 697
martyrs 5:609, 610, 678
Marwan II 6:769
Mary, veneration of 5:678, 680, 681
Mary of Burgundy 8:1131, 1132–1133, 1133
Masaccio, Tommaso 10:1401, 1403–1404
Masai people 9:1264, 1264
masks, theatrical 3:318, 320, 320, 321, 4:555
Masolino 10:1403
Massachusetts Bay Colony 10:1383
massacres 2:213, 214, 216, 4:502, 529, 5:643
Masudi, Al- 6:781
mathematics
Alexandria and 3:404, 407–408
astronomy and 3:409, 410
Babylonians and 1:119
Byzantine Empire and 9:1174–1175
Greek philosophy and 3:361
India and 7:926, 961–962
Islamic world and 6:782, 783–784
medieval Europe and 10:1390, 1391
Pythagoras and 3:357, 358
Sumerians and 1:69
Matilda 8:1049, 1051, 1051, 1063
matrilineal societies 7:988
Matthias Corvinus 9:1216
Mauretania 4:483, 522
Maurice 9:1165
Mauricius 6:735
Mauryan India 7:927–929, 930, 960, 963, 965

Mauryan stone sculpture 7:927
mawali, rebellion of 6:768
Maxentius 5:611, 628
Maximian 5:607, 610
Maximilian I 8:1131, 1132–1133
Maximinus 5:598
Maximus, Magnus 5:614, 615
Maya 10:1302, 1304, 1309, 1312–1323, 1314, 1421
Mayapán 10:1315, 1323
Mayflower 10:1381
Mayflower Compact 10:1381, 1383
mayors, Merovingian dynasty and 6:790–791
Mbuti people 9:1256
Mecca
Adb al-Malik and 6:767, 768
Africa and 9:1271
Islam and 6:740, 749
Mohammed and 6:736, 746, 747
pre-Islamic Arabia and 6:738–739
Medea (Euripides) 3:325
Medes 1:122, 2:217, 221, 232–233, 233–234, 244, 3:326
Medici, Cosimo de' 10:1401
Medici, Lorenzo de' 8:1096, 10:1396, 1401, 1403
medicine
Alexander the Great and 3:384
Alexandria and 3:410–411
Athens and 3:372
Babylonians and 1:119
Black Death and 8:1085
Hippocrates and 3:352
India and 7:926
Islamic world and 6:783
medieval Europe and 10:1390, 1391
Medina 6:736, 745–746, 747, 764
meditation 7:948, 951
Mediterranean Sea 6:779–780, 814, 817, 8:1019, 9:1163, 1252, 1253, 1255, 10:1360
Medjay tribespeople 1:89
Megacles 3:300–301, 304
megalithic cists 7:927
megaliths 1:18–31, 38–39, 10:1307
megarons 2:184, 189
Mehmed I 9:1246
Mehmed II 9:1246, 1247, 1249, 1250
Mehrgarh 7:918
Melanesia 7:982, 987
Melqart 2:206
Memphis 1:73, 2:199
Menander 3:325, 407, 407, 4:557
Mencius 7:887, 890, 891
Mendaña, Álvaro de 7:988
mendicant friars 8:1042
Menelaus 2:182, 194
Menelik I 9:1269
Menes 1:73
menhirs see standing stones

mental illness, emperors and 4:518, 519, 520–521
Mentu 1:81
Mentuhotep II 1:81, 82, 82
Mentuhotep III 1:82
Mercator 10:1368
mercenaries
Alexander the Great and 3:388–389
Egypt and 1:107
Fatimid dynasty and 6:774
Greece and 3:294, 303
Greek colonies and 4:461
Hittites and 2:157
Hundred Years' War and 8:1107
Italian city-states and 8:1096
Tang dynasty and 7:902
merchants 2:175, 8:1087, 10:1327–1328
see also trade
Mercia 9:1196, 1198
Merneptah 1:106, 2:225, 229
Merneptah stele 2:224–225, 225
Merodach-baladan 1:122
Merodach-baladan II 2:217, 218–219
Meroë 5:585, 586, 9:1266, 1269
Merovingian dynasty 5:654, 6:788, 790–793, 794, 808
Mese 5:616, 617
Mesoamerican region 10:1304
see also specific cultures
Mesolithic period 1:6, 6–11, 14, 17
Mesopotamia
Aramaeans and 2:212
Babylonians and 1:110–125
Byzantine Empire and 9:1175–1176
Egypt and 1:72, 99
Indus Valley civilization and 7:918, 920
Islamic world and 6:754, 755, 768
metalwork and 1:32
Mongols and 9:1228, 1235
Neolithic period and 1:16, 22
Ottoman Turks and 9:1242, 1252
Parthians and 5:584–585
Persians and 6:729
Roman Empire and 4:540, 5:594–595, 596
Sumerians and 1:54
Tamerlane and 9:1229
Messalina 4:523
Messana 4:464
Messenia 2:258
metals, sources of 2:164
metalwork
Africa and 9:1261, 1263, 1265, 1266
Akkadian 1:61
Celtic 1:50
Greece and 2:162, 172
Hallstatt culture and 1:45, 47
Hittites and 2:156, 158

Iberian 1:49–50
pre-Columbian cultures and
10:1305–1306, *1310*, 1310
Southeast Asia and 7:972, 974
Sumerian 1:65
Metaphysics (Aristotle) 3:354
Metcaurus River, Battle of 4:474
Metellus, Caecilius 4:483
Metellus, Quintus Caecilius 4:478
Metellus Pius 4:488
metempsychosis 3:357
Mevlana Tekkesi 9:*1233*
Mexica people 10:1324, 1334
Michael I 6:803, 9:1171, *1172*
Michael II 9:1171–1172
Michael III 9:1173, 1177
Michael IV 9:1178
Michael V 9:1178
Michael VII 9:1179
Michael VIII 9:1181, 1193
Michael Cerularius 6:840
Michael Paleologus 8:1068
Michelangelo 8:1096, 10:1402,
1403, 1404, 1406
Michelozzo 10:1401
Michelsberg culture 1:18
microliths 1:9–10
Micronesia 7:982, 984, 987–988
Middle Ages
crises in 8:**1082–1093**
India and 7:**960–971**
leagues and alliances during
8:**1094–1101**
popes and emperors during
8:**1058–1069**
rulers of the 13th century CE
8:**1070–1081**
urban Europe and 8:**1026–1043**
middle and late Byzantine Empire
9:**1168–1181**
Middle Egyptian language 1:103
Middle Empire, Assyria 2:208,
210–212
Middle Kingdom, Egypt 1:**78–
91**
Middle Minoan period 2:172
Middle Stone Age *see* Mesolithic
period
Middle Way 7:951
migrations
Africa and 9:1263, 1264, 1265
early Byzantine Empire and
9:1158, 1160–1161
pre-Columbian cultures and
10:1302, 1304, 1323, 1350,
1352, 1357, 1359
Mihirakula 7:962–963
Milan 8:1061, 1096
Miletus 3:303, 327, 352, 354
military coups *see* coups d'etat
military forces
Africa and 9:*1268*, 1270, *1273*,
1274, *1277*
Agincourt, Battle of, and 8:1111
Alexander the Great and 3:*385*,
388–389, 394

archers 6:*728*, 728, 9:1220–1221
Aryan people and 7:924
Assyrians and 2:210–211, 213,
214, 214, 216
Athens and 3:306, 331
barbarian invaders and 5:658
Bedouin nomads and 6:751
Berber peoples and 9:1235
Britain and 5:663, *664*
Bulgar people and 9:1176, *1177*,
1178
Byzantine Empire and 5:612,
612–613, 625, 671, 673, 9:1163,
1165, 1168, 1170, 1171, 1174,
1175, 1176, 1178–1179
Carthage and 4:464
cavalry 4:462
Charlemagne and 6:*799*, 799
Charles Martel and 6:792
children and 9:1230, 1236, 1255
China and 7:875, 877, *881*, 881,
902, 903
Crécy, Battle of, and 8:1106
crusades and 9:1184–1185, *1187*,
1187
cultural influence in Roman
provinces and 4:547
early Rome and 4:446, 449–550,
454, 456–463, 484
Egypt's New Kingdom and
1:99–100, 105, 107
equestrians and 5:601
First Persian War and 3:329–330
Germanic peoples and 4:*547*,
5:641–642, 643, 645–646, 653,
660, 665, 6:808
Hittites and 2:157, *157*, 158
hoplites 2:265, 3:304, 330, *336*,
369, *376*, 382–383
Huns and 9:1161
India and 7:928
Ionian rebellion and 3:326–327
Islamic culture and 6:785
Italian rebels and 4:485–486
Janissaries 9:1230, 1245, 1247,
1249, 1255
Japan and 7:911, 912, 913–914,
916
Jewish people and 4:*541*
Khosrow I and 6:735
Kiev and 9:1211
Knights Hospitaller 8:1014, 1101
Knights Templar 8:1014, 1018,
1079, 1079, *1080*, 1080
Macedonia and 3:383, 386, *387*,
387, 4:478
Mamluk dynasty and 9:1236,
1238, 1251–1252
Mari and 1:115
Medes and 2:232
mercenaries 3:294, 303, 388–389
Mongols and 7:904, 9:1215,
1219, 1220–1222, 1223, *1227*,
1237, 1238, 1240
Mycenaeans and 2:189, 191
Normans and 8:1023

Ottoman Turks and 9:1250, *1254*
Otto the Great and 6:831
Parthians and 6:*728*, 728
Persians and 2:*237*, 237, 3:332
Praetorian Guard 4:517,
519–520, *521*, 521, 532
pre-Columbian cultures and
10:1324, 1327, 1328–1329,
1329, 1341, *1349*
Reconquista and 8:1017–1018
religious orders and 8:1014, 1025
Roman emperors and 4:493, 494,
504, 506, 511–513, 520–521,
536, 537–538, 539–540,
542–543
Roman Empire and 5:582,
593–594, 604, *605*, 607, 608
Rome and 4:484
Samites and 4:*461*
Second Persian War and 3:336,
337, 339
Seljuk Turks and 9:*1234*,
1240–1241
Sparta and 2:258, 260, 261, 263
succession of Roman leadership
and 4:532–533, 538, 5:592–593
Thebes and 3:382–383
tyranny and 3:294
Vikings and 9:1198
military tribunes 4:453
Milos 2:167, 169
Miltiades 3:330
Milvian Bridge, Battle of 5:628
Mimar Sinan 9:1255
mime, Roman theater and 4:555
Min 1:81–82
Minamoto Yoritomo 7:914, *916*
minarets 6:*786*, 786
minerals, sources of 2:164
Ming dynasty 7:905, 10:*1414*,
1414, 1416, 1419, 1420, 1421
mining
Anatolia and 3:328
Athens and 3:331, 348
Bronze Age and 1:37
copper 1:94
flint 1:19, 23
Hittites and 2:156
Phoenicians and 2:200
salt 1:45
Teotihuacán and 10:1308
tin 1:*36*
Minoans 2:167, 168, **170–181**, *173*,
3:310
Minos 2:170, 176
Minotaur 2:170, *171*, 176
Minyan people 2:163–164
miracles, Christianity and 5:690,
696
Mirandola, Pico della 10:1401,
1403
mirror, Chinese 7:*885*, 895
missi dominici (lord's messengers)
6:810
missionaries 6:791, 7:929, 930,
957–958, 967, 9:1230, 1233

Mississippians 10:1350, *1352*, 1357
Mitanni Empire 1:99, 101, 120,
2:210
Mithridates VI 4:*485*, 486, 487,
488–489, 490
Mitla 10:1310
Mixtec people 10:1302, 1310,
1334
models, Egyptian 1:*74*, *81*, 84–85,
86, *91*
Mohács, Battle of 9:1252, 10:1418
Mohammad ibn Tughluq 7:969,
971
Mohammed 6:**736–751**, *737*, *741*,
746, *750*, 764, 769
Mohammed Shah 9:1223
Mohawk people 10:1356
Mohenjo-Daro 7:918, *919*, 920,
920–921, 923
Mohesh 9:1277
Mohica people 10:1302, *1305*
moksha (release) 7:937
Molay, Jacques de 8:1080
molds, copper tools and 1:32, 35
Mona Lisa (da Vinci) 10:1405
monasteries
Basil of Caesarea and 5:693, *694*
Benedict of Nursia and 5:699–
701
Buddhism and 7:*892*, 902, 946,
954–955, 956, 959
Byzantine Empire and 9:1175
education and 6:804, 10:1387
India and 7:*964*
medieval Europe and 6:814, 816,
825, 826, 826, 838, 8:1035,
9:1196, 1201
Pachomius and 5:692
preserving knowledge and 5:661,
665
Sufism and 9:*1233*
see also convents
monasticism, appeal of 5:**688–
701**
monastic rules 5:692, 693–694,
699–701, 6:825, 826, 7:954
money *see* currency
moneychanging 8:1031, 1032–1033
moneylending 4:466, 6:784,
8:1033
Mongolia 9:*1221*
Mongols 9:**1218–1229**, *1219*,
1220, *1224*, *1237*
China and 7:902, 904
development of states and
10:1414
Islam and 9:1238, 1240
Islamic world and 6:764, 775,
7:969, 9:1230, 1235–1238,
1240, 10:1360, 1362
Japan and 7:916, *917*
Mamluk dynasty and 9:1230,
1236–1237, 1238
Ottoman Turks and 8:1082
Russia and 8:1101, 9:1211,
1214–1215, *1215*, 1216

monks, Buddhist 7:*954*

Monophysitism 5:625, 626, 627, 670, 6:766–767, 9:1163

monotheism 1:*100*, 101–102, 2:228, 241–242, 10:1354

Mon people 7:978

Monte Albán 10:1309

Monte Cassino 5:699, *700*, *701*, 6:825

Monteverdi, Claudio 10:*1407*, 1407

Montezuma I 10:1334

Montezuma II 10:1334, 1335

Montfort, Simon de 8:1025, 1076, 1077

monumental gateway, Tiwanaku 10:*1311*

morality, Buddhism and 7:953

Morat, Battle of 8:1132, *1132*

More, Anthony 10:*1381*

More, Thomas 8:1124, 10:1397

Morocco, trade and 10:1366

mortification 5:695

mosaics

  Byzantine Empire and 5:*667*, *673*, *674*, 9:*1164*

  Christianity and 5:*679*

  Fourth Crusade and 9:*1193*

  gladiators in 4:*551*

  Hagia Sophia and 5:672, 9:*1159*, *1178*, *1180*

  Macedonian Renaissance and 9:*1180*

  Minoan 2:*171*

  pre-Columbian cultures and 10:1310, 1315

  Roman 2:*194*, *250*, 3:*389*, 5:*591*

  Rome and 4:*477*

  Saint Sophia's Cathedral and 9:*1209*

  Sumerian 1:56

  Umayyad Mosque and 6:*767*

  Venetian 2:*223*

Moscow 9:1215, 1217

Moses 2:227, 228, 228, 229, 3:*297*, 6:748, 749

Mosque of Ahmed ibn Tulun 6:774

Mosque of Mohammed Ali 6:*745*

mosques

  Abu Dulaf Mosque 6:*786*

  Africa and 9:*1270*

  Dome of the Rock 6:*768*, 768, 769

  Hagia Sophia and 5:672

  Medina and 6:745, 746

  in Mesopotamia 6:*755*

  Mosque of Ahmed ibn Tulun 6:*774*

  Mosque of Mohammed Ali 6:*745*

  Ottoman Turks and 9:1247, 1255

  in Persia 6:*753*

  Qarawuyin Mosque 9:*1241*

  Southeast Asia and 7:*981*

  Umayyad Mosque 6:*765*, 767

Mosul 1:*57*

mound builders 10:1357

Mount Olympus 3:310, 314

Mount Uhud, Battle of 6:746

Mount Vesuvius 4:535, 536

mowing tools 1:11

Mpande 9:1277

Mstislav 9:1211

Mu'awiyah 6:756–757, 758, 764, 776

mud-brick architecture 9:*1270*

muezzins 6:743, *744*

Mughal dynasty 9:1229, 1232

Mughal Empire 7:930, 970, 971, 10:*1411*, 1414, *1418*, 1418

Muhammad of Ghur 7:968, 970

Muisca people *see* Chibcha people

mummies 1:96, 7:*874*, 874, 10:*1340*

Munda, Battle of 4:499

Murad I 9:*1245*, 1245, *1246*, 1255

Murad II 9:1246, *1249*

murals *see* frescos; painting

Murasaki Shikibu 7:913

murders, Nero and 4:525, 527

Mursilis I 1:120, 2:150, 152

Mursilis II 2:152–153

Muscovy 8:1084, 1101

Muses 3:412

Museum of Alexandria 3:392, 398, 404, 406–407, *411*

music and dance

  Babylonians and 1:*117*

  early Africa and 9:1259, *1261*

  Egypt and 1:90

  Greek drama and 3:320

  Gregorian chant 5:700

  Hittites and 2:158–159

  Mali and 9:1272

  medieval Europe and 10:1394

  Ptolemy of Alexandria and 3:410

  Pythagoras and 3:357, 358

  religious festivals and 3:318

  Renaissance and 10:1407–1408

  Rome and 4:555, *557*

  sankyo (musical instrument) 9:*1274*

  Sioux people and 10:*1356*

  Sparta and 2:264

  Sufis and 9:1230, 1233

Muslims *see* Islam; Islamic world

Mustansir, Al- 6:775

Mu'tasim, Al- 6:786

Mutawakkil, Al- 6:*786*

Mutazilites 6:772–773

Mutina, Battle of 4:502

mutinies, Alexander the Great and 3:394

Muwatallis 2:153

Mwene Mutapa Empire 9:1276, 1277

Myanmar 7:*953*, *958*, 958, 967, 977, 978

Mycenae 2:182–195, *187*

Mycenaean civilization, maps of 2:*185*

Mycenaeans

  Cycladic people and 2:169

  Greece and 2:246, 264, 266, 3:310

  Iron Age and 1:40–41

  Minoans and 2:172, 181

  Phoenicians and 2:196

  tombs and 2:185–186

  Troy and 2:194, 195

  writing and 2:204

Mylae, Battle of 4:467, *468*

mystery religions 3:315–316, 5:680

mysticism 5:684

mythology

  Carthage and 2:200

  Greece and 2:167, 176

  Greek 1:69

  Hittites and 2:159, 160

  Minoans and 2:170

  Roman 4:438–439, 456–458, 526

  Sumerian 1:66, 69

  see also gods and goddesses

Mzilikazi Kumalo 9:1277

N

Nabatean kingdom 6:736

Nabis 3:403

Nabonidus 1:125, 2:234

Nabu-nasir 1:122, 2:216

Nahavand, Battle of 6:755

Nahuatl language 10:1335

Nak people, terra-cotta bust and 9:*1257*

Namib Desert 9:1260

Nancy, siege of 8:1132

Nanda dynasty 7:928

Napata 9:1266

Naples 4:473, 5:675, 8:1019, 1096

Nara 7:917

Naram-Sin 1:60–61, *61–62*, *63*

Narasimhavarman I 7:965

Narcissus 4:522, 523

Narmer 1:73

Narses 5:675, 676

Nataraja 7:*966*

nation-states, development of 10:1414

Native Americans 9:1207, 10:1348–1359, 1380, 1382, 1383

  see also specific tribes

Natufian culture 1:10–11, 13

natural disasters 2:167, 168, 169, 181, 192, 210, 4:535

nature deities 2:160

Nauru 7:982

naval power

  Antony and Cleopatra and 4:503

  Athens and 3:331, 340

  blood games and 4:552

  Byzantine Empire and 9:1176, 1181

  China and 7:904

  Delian League and 3:341

India and 7:966

Islamic world and 6:763

Italian city-states and 8:1025, 1034, 1036

medieval Europe and 6:814, 817, 10:1365

Mylae, Battle of 4:*468*

Ottoman Turks and 9:1244, 1247, 1249, *1251*, 1253, 1255, 10:1418

Peloponnesian War and 3:368, 370, 376, 378

piracy and 4:489

Portugal and 10:1364, 1366–1367, 1369–1371

Punic Wars and 4:465, 467, 468–469, 470, 473

Salamis, Battle of 3:334, 336

Second Persian War and 3:332–333

Thucydides and 3:377

triremes (warships) and 3:331, 334, *339*, 339

Vandals and 5:652, 653

Vikings and 9:1196, 1201, *1202*, 1202

Navarre 8:1016

navigation

  medieval Europe and 10:1363–1364, 1365, 1367, 1391

  Phoenicians and 2:200–201, 202

  Polynesia and 7:985

  Vikings and 9:1202

Nawfal, Waraqah ibn 6:741

Nayarit culture 10:1307

Ndebele people 9:1277

Ndwandwe people 9:1277

Neanderthals 1:*8*, 9, 2:208

Nebuchadnezzar I 1:121

Nebuchadnezzar II 1:124, 2:231

Necho 2:201

Nedao, Battle of 5:651

Nefertiti 1:*103*

Neo-Hittites 2:155

Neolithic period

  agriculture and 1:12, 13

  China and 7:870–871

  culture and 1:14–17

  early humans and 1:6–17

  funnel-beaker culture and 1:18–24

  Greece and 2:162, 164–165

  megaliths and 1:24–31

  Minoans and 2:170, 172

  Pacific islands and 7:987

  tools and 1:6–7

Neolithic Revolution 1:14, 7:871

Neoplatonism 5:683, 684, 6:783

Nepal 7:950

Nero 4:516, *517*, 524–525, *527*, 527–529, 531, 5:678

Nero, Gaius Claudius 4:474

Nero, Tiberius Claudius 4:510

Nerva, Marcus Cocceius 4:538

Nestorianism 6:734

Nestorius 5:678, 680, 6:734, 9:1163
Nestor's Palace 2:187, 189
Netherlands 10:1371, 1378, 1409
Neutria 6:791
Neville, Anne 8:1120
Neville, Richard (earl of Salisbury)
    8:1116, 1117, 1118
Neville, Richard (earl of Warwick)
    8:1116, 1117, *1118*,
    1119–1122, *1122*
New Caledonia 7:982, 984
New Carthage 4:474
"New Comedy," Greek 3:325
New Empire, Assyria 2:208,
    212–213, 215–221
New England 10:1383
Newgrange burial mound 1:*25*, 25,
    26
New Guinea 7:982, 984, 985
New Kingdom, Egypt 1:91,
    92–109, 2:152–153
New Persian Empire 6:**726–735**
New Stone Age *see* Neolithic
    period
New Zealand 7:982, 985, 988, *989*,
    10:1410
Nicaea 9:1187, 1242
Nicaea, Council of 5:*624*, 625,
    628–630, *631*, 631, 633, 9:1162,
    1168
Nicaea, Seventh Council of
    6:811
Nicene Creed 5:629, 630, 6:840
Nicephorus I 9:1170–1171
Nicephorus Phocas 9:1175
Nicholas of Cusa 10:1398
Nicias 3:373, 374, 376
Nicomedia 9:1242, 1244
Nicopolis, Battle of 9:1245, *1248*,
    1248
Niger-Kordofanian languages
    9:1264
Nihon shoki (Chronicles of Japan)
    7:908–909
Nika Revolt 5:670, 671, 672, 674,
    9:1164
Nile River 1:70, 78, 86, 5:*587*,
    9:1195, 1260, 1266
Nilo-Saharan languages 9:1259,
    1264
Nilotic languages 9:1264
Nimrud 2:208, *209*, 213, 215, 216,
    217, *218*
Niña 10:1372, 1374
Ninevah 1:122, 2:208, 218,
    219–220, *220*, 221, 232
nirvana 7:953–954
Noah's Ark 2:224
nobility
    Athens and 2:266, 269
    Aztecs and 10:1324, 1326, 1327,
        1331, 1332
    civil strife and 4:486–487
    clothing and 10:1344–1345
    Greek poleis and 2:249, 251,
        253

Incas and 10:1340, 1344
    Kiev and 9:1213
    landownership and 4:476
    Minoans and 2:175
    North American peoples and
        10:1358
    political power of 4:488
    reform movements and 4:479,
        481, 482
    senate and 4:455
    Vikings and 9:1205
    see also aristocracy; patricians
nobility of character, Confucianism
    and 7:885–886
No drama 7:*907*
Nogaret, Guillaume de 8:1081
Nok people 9:*1257*, 1261, 1263,
    1265, 1269
nomadic peoples
    Asian nomads 9:1208
    Bedouin people 6:736, *738*,
        738–739, *739*
    development of states and
        10:1414
    India and 7:924–925, 962–963
    Mongols 9:*1224*
    plunder and 9:1238, 1240
    pre-Columbian cultures and
        10:1312, 1324, 1350,
        1358–1359
    Russia and 9:1208, 1213
    Sayfuwa people 9:1273–1274
    Turkic people 9:1230, 1232
nomarchs (provincial governors)
    1:77, 78, 80, 83
"non-doing," Taoism and 7:888
non-Muslims, Islam and 6:746, 747,
    754, 766–767, 773
nonviolence 7:948, 958
Normandy 6:826, 8:1044, 1046,
    1113, 9:1200
Normans 8:1023, 1024, 1025
    Byzantine Empire and 9:1178,
        1181
    England and 8:1047, 1048–
        1049
    Vikings and 9:1200
Norsemen *see* Vikings
North America
    peoples of 10:**1348–1359**
    settlement of 10:1379–1381,
        1382, 1383, 1410
    Vikings and 9:1206–1207
Northampton, Battle of 8:1117
northeastern tribes 10:1356–
    1357
northern Europe
    paganism and 8:1025
    Renaissance and 10:1408–1409
    trade and 8:1033–1034
    see also specific countries
Northern Marianas Islands
    7:982
Northern Passage, search for
    10:1378
Northern Plateau region 9:1260

North Semitic alphabet 2:204
Northumbria 9:1196, 1198
Norway 8:1098, 1098–1099, 1100,
    9:1199, 1204, 1205
notaries 8:*1043*
Novgorod
    Estonia and 9:1217
    fortifications and 8:*1101*,
        9:*1214*
    government and 9:1211
    Kiev and 9:1213
    Mongols and 8:1101, 9:1214
    Moscow and 9:1215, 1217
    trade and 9:1208
Nubia
    Africa and 9:1266, 1268
    Egypt and 1:77, 83, 87, 89, 92,
        94, 95, 109, 9:*1268*
    pottery and 9:*1262*
    pyramids and 5:*585*, 9:*1269*
    Roman Empire and 5:586, 588
Numa Pompilius 4:440, *446*, 549
Numerian 5:606
Numidians 4:479, 481, 483
Nur ad-Din 9:1191
Nut 1:*106*

O
"oath helpers" 5:662
oaths of allegiance 6:808, 810, 819,
    821, 842
Oba Ozolua 9:1274–1275
obedience, monasteries and 5:694
obelisk, Egyptian 5:*617*
observatories, Toltecs and 10:1318
obsidian 2:167, 10:1308
Oceanic languages 7:988
Octavia 4:527
Octavian 4:497, *499*, 501–502, 503
    see also Augustus Caesar
Octavius, Marcus 4:480
Odin 9:1205
Odoacer 5:646, *647*, 647, 9:1163
Odo of Aquitaine 6:761, 792
Odo of Cluny 6:826
Odo of France 6:827
Odo of Metz 6:807
Odysseus 2:182, *193*, *194*, 194, 3:*406*
Odyssey (Homer) 2:182, 192, 194,
    248–249, 256, 3:313, 404, *406*,
    6:732
Oedipus at Colonus (Sophocles)
    3:323–324
Oedipus Rex (Sophocles) 3:323,
    324, 324
offerings, religious 1:19, 24, 25, 85,
    3:312
Ogotai 9:1214, 1223, 1227
Olaf IV 8:1099
Old Babylonian period 1:110
"Old Comedy," Greek 3:325
Old Empire, Assyria 2:208
Old Kingdom, Egypt 1:**70–77**
Old Persian language 2:243
Old Stone Age *see* Paleolithic
    period

Oleg 9:1201, 1203, 1210, *1211*,
    1211
Olga 9:1203, 1210
oligarchy 3:298, 348, 378–380,
    8:1036–1037
olive oil 3:302
Olmec people 10:1302, *1304*,
    1305, *1306*, 1306–1307, *1307*,
    1309
Olympias 3:384, 386
Olympic Games 3:330, 4:527
Omar bin Khattab 6:752, 754, 755,
    758, 764
Oneida people 10:1356
One Thousand and One Nights
    6:780, *780*, 781, 787
Onin War 7:917
On Nature (Anaxagoras) 3:356
Onondaga people 10:1356
On the Holy Spirit and Moralia (Basil
    of Caesarea) 5:695
opera 10:*1407*, 1407
Oppert, Jules 1:67
oppida *see* city-states
Optics (Ptolemy) 3:410
optimates (aristocrats) *see* nobility
oracle bones *see* divination
oracles 2:255, 3:297, 313, 315,
    331
oral traditions 9:1264, 1271,
    10:1336
orators 3:380
Oresteia trilogy (Aeschylus)
    3:322–323
Orestes 5:647
Orfeo (Monteverdi) 10:1407
Orhan 9:1242, 1244
original sin 5:685, 687
Orléans, siege of 8:1110, *1112*,
    1112
ornamental stone, Viking 9:*1204*
orphans, Islam and 6:740
Orsini, Latino 8:*1020*
Ortakoi Camii 5:*623*
orthodox Christianity
    Athanasius of Alexandria and
        5:695–696
    barbarian invaders and 5:658,
        660
    Justinian I and 5:670
    Russia and 9:1212, 1215
    Vandals and 5:653–654
    see also doctrinal disputes; Roman
        Catholic Church
Orthodoxy, Council of 6:811,
    9:1173
Oscans 2:252
Osiris 1:84, 106
Osman I 9:1241, *1243*
Ostia, amphitheater at 4:*466*
ostracism, Athens and 3:306, 342
Ostrogoths 5:640, 645–646, 648
    eastern Roman Empire and
        5:626, 666, 669
    Huns and 5:648, 649
    Italy and 5:673

Othman ibn Affan 6:743–744, 755–756, 758, 764
Otho, Marcus Salvio 4:527, 532, *536*
Otto I 6:830, *831*, 831, 832, 8:1022
Otto II 6:832, *835*, 836, 9:1176
Otto III 6:832, 834–835, *836*
Otto IV 8:1055, *1057*, 1065, *1066*
Ottoman Empire, map of 9:*1244*
Ottoman Turks 9:**1242–1255**
　Anatolia and 9:1241
　Byzantine Empire and 5:618, 672, 9:1181, 1215
　crusades and 9:1195
　development of states and 10:1414
　Hungary and 9:1216
　Islamic world and 6:764, 775
　Kanem–Bornu Empire and 9:1274
　medieval Europe and 8:1082, 10:1360, 1418
　Tamerlane and 9:1229
　warfare and 10:1419
　White Sheep Turks and 9:1240
Otto of Brunswick *see* Otto IV
Ötzi 1:32, *34*
Ovid 4:510–511, *512*, 526
Oyo 9:1275

P
Pacal 10:*1316*, 1322
Pachacuti Inca Yupanqui 10:1338–1339
Pachomius 5:691–692
Pacific cultures 7:**982–989**
Pacific islands
　map of 7:*984*
　settlement of 10:1410
Pacific Northwest tribes 10:1357–1358
Pacific Ocean, European explorers and 10:1377–1378
Paderborn, diet at 6:797, 798
paganism
　Africa and 9:1269, 1270
　Augustine and 5:687
　Christianity and 5:632–634, 635, 636, 691
　crusades and 9:1182
　Europe and 8:1082, 9:1182, 1196, 1204, 1216
　Iceland and 9:1204
　Lithuania and 8:1100, 9:1216
　northern Europe and 6:839, 8:1025, 1101
　pre-Islamic Arabia and 6:736, 739, 742–743
　Saxons and 6:796

Theodosius I and 5:636–637
Vikings and 6:809, 9:1196
see also gods and goddesses; religious beliefs
Pagan kingdom 7:978, *980*
painting
　Macedonian Renaissance and 9:1180
　Minoans and 2:178
　perspective and 10:1403–1404
　portrait painting 10:1404, 1405, 1406
　pre-Columbian cultures and 10:1305, 1308, 1315
　Renaissance and 10:1402
　Venice and 10:1406
Paiute people 10:1359
Pakistan 7:874, 966
Palace of Minos *see* Knossos
palaces
　Assyrians and 2:213, 215
　Constantinople and 5:619, 621
　Israelites and 2:231
　Kublai Khan and 9:1226
　Maya and 10:1318
　Minoans and 2:172–173, 175, 178
　Mycenaeans and 2:184, 187, 189, 246
　Nero and 4:528
　Persians and 2:234, *236*, 240
Pala dynasty 7:963
Palatine Chapel 6:*807*, 807
Palatine School 6:804
Palau 7:982
Palenque 10:1315
Paleolithic period 1:6, 6–7, 2:162, 208, 7:871
Palestine
　Byzantine Empire and 9:1181
　crusades and 8:1082, 9:1182, 1187, 1195
　Egypt and 1:92, 94
　Ottoman Turks and 9:1252
　Palmyra and 5:602
　Philistines and 2:222
　Seleucid dynasty and 3:400
　Seljuk Turks and 9:1234
　Umayyad caliphate and 6:768
Palestrina 10:1407
palisades 10:1357
Pallas 4:522
Pallava dynasty 7:965
Pallene, Battle of 3:301
Palmero 8:1022
Palmyra 5:*597*, 601, *602*, 603
Pamir 7:901
Pamplona 6:798
Panathenaea 3:301
Pandya dynasty 7:966
Panehsi 1:107
Panipat, Battle of 7:970
Pannonia 5:666, 669
Panormus 4:468
Papal Palace, Avignon 8:*1083*, 1088

Papal States 8:1064, 1065, 1072, 1096
paper 7:899, 10:1319, 1328
Papinian 5:594
papyrus 1:88
paradoxes, Greek philosophy and 3:360
Paris 6:832, 8:1039, 1112, 1113, 9:1199–1200, *1201*
parliament, English 8:1076, 1077, 1108, 1118, 1131
Parmenides 3:355, 358, 360, 362–363
Parni 6:728
Parrot, André 1:114
Parseeism 6:731
Parsura *see* Persians
Parthenon 3:340, *346*, 349, 351
Parthia 4:496, 513, 529, 540, 544, 6:728
Parthians 5:*586*, 6:*728*, 728
　Roman Empire and 5:584–585, 589, 594–595, 596
　Sassanid Empire and 6:726
　Seleucid Empire and 3:401, 5:586
Parts of the Universe, The 6:784
Parvati 7:945, 963
Pasargadae 2:234, *236*, 3:393
Paschal II 6:843–844
passage tombs 1:*25*, 25, *26*, 27–28
Pataliputra 7:960
Patinier, Joachim 4:*526*
patriarchs 5:632
patricians 4:446, 446–447, 448, 449, 452
patrilineal societies 7:987
patrons, Renaissance and 10:1400–1401, 1403, 1404, 1405, 1406
Paul 4:530, 5:683, 686
Paula 5:697
Paul of Thebes 5:688, *689*
Paulus, Lucius Aemilius 4:472
Pausanias 3:337, 379
Pavia 6:796
pax Augusta 4:511–513
Pax Nicephori 9:1171
payments, government service and 3:344
payments, trade and 2:202–203
Peace (Aristophanes) 3:378
Peace of Anatolius 5:649
Peace of Antalcidas 3:382
peace of God 8:1018
Peace of Nicias 3:373, 378
peace treaties 4:469, 474–475, 478, 513
Peasants' Revolt 8:1108, *1109*, 1109
peasants' revolts 8:1086, 1107, 1116
peat bogs 1:10, 19
Pecheneg people 9:1203, 1210
pedagogues 4:557
Peisistratus 3:300–301
Peking Man 7:870, *873*
Pelagius (monk) 5:685

Pelagius (pope) 5:*687*
Peloponnesian League 3:368, 370, 373
Peloponnesian War 2:239, 250, 254, 3:342, 344, 362, 368–383
penance 5:639, 682, 6:842–843, *843*, 845
People's Crusade 9:1184
peoples of North America 10:**1348–1359**
Pépin (mayor) 6:791–792
Pépin (son of Charlemagne) 6:802
Pépin of Aquitaine 6:812
Pépin the Short 6:794, 795, 8:1020
Pepy I 1:78
Pepy II 1:78
Perdiccas 3:386, 396
perfume makers 6:779
Pergamum 3:401, 4:476, 482
Peri, Jacopo 10:1407
Periander 3:295, 296, 298, 299
Pericles 3:*341*
　Acropolis and 3:342
　Athenian culture and 3:348–349
　democracy and 3:346–347
　Greek philosophy and 3:356
　Peloponnesian War and 3:370, 371
　rhetoric and 3:345
　upbringing of 3:340
Pericles, Age of 3:**340–351**
Period of the Warring States (China) 7:877, *885*, 906
Period of the Warring States (Japan) 7:917
perioikoi (neighbors) 2:258, 260–261, 3:403
persecution
　Christianity and 5:609, 610, 628, 635, 678
　hermits and 5:688
　pagans and 5:636–637, 639
Persephone 3:315–316, *317*
Persepolis 2:*240*, 240, *241*, 245, 3:*338*, 390, 393
Perseus 4:478
Persia
　Babylon and 1:125
　Byzantine Empire and 9:1165
　Egypt's New Kingdom and 1:109
　Islam and 6:*753*, 768, 769, 771
　Islamic world and 9:1232, 1234, 1238, 1240, 10:1415, 1418
　Khoresm Empire and 9:1223
　Mongols and 9:1228, 1229, 1235–1236, 1240
　Ottoman Turks and 9:1252
　Tamerlane and 9:1229
Persian Empire 6:**726–735**
　Achaemenid dynasty and 6:726
　Byzantine Empire and 6:752
　Islam and 6:751, 754, 755, 757, 776
　map of 2:*235*
　taxation and 6:779

Persian Gulf 3:394–395
Persians 2:232–245
  Alexander, Severus, and
    5:597–598
  Alexander the Great and 3:385,
    389–391, 393, 393–394, 395
  Athens and 3:305, 309, 341, 342,
    368
  Byzantine Empire and 5:613,
    625, 666, 670–671, 675
  Diocletian and 5:607
  Islamic world and 6:785
  Manichaeism and 5:682
  Palmyra and 5:602
  Parthians and 5:584, 585,
    6:728
  Peloponnesian War and 3:376
  Persian Wars 3:326–339
  Philip I 5:599
  Phoenicians and 2:207
  Sparta and 3:381–382
Persians (Aeschylus) 3:323
Persian Wars 2:264, 3:326–339, 329
Persis 6:726, 728
personal appearance
  Egyptians and 1:108
  Hittites and 2:150, 156
  Minoans and 2:178–179
  pre-Columbian cultures and
    10:1323, 1331, 1345, 1358
personal property, North American
    peoples and 10:1352
perspective, painting and
    10:1403–1404
Pertinax, Helvius 5:592
Peru, agriculture in 1:14
Pescennius Niger 5:592, 592, 616
Petén 10:1312
Peter 4:530, 5:609, 6:840
Peter III of Aragon 8:1075
Peter the Cruel 8:1107
Peter the Hermit 9:1185
Petrarch 8:1088
petroglyphs 10:1351
Phaedo (Plato) 3:365
Phaistos, palaces at 2:178
phalanxes 3:386, 387, 387, 389,
    4:478
pharaohs
  afterlife and 1:85
  Egypt's Middle Kingdom and
    1:78, 80, 83, 89, 91
  Egypt's New Kingdom and 1:99,
    100
  Egypt's Old Kingdom and 1:73,
    74
  literature and 1:88
  see also specific pharaohs
Pharisees 4:541
Pharsalus, Battle of 4:496
Phidias 3:349, 351
Philae 9:1266
Philip I (France) 9:1185
Philip I (Philip the Arabian) 5:598,
    599
Philip I (West Francia) 6:828

Philip II (Macedonia) 3:383, 383,
    384, 386
Philip II Augustus (France) 8:1055,
    1057, 1067, 9:1192
  development of France and
    8:1044, 1052, 1054–1055,
    1057
  marriages of 8:1066–1067
  Otto of Brunswick and 8:1065
  Richard I (the Lionheart) and
    8:1056
Philip III (Burgundy) 8:1127
Philip III (France) 8:1078–1079
Philip III (Macedonia) 3:396
Philip IV (France) 8:1079, 1080,
    1081, 1087, 1133
Philip V (Macedonia) 4:476, 478,
    478
Philip VI (France) 8:1102, 1106
Philip of Swabia 8:1065
Philip the Bold 8:1126
Philip the Good 8:1110, 1113
Philistines 2:222, 230
Philoctetes (Sophocles) 3:323
philosophy
  China and 7:877, 879, 882–893,
    903
  Christianity and 5:633, 634, 639,
    682–685
  Greek 3:348, 352–367, 411–413,
    5:661
  Hinduism and 7:964
  humanism 10:1392–1393, 1395,
    1396, 1397
  Islamic world and 6:781–783
  Neoplatonism 5:684
  Persians and 6:735
  Stoicism 4:557
  see also Buddhism; religious beliefs
Phocas 9:1165
Phoenicians 2:196–207, 198–
    199
  Alexander the Great and 3:391
  alphabet and 2:248, 252
  Assyrians and 2:213, 216, 217
  Babylon and 1:124
  Canaan and 2:222
  Carthage and 4:464
  Cycladic culture and 2:169
  Greece and 2:255, 3:310, 332
  Israelites and 2:231
  metalworking and 9:1261
  Seleucid Empire and 5:586
  trade and 1:49
phonetic writing 1:68
Phraortes 2:232
Phrynichus 3:321–322
phylae (governmental divisions)
    3:306, 307
pictographic writing 1:68, 10:1328,
    1328
  see also hieroglyphic writing
Picts 5:584, 595, 663, 664
Pietàs (Michelangelo) 10:1403,
    1404
Pilate, Pontius 4:507–508, 530

pilgrimages
  Buddhism and 7:955
  crusades and 9:1182
  Islam and 6:742, 746, 747, 749,
    769, 786, 9:1271
pillars, Buddhist 7:928, 929, 930,
    930, 958
Pillow Book, The (Sei) 7:913
Pinta 10:1372, 1374
piracy 4:464, 489, 490, 6:779,
    780
Piraeus 3:349, 370, 371, 372
Pisa 8:1025, 1034, 1036–1037
Piso, Gaius Calpurnius 4:529
Piso Licinianus 4:532
pitcher, Anasazi 10:1350
Pithekoussai 2:256
Piye 1:109
Pizarro, Francisco 10:1347, 1347,
    1421
plague
  Black Death 8:1084, 1084–
    1086, 1085, 1086, 1105,
    1108, 1109
  Peloponnesian War and 3:344,
    370–371, 372
  Rome and 4:544
plankhouses 10:1358
Plataea, Battle of 2:239, 3:336, 337,
    337, 340
Plato 3:353, 10:1388
  Academy and 3:365, 367
  democracy and 3:347–348
  Heracles and 3:355
  humanism and 10:1393, 1395
  Islamic world and 6:782, 783
  Neoplatonism 5:684
  preserving knowledge of 5:661
  Renaissance and 10:1404
  Socrates and 3:362, 364, 365
  Sophists and 3:361, 412
  Sparta and 2:264
Platonic Academy 10:1393
playwrights see dramatists
plebians
  Clodius, Publius Pulcher, and
    4:494
  concilium plebis (council of the
    plebians) 4:451, 455, 480
  Domitian and 4:536–537
  early Roman republic and
    4:450–451
  early Rome and 4:446, 446–
    447
  legal system and 4:452–455
  political power of 4:488
  senate, Roman, and 4:449
Pliny the Elder 4:536
Pliny the Younger 4:536, 556
Plotinus 5:684
plows 1:21, 3:302, 8:1026, 1028
plumbing and water supplies
  aqueducts 5:620, 670, 675, 676
  Constantinople and 5:619, 620
  Cycladic culture and 2:169
  Hittites and 2:154

India and 7:918
  Khmer people and 7:976–977
  Minoans and 2:174, 175
  Mycenae and 2:184
  Persians and 6:735
  pre-Columbian cultures and
    10:1316, 1332
  Rome and 5:675, 676
  Saint Anthony's Monastery and
    5:691
  see also irrigation
Plutarch 3:384, 4:438
Plymouth Colony 10:1381, 1383
Pocahontas 10:1382, 1382
poetry
  Bedouin people and 6:738
  China and 7:887, 901
  Greece and 3:318, 355, 358,
    406–407, 412
  Hinduism and 7:940, 944
  India and 7:935, 961, 963
  Islamic world and 6:766, 767,
    9:1233
  Japan and 7:912
  medieval Europe and 6:798, 801,
    10:1394
  Persians and 6:732
  Roman Empire and 4:556
  see also literature and writings
Poitiers, Battle of 8:1105
Pola Island 7:985
Poland 6:835, 836, 8:1084, 1100–
    1101, 9:1213, 1216, 1217, 1227
poleis see city-states
Politian 10:1403
political intrigue, Louis XI of
    France and 8:1130
political power
  barbarian invaders and 5:660
  Buddhist monasteries and 7:955
  Byzantine Empire and 9:1158
  Carolingian Empire and
    6:826–827
  conquered people and 4:463
  democracy and 3:304
  development of states and
    10:1415–1416
  English parliament and 8:1108
  Inquisition and 8:1019–1020
  Japan and 7:909, 913–914
  Machiavelli, Niccolò and
    10:1396
  mandalas and 7:975–976
  Merovingian dynasty and 6:788,
    790–791
  Mongol China and 9:1224
  pre-Columbian cultures and
    10:1323, 1326
  religious beliefs and 10:1415
  Roman Catholic Church and
    6:824–825, 835, 8:1058, 1061,
    1064, 1075, 1081, 1086, 9:1170,
    1191
  Roman emperors and 4:493, 496,
    504, 506, 515, 517, 522
  Rome and 4:450–451, 458, 488

political power (*continued*)
 social classes and 4:446–455,
  488
 trade guilds and 4:550
 western schism and 8:1089
 see also government
Polo, Marco 8:*1098*, 9:*1179*, 1224,
 1225, 1225, 1226, 10:1362,
 1363
Polovtsi people 9:1214
Polycrates 3:356
Polynesia 7:974, 982, *983*, *985*, 985,
 988
polytheism *see* gods and goddesses
Pompeii 4:*449*, *531*, 535, 536, *537*,
 553, *556*
Pompeius, Gnaeus *see* Pompey
Pompeius, Gnaeus (son of Pompey)
 4:499
Pompeius, Sextus 4:499, 502–
 503
Pompey 4:*490*
 Augustus Caesar and 4:506
 Cicero and 4:490–491
 Egypt and 4:496, 497, 498
 first triumvirate and 4:493–494,
  495–496
 Parthia and 5:585
 Roman republic and 4:488,
  499
 Seleucid Empire and 5:586
 theater and 4:555
Pompey's Pillar 3:*400*
Pomponius, Marcus 4:471
pontifex maximus 4:493, 502
Pont Saint-Bénézet 8:*1088*
Pontus 4:*485*, 486
popes
 Byzantine Empire and
  6:799–800, 802, 9:1167, 1170
 Carolingian dynasty and 6:794,
  794–795
 Constantine I and 5:628
 development of the church and
  5:632
 emperors and 8:**1058–1069**
 Frederick II and 8:1072–1073
 Holy Roman Empire and 6:834,
  837, 839, 841–845
 Renaissance and 10:1406
 Rome and 8:1037–1038
 Tordesillas, Treaty of, and
  10:1375–1376
 western schism and 8:1082, 1089,
  1091–1093
 see also crusades; Roman Catholic
  Church; specific popes
Popol Vuh (Book of the
 Community) 10:1317, 1322
Poppaea Sabina 4:525, 527
populares (advocates of the people)
 4:481
population
 Black Death and 8:1084–
  1086
 China and 10:1419

city-states and 8:1036, 1039
Constantinople and 5:616, 618,
 9:1161
crusades and 9:1182
Dark Age Greece and 2:246
Great Zimbabwe and 9:1276
growth of 8:1026, 1082
Iceland and 9:1204
Neolithic period and 1:15
North American peoples and
 10:1348, 1350, 1351
pre-Columbian cultures and
 10:1307, 1332, 1336
Rome and 4:548
portrait painting 10:1404, 1405,
 1406, 1409
Portugal
 Africa and 9:1275, 1276, 1277
 exploration and 8:1093, 10:*1362*,
  1364, 1366–1367, 1369–1371
 medieval Europe and 8:1020
 Pacific islands and 7:988–989
 pre-Columbian cultures and
  10:1311
 Southeast Asia and 7:981
 Tordesillas, Treaty of, and
  10:1375–1376
 trade and 10:*1417*, 1418
Poseidon 2:167, 176, 190, 3:314
postal service, Persians and 2:245
Postclassic period, pre-Columbian
 cultures and 10:1304, 1309,
 1310, 1316, 1318
Postumas, Marcus 5:601
potlatch festivals 10:1358
pottery
 African 9:1259, *1262*
 bell-beaker culture and 1:*19*, 31
 Bükk culture and 1:*16*
 China and 7:870, 871–872
 corded-ware culture and 1:31
 Crete and 2:172
 funnel-beaker culture and
  1:18–19, 21
 Greece and 3:296, *298*, 301, *308*
 Hallstatt culture and 1:47
 India and 7:924, 927
 Japan and 7:906, *909*
 Minoans and 2:170, 173, 180
 Minyan people and 2:163
 Neolithic period and 1:16–17
 Pacific islands and 7:984, 987
 pre-Columbian cultures and
  10:1305, 1310, 1311, 1314,
  1315, *1323*, *1350*, 1350, *1352*
 Rössen and Michelsburg cultures
  and 1:18
 Sumerian people and 1:65
 Thera and 2:168
pottery wheels 7:872, 906
Poulnabrone dolmen 1:25
poverty
 Athens and 3:298, 300
 Constantinople and 5:621, 622
 Dark Age Greece and 2:246, 248
 Rome and 4:481–482, 548

Powhatan 10:1356, 1382
Praetorian Guard
 Caligula and 4:519–520, *521*,
  521
 Caracalla and 5:596
 Elagabalus and 5:597
 Galba, Sulpicius, and 4:532
 Pertinax, Helvius, and 5:592
 Postumas, Marcus, and 5:601
 Severus, Septimius, and 5:594
 Tiberius and 4:517
praetors 4:453, 470
 see also consuls
Prajapti 7:938
prayer
 Benedict of Nursia and 5:700
 Cycladic people and 2:166
 Greece and 3:312
 Hittites and 2:159
 Islam and 6:742, *743*, 749
 monasteries and 5:693, 694,
  6:824, 826
 muezzins and 6:743
Preclassic period, pre-Columbian
 cultures and 10:1304, 1306–
 1307, 1309, 1312, 1314, 1316
pre-Columbian cultures
 10:**1302–1311**
 see also specific cultures
predestination 5:685, 687
Predynastic period, Egypt 1:76
prefectures, Roman Empire and
 5:612
Prempeh I 9:1275
Prester John 9:1225, 10:1360
pretenders, Roman leadership and
 5:611
Preveza, Battle of 9:1253, 1255
Priam 2:193, 194
priestesses, Rome and 4:441
priests
 Assyrians and 2:217, 218
 Aztecs and 10:1326, *1327*, 1328,
  1331
 Babylonians and 1:119
 brahmins 7:925, 927, 946
 Bronze Age and 1:38, 39
 Chibcha people and 10:1310
 China and 7:873
 Christian 5:609, 685
 Egyptians and 1:74, 85, 100,
  107
 Greece and 3:312, 313, 315
 Hittites and 2:159, 160
 Incas and 10:1345
 India and 7:924
 Maya and 10:1318–1319, 1323
 Mycenaeans and 2:190
 North American peoples and
  10:1354
 pagan 5:596–597
 Persians and 2:244
 Sumerians and 1:65
primogeniture 6:828
Prince, The (Machiavelli) 10:1396,
 1397

princeps (first citizen) 4:506
 see also emperors, Roman
princes, Richard III and 8:1123,
 1124
printing, China and 7:901
printing presses 10:1391–1392,
 1408
prisoners of war, Aztecs and
 10:1328, 1329, 1330
professions, Sumerians and
 1:69
Prometheus Bound (Aeschylus)
 3:323
property rights
 Athens and 2:267, 269
 Babylonians and 1:113
 early Byzantine Empire and
  9:1165
 early Rome and 4:449, 453,
  550
 monasteries and 5:694, 700
 serfs and 6:823
 women and 5:664
 see also landownership
prophesy, Aztecs and 10:1335
Prophesy of Neferti (Egyptian text)
 1:82–83
prophets 6:741, 748
propoganda 6:785, 795
Propylaea 3:349
proscription lists 4:487, 502
prostitution 5:674
Protagoras 3:349, 352
Protestant Reformation 10:1393,
 1415, 1415
provinces
 Antoninus Pius and 4:544
 Assyrians and 2:217
 Augustus Caesar and 4:504, 506,
  514
 Aztecs and 10:1327
 civil strife and 4:532
 Claudius I and 4:522
 daily life in 4:546–547
 Domitian and 4:537–538
 Egypt 4:503
 Gaul 4:494–495
 Hadrian and 4:542–543
 imperial provinces 4:507–508
 Incas and 10:1340, 1343
 Macedonia and 4:478
 Nero and 4:531
 Persians and 2:236, 238, 245
 Pompey and 4:490–491
 Punic Wars and 4:470
 rebellion in 4:528–529, 531
 Roman Empire and 5:590, 594,
  604, 607–608
 Trajan and 4:538–539, 540
 Vespasian and 4:534–535
Provisions of Oxford 8:1076
Prusias II 4:475
prytane system (government
 administration) 3:307–308
Psamtik I 1:109
Pskov 9:1215, 1217

Ptolemaic dynasty 4:497
Ptolemy I 3:396, *398*, 398, 404,
    4:497
Ptolemy II 3:398, 404
Ptolemy XII Auletes 4:497
Ptolemy XIII 4:497, 498
Ptolemy of Alexandria 3:*405*,
    409–410, **10**:1368, 1372,
    1390–1391, *1391*, 1397
public assembly
    Athens and 2:267, 269, 3:304,
        306–307, 308–309, 344, 345,
        380
    early Rome and 4:449–550,
        451–452
    Sparta and 2:262–263
    see also senate, Roman
public opinion
    Roman emperors and 4:500, 516,
        531, 532
    tyranny and 3:294
public safety 4:509, 532, 550
public services 7:903, 958
public works, Incas and 10:1341,
    1347
Publius Aelius Hadrianus *see*
    Hadrian
Pueblo Bonito 10:*1351*, 1351
Pueblo people 10:1358, *1359*
pueblos 10:1348, 1350, *1351*, 1351
Pulakesin I 7:966
Pulakesin II 7:966
Pulcheria 5:666, *669*
Pulu *see* Tiglath-pileser I
Punic Wars **4**:464–475
punishments
    Assyrians and 2:212
    Aztecs and 10:1326–1327
    Code of Hammurabi and 1:113,
        115–116, 119
    Constantine I and 5:635
    early Rome and 4:441, 451, 453
    Germanic peoples and 5:662,
        664
    Greece and 2:260
    Hittites and 2:161
    Persians and 2:244
    Roman republic and 4:490
    see also legal systems
Punt 1:77, 98
Punta Arenas 10:*1380*
Puritans 10:1381, 1383
Purusha 7:936
Pushyamitra Shunga 7:929
Pydna, Battle of 4:478
Pylos 2:182, 187, 191
Pylos, Battle of 3:371
Pyramid of the Moon 10:*1308*
Pyramid of the Sun 10:*1308*, 1308
pyramids
    Egyptian 1:73–74, *75*, 75, 77, 78
    Nubian 5:*585*, 9:*1269*
    pre-Columbian cultures and
        10:1305, 1307, *1308*, 1308,
        1333
    see also ziggurats

Pyramid Texts 1:74, 77
Pyrrhic victories 4:462–463
Pyrrhon of Elis 3:412
Pyrrhus 4:461–462, *463*
Pythagoras 3:356–357, *358*, *359*
Pythia 3:313, 315
pyx, Córdoban 6:*773*
pyxis (jewelry box) 3:*350*

Q

Qarakhanid people 9:1232
Qarawiyin Mosque 9:*1241*
Qin dynasty 7:877, 879, 881, 891,
    893, 894
quadrants 10:1365
quaestors 4:451
Quaraish tribe 6:740, 743, 744, 752,
    755, 766
Quechua language 10:1336
Quechua people 10:1336
questions, Socrates and 3:362–363,
    364
Quetzalcoatl 10:*1303*, 1318, 1335
quipucamayoc (administrators)
    10:1341, *1343*
quipus (accounting system) 10:1341,
    1343
Qutb Minar 7:969, *970*
Qutb-ud-Din Aybak 7:968–969,
    970

R

race 7:874, 924
Rachel 2:226, 227
Radha 7:945
Rajaraja I 7:966
Rajendra I 7:966
Rajputs 7:963
Raleigh, Walter 10:1380, *1381*
Rama 7:*942*, 942, 943, 944
Ramadan 6:749
Ramesside period 1:105–107
ramming, naval warfare and 3:339,
    4:467
Ramses I 1:105
Ramses II 1:106, 2:153, 229
Ramses III 1:106–107, *107*
ransoms 8:1056, 1111
Raphael 10:1404, 1406
Rasthrakuta dynasty 7:966
Raven Floki 9:1204
Raydaniyya, Battle of 9:1252
Raymond IV of Toulouse 9:1185,
    1187, 1188–1189
Raymond VI of Toulouse 8:1025
Rea Silvia 4:438, *443*
rebellions
    China and 7:890, 894, 897, 898,
        899, 905
    in Italian cities 4:485–486
    Jewish people and 4:541
    provinces and 4:534–535
    Roman emperors and 4:528–529,
        531, 537, 540
    Spartacus and 4:489–490
    see also civil strife

Reconquista 6:762, 770,
    8:1014–1025, 1082, 9:1235,
    10:1364
Red Eyebrows 7:898
Redjedef 1:74
Reformation 8:1094
reform movements, Roman
    Catholic Church and *see*
    church reform movements
reform movements, Roman
    republic and 4:479–481,
    481–482, 490
regencies
    Han dynasty and 7:896–897,
        898–899
    Macedonian Empire and 3:396
    Nero and 4:524–525
Regimen in Acute Diseases
    (Hippocrates) 3:411
regional differences
    Christianity and 5:681
    Islamic world and 6:773
    North American peoples and
        10:1356–1359
reincarnation 5:682, 685,
    7:937–938, 946, 9:1194
Rekhmire 1:99
relay runners, Incas and 10:1346,
    1347
relics, Christian 5:695, 6:735
relief sculptures
    Assyrian 2:*201*, *212*, *215*, 215,
        221, *231*
    Greek 2:*262*, *265*, 3:*307*, *317*
    Hittites and 2:158
    India and 7:*928*, *940*, *961*
    Palmyra and 5:*602*
    Parthians and 6:*728*
    Persian 2:*233*, *239*, 240, 3:*338*,
        5:*600*, 6:*729*, 729
    Phoenician 2:205
    Pictish 5:*664*
    pre-Columbian cultures and
        10:*1318*
    Roman 4:*480*, *515*, *541*, *547*,
        550, 5:*605*, *681*
    Sicily and 8:*1023*
    Southeast Asia and 7:*973*
    Syrian 5:*597*
religion, feudalism and 6:823–824,
    825
religious beliefs
    afterlife and 4:526
    Akkadians and 1:61, 61–62
    Aryan people and 7:926
    Assyrians and 2:211, 218
    Aztecs and 10:1329–1331,
        1334
    Babylonians and 1:117, 119
    barbarian invaders and 5:658,
        660
    Bronze Age and 1:38–39
    Buddhism 7:902, 928–929, 930,
        946–959
    Byzantine Empire and 5:670
    Celtic people and 1:46, 52

China and 7:873, 892, 893, 904
Confucianism and 7:886
Egypt and 1:74, 75, 84, 95, 100,
    101–102, 104
Etruscans and 4:445
European settlers and 10:1381,
    1383
funnel-beaker culture and 1:19,
    24
Germanic peoples and 5:648, 654
Greek 3:**310–317**
Hinduism 7:927, **932–945**
Hittites and 2:159–160
Incas and 10:1340–1341, 1343,
    1344
India and 7:920, 925, 931, 967
Israelites and 2:225–226, 227,
    228, 229
Jainism 7:927, *931*, 948
Japan and 7:909, 909–910, 911
Manichaeism 5:682, 6:730–731,
    733
Maya and 10:1317, 1320, 1322
Minoans and 2:176–177, 178, 180
Mycenaeans and 2:190
Neolithic period and 1:26,
    27–28, 29
North American peoples and
    10:1354–1355, 1358
Pacific islands and 7:987, 988
paganism 5:632–634, 635, 636,
    636–637, 687, 691
Persians and 2:241–244
Phoenicians and 2:206
pre-Columbian cultures and
    10:1302, 1309, *1311*
pre-Islamic Arabia and 6:736,
    741
Pythagoras and 3:356–357
Renaissance and 10:1326,
    1403–1404
Rome and 4:493, 511,
    5:596–597, 599, 601
Scholasticism and 10:1384,
    1386–1390
Scythians and 1:51
Shintoism 7:910
Southeast Asia and 7:975, 979,
    981
Sparta and 2:264
Sumerians and 1:56, 62, 64, 65,
    66, 69
warfare and 10:1414–1415
Zoroastrianism 6:726, 730, 731,
    733
    see also burial practices;
        Christianity; gods and
        goddesses; Islam; Judaism
religious festivals 3:301, 312, 315,
    318, 320
religious law, Ottoman Turks and
    9:1250
religious orders
    agricultural improvements and
        8:1029
    education and 10:1384

religious orders (continued)
  Henry the Navigator and
    10:1366
  medieval Europe and 8:1035
  mendicant friars and 8:1042
  military forces and 8:1014, 1025,
    1080, 1080, 9:1190
  Safavid Empire and 10:1418
  Sufis and 9:1233
  see also monasteries
religious rituals
  mystery religions and 3:315–
    316
  pre-Columbian cultures and
    10:1343, 1345, 1353, 1354
  Vedas and 7:935
religious sects 3:356–357
religious tolerance
  Buddhism and 7:930
  Byzantine Empire and 5:613,
    614, 9:1160, 1166–1167,
    1172
  Charlemagne and 6:810
  Christianity and 9:1160
  Frederick II and 8:1070
  iconoclasm and 9:1166–1167,
    1172
  Islamic world and 6:747, 766–
    767, 9:1238
  Kushan India and 7:931
  Mongols and 9:1226
  Normans and 8:1023, 1025
  Ottoman Turks and 9:1245, 1249,
    1250, 10:1418
  Persians and 6:733–734
  Southeast Asia and 7:979
religious visions 6:741–742, 8:1112,
  9:1188
reliquaries 6:789, 9:1171
Rembrandt van Rijn 10:1409
Remus 4:438, 438–439, 439
Renaissance 8:1093, 1094, 1096,
  1099, 10:1398–1409
republic, Roman 4:447–455,
  488–503
Republic, The (Plato) 3:347–348,
  367
resettlement policies, Incas and
  10:1343
Re 1:74, 101–102
Resurrection of the Son of Theophilus
  (Masaccio) 10:1401, 1403–
  1404
Revellers (Aristophanes) 3:325
revolution and reform, Rome and
  4:476–487
Rheims 8:1112
rhetoric 3:345, 361, 362, 411–412,
  4:557
  see also orators
rhino horn cup, Chinese
  10:1414
Rhodes 3:396, 4:476, 9:1195,
  1195, 1251, 1252, 1255
Riade, Battle of 6:830
Rib-Addi 1:101

Richard I (the Lionheart) 8:1054,
  1056, 1056, 1076, 9:1192
Richard II 8:1108, 1109, 1114
Richard III 8:1120, 1123, 1124,
  1125, 1125
Richard of Gloucester see
  Richard III
Richard of York 8:1116–1118,
  1123, 1124
Richard the Kingmaker see
  Neville, Richard (earl of
  Warwick)
riches of Islam 6:776–787
Rig Veda 6:731, 7:925, 935
Ripon Cathedral 8:1046
rise and fall of African empires
  9:1266–1277
rise of Islam 6:752–763
ritsuryo system 7:910–911
River Garonne, Battle of 6:761,
  792
roadbuilding 1:21
roads 2:177, 245, 3:301, 4:508,
  10:1346, 1347
Roanoke Island 10:1380
Robert I 6:827
Robert Guiscard 8:1023, 1024,
  1024
Robert of Flanders 9:1185
Robert of Gloucester 8:1051
Robert of Normandy 6:828
Robert the Bruce 8:1077
Robert the Pious 6:827
Robert the Strong 6:827
rock paintings, San people and
  9:1262
Roderick 6:760
Roger I 8:1023, 1023, 1025
Roger II 8:1025
Roggeveen, Jacob 7:986, 989
Roland 6:798, 801
Rolfe, John 10:1382
Rollo 6:817, 819, 8:1023
Roman allies 4:482
Roman baths 4:524, 553, 554
Roman Catholic Church
  Arnold of Brescia and 8:1040
  Becket, Thomas, and 8:1053
  Burgundy and 8:1129
  Charlemagne and 6:788, 807
  crisis in 8:1086–1089, 1090,
    1091–1093
  eastern Europe and 9:1216
  education and 10:1387, 1388
  feudalism and 6:822, 823–824,
    826
  Franks and 5:656, 657, 6:791–
    792
  Greek philosophers and
    10:1389
  Holy Roman Empire and
    6:835
  humanism and 10:1397, 1400
  Inquisition and 8:1019–1020
  Japan and 7:917
  landownership and 6:790, 792

mendicant friars and 8:1042
moneylending and 8:1033
music and 10:1407
Ostrogoths and 5:648
Otto I and 6:830–831
political power and 6:824–825,
  835, 8:1058, 1061, 1064, 1075,
  1081, 1086, 9:1170, 1191
Protestant Reformation and
  10:1415
Renaissance and 8:1099
Rome and 8:1037
taxation and 8:1079, 1081
Vandals and 5:653–654, 671
Visigoths and 5:645
Vulgate Bible and 5:697
warfare and 8:1018
western schism and 8:1089,
  1091–1093
  see also Christianity; church
  reform movements; crusades;
  popes
Romance languages 5:665
Roman Empire
  Africa and 9:1266, 1269
  barbarian invaders and 5:640–
    657
  Charlemagne and 6:799, 808
  China and 7:899
  Christianity and 5:609, 634, 636,
    687, 695–696
  daily life in 5:658–665
  decline of 5:590–603
  disintegration of 5:604–615
  edges of 5:582–589
  Germanic peoples and 1:53
  India and 7:931
  Islamic world and 6:751
  Persians and 6:728, 729, 733,
    734
  see also Byzantine Empire;
  emperors, Byzantine; emperors,
  Roman; Holy Roman Empire;
  Rome
Romanian language 4:540
Romanization policy 4:522
Romans 2:195, 200, 202, 207, 252
Romanus II 9:1169, 1175
Romanus III 9:1178
Romanus IV 9:1178–1179
Romanus Lecapenus 9:1174,
  1175
Rome
  Augustus, Age of, and 4:504–515
  Aurelian Wall 5:603
  Byzantine Empire and 5:675,
    676
  Celtic people and 1:50, 52
  Christianity and 5:609, 678
  city of 4:508–509
  daily life and 4:548–557
  early history of 4:438–455
  early wars and conquests of
    4:456–463
  end of the republic and 4:488–
    503

expanding the empire and 4:532–
  547
fires in 4:527–528, 535, 548
Germanic people and 1:53
Holy Roman Empire and
  6:834–835, 840, 843, 844
Islamic world and 6:780
Julio-Claudian emperors and
  4:516–531
legal system and 5:664
maps and 4:491, 534
medieval Europe and
  8:1037–1039, 1040, 1060–
  1061
origins of 4:438
popes and 8:1088–1089
Punic Wars and 4:464–475
Renaissance and 10:1398,
  1406
republic and 4:447–455, 488–
  503
revolution and reform and
  4:476–487
Vandals and 5:653
Visigoths and 5:643, 645
warfare and 4:456–463
  see also Italy; Roman Empire
Romulus 4:438, 438–439, 439–440
Romulus Augustulus 5:647, 647,
  9:1163
Roncesvalles, Battle of 6:798–799,
  801, 801
roofboxes, passage tombs and 1:25
Rössen culture 1:18, 21
Roussillon 6:762
Roxana 3:396
Rubicon, crossing of 4:495, 496
Rudolf of Burgandy 6:827
Rudolf of Swabia 6:843, 844
Rudra 7:939
Rufinus 5:666, 668
rulers of the 13th century CE
  8:1070–1081
rules, university students and
  10:1386
ruling classes
  Bronze Age and 1:38
  Celtic people and 1:50, 52
  Egypt and 1:73, 78, 80, 81
  Hallstatt culture and 1:48
  Scythians and 1:51
  Sumerians and 1:56–57
  see also government
Rum 9:1234, 1241
Rurik 9:1200, 1201, 1208, 1210,
  1210
Russia 8:1101, 9:1175, 1177,
  1208–1217, 1223, 1227–
  1228
Rutilus, Marcius 4:453–454
Rwanda 9:1275–1276

S
Sabaea 9:1268–1269
Sabine people 4:439–440, 443,
  444

sacerdotal writing 2:204
Sacrifice of Isaac, The (Caravaggio)
2:*226*
sacrifices
    Aryan people and 7:926, 932,
        934
    Christianity and 5:635
    Greece and 3:312, *313*
    Vedic religion and 7:936, 946
    see also human sacrifice
sacrilege, Alcibiades and 3:376
Sadducees 4:541
sadhu (holy man) 7:*938*
Safavid Empire 10:1414, 1415,
    1418, 1419
Safavid people 9:1240, 1252
Sahara Desert 5:589, 9:1260
sails, medieval ships and 10:1369
Saint Anthony's Monastery 5:*691*
Saint Michael's Monastery
    9:*1213*
Saint Peter's Basilica 10:1406
saints
    Buddhism and 7:956, 957
    Byzantine Empire and 9:1175,
        1180
    Christianity and 5:656, 678, 688,
        690, 691–695, 696–697,
        699–701
Saint Sophia's Cathedral 9:*1209*
Saint-Victor, Abbey of 5:696
Sajo River, Battle of 9:1227
Saka people 7:929
Sakya clan 7:946
Saladin 6:774, 8:1056, 1068,
    9:*1191*, 1191, *1192*, 1234,
    1235, 1236
Salamis, Battle of 2:239, 3:*334*, 334,
    336, 339, 340
sale, Holy Roman emperorship
    and 5:592
Salian dynasty 6:836–837, 839,
    841–845
Salian Franks 5:654
Salonika 9:1246
salt mining 1:45
Samaria 2:217, 231
Samarkand 6:763, 7:895, 9:1223,
    1228, 1229
Samarra 6:776, 786, 787
Samnites 4:460–461, *461*
Samoa 7:982, 984
Samos 3:*331*, 356
Samsu-ilina 1:120
Samu-abu 1:110
Samudra Gupta 7:960
Samuel 2:230
Samuel of Bulgaria 9:1176, 1178
samurai 7:913–914, 916
Sanatana Dharma (Eternal Law) *see*
    Hinduism
Sancho II 8:1017, 1021
Sancho III 8:1016
sanctuaries *see* temples
Sanctuary of Athena Pronaia
    3:*316*

Sangallo, Giuliano da 10:1403
Sanhaja Berber people 9:1271
sankyo (musical instrument)
    9:*1274*
San Lorenzo 10:1306–1307
San people 9:1256, 1262, 1264,
    1265, 1275, 1277
San Salvador 10:1374
Sanskrit 7:940, 971, 975
Santa Maria 10:1372, 1374
Santorini *see* Thera
Sappho 2:*250*
Saracens 8:1020, 1022
Sarai (Mongol capital) 9:1215,
    1228
Sarai (Sarah) 2:225, 226
Sarasvati 7:940, 945
Sarasvati-Ghaggar river system
    7:923
Sardinia 4:469, 470, 5:653, 8:1019,
    1025
Sardis 2:234, 3:327
Sargon 1:59–61, 114
Sargon II 2:155, 217–218, 231
Sarmatians 1:48, 4:539
Sarnath, temple at 7:*950*
Sassanid dynasty 5:585, 613,
    6:726–735, 755
Satavahanihara 7:929
Satavhana kings 7:965
satire 3:325, 378
satrapies *see* provinces
Saturnius 4:537, 538
satyr plays 3:320, 324
Saud, Abdul Aziz ibn 6:775
Saudi Arabia 6:775
Saul 2:230
Saxons 5:663, 6:792, 796–797,
    800
Saxony 6:819, 829, 836, 8:1094
Sayfuwa people 9:1273, 1273–
    1274
Sayyid dynasty 7:970
Scaevola, Mucius 4:456, *459*
Scandinavia 8:1082, 1098–1100,
    9:1196, 1201, 1205
Scheffer, Ary 6:*800*
Scheherazade 6:781
Schliemann, Heinrich 2:163,
    182–183, 184, 185, 186,
    192–193, 195
Scholasticism and humanism
    10:1384–1397
Schoolmen 10:1388–1389
School of Athens, The (Raphael)
    3:*353*, 10:1404
School of Miletus 3:352, 354
sciences
    Babylonians and 1:119
    Byzantine Empire and
        9:1174–1175
    Egyptians and 1:77
    Europe and 10:1390–1391, 1395,
        1398
    Greeks and 3:361, 404, 407–
        408

India and 7:961–962
    Islamic culture and 6:782, 783
    see also astronomy; mathematics;
        medicine
Scipio, Ganaeus Cornelius 4:474
Scipio, Publius Cornelius 4:471,
    473–474
Scipio, Quintus Metellus 4:496, 498
Scipio Aemilianus 4:481, *482*, 482
Scipio Africanus 4:*470*, *472*, 474,
    475, 480
Scotland 8:1077, 1098
Scots 5:663
scribes 2:176, 10:1328
scriptures
    Buddhism and 7:*953*, 957
    Vedas and 7:932, 935, 936–937,
        937–938, 940, 945, 946
    see also Bible; Koran
sculpture
    Assyrian 2:213, 215
    Aztecs and 10:*1329*, 1333
    Babylonian 2:*219*
    Greek 2:*163*, *166*, *257*, *259*,
        267
    Hittite 2:*151*, *152*, *154*, *155*,
        158, *159*
    Mayan architecture and 10:1315
    Minoan 2:179
    Olmec people and 10:*1306*,
        1307, 1307
    Persian 2:*245*
    pre-Columbian cultures and
        10:1305, 1307, 1310
    Renaissance and 10:1404,
        1406
    Toltec people and 10:*1309*,
        1309
    see also relief sculptures
scurvy, European explorers and
    10:1377
Scythians 1:46, *48*, 48–49, *49*, 51,
    2:232, 238
seafaring
    Athens and 2:264
    Corinth and 3:295, 296
    Dong Son civilization and 7:974
    Pacific islands and 7:985, 987
    Phoenicians and 2:196, 198–199,
        200–202
    Southeast Asia and 7:972, 976
    trade and 3:304
    see also ships and shipbuilding
Sealand dynasty 1:120
sea levels 7:906, 921, 972, 10:1348
seals 2:180, 181, 3:*339*
Sea Peoples 1:44, 106, 107, 2:153,
    155, 192, 210, 222, 230
seasonal camps 1:6
seasons, Mayan calendars and
    10:1320
Sebastian 5:*610*
Sebetwane 9:1277
Second Crusade 9:1189–1191,
    1190
Second Dynasty of Isin 1:121

Second Intermediate period, Egypt
    1:90–91
Second Macedonian War 4:476,
    478
Second Persian War 3:330–339
Second Punic War 4:470–475, 476,
    478
second triumvirate 4:502–503
secularism, Greek 3:352
    see also philosophy
seiges 3:386, 391
Sei Shonagon 7:913
Sejanus 4:517–518
Seleucid dynasty 3:399, 400, 401,
    402, 5:584–585, 586
Seleucid Empire 4:476
Seleucus I 3:*391*, 398, 399, *401*,
    401, 5:586, 7:928
Seleucus IV 5:586
self-denial, monasteries and 5:693,
    695
Selim I 9:1249–1252
Selim II 9:1255
Seljuk Turks
    Byzantine Empire and
        9:1178–1179, 1181
    crusades and 9:1182, 1184, 1187,
        1187–1188, 1189, 1190–1191
    Islamic world and 6:773, 774,
        9:1230, 1232, *1234*, 1234
    Mongols and 9:1235
    Ottoman Turks and 9:1242
Semi-Arianism 5:630, 631
Semitic languages 9:1258
Semitic people 1:54, 89, 2:229, 252,
    3:310, 9:1268–1269
    see also Israelites
Sempach, Battle of 8:*1096*
Sempronius Longus 4:471
senate, Roman
    Christianity and 5:634, 636
    civil strife and 4:486
    Curia 4:*455*
    decline of Rome and 5:590,
        598
    early republic and 4:448, 449
    early Rome and 4:440
    emperors and 4:496, 498, 500,
        500–501, 504, 506–507, 517,
        522, 531, 533–534, 535–536,
        538–539, 544
    first triumvirate and 4:495
    kings and 4:444, 446
    military forces and 4:493
    plebians and 4:454–455
    reform movements and
        4:480–481, 482
    Samnites and 4:460
    succession of Roman leadership
        and 4:532
Senebtyfy 1:*84*
Seneca 4:524, 525, 527, *529*, 529,
    555
Seneca people 10:1356
Sengoku period 7:917
Sennacherib 2:217, 218, *231*, 231

Seqenenre 1:91, 92
Serapeum 5:636–637
Serbia 9:1177, 1245
serfdom 5:606
serfs 6:819, 821, 822, 823, 8:1041
Sergius III 6:826
Sertorius, Quintus 4:488
Servius Tullius 4:442
Sesostris I 1:79, 83–84, 87
Sesostris II 1:87
Sesostris III 1:87, 89
Seti I 1:96, 105–106
Setnakht 1:106
settlement
    early humans and 1:6
    English 6:816
    Natufian culture and 1:11
    Pacific islands and 7:984–985, 987
    worldwide 10:1410, 1414
Seven Against Thebes (Aeschylus)
    3:323
Seventh Crusade 9:1236
Severan Arch 5:593
Severan dynasty 5:593–596
Severus 5:610, 611
Severus, Septimius 5:585, 592–595,
    593, 616, 618
Severus, Sulpicius 5:696
Seville 6:760, 8:1017
sewers see plumbing and water
    supplies
Sforza, Francesco 8:1096
Sforza, Ludovico 10:1404, 1405,
    1405
Shabaka 1:109, 9:1266
shaft tombs 2:185–186
Shahi dynasty 7:969
Shah-nameh (The Book of Kings)
    6:732
Shahryar 6:781
Shaka 9:1277, 1277
Shakespeare, William 3:407
Shalmaneser I 2:210
Shalmaneser III 2:207, 213,
    215–216
Shalmaneser V 2:217
shamans, early Africa and 9:1262
Shamshi-Adad I 1:115, 2:208,
    210
Shandong Peninsula 9:1222
Shang Di 7:873
Shang dynasty 1:33, 35, 7:871, 873,
    875, 876
Shang Yang 7:877
Shankara 7:964
Shapur (brother of Ardashir I)
    6:726
Shapur I 5:600, 601, 6:726, 729,
    729, 730, 730, 731, 733,
    7:931
Shapur II 5:613, 6:733, 733
Sharkalisharri 1:62
Shauska see Ishtar
shawabti figures 1:87
sheikhs, Bedouin nomads and
    6:738

Sheshonk 1:109
Shi Huang Di 7:877, 879, 879
Shi'ite Islam 6:757, 758, 758, 767,
    769, 773, 786, 10:1415
Shi-ji (Records of the Grand
    Historian) (Sima Qian) 7:886,
    899
Shiloh, sanctuary at 2:229
Shintoism 7:910
ships and shipbuilding
    China and 10:1419, 1420
    European conquests and 10:1421
    Islamic world and 6:777,
        779–780
    longships, Viking 6:809, 9:1196,
        1202, 1202, 1204
    medieval Europe and 6:809, 814,
        817, 10:1363, 1367, 1369
    Minoans and 2:172
    Phoenicians and 2:198, 201, 205
    Rome and 4:465, 466, 467
    Vandals and 5:652
ships' logs 2:202, 205
shipwrecks 5:589
Shi Shu (Four Books) 7:887
Shiva 7:920, 937, 938, 939, 940,
    943, 943, 945, 963, 966
shoemakers 2:266, 3:303, 4:550
shoguns (military commanders)
    7:914, 916–917
Shomu 7:912
shopkeepers 4:480
Shotoku 7:910
Shravakayana Buddhism 7:956
shrines
    Buddhist 7:930, 950, 951, 955
    household 4:449
    Incas and 10:1343
    Mycenaeans and 2:190
shudras (laborers and servants)
    7:925, 927, 946
Shu dynasty 7:899, 900
Shulgi 1:63, 65
Shunga dynasty 7:929
Shutruk-Nahhunte I 1:121
Siberia 10:1302, 1304, 1348
Sichelgaita 8:1024
Sicilian Vespers 8:1074–1075,
    1075
Sicily
    Aragon and 8:1019
    Byzantine Empire and 5:673,
        9:1163
    Greece and 2:254, 3:296,
        373–374, 376
    Holy Roman Empire and
        8:1060, 1063, 1064, 1070,
        1072, 1073–1075, 1096
    Innocent III and 8:1065
    medieval Europe and 6:817
    Mongols and 9:1200
    Normans and 8:1023, 1025
    Ottoman Turks and 9:1255
    Punic Wars and 4:467, 468–469,
        470, 473
    Rome and 4:462, 464–465

Saracens and 8:1020, 1022
    Vandals and 5:653
Siddharta Gautama see Buddha
sieges
    of Antioch 9:1187, 1188
    of Baghdad 6:772, 775
    of Belgrade 9:1254
    Carthage and 4:481
    of Constantinople 6:762, 763,
        9:1172, 1247
    of Damascus 9:1190
    of Jerusalem 9:1189
    Mongols and 9:1222
    of Nancy 8:1132
    of Orléans 8:1110, 1112, 1112
    of Paris 6:832, 9:1199–1200,
        1201
    of Rhodes 9:1255
    Rome and 5:675
    of Seville 6:760
Siffin, Battle of 6:756
Sigismund of Hungary 9:1248,
    1248
Sigurd's Helmet 9:1197
Silbury Hill 1:28, 31
Silius, Gaius 4:523
silk 5:589
Silk Road 5:589, 7:898, 899
silver artifacts 2:156, 7:901, 902,
    9:1232, 10:1421
silver mining 4:466
Sima Qian 7:886, 899
Sima Yan 7:900
Simeon of Bulgaria 9:1177
Simeon Stylites 5:695, 695
simony 6:838, 839, 8:1086–1087,
    1088
Simpson, James H. 10:1351
Sinai Peninsula 1:83
Sindbad and the Old Man of the
    Sea 6:780, 780
single-grave culture 1:28, 31
Sinhalese people 7:929
Sioux people 10:1354, 1356, 1356
Sirat Rasul Allah (The Life of God's
    Prophet) 6:739
Sistine Chapel 10:1406
Sita 7:942, 943, 944, 945
Six Dynasties period 7:899–900
Skanda Gupta 7:962
skandhas (elements) 7:952–953
Skara Brae 1:30, 30
skenes, Greek drama and 3:320
Skepticism 5:683
Skeptics 3:412
slash-and-burn agriculture 1:16,
    19, 10:1312
slavery
    Africa and 9:1272, 1274–
        1275
    agriculture and 4:476
    Assyrians and 2:214
    Babylonians and 1:115
    Carthage and 4:469

Celtic people and 1:50
China and 7:877
Christianity and 5:635
debts and 4:453, 455
early Rome and 4:446
Egyptians and 1:86
Germanic peoples and 5:664
Greece and 2:253, 255, 266–
    267, 3:308, 347, 403
Islam and 6:743
Japan and 7:911
Macedonia and 3:388
Mycenaeans and 2:189
Peloponnesian War and 3:376
Portuguese traders and 10:1367
pre-Columbian cultures and
    10:1326–1327, 1358
Punic Wars and 4:481
Roman Empire and 5:606
Spartacus and 4:489–490
Sumerians and 1:57
Vikings and 9:1196, 1205
Slavic peoples
    Bulgarian Empire and 9:1177
    Byzantine Empire and 5:625,
        677, 9:1165
    Charlemagne and 6:797–798
    East Francia and 6:828
    Otto the Great and 6:831
    Russia and 9:1208
    Vikings and 9:1196, 1200–1201,
        1203
sleds, Neolithic period and 1:21
slit-drums 10:1310
Sluys, Battle of 8:1103, 1104
smelting 1:32, 37, 41
Smendes 1:107
Smenkhkare 1:104
Smith, John 10:1381, 1382, 1382,
    1383
smiths 1:36–37, 6:780–781
Snefru 1:74, 83
soapstone seals 7:920, 923, 934
social classes
    arts and 10:1400–1401, 1403
    Babylonian 1:113, 115–116
    Carolingian Empire and 6:808
    China and 7:873
    clothing and 10:1344–1345
    Constantinople and 5:623
    Egyptian 1:77, 86, 97, 99–100
    feudalism and 6:821–822
    Greece and 3:298, 299, 300–301,
        304, 367
    India and 7:918, 924–925, 927
    Islamic world and 6:743–744,
        768
    Japan and 7:911, 917
    landownership and 4:476
    medieval Europe and 8:1078,
        1086
    military forces and 4:484
    pre-Columbian cultures and
        10:1316, 1326
    Roman Catholic Church and
        6:825

Rome and 4:446–447, 446–455, 479–481, 481–482, 488, 492, 542, 543
Sumerian 1:56–57
Vikings and 9:1205
social clubs 4:550
social mobility 6:822, 823
social structure
barbarian invaders and 5:658, 660
Confucianism and 7:884, 885–886, 890, 894
early Africa and 9:1259, 1261
Greece and 2:246, 251, 253, 258, 260–261, 266–267
Greek colonies and 2:256
Hittites and 2:155–156
Minoans and 2:175–177
Mycenaeans and 2:189, 191
pre-Columbian cultures and 10:1306, 1307, 1310, 1318–1319, 1324, 1326–1327, 1340, 1343–1344, 1353, 1357–1358
Rome and 5:593–594, 595
Society Islands 7:982
Socrates 3:348, 356, 361, 361–365, 362, 363, 366, 373
Socratic irony 3:363
Soga clan 7:910
Soissons, Battle of 5:659
solar calendars 10:1320
solar eclipses 3:354, 356
Solomon 2:198, 199, 223, 231
Solomonid dynasty 9:1268, 1269
Solomon Islands 7:982
Solon 2:267, 267, 269, 3:294, 298, 328, 328
Solutrean people 1:11
Somerset, duke of 8:1116
Somnath, temple at 7:968, 969
Song dynasty 7:902–904, 904, 9:1224, 1226
Songhai 9:1272–1273, 10:1418
Song of Roland 6:798, 801, 801
Sont Strait 8:1097
Sophism 3:348, 361, 362, 364, 411–412
Sophocles 3:323–324, 349
Soshangane 9:1277
souls 7:952–953, 964
south African kingdoms 9:1277
South America
European explorers and 10:1375–1376, 1377
Incas and 10:1336–1347
legal systems and 5:677
pre-Columbian cultures and 10:1302
settlement of 10:1410
Spanish conquistadores and 10:1419, 1421
Southeast Asia 7:972–981, 974, 9:1226
southeastern tribes 10:1357
Southern Song era 7:903–904
southwestern tribes 10:1358–1359

Spain
absolute monarchies and 8:1094
barbarian invaders and 5:643, 645, 652, 660
Byzantine Empire and 5:618, 676, 9:1163
Carthage and 4:469, 470–471, 474
Charlemagne and 6:798, 801
Charles Martel and 6:792
crusades and 9:1182
Greece and 2:254
Incas and 10:1342, 1347
Islamic world and 6:759–760, 768, 770, 771, 785, 9:1235, 1238
Phoenicians and 2:196, 200
pre-Columbian cultures and 10:1311, 1323, 1333, 1334, 1335
Reconquista and 6:762, 8:1016–1020, 1082
Rome and 4:482, 488, 493, 496, 499, 504, 513, 529, 531
smiths in 6:780–781
Southeast Asia and 7:981
Tordesillas, Treaty of, and 10:1375–1376
weapons and armor of 10:1419, 1421
Spanish Wars 4:479
Sparta
Athens and 2:258–268, 261, 3:302, 340, 342, 348
citizenship and 2:253
Cleomenes III and 3:403
colonization and 2:251
First Persian War and 3:329, 330
military forces and 2:265
Peloponnesian War and 3:342, 344, 368–383
Persians and 2:239, 3:326
Plataea, Battle of, and 3:337
Second Persian War and 3:331, 334, 336
Thermopylae, Battle of, and 3:333
Troy and 2:182
tyranny and 3:294
Spartacus 4:489–490, 492
Spartan Confederacy 3:342, 344
spearthrowers 1:7
spear-tips 7:872
specific gravity 3:408, 410
speechmaking, North American peoples and 10:1355
spelling and grammar, medieval Europe and 10:1394
spending, government 4:516–517, 520, 531, 532–533, 534, 539, 5:595
sphinxes, Persian 2:233
Spice Islands 7:980, 981, 10:1362, 1363, 1371, 1376, 1377

spice trade 7:931, 980–981, 10:1362–1363, 1370–1371
spies, Aztecs and 10:1328
spinning 3:349
spirits, Greek 3:310–311
Spitsbergen Islands 10:1378
sports 2:169, 177, 5:622, 624
see also games
Sri Ranganathaswamy Temple 7:941
Srivijaya mandala 7:976, 977
Stabiae 4:535, 536
stag, carving of 1:15
stained-glass windows 5:697, 6:815, 8:1036, 1067
St. Albans, Battle of 8:1116
Stamford Bridge, Battle of 8:1048
Standard of Ur 1:58, 59
standing stones 1:20, 24, 25–27, 27, 29, 29
states, China and 7:875, 877, 879, 882, 894, 899
Statilia Messalina 4:527
statues see relief sculptures; sculpture
statues, Easter Island and 7:986, 986
statuettes 1:7, 2:165–166, 167, 179, 190, 248
status symbols, Bronze Age and 1:37–38
Stauracius 9:1171
steam turbines 3:408, 409
Stefan Dusan 9:1245
steles
Akkadian 1:60–61
Assyrians and 2:213
Canaan and 2:229
Code of Hammurabi and 1:112, 113, 116
Egyptian 1:85
Greece and 3:327
of Naram-Sin 1:63
pre-Columbian cultures and 10:1305, 1319
Stephen 5:678, 687
Stephen I (Hungary) 6:837
Stephen II (pope) 6:794, 795
Stephen III (pope) 6:796, 798
Stephen of Blois 8:1051
Step Pyramid 1:73, 75, 75
Steuben, Charles 6:762
Sthaviras (Elders) 7:956
Stilicho 5:642, 654
Stilicho, Flavius 5:637, 666
Stoicism 3:413, 4:544, 555, 557
stone, tools and 1:6
Stone Age see Neolithic period; Paleolithic period
stone circles 1:26–27, 29
Stonehenge 1:26, 29, 29
stonemasons 2:158
stone sculptures, pre-Columbian cultures and 10:1306, 1307, 1309, 1329

stone tools 9:1256
Story of Sinuhe (Egyptian text) 1:83–84
Strabo 9:1266
Stralsund, Treaty of 8:1098
strategoi (commanders-in-chief) 3:345, 373, 377
student life, medieval Europe and 10:1384, 1386
stupas 7:950, 951, 955
stylites (pillars) 5:695
Styx 4:526, 526
succession
Antonine emperors and 4:538
Byzantine Empire and 5:624, 669, 6:763, 9:1158
caliphs and 6:755–756, 756–757, 758, 764, 771, 772
Capetian dynasty and 6:827, 827–828
Carolingian Empire and 6:803, 811, 812–813, 817–818
Chinese dynasties and 7:875, 896–897
Holy Roman Empire and 8:1058
Hundred Years' War and 8:1102–1113
Julio-Claudian emperors and 4:516, 517–518, 519, 521
Mamluk dynasty and 9:1237–1238
Merovingian dynasty and 6:788
Mongols and 9:1218, 1227
political leadership and 10:1340, 1415–1416
Roman leadership and 4:515, 532, 543, 5:590, 595, 598, 599, 603, 610–611, 612
Russia and 9:1212–1213
Wars of the Roses and 8:1114–1125
Suevi people 1:53
suffering, Buddhism and 7:950–951, 953
Suffolk, duke of 8:1116
Sufis 9:1230, 1233
Sui dynasty 7:900–901
Süleyman (son of Orhan) 9:1244–1245
Süleyman I 9:1250, 1252, 1252, 1253, 1255, 10:1419
Sulla, Lucius Cornelius 4:483, 486, 486–487, 488
Sulpicianus 5:592
Sulpicius, Publius 4:486
Sumatra 7:967, 975
Sumer 1:62, 123, 2:208, 225
Sumerian people 1:54–69, 118
Sumerian world, map of 1:56
Summa Theologiae (Aquinas) 10:1389, 1389
Sun Chariot of Trundholm 1:38
sundials 3:354, 410
Sundiata Keita 9:1271
Sunni Ali 9:1272

Sunni Islam 6:758, 764, 766, 767, 772, 10:1415
sun worship 1:39, *100*, 101–102
Suppiluliumas I 1:104–105, 2:152
Suppliants (Aeschylus) 3:323
supplies, warfare and 3:374, 394–395
Susa 2:221, 3:390, 393, 395
Svyatopolk the Accursed 9:1212
Svyatoslav 9:1203, 1210
Swabia 6:819, 829, 8:1094
Swabian League of Cities 8:1094
Swahili 9:1264, 1275
Sweden 8:1098, 1098–1099, 1100, 9:1199, 1200–1201, 1203, 1205, 1217
Sweyn Forkbeard 6:816, 819, 8:1046, 9:1198–1199
Swiss Confederation 8:1094, *1096*
Switzerland 8:1132
Swordbrothers 8:1025
Sylvester I 5:*630*, 9:*1161*
Sylvester II 6:834
Sylvester III 6:837
Symmachus 5:636, 683
syncretism 3:403
Syracuse 2:*254*, 254, 3:373–374, *375*, 376, 408, 4:464, 473
Syria
　Aramaeans and 2:212
　Assyrians and 2:215–216, 217, 219
　Ayyubids and 9:1234
　Babylonians and 1:124
　Byzantine Empire and 9:1165, 1175–1176
　Christianity and 5:625
　Constantinople and 5:621
　Hittites and 2:150, 152, 153
　Islamic world and 6:768
　Jewish people and 3:400
　Mongols and 9:1229, 1236
　Neo-Hittites and 2:155
　Ottoman Turks and 9:1242, 1252
　Palmyra and 5:602
　Persians and 6:729
　Phoenicians and 2:196
　religious beliefs and 2:159, 5:596
　Rome and 4:475, 490, 495, 513, 540
　Seleucid dynasty and 3:399, 5:586
　Seljuk Turks and 9:1232
　Semitic people and 2:222
　spread of Islam and 6:754, 757

T
Tacitus 4:516, 525, 5:582, 606, 660, *662*, 6:808
Tahiti 7:982, 987, 989
Taika Reforms 7:910–911
tailors 8:*1036*
Taj Mahal 10:1419
Takauji 7:916–917
Tale of Genji, The (Murasaki) 7:913

Talha 6:743–744
talisman, gold 6:*797*
Tamarshak language 9:1264
Tamerlane 7:969, 970, 8:1082, 9:*1228, 1229*, 1229, 1238, 1240, 1245–1246
Tamil people 7:965–966
Tamralipti 7:967
Tanaquil 4:441, 442
Tangaroa 7:*983*
Tang dynasty 7:*895, 899, 901*, 910
Tang Empire, map of 7:*900*
Tanit 2:206
Tannenberg, Battle of 8:*1100*, 1100–1101, 9:1217
Tantalus 4:526
Tantric Buddhism 7:959
Tao 7:884, 885, 886, 888
Taoism 7:877, 886, 888, 889, 890, 892, 901, 902, 975
Taoist societies 7:899
Tao Te Ching (Lao-tzu) 7:886, 888, 889, 892
tapestries 5:*646, 659*, 10:*1371*
Tarascans 10:1302, 1310
Tarasius 9:1168
Tarentum 3:374, 4:461–462, 463, 464, 473
Tariq ibn-Ziyad 6:759
Tarquinius Priscus, Lucius 4:441–442
Tarquin the Proud 4:438, 442, *447*
Tartars 2:242
Tarunza 2:*152*
Tasman, Abel 7:989
tattoos 7:987
Tavarone, Lazzaro 10:*1376*
taxation
　Africa and 9:1271
　Assyrians and 2:216, 217
　barbarian invaders and 5:658
　Byzantine Empire and 5:608, 612, 676, 9:1161, 1164, 1170, 1175
　China and 7:877, 879, 894, 895, 896, 897, 901–902, 904
　cities and towns and 8:1034, 1039
　Egypt and 1:77, 86, 105
　England and 8:1050, 1056, 1067, 1109, 1116
　France and 8:1079, 1081
　Greece and 3:301
　Hittites and 2:158
　Holy Roman Empire and 8:1072
　Incas and 10:1341
　India and 7:928
　Islamic world and 6:746, 759, 768
　Japan and 7:911, 913
　Kievan Rus and 9:1211
　Mongols and 9:1220, 1222, 1226

Ottoman Turks and 9:1249, 1250
　Persians and 2:238, 245, 6:735
　Roman Empire and 4:508, 525, 534, 546, 5:595, 596, 604
　Rome and 4:476, 479, 534
tax collectors 5:604
teaching methods, medieval universities and 10:1387, 1388–1389
technology
　agriculture and 8:1026, 1028–1029
　barbarian invaders and 5:658
　Egypt and 1:90
　European conquests and 10:1421
　Leonardo da Vinci and 10:1405
　mathematics and 3:407–408
　navigation and 10:*1365*, 1365
　pre-Columbian cultures and 10:1302, 1345
　textiles and 8:1030
　warfare and 10:1419
Tefnakhte 1:109
Telepinu 2:160
Tell es-Sultan 1:13
tells 1:67
Temple of Apollo (Corinth) 3:*299*
Temple of Apollo (Syracuse) 3:*375*
Temple of Athena Nike 3:*347*, 349
Temple of Ceres 2:*253*
Temple of Hera 2:*247*
Temple of Hercules Victor 4:*487*
Temple of Poseidon 3:*315*
Temple of Solomon 6:769
Temple of the Muses *see* Museum of Alexandria
Temple of the Sun 10:*1341*, 1346
Temple of the Warriors 10:*1321*
temples
　Angkor Wat 7:977, *978*
　Assyrians and 2:216, 217
　Byzantine Empire and 5:618, 636–637
　Egypt and 1:75, 81–82, 87, 95, 98, 100, 101, 104, 106
　Greece and 3:311–312
　Hittites and 2:154
　India and 7:*933, 941, 945, 950*, 961, *965*, 965, 966, *967*, 968, *969*
　Israelites and 2:229, 231
　Maya and 10:1315
　Mecca and 6:738–739
　Minoans and 2:180
　Mycenaeans and 2:190
　Persians and 2:234, 236
　Phoenicians and 2:206
　pre-Columbian cultures and 10:1302, *1303*, 1310, *1313*, 1315, 1316, 1318, *1319, 1331*, 1335, *1341*, 1342, 1346, 1350

Rome and 4:451, *487*, 511, 520, 555, 5:597, *613*
Southeast Asia and 7:*973*, 980
Sumerian 1:56, 64, 66
tenant farmers 5:606, 608
Ten Commandments 2:227, 228, 229
Tenochtitlán 10:1324, *1325, 1332*, 1332, 1333, 1416, 1419
Tenzin Gyatso *see* Dalai Lama
Teotihuacán 10:1302, *1303*, 1307–1309, *1308*, 1316
Tepanec people 10:1324, 1334
tepees 10:1352, *1355*
terraces, agriculture and 10:1304
terra-cotta artifacts
　Africa and 9:*1257*
　Byzantine Empire and 9:*1181*
　China and 7:*881*, 881
　Greece and 2:*248*
　India and 7:*920, 924, 926*
　Japan and 7:*909, 912*
　Mycenaeans and 2:*190*, 190
　Nok people and 9:*1257*, 1261, 1263
　Phoenicians and 2:*197*
Tertullian 5:680–681, *682*, 682
Testament of Ardashir, The 6:730
Testry, Battle of 6:791
Tetrabiblos (Ptolemy) 3:410
tetrarchy 5:607–608, *608*
Tetricus 5:601
Teutoburg Forest, Battle of 4:514
Teutonic Knights 8:1025, 1100, 1101, 9:1216, 1217
Teutons 4:483, 485
Tewksbury, Battle of 8:1122, *1123*
Texcatlipoca 10:1329
Texcoco 10:1324
textiles
　Africa and 9:1271
　China and 7:874
　Greece and 3:302
　Islamic world and 6:781, 9:*1231*
　Japan and 7:906
　medieval Europe and 8:1029–1030, *1031*
　Mycenaeans and 2:189
　Pacific islands and 7:987
　Phoenicians and 2:198, 202
　pre-Columbian cultures and 10:1306, 1310, 1311, 1314, 1323, 1345
textual criticism 3:404, 406
Tezcatlipoca 10:*1333*, 1334
Thailand
　Ayutthaya dynasty and 7:977
　Bronze Age and 1:33, 35
　Buddhism and 7:*954*, 958
　Chiang Mai dynasty and 7:977
　early humans and 7:972
　statues and 7:*947, 976*
　Thai people 7:978
Thales of Miletus 3:352, *354*
Thanksgiving 10:1383

Thasos 2:257

theater *see* drama

Theater of Dionysus 3:*321*

theaters
  Greek 2:*254*, 3:318, 320, *321*
    Roman 4:553, 555

Thebes (Egypt) 1:81, 91, 92, 95,
    100, 103, 106, 107, 109

Thebes (Greece) 3:342, 382, 382–
    383
  Macedonia and 3:386, 388
  Mycenaeans and 2:182

Themistocles 3:331, 334

theocracy, Tibet and 7:959

Theocritus 3:406–407, 4:512

Theodemir 5:645

Theodora 5:670, 671, *674*, 674,
    9:*1172–1173*, 1244

Theodoric I 5:645

Theodoric the Great 5:645–646,
    647, 648, 650–651, 660, 661,
    669, 673

Theodosius I 5:*615, 635, 637,*
    638
  Christianity and 5:630, 632
  division of the Roman Empire
    and 5:666
  massacre and 5:637, 639
  military leadership and 5:614–615
  paganism and 5:636–637
  Roman Empire and 9:1158, 1160
  Visigoths and 5:640, 643

Theodosius II 5:618, 649, 666,
    668, *680*, 6:763, 9:1161–1162

Theodosius III 9:1165

Theodosius the Elder 5:614

Theogony (Birth of the Gods)
    (Hesiod) 3:313

theology
  Christian 5:**678–687**, 696
  Islamic 6:782–783

Theophano 9:1175, 1176

Theophanu 6:832

Theophilus 9:1172, *1174*

Thera 2:167, *168*, 168, 169

Theravada Buddhism 7:956, 957,
    958, 981

Thermopylae, Battle of 2:264,
    3:332, 333

Theseus 2:*171*, 176, 264

Thespis 3:318, 321

Thessalonica, massacre at 5:637,
    639

Thessaloniki 9:*1177*, 1181, 1245

thetes (laborers) 2:266, 267, 3:304,
    344

Thingvellir 9:*1205*

Third Crusade 8:1063, 9:1192

Third Intermediate period, Egypt
    1:107, 109

Third Macedonian War 4:478

Third Palace period, Minoan
    2:181

Third Punic War 4:479, 481

Thirty Tyrants 3:378–379, *380*,
    380

tholos tombs 2:186–187, 188

Thomas Aquinas 10:*1388, 1389*,
    1389–1390

Thomas the Slav 9:1171–1172

Thomsen, Christian 1:42, 45

Thor 9:*1203*, 1205

Thrace 4:522, 5:649

Thracians 2:257, 3:326, 384, 385

Thrasybulus 3:299, 379

Three-Age system 1:45

Three Doctrines 7:892

Three Kingdoms 7:899–900

throne, Charlemagne and 6:807,
    807

Thucydides 3:352, 371, 372, *377*,
    377

Thurii 3:349, 4:461

Thuringians 6:792, 797

Thutmose I 1:*95*, 96, 98

Thutmose II 1:96, 98

Thutmose III 1:92, 98, 98–99

Thutmose IV 1:99

Tiberius 4:513, 515, 516–519, *518*,
    519

Tiber River 4:*448*, 508

Tibet 7:901, 959, 963

Tibeto-Burman languages 7:972

Tibur 6:835

Tigellinus 4:527

Tiglath-pileser I 2:210, 216–217,
    219

Tiglath-pileser III 1:122

Tigris River 6:*787*

Tijing 7:967

Tikal 10:*1313*, 1315, *1316*

tile, Corinthian 3:*298*

timber, trade in 2:198

Timbuktu 9:1271, 1273

Timur the Lame *see* Tamerlane

tin 1:32–33, 35, *36*, 2:200

Tintoretto 10:1406

Tirnova 9:1245

Tiresias 3:*406*

Tiryns 2:182, 184, 187, *189*

Titian 10:*1406*, 1406

titles
  Byzantine Empire and 9:1167
  emperors of Rome and 4:506,
    5:592, 607
  Holy Roman Empire and
    6:836
  India and 7:931, 960
  Otto III and 6:834
  Russia and 9:1215
  Sassanid dynasty and 6:726

Titus 4:535

Titus Aelius Antoninus *see*
    Antoninus Pius

Titus Flavius Vespasianus *see*
    Vespasian

Titus Tatius 4:439

Tiwanaku people 10:1310–1311,
    1311

Tizoc 10:1334

Tlacopán 10:1324

Tlaloc 10:1329, 1332

Tlalocan 10:1308

Tlaltecuhtli 10:1329

tobacco 10:1352, 1381

Tolbiac, Battle of 5:*655*

Toledo 8:1016, 1017

tolls, desert trade routes and
    6:779

Toltec people 10:1302, *1309*,
    1309, 1318

tomahawks 10:*1353*

tombs
  of Archimedes 4:*473*
  of Askia 9:*1272*, 1273
  of Cyrus the Great 2:*238*
  Egypt and 1:73, 82, *88*, 95–96,
    104, *109*, 4:*452*
  Japan and 7:909
  of Mahmud of Ghazi 7:*968*
  Mycenaeans and 2:185–187
  Persians and 2:234
  Phoenicians and 2:204, 207
  Pontus and 4:*485*
  pre-Columbian cultures and
    10:1305
  of Rollo 6:*817*
  see also burial practices

tomo (communities of workers)
    7:909

Tonatiuh 10:1329

Tonga 7:982

tools
  Africa and 9:1256, *1263*, 1263
  agriculture and 1:12, 21–22
  bronze 1:*37*, 40, 2:167, 172
  China and 7:870, 871, 877
  copper 1:32, 34
  early humans and 1:9–10, *11*
  flint 1:*23*, 23
  iron 1:42, *43*, 44, 47
  Japan and 7:906
  metal 1:31
  Natufian culture and 1:11
  Neolithic period and 1:15, *17*
  Pacific islands and 7:985, 986, 987
  pottery and 1:21
  pre-Columbian cultures and
    10:1304, 1308, 1315, 1331
  Southeast Asia and 7:972, 974

Toramana 7:962

Torres, Luis Váez de 7:988–989

Tosar 6:730

Toscanelli, Paolo 10:1395, 1397

totem poles 10:1358

Totila 5:675, 676

Toulouse 8:1025

Tours, Battle of 6:761–762, *762*,
    768, 792, 793, *795*

Tower of London 8:*1124*

towns and villages
  Athenian government and 3:307,
    308
  Bronze Age and 1:40
  Celtic people and 1:52
  Cycladic people and 2:167
  Egyptian 1:86
  funnel-beaker culture and 1:19

Greece and 2:162, 246, 249, 251

Hittites and 2:158

Iberian people and 1:50

Mesopotamia and 1:54

Minoans and 2:177–178, *178*

Minyan people and 2:164

Sparta and 2:263–264

see also cities and towns

Towton Field, Battle of 8:1119

Trachiniai (Sophocles) 3:323

trade
  Africa and 9:1266, 1269, 1271,
    1272, 1273, 1274, 1276,
    10:1367
  Akkadian Empire and 1:59–60
  Alexandria and 3:392
  annual fairs and 8:1030–1032
  Arabia and 5:587
  Assyrians and 2:208, 211
  Athens and 3:301
  barbarian rulers and 5:665
  Bedouin nomads and 6:738
  Bronze Age and 1:33, 36, 37
  Byzantine Empire and
    5:618–619, 9:1162, 1164
  caravans and 6:740–741, *749*,
    776
  Carthage and 2:200, 4:464
  China and 5:589, 7:898, 899, 901,
    903, 10:1420
  cities and towns and 8:1034
  Corinth and 3:295–296, 298, 342
  Cycladic people and 2:167, 169
  deserts and 6:776, 778, 779
  disintegration of the Roman
    Empire and 5:604
  Dutch and 10:1371
  education and 10:1384
  Egypt and 1:87, 101
  Etruscans and 4:445
  Greece and 2:162, 248, 253–254,
    3:302, 304
  Greek colonies and 2:257
  guilds and 8:1041, 1043
  Hallstatt culture and 1:45, 47
  Hanseatic League and 8:1094,
    1095, 1097
  Iberian people and 1:49
  India and 5:589, 7:918, 920, 921,
    931, 946, 966
  Iron Age and 1:44
  Islamic world and 6:767, 774,
    776, 784, 787, 9:1230
  Israelites and 2:231
  Japan and 7:917
  Lydia and 3:328
  Mari and 1:114
  Mecca and 6:739
  Minoans and 2:175
  Mohammed and 6:740–741
  Mongols and 9:1224, 1225
  Mycenaeans and 2:191
  Neolithic period and 1:15
  networks 8:1033–1034
  Phoenicians and 2:196, 198,
    198–199, 202–203, 222

trade (*continued*)
  Portugal and 10:1364, 1366, 1370–1371, *1417*
  pre-Columbian cultures and 10:1308, 1309, 1316, 1327–1328
  Rome and 4:466, 489, 546, 548
  Russia and 9:1208, 1210, 1213
  Samarra and 6:786
  seagoing traders and 6:779–780
  slavery and 9:1274–1275
  Southeast Asia and 7:975, 976, 977, 978, 980, 980–981
  Troy and 2:192, 195
  Vikings and 9:1196, 1200, 1201, 1203
  Wars of the Roses and 8:1117
trade guilds 4:548, 550
trade laws 1:116
trade networks 8:1033–1034
trade routes, European expansion and 10:1362–1364
trading posts 2:199, 208, 253–254, 8:1097, 10:1367
tragedy
  Aeschylus and 3:322–323
  Euripides and 3:324–325
  Greek drama and 3:318, 320, 321–322
  Roman theater and 4:555
  Sophocles and 3:323–324
tragoidos (goat bard) 3:318
Trajan 4:538–540, *539*, 5:582, 585, 6:728, 736
Trajan's Arch 4:*540*, *541*
Trajan's Column 4:540, *542*
translations
  of ancient texts 10:1390–1391, 1393
  of Bible 5:697
  of Greek literature 5:661
transmigration of souls 5:685
transportation 1:37, 10:1316, 1327
traps and snares 1:9
Trasimene, Battle of 4:471–472
treason, charges of 4:518–519, 519–520
Treasure of El Carambolo 1:50
Treasury of Atreus 2:187, *188*, 188
treaties
  of al-Hudaybiyah 6:746
  of Arras 8:1113, 1126, 1128
  of Bretigny 8:1107–1108
  of Clair-sur-Epte 6:819
  of Eternal Peace 5:671
  of Margus 5:649
  of Paris 9:1194
  of Stralsund 8:1098
  of Tordesillas 10:1375–1376
  of Troyes 8:1110
  of Verdun 6:813
  of Worms 6:844
Treatise on Pastoral Care (Gregory) 6:820

Trebia River, Battle of 4:471
Trebonian 5:677
Tres Zapotes 10:1306, 1307
trial by ordeal 5:662, 8:1078
tribal councils, Germanic peoples and 5:660
tribes, North American peoples and 10:1348, 1350, 1352–1353, 1356
tribunes 4:451, 480, 506
tribute
  Byzantine Empire and 5:671
  Charlemagne and 6:798
  China and 7:903
  England and 8:1046
  Greece and 3:341, 381
  Huns and 5:651, 9:1161–1162
  India and 7:960
  Islamic Spain and 8:1016
  medieval Europe and 6:830
  Mongols and 8:1101, 9:1215, 1222, 1228, 1235
  Ottoman Turks and 9:1245
  Persians and 6:726
  pre-Columbian cultures and 10:1324, 1327, *1328*, 1334, 1356
  Rome and 4:469, 478, 497, 508
  Saracens and 8:1022
  Seljuk Turks and 9:1179
  Vikings and 6:818–819, 9:1201
trigonometry 3:410
trimurti concept 7:938–939
Trinity 5:628–629, 631, *633*, 633
Tripitaka 7:*953*, 957
Tripoli 9:1189, 1255, 1273
triremes (warships) 3:331, 334, *339*, 339
Troy 2:182–183, 192–195, *195*, 4:438
Truce of Tours 8:1113
Tsonga people 9:1277
tsunamis 7:965
Tuamotu Archipelago 7:982
Tuareg tribe 6:*749*
Tudor, Henry *see* Henry VII (England)
Tughluq dynasty 7:969, 970
Tukulti-Ninurta I 1:120–121, 2:210, 211
Tukulti-Ninurta II 2:212
Tula 10:1309
Tullus Hostilius 4:440
tumuli see burial mounds
Tumulus culture 1:36, 40
Tumulus period *see* Yamato period
tundra landscapes 1:8
Tunisia 5:*588*
Tupac Amaru 10:1347
Turkestan 6:763, 776, 7:901
Turkey 6:775
Turkic people 9:1165, 1168, 1229, 1230, 1232, 1240
Turkish empires and the Islamic world 9:**1230–1241**

Tuscarora people 10:1356
Tutankhamen 1:92, 104, *105*, *106*, 9:*1268*
Tuvalu 7:982
Twa people 9:1256
Tyler, Wat 8:1108, *1109*, 1109
typhoons, Japan and 7:916, *917*
tyranny and democracy 3:**294–309**
tyrants 2:253, 3:326, 327, 345, 367, 378–380, 403, 4:442
Tyre 2:196, 197–198, 200, *204*, 206, 3:391
Tyrell, James 8:1124
Tyrolean ice man *see* Ötzi
Tyrrhenians 4:445
Tyrtaeus 2:258
Tzintzuntzan 10:1310

U
Uazactún 10:1315
Ubayd Allah 6:774
Ubbi 9:1196, 1198
Ugarit 2:196, *206*, 252
Uighur people 9:1220
uji (clans) 7:909, 910
Ujjain 7:927
Ukraine 9:1210
Ulama ball game 10:*1317*, 1317, 1318
Ulfsson, Gunnbjörn 9:1204, 1206
Umako 7:910
Umayyad caliphate 6:764, 766–769, 770, 776, 785
Umayyad Mosque 6:*765*, 767
Umbrians 2:252
Umma 1:58
Unas 1:74
Unetician culture 1:36
unification of Japan 7:908–909
Union of Kalmar 8:1099–1100
unions, tribes and 10:1356
universities, medieval Europe and 10:1384, *1386*, *1388*
untouchables 7:923, *925*, 959
Upanishands (private lessons) 7:935, 936–937, *937*–938, 946
Upper Egypt 1:72
Ur 1:57–58, 114, 2:225
Ur III period 1:63, 65–66
Urartu 2:216, 217
Urban II 9:1182, *1183*, 1184, *1187*, 1187
Urban VI 8:1089, 1091
urban Europe, growth of 8:**1026–1043**
urbanization *see* cities and towns
urban planning 5:618–619, 7:918, 920–921, 10:1307–1308, 1315–1416
Ur-Nammu 1:63, 111
Urnfield culture 1:39–40
urn, Villanovan 4:*550*

Urqon 10:1338
Uruinimgina 1:58
Uruk 1:54, 57, 62, 65, 123
Uru-Salem *see* Jerusalem
Usha 7:945
Utopia (More) 10:1397
Utuhegal 1:63
Uxmal 10:1315, *1317*
Uyghur people 7:874

V
Vac 7:940, 945
Vacarius, Roger 10:1384
vacuum, Greek philosophy and 3:358, 360, 361
vaishyas (farmers and traders) 7:925, 946
Vajrayana Buddhism *see* Tantric Buddhism
Valencia 8:1021
Valens 5:614, 620, 630, 631, 640, 643
Valens Aqueduct 5:619, *620*, 620
Valentinian I 5:613–614, 634
Valentinian II 5:614, 615, 634, 636
Valentinian III 5:650, 653
Valerian 5:601, 6:726, 729, *730*
Valerius Laevinus 4:478
Valhalla 9:*1204*
Vallabha 7:964
Valley of the Kings 1:95–96, *96*, 97
Valois family 6:827
Vandals 5:603, 649, 652–654, 660, 669, 671, 673, 687
Vanuatu 7:982
Vardhamana *see* Mahavira
Varna, Battle of 9:1246
Varro, Gaius Terentius 4:472
Varuna 7:*936*
Vasari, Giorgio 10:1402, 1403
vase illustrations, Greek 3:*302*, *303*, *306*, *313*, *319*, *336*, *342*, *369*, *371*, *406*
vases 2:*193*, *251*, *266*, 7:*904*
Vasily II 9:1215
Vasily III 9:1217
Vasnetsov, Victor 9:*1211*
vassals 6:808, 819
vassal states, Hittites and 2:152
Vayu 7:936
veche (city council) 9:1211, 1215
Vedanta school of philosophy 7:964
Vedas 7:927, 932, 935, 936–937, 937–938, 940, 945, 946
Vedda people 7:929
Vedic religion 7:932, 934, 938–939, 945, 946, 952, 967
  see also Hinduism
Vega, Lope de 8:1021
Venice
  Byzantine Empire and 8:1082, 9:1181
  Fourth Crusade and 8:1068, 9:1192

Middle Ages and 8:1096
Ottoman Turks and 9:1245, 1246
Polo, Marco, and 8:*1098*, 9:1225, 10:*1363*
Renaissance and 10:1406–1407
spice trade and 10:1362–1363
Venus 4:*537*
Venus of Brassempouy 1:7, *10*
Venus of Willendorf 1:7, *9*
Vermandois 8:1054
Veronese 10:1406
Verrazzano, Giovanni da 10:1379
Verres, trial of 4:491–492
Verrocchio, Andrea del 10:1403
Versinicia, Battle of 9:1171
Verus, Lucius 4:543, 544, 6:728
Vespasian 4:529, 533–535, 541
Vespo della Beata Virgine (Monteverdi) 10:1407
Vespucci, Amerigo 10:1375–1376
Vesta 4:441, 5:597
Vestal Virgins 4:438, 441
Vibius Pansa 4:502
Victor IV 8:1062
Victory, statue of 5:634, 636
Vienna 9:1216, 1252
Vietnam 7:896, 901, 972, 974, 975, *977*, 977–978, 980
Vijaya 7:929
Vijayanagar, kingdom of 7:971
Vikings 6:*809*, *816*, 9:**1196–1207**, *1199*
England and 8:1046
exploration and 10:1363
medieval Europe and 6:809, 811, 814, 818–819, 820
Russia and 9:1208, 1210
Scandinavia and 8:1098
villages *see* cities and towns; towns and villages
villages, North American peoples and 10:1350, 1352, 1355, *1355*
Villanovans 4:445, *457*, *550*
villas, Minoan 2:177–178
Vima Kadphises 7:931
Vinland 9:1207
Viracocha (god) 10:1341
Viracocha (king) 10:1336
Virgil 2:200, 3:406–407, 4:438, 510, 512, 526, 557
Virginia Company 10:1381
virtue 3:362, 413
Visconti family 8:1096
Vishnu 7:938–939, *940*, 940–942, *941*, 960, *965*, 975
Visigoths
Byzantine Empire and 5:614
Clovis I and 5:*646*
crafts of 5:*645*
Franks and 5:654, 657
Huns and 5:648, 650–651
Islamic world and 6:759, 760
Roman Catholic Church and 5:660

Rome and 5:640–641, *641*, 641–643, 644, 687
Spain and 5:660, 676
Visva-Karman 7:934
Vitellius, Aulus 4:532–533
viziers (chief ministers) 1:77, 78, 94, 99
Vladimir Monomachus 9:1211, 1213
Vladimir the Great 9:1203, 1210, 1212–1213
Vladislav of Lithuania 8:1100
volcanic eruptions 2:167, 168, 169, 181
Volga River 9:1203, 1208
voting 3:306, 10:1355
votive figures 2:166
voyages of discovery, map of 10:*1374*
Vulgate Bible 5:697

W
Wadai 9:1273, 1274
Wagadou *see* Ghana
wages 1:116, 8:1086, 1109
Wailing Wall 4:535
Wai Wang 9:1222
Wakefield, Battle of 8:1118–1119
Waldemar IV 8:1098–1099
Waldseemüller, Martin 10:1376
Wales 8:1077
Walid, Al- 6:768
Wallia 5:643, 645
Wallis, Samuel 7:989
wall paintings 9:1259, *1261*
Wampanoag people 10:1383
Wang Mang 7:897–898
Waqidi, Al- 6:739
war booty 3:304, 390, 4:459, 466, 5:604, 6:729, 755, 814
warfare
Akkadians and 1:60, 62
Alexander the Great and 3:384–391, 393–395
Alfred the Great and 6:820
Assyrians and 2:210, 212–213
Babylonians and 1:110
Bedouin nomads and 6:738
Bronze Age and 1:40
Burgundy and 8:1130–1133
Celtic people and 1:50
cities and towns and 8:1041
comitia centuriata and 4:450
dynastic succession and 10:1415–1416
Egypt and 1:77, 87, 92, 94, 98, 99, 105, 106, 107, 109, 2:225
feudalism and 6:822–823
France and 8:1079
Germanic people and 1:53
Greece and 2:258, 3:302, 303, 4:456
guerrilla warfare 6:797, 8:1113
Hallstatt culture and 1:47
Hanseatic League and 8:1097, 1098

Hittites and 2:150, 152, 153, 157
Holy Roman Empire and 8:1073
Islam and 6:744, 746, 751, 752, 754, 755–757, 768
Israelites and 2:230, 231
Macedonia and 4:476
Medes and 2:232
Mughal Empire and 10:*1418*
Persians and 2:232, 233–234, 238–239, 3:381–382, 6:726, 729, 733, 735
pre-Columbian cultures and 10:1308, 1318, 1324, 1328–1329, 1334, 1336, 1338–1339, 1356
religious beliefs and 8:1018, 10:1414–1415
Rome and 4:456–463, 488–489
Saxons and 6:797
Scythian people and 1:49
sieges 3:386, 391, 6:760, 762, 763, 772, *775*, 832
Sumerian people and 1:57, 58–59, 65–66
supplies and 3:374, 394–395
technology and 10:1419
Troy and 2:194, 195
see also military forces; naval power; specific wars and battles
Warka Vase 1:*65*
warships 3:331, 334, *339*, 339, *371*
Wars of the Roses 8:**1114–1125**
Wasps (Aristophanes) 3:378
water, natural philosophy and 3:354
wealth
Assyrians and 2:208
Athens and 3:348
Greeks and 2:251, 269
Minoans and 2:180
Rome and 4:446, 449, 450, 507, 548
weapons and armor
Africa and 9:*1274*
Berber peoples and 9:1235
breastplates 4:*465*, 9:*1274*
Bronze Age and 1:38
Carthaginian 4:*465*
Celtic people and 1:46, 4:*460*
Charlemagne and 6:799
Copper Age and 1:32, 34
Egyptian 1:90
European conquests and 10:1419, 1421
Frankish 5:*657*
gladiators and 4:*531*, *552*
Greek 2:265
Greek fire 6:762
hand grenades 9:*1181*
Iron Age and 1:42
Islamic Spain and 6:780–781
Japan and 7:909, 917, 10:*1416*
Macedon and 3:387

medieval Europe and 8:1105, 1106
Mongols and 9:1220–1221
Parthians and 6:728
pre-Columbian cultures and 10:1329, *1353*
Rome and 4:449, 462, 484
Vikings and 9:*1197*
Villanovan 4:*457*
see also military forces
weaving *see* textiles
Wei dynasty 7:899, 900
weights and measures 1:119, 2:212, 238, 7:879
Wessex 6:820, 9:1196, 1198
west African kingdoms 9:1274–1275
western Roman Empire *see* Roman Empire
western schism 8:1089, 1091–1093
Western Xia people 9:1222
West Francia 6:813, 828
West Kennet Long Barrow 1:27–28, *28*
wheeled wagons 7:874
wheels 1:21–22, 65, 10:1304–1305, 1333
White Huns *see* Hephthalites
White Sheep Turks 9:1240
Widukind 6:797, *800*
wigwams 10:1352, 1357
William I (England) 8:*1045*, 1047, 1047–1048, *1049*, 1050
William II Rufus 8:1049
William of Aquitaine 6:826
William of Bavaria 8:1128
William of Normandy *see* William I (England)
Willigis 6:834, 835
wills 4:501, 515
windmills 6:780, 8:1028
wine 2:244
wine vessel, Chinese 7:*876*
winter solstice 1:25, 10:*1345*
Winthrop, John 10:1383
Wise Men 5:*681*
witchcraft, Germanic peoples and 5:662
wives, pharaohs and 1:95, 96, 98
Wladyslaw I 8:1100
Wladyslaw II 8:1100, 9:1216
Wladyslaw III 9:1246
women
Africa and 4:453, 9:1259
Assyrians and 2:212
Babylonian 1:113, 118
Byzantine Empire and 5:674
China and 7:903
Egyptian 1:108
Germanic peoples and 5:664–665
Greece and 2:263, *268*, 268, 3:308, 321, 350
Greek colonies and 2:256
medieval Europe and 10:1387
Minoans and 2:179

women (*continued*)
pre-Columbian cultures and 10:1344, 1345
religious communities and 5:692
wooden sculptures 7:*987*, 9:*1175, 1271, 1276*
Woodville, Anthony 8:1123
Woodville, Elizabeth 8:1120, 1122, 1123, 1124, 1125
wool exports 8:1102
Woolley, Leonard 1:57, *67*
work specialization 1:36–37, 38, 70
see also employment; labor
world in the early 16th century CE 10:**1410–1421**
Worms, council at 6:841
wrestlers 2:*262*
writing
Africa and 9:1264
Carolingian miniscule script 6:806
China and 7:873, 876, 877, *879*, 899
cuneiform 1:60–61, 67, *68*, 68, 69, 119
demotic 1:88
Germanic peoples and 5:658, 665
Greek 3:315
Greeks and 2:248–249, 253
hieratic 1:88
hieroglyphic 1:72–73, 88
Hittites and 2:150, 160–161
Indus Valley civilization and 7:920, 923
Japan and 7:910, *915*, 915

Minoans and 2:176, 179, 180–181
Mongols and 9:1222
Mycenaeans and 2:182, 186, 189
Persians and 2:236
Phoenicians and 2:203–204
phonetic 1:68
pictographic 1:68
pre-Columbian cultures and 10:1305, 1319, *1328*, 1328, 1336
printing press and 10:1391–1392
systems of 2:252
see also alphabets; literature and writings
Wu Ding 7:876
Wu dynasty 7:899, 900
Wu Jing (Five Classics) 7:887
Würzburg, Diet of 6:844
Wu Ti 7:895–897, *897*, 899

X

Xanthippus 3:340, 4:467–468
Xenophanes 3:355, *357*
Xenophon 3:303, 362
Xerxes I 2:237, 239, 240, 3:330–331, 331–332, 334, 336, 390
Xia dynasty 7:873, 875, 9:1223
Xin dynasty 7:897–898
Xinjiang mummies 7:*874*, 874
Xiongnu people 7:895
Xi Xia tribe 7:903
Xunzi 7:891, 894

Y

Yabahya 2:219
Yadava people 7:943

yaghbus (sub-kings) 7:931
Yagul 10:1310
Yamato period 7:909, *909*–910
Yamuna 7:945
yanacona (social ranking) 10:1344
Yang Jian 7:900–901
Yang-sho culture 7:870, 872
Yangtze River 7:*878*, 878
Yarmuk River, Battle of 6:755
Yaroslav the Wise 9:1211, 1212
Yathrib *see* Medina
Yavuz the Grim *see* Selim I
Yayoi period 7:906, 909
Yazdegerd I 6:734
Yazdegerd III 6:735, 755
Yazid I 6:*757*, 757, 764, 767
Yazilikaya sanctuary 2:*155*, 160
Yellow River 7:878, 898
Yellow Turbans 7:899
Yemen 9:1269
Yenking 9:1222
Yin 7:873, 876
York, house of 8:1114, *1115*
Yoruba people 9:1275
Yuan dynasty 7:904, 9:1226
Yue Qi nomads 7:929
Yung-lo 10:1420
yurts 9:*1223*
Yu the Great 7:873

Z

Zachary 6:794, 795
Zaghawa people 9:1273
Zama, Battle of 4:475, *475*
Zamasp 6:734

Zangi, Imad ad-Din 9:1189, 1190
Zannanza 1:105
Zápolya, John 9:1252
Zapotecs 10:1302, 1309
Zaragoza 6:798
Zarco, João Gonçalves 10:1366, *1367*
Zealots 4:541
Zen Buddhism 7:958–959
Zeno 5:*626*, 626, 645–646, 647, 653, 669, 9:1162, 1165
Zenobia 5:*602*, 602, 603
Zeno of Citium 3:413, 4:557
Zeno of Elea 3:360, 362–363
zeugitai (farmers) 2:266, 267, 3:304, 344
Zeus 2:167, 190, 3:*301*, 310, 313, 314, 393, 403, 412
Zhang Qian 7:895
Zhao Kuangyin 7:902
Zhou dynasty 7:873, 875, 877, 882, 884, 887, 889, *890*
Zhou period 7:*872*
Zhuangzi 7:889
Zhu Yuanzhang 7:905
Ziggurat of Ur 1:*58*
ziggurats 1:56, 124, 2:*209*
Zimrilim 1:114, 2:224
Zoe (daughter of Constantine VIII) 9:*1178*, 1178
Zoe (mother of Constantine VII) 9:1174
Zoroaster 2:241–243
Zoroastrianism 6:726, 730, 731, 733, 734, 735
Zulu people 9:1265, *1277*, 1277
Zurbarán, Francisco de 9:*1187*